Time Out

1000 Films

to change your life

timeout.com

Published by Time Out Guides Ltd, a wholly owned subsidiary of Time Out Group Ltd.
Time Out and the Time Out logo are trademarks of Time Out Group Ltd.

© **Time Out Group Ltd 2006**

10 9 8 7 6

This edition first published in Great Britain in 2006 by Ebury Publishing
Ebury Publishing is a division of The Random House Group Ltd,
20 Vauxhall Bridge Road, London SW1V 2SA

Random House Australia Pty Limited 20 Alfred Street, Milsons Point, Sydney, New South Wales 2061, Australia
Random House New Zealand Limited 18 Poland Road, Glenfield, Auckland 10, New Zealand
Random House South Africa (Pty) Limited Isle of Houghton, Corner Boundary Road & Carse O'Gowrie,
Houghton 2198, South Africa

Random House UK Limited Reg. No. 954009

Distributed in USA by Publishers Group West
1700 Fourth Street, Berkeley, California 94710

Distributed in Canada by Penguin Canada Ltd
10 Alcorn Avenue, Toronto, Ontario, Canada M4V 3B2

For further distribution details, see www.timeout.com

ISBN 978-0-091936-48-8

A CIP catalogue record for this book is available from the British Library

Colour reprographics by Icon, Crowne House, 56-58 Southwark Street, London SE1 1UN

Printed and bound by Firmengruppe APPL, aprinta druck, Wemding, Germany

Papers used by Ebury Publishing are natural, recyclable products made from wood grown in sustainable forests

Time Out Guides Limited
Universal House
251 Tottenham Court Road
London W1T 7AB
Tel + 44 (0)20 7813 3000
Fax + 44 (0)20 7813 6001
Email guides@timeout.com
www.timeout.com

Editorial

Editor Simon Cropper
Deputy Editors Janice Fuscoe, Andrew Humphreys
Consultant Editor Gareth Evans
Editorial Assistant Alexia Loundras
Proofreader John Pym

Editorial/Managing Director Peter Fiennes
Series Editor Sarah Guy
Deputy Series Editor Cath Phillips
Business Manager Gareth Garner
Guides Co-ordinator Holly Pick
Accountant Kemi Olufuwa

Design

Art Director Scott Moore
Art Editor Pinelope Kourmouzoglou
Senior Designer Josephine Spencer
Graphic Designer Henry Elphick
Digital Imaging Dan Conway

Picture Desk

Picture Editor Jael Marschner
Deputy Picture Editor Tracey Kerrigan
Picture Researcher Helen McFarland

Advertising

Sales Director & Sponsorship Mark Phillips
Sales Manager Alison Wallen
Advertising Sales Michelle Clements, Jason Trotman
Advertising Assistant Kate Staddon
Copy Controller Amy Nelson

Marketing

Group Marketing Director John Luck
Marketing & Publicity Manager, US Rosella Albanese

Production

Production Director Mark Lamond
Production Controller Marie Howell

Time Out Group

Chairman Tony Elliott
Managing Director Mike Hardwick
Financial Director Richard Waterlow
General Manager Nichola Coulthard
Art Director John Oakey
Online Managing Director David Pepper
Production Director Steve Proctor
IT Director Simon Chappell

The editors wish to thank the following for advice and assistance: Derek Adams, Dick Arnell, Yuko Aso, James Bell, Holly Bowman, Feargal Byrne, Katie Clarke, Nadia Costes, Isabelle Dassonville, Will Fulford-Jones, Marcy Gerstein, Alistair Griggs, Mike Gubbins, Robert Lepage, Nick Marston, Anna Norman, Rowan Pelling, Gill Plummer, Lisa Ritchie, Chris Salmon, Sammie Squire and Christina Withers; John Pym; Geoff Andrew, Tom Charity and Tony Rayns; Katsue Tomiyama and Koyo Yamashita of Image Forum, Tokyo; Nagisa Oshima, for permission to adapt a passage from his book *Taiken Teki Sengo Eizoron* (*Post-War Cinema From My Perspective*); staff and students of the Script Factory, London; and all the film-makers, actresses, actors, writers and artists whose contributions make up this book.

Photography by: All pictures provided by Photofest NYC except the following: page 3 Culver Pictures Inc./ Superstock, page 237 Eric Gaillard/Reuters/Corbis, page 247 Time & Life Pictures/Getty Images.

Contents

Introduction

Dumb and Dumber, a life-changing film? Surely not? And how about *Basic Instinct*? *Carry On, Emmanuelle*? *Raiders of the Lost Ark*? Or *The Cameraman's Revenge*, a 12-minute Russian short made nearly a century ago? 'Come on,' you might reasonably think, flicking through this book's index, 'only big guns of the calibre of *Citizen Kane, La Grande Illusion, The Godfather* and *Seven Samurai* deserve to have that sort of claim made about them.' So, is the book you're holding merely another one of those tomes with a tiger title and nothing in the tank but fumes?

We hope not. To begin with, we make no suggestion that every film mentioned in the following 240 pages is 'good', or even 'worthy'. Secondly, this book does not have a special interest in the critical or popular stock of any given film – though it's not short of praise for hundreds of movies we think anyone would enjoy watching. Instead, it's about the ways – even ways their makers may not have foreseen – that films go to work on us. As for 'life-changing', a notion peddled all too fraudulently these days – well, that will depend on who you are and how you measure the term (of which more in a moment).

We reckon there are already quite enough generalist movie books organised by genre – chapter on the Western, chapter on the road movie, chapter on horror flicks, and so on. More interesting, we argued, to look at films through the emotions they trigger: the instant, unthinking, gut reactions, the Geiger counter clicks of a movie's power. That's why *1000 Films* is shaped by the nine emotions people are most likely to feel at the cinema; there's one chapter dedicated to each. And a tenth chapter, entitled Food for Thought, assesses the thinking responses that are often just a short distance behind the visceral ones.

Each chapter begins with a wide-ranging survey, by a leading film critic, of the particular emotion's cinematic history. The remaining two thirds of the chapter serve up a rich and varied mix of material: shorter pieces that give the emotions a sidelong look; 'Moving picture' testimonies, wherein major directors, actresses, actors, writers and others tell us about their life-changing experiences at the movies; 'Critics' choice' boxes, compiled by the editors, each listing ten notable films with a particular theme; and a handful of other boxes on aspects of film-going. In addition, sprinkled throughout the book are six untethered 'Bigger picture' studies of major stars, the Cannes film festival and contemporary British animation.

There are overlaps, of course. A film that makes its viewers feel contempt may well make them feel anger; joy and exhilaration are close companions, too, as are sadness and regret. Like the man said, that's part of the fun. *1000 Films to change your life* can be treated as you would a DVD: you can read it from start to finish, open it at random and dive in, jump from one part to another, make your own edit.

But back to the 'change your life' business. A movie's emotional impact can be coercive (like having your arm twisted) or less so (like having your heartstrings gently plucked). It's clear, judging from the remarks made by this book's contributors, that *Singin' in the Rain* and *2001: A Space Odyssey* have changed the lives of a lot of people – but who's to deny any film, even a film stunted in one way or another, that sort of power? It might be a tiny detail that tips you, and the effects need not be immediately obvious. A film, as a line by Seamus Heaney wonderfully puts it, can 'catch the heart off guard and blow it wide open'.

And 1000? Well, we had to stop somewhere. (Confession: there are, in fact, 1158 films mentioned in *1000 Films*.) Happy viewing!

This book's big brother, the annual *Time Out Film Guide* (£22.50/$34.95), is an essential reference book for any film-goer. It reaches into every corner of cinema – classic silents, the Hollywood mainstream, contemporary cinema of the Far East, decades-old B-movie horrors, and more. It contains well over 16,500 reviews, all of which are available online at www.timeout.com/film.

Joy

'What a glorious feelin',
I'm happy again'
Singin' in the Rain

Joy

A User's Manual

Trevor Johnston finds no shortage of reasons to be cheerful at the movies.

Catholicism hasn't worked, Judaism has failed him, Krishna didn't cut it either. For Woody Allen's despairing comedy writer in *Hannah and Her Sisters*, the answer is Marx. That's Groucho, Chico, Harpo and Zeppo Marx, by the way, since it's during a matinée of *Duck Soup* that he finally pulls out of an existential tailspin precipitated by a recent medical scare. Watching the inspired tomfoolery unfold in this classic Hollywood comedy of the '30s, Allen catches himself laughing, and suddenly, as his voiceover explains, it all starts to make sense: 'Look at the people up there on the screen, they're so funny… What if the worst were true, there's no God, you only go around once, and that's it? Well, don't you want to be part of the experience? It's not all a drag. I should stop ruining my life looking for answers I'm never going to get, and just enjoy myself while it lasts…'

Not everyone, it has to be admitted, will find a reason to live from the madcap cadences of 'Hail Freedonia!', but the general principle surely holds good. The great positive movie moments can and do take you out of yourself, lift your mood, crack a smile, raise your spirits. Sure, it's not always a matter of piercing the dark clouds of life-threatening gloom, sometimes it might be decidedly frivolous, like quietly chuckling to yourself in the supermarket on remembering the cherishable idiocies of spoof disaster flick *Airplane!* – 'Roger, Roger. What's our vector, Victor?' From timeless classics to such jolly fluff, it seems there's always a teeming miscellany of cinematic felicities jostling in our subconscious.

True, the absolutely searingly affirmative charge erupting from the reconciliation of fractious marrieds Ingrid Bergman and George Sanders in Rossellini's *Viaggio in Italia*, for instance, isn't something to be encountered every day, yet the epiphanies of a lifetime's viewing really do build into a mental archive of just so many of filmic joys. From Marilyn's grin-inducing 'Boo-boo be-doo' ornamenting her torchy 'I Wanna Be Loved by You' in *Some Like*

JOY

It Hot, to the heartening insights of a Frank Capra or Yasujiro Ozu, it's all in there and waiting for just the right moment of recall.

Trying to make sense of it in short order seems quite as exhilarating and arbitrary as the wonderful whizz through the Louvre in Godard's *Bande à part*. There's the ecstatic expression of romantic love in FW Murnau's 1927 silent masterpiece *Sunrise*, for example, where back-projection transmutes the loving couple's walk through the city into a rural idyll, before a brilliant cut shows they're kissing, blissfully self-absorbed, in the midst of a traffic-thronged thoroughfare. Very different, yet equally joyous in its own way is the soaring exuberance of Gene Kelly merrily splashing through the title number in *Singin' in the Rain*, or Audrey Tautou's adorable *Amélie* listing among her individual peccadilloes an eager penchant for cracking the crystalline sugar crust on crème brûlée. Even more potently emotive perhaps is the parental reunion which brings *The Railway Children*, Lionel Jeffries's much-loved chronicle of an eventful Edwardian summer, its cheeringly appropriate closure, or, say, the sequence of a child borne aloft on his father's shoulders with which Satyajit Ray ends *The World of Apu*, a stirring note of Bengali hope and expectation after three films of epochal privation and perseverance. Then again, sometimes it's just the sheer aesthetic joy of a director's accomplishment which glitters

JOY

Uplift, courtesy of Gene Kelly:
Singin' in the Rain

in the memory, whether it's the unforgettable magic-hour light pervading the amber waves of Texas wheat in Terrence Malick's *Days of Heaven*, Hitchcock's brilliantly mischievous cut whisking *North by Northwest* from the jeopardy of Mt Rushmore to a pre-coital Cary Grant and Eva Marie Saint, or the newly iconic Abbas Kiarostami images of a car exquisitely framed on its zigzag trajectory through remote Iranian terrain in *The Wind Will Carry Us*. The hits, as they say, just keep on coming.

There is though, a definite shape to the cinema's history of happiness, with the great silent comedians and the golden age of the Hollywood musical providing a particularly fertile patch. Indeed, the silent era almost seems predicated on the power of comedy to bring ready entertainment to the masses, developing the instant whammy of the Mack Sennett shorts into an enduring art form thanks to the genius of Keaton and Chaplin. Without the hindrance of dialogue, there's just such a purity of expression in Buster's discreet romanticism and inch-perfect elastic grace – the locomotive chase in *The General* is an unparalleled highlight for its inspired conception and fearless execution – or indeed the balletic whimsicality of Charlie at his best. Chaplin's sometimes full-on emotionalism has drawn disdain from snooty critics, but the big finish to *City Lights* is still a marvel. After the tension of whether the flower girl, whose sight the kindly tramp helped restore, will recognise him now she can see, it's the simple touch of a hand which finally makes the magic connection, and his innate generosity of spirit is gladly repaid.

By 1931, when *City Lights* appeared, economic Depression was biting, and movies more than ever before became a source of feelgood balm. With sound technology finding its feet, musicals were in, matching the craft of the great Broadway tunesmiths to the specifically cinematic choreography of Busby Berkeley's extravagantly visualised production numbers. A treasure like *Gold Diggers of 1933* wraps its backstage melodrama around a string of such terpsichorean follies, notably 'We're in the Money', which flaunts the outrageous ambiguity of chorines disporting themselves dressed as gold coins in front of an audience who barely had pennies to rub together. Since the musical as a genre is so wholly dedicated to

"**'New York, New York! It's a wonderful town!' proclaim sailors Gene Kelly, Frank Sinatra and Jules Munshin – and who are we to argue?'**

offering undemanding pleasure, it's instructive to trace its relationship with the turbulence of mid-20th century history. Both during World War II and the following decade, you can see how the genre enshrined an idealised vision of domesticity as a bulwark against the horrors darkening the collective psyche in the real world beyond, while still giving us a host of true anthology moments. The acme might indeed be Vincente Minnelli's still tremendously touching *Meet Me in St Louis*, where the optimism of the 1904 World's Fair, the loving enclave of a well-to-do household and the youthful romantic zing expressed by budding Judy Garland in 'The Trolley Song' create a joyful paean to the Good Old Days, made even more affecting in dramatic terms by the threat that dad's new job might have to move everyone to New York. The joy we feel when this doesn't happen must tell us something about our own deep-rooted longing for the sort of cosseting certainties of home, hearth and security that the film represents with such apparent sincerity.

For sheer joie de vivre, the sweet spot for musicals around 1950 or so takes some topping. 'New York, New York! It's a wonderful town!' proclaim sailors Gene Kelly, Frank Sinatra and Jules Munshin as they hit authentic Big Apple locations in Kelly and Stanley Donen's *On the Town* – and who are we to argue? Kelly, Donald O'Connor and Debbie Reynolds's 'Good Morning!' number from the same directing duo's *Singin' in the Rain* is almost as

JOY

irrepressibly zesty as the title show-stopper, while among the myriad highlights of Minnelli's *An American in Paris* is painter Kelly's soaring declaration to gamine Leslie Caron that 'Our Love Is Here to Stay'.

Well, sorry Gene, but it wasn't. Although musicals continued to create moments of sheer exultation, including Audrey Hepburn's celebratory 'I Could Have Danced All Night' from *My Fair Lady*, and the undeniably rapturous alpine opening (whatever your feelings may be about the rest of the film) to *The Sound of Music*, its tenure was altered by the fundamental social changes of the world beyond. Even so, it's not like these great artists worked in isolation. Donen and Kelly's *It's Always Fair Weather*, surely the most under-appreciated classic musical of all, springs its just-about-optimistic resolution from the post-war disillusionment of a trio of old army buddies. Kelly's roller-skating athleticism during his big number 'I Like Myself' is the supreme moment here, not only for its freewheeling élan, but also for its emotive declaration of self-respect in a world going slowly rotten.

Of course, what's really happening in this instance is that the song touches us more deeply exactly because it's framed by the recognition of a troubled universe. It's the same productive tension which has allowed film-makers to create their most joyous moments through stories where the protagonists almost, but not quite, lose everything. Take a closer look at Capra's *It's a Wonderful Life*, one tough movie for much of its running time, since it shows how irrepressibly decent James Stewart has had to sacrifice his own dreams of travel and achievement to sustain his family's loan company on which the local community depends. Decades of self-denying service lead him to, well, contemplate suicide from a bridge at Christmas since his insurance policy seems the only thing able to rescue the operation from financial doom. Not such a wonderful life then, after all, until Henry Travers's passing trainee angel shows him the corruption and misery which would have overrun his home town Bedford Falls had he not been born. The climactic affirmation of genuine friendship and mutual reliance is so affecting precisely because it's so darn hard-won.

The triumph over – and thus sublimation of – this fear of loss, which is at the heart of Capra's film, possibly also explains the enduring potency of parental reunions on-screen. Not just in *The Railway Children*, of course, it's a motif common to classic adaptations of children's literature from *Little Women* (choose from George Cukor in 1933, Mervyn LeRoy in 1949 and Gillian Armstrong's 1994 versions, each excellent in its own way) to *A Little Princess* (Alfonso Cuarón's pictorially ravishing 1995 adaptation is far too magical to be the exclusive domain of younger viewers), and it seems to bring a joyful lump to the throat almost every time. Possibly raising the stakes here is the fact that we tend to see these films when we're children, often bouncing on the seats beside mum and dad, thus intensifying the emotional impact of the separation/reunion narrative arc (and explaining the ultimate trauma of seeing Bambi's mother take a fatal bullet). Participating in these filmic experiences as families seems to deepen their effect, and it's this aesthetic of shared pleasures which Disney and latterly Pixar's animated output have so joyously made their own, from the jazzy exuberance of *The Jungle Book* to the sense of community and daring adventure uniting Woody, Buzz Lightyear and cohorts in the *Toy Story* diptych. The same goes for the stop-motion plasticine pleasures of Nick Park's Aardman Animation too of course, the escaped oven skiing on the moon in *A Grand Day Out* with Wallace and Gromit a typically gambolsome moment.

The unfortunate truth is that this is by no means a universal experience in a society where dysfunctional families are now a hard reality. Which is precisely where the special resonance of Spielberg's *E.T. The Extra-Terrestrial* comes in – a film about the end of childhood innocence which somehow leaves us feeling utterly restored. Ahead of Henry Thomas's guileless Elliot lies the neuroses of adolescence and the dislocation of adult relationships (as represented by his one-parent household), but in the meantime it's his unselfish gestures of companionship towards another lost child, albeit of the interstellar variety, that makes the crucial difference in the latter's long journey home. The scene where the BMX-riding kids and their diminutive alien passenger evade the sinister government agents by rising into the skies of suburbia achieves a genuine emotional lift-off that relatively few modern movies have matched, the supposed dedication of the post-*Star Wars* industry to feelgood manipulation notwithstanding.

Still, it would be grossly misleading to suggest that we live at a time where the cinema is simply dominated by calculating and unfeeling acts of commerce, since the ever-developing festival circuit and our ever expanding DVD shelves probably make this a golden age for the discerning viewer. That said, although myriad golden moments from recent celluloid history easily come to mind – Paul Giamatti enjoying his Cheval Blanc under the table at a burger joint in *Sideways*, the couple water-skiing under the bridges of Paris during a fireworks display from *Les Amants du Pont-Neuf*, or even the scene in *Chungking Express* where Faye Wong flies a toy 747 around someone else's apartment – classic Hollywood fare continues to exert its glamorous spell over the collective imagination. Taking, for the sake of argument, the seasonal television schedules as a workable index of our cinematic affections, it really is a question of rounding up the usual suspects. There'll be *The Wizard of Oz, Casablanca, It's a Wonderful Life, Some Like It Hot, The Philadelphia Story* and *Singin' in the Rain* to name only the most obvious titles, and it's as if this desire to encapsulate the cornucopia of Hollywood's back catalogue in just a few ultra-canonical movies merely serves to underline our need for the guaranteed joy and bolstering thematic certainties that these endlessly repeatable movies provide.

Isn't it just a bit restrictive however, when the cinema's reach is so wide, to pore over the same old clips and enthuse over the same old lists, as if the cinematic happy pills of *Casablanca* and company were the only ones available on the shelves? No matter how central these reliable remedies might be, there's still more room in the medicine cabinet after all. We will always have Paris, that's for sure, but in the hope that we might also eventually be arguing over '*The 100 Best Movies You Should See Because They're Wonderful Even If You've Never Heard of Them*', here are just a handful of suggestions for joy-inducing alternative therapy. Not tested on animals, just this particular film enthusiast…

Joy in 20 films

Le Million (1931)
Who wants to be a millionaire? The starving young artist in René Clair's deliciously frisky, wildly innovative musical milestone, that's who. But he's left his winning lottery ticket in his jacket pocket.

Love Me Tonight (1932)
Taking the baton offered by Clair and running with it is Rouben Mamoulian's effervescent musical pick-me-up, wherein humble tailor Maurice Chevalier falls for princess Jeanette MacDonald. And as an unforgettable tracking shot glides through the number 'Isn't It Romantic?', it seems the whole world's in love too.

Ninotchka (1939)
'Garbo laughs!' exclaimed the posters, and well she might – what with charming flâneur Melvyn Douglas offering suave tuition in awakening the visiting commissar's Soviet-suppressed pleasure nodes. Director Ernst Lubitsch conducts proceedings on the backlot Gay Paree with his usual wisdom and grace.

A Matter of Life and Death (1946)
Forget Patrick Swayze and Demi Moore, here's a genuine passion transcending the boundaries of this world and the next. The celestial court decides the fate of shot-down air force pilot David Niven and radio operator Kim Hunter as mavericks Michael Powell and Emeric Pressburger take the viewer on a stairway to heaven.

Kind Hearts and Coronets (1948)
Serial murder was rarely this delightful, as elegant schemer Dennis Price takes extreme measures to secure the title he believes is rightly his, and Alec Guinness plays every single one of his aristocratic victims. Very dry, very dark, astonishingly modern, and in purring Joan Greenwood it certainly has a temptress to kill for.

Born Yesterday (1950)
Judy Holliday. She's funny. She's just funny. You could watch her reading the telephone book, but Hollywood never got round to filming it; so make do instead with her timeless rendition of the blonde who's not as dumb as she looks, giving mob kingpin Broderick Crawford and journo William Holden the run-around.

The Flavour of Green Tea over Rice (1952)
Only Yasujiro Ozu could make the preparation of the most simple meal together a moving affirmation of the renewed bonds between husband and wife divided by subtle class tensions. Simple, timeless mastery.

JOY

So ecstatic you'll cry: Chihiro meets a friend from the past in **Spirited Away**

Umberto D (1952)

Is this the Italian Neo-Realist *It's a Wonderful Life*? A cash-strapped retired civil servant tries desperately to hold on to his dignity, but can't quite end it all because there's his little terrier to think of. It sounds sentimental, but Vittorio De Sica's film is truly elemental in its determination to strip everything down to the urge to love that makes us human.

Mon Oncle (1958)

Man's eternal quest to create a better world for himself is all very well, but what's more human: (a) a modern high-tech mansion, or (b) Tati's Monsieur Hulot, a pipe-puffing old bodger creating unwitting chaos? If you answered (a), you definitely need to catch up with this sustained exercise in painstakingly mounted hilarity.

Pillow Talk (1959)

When the much-needed monograph 'The Joy of Fluff' comes to be written, Doris Day will need a chapter to herself. She's so utterly relaxed on screen, it's hard not to have fun with her, and though the series of 'sex' comedies which began here certainly out-stayed their welcome, this neatly turned frolic with Rock Hudson and a shared phone line is a real tonic for a wet Sunday afternoon.

Jules et Jim (1961)

Boy meets girl meets boy in François Truffaut's considered period romance, revolving around the tantalising caprices of Jeanne Moreau (variously described by the boys as 'a force of nature', 'a queen', 'a catalysm'). Sweet sadness seems etched into every fibre of leading man Oskar Werner, but the music of Georges Delerue supplies everyone with enough lush melancholy and exuberant zip for three movies.

Pierrot le Fou (1965)

Guns, Belmondo on the run, typically Godardian suggestions of a thriller plot, an epochal Sam Fuller

teenage emotions. The classic bit: on his big date neither he nor she knows what to say, so they talk in numbers.

Down by Law (1986)
Only Jim Jarmusch knows how he can play it so deadpan cool yet create something so life-affirming (though he'd probably hate the term). This is the black and white one with Tom Waits, Roberto Benigni and John Lurie as escaped convicts in the Deep South. And altogether now: 'You scream, I scream, we all scream… for ice cream!'

Tampopo (1986)
A worthy paean to the joys of the gourmand, Juzo Itami's freewheeling romp is based around the triumph of a no-hope ramen shop against all the odds. Hats off to the tramps foraging for half-drunk bottles of claret in the bins of a top restaurant, and respect to the elderly noodle sensei who whispers a lover's 'Later…' to the pork slices in his bowl of chashumen.

My Neighbour Totoro (1988)
Hayao Miyazaki's *Spirited Away* remains better known, but this is the true masterpiece by the animator all other animators look up to. A childhood in the country while mum's in hospital, a very large furry friend in the forest and – what's that? A cat? A bus? Both, in fact. You have to see it.

Toto the Hero (1991)
Thomas is convinced he was switched at birth with Alfred, the rich boy next door, and has had the life she should have lived denied him. As Jaco Van Dormael's amazing first feature unfolds however, the protagonist's joys and anxieties, tiny triumphs and disappointments become so real to us, it's like a celebration of film's ability to celebrate life through the inspired assemblage of small things. A marvel to this day.

The Long Day Closes (1992)
Fragments of a '50s Liverpool working-class boyhood on the cusp of adolescence, shaped by a master film-maker so we feel every happy-sad moment of it, from a mother's unconditional love right down to the sunlight on the carpet. The evocation of going to the pictures is so palpably jubilant, it'll burst the heart of every true cinema lover.

Abouna (2002)
The departure of an errant father leaves his two small sons to get their heads round life without him in this truly beautiful offering from Chaddean film-maker Mahamat-Saleh Haroun. There's longing here, but wry comedy too, as the effortlessly natural performances, vibrant colour palette and gently melancholy music from Malian guitar hero Ali Farka Touré combine with such evident rightness, one's only response is to tremble with pleasure.

cameo and Anna Karina singing 'Sans Lendemain' in a blue robe while making coffee in a red pot in a white room. And the world stops. Sigh.

Les Demoiselles de Rochefort (1967)
The greatness of Jacques Demy's musical lies in its acknowledgement that the days of musicals are over. Hence the hallucinatory sight of the real Gene Kelly in pink to match the painted fire hydrants dotting transformed French provincial streets. Meanwhile Michel Legrand's achingly beautiful score plus scintillating singing siblings Catherine Deneuve and Françoise Dorléac assemble the movie equivalent of fine champagne.

Gregory's Girl (1980)
'Modern boys, modern girls… it's good,' reckons John Gordon Sinclair's shy Glasgow schoolboy on the latest undeniably female addition to the football team. She plays havoc with his hormones in this wonderfully observant chronicle of tongue-tied

'The gasp-inducingly beautiful Gong Li' (*centre*), in **Raise the Red Lantern**

JOY

Isabella necessities

Isabella Rossellini selects the eight films she couldn't be without.

The Circus (1928)

I love circuses, and always try to get myself and my kids out for at least one afternoon under the big top every year – but maestro Charlie Chaplin's *The Circus* I watch with a rapture that exceeds pleasure and pushes into exquisite agonies. I've read somewhere that Chaplin didn't care for this project – I know he had a nervous breakdown during or just after production – but sometimes he was just wrong about his own work: *why* did he re-edit his silent masterpieces decades later when improvement upon such loveliness was simply impossible? The Little Tramp's high-wire act with a swarm of sadistic monkeys crawling all over him seems to distil *1001 Nights* under one big top, and the ending is as poignant as anything this side of *City Lights*.

Notorious (1946)

My personal favourite of all my mother's movies. I think even the title opens up so many emotional compartments for me, for I was born during my mother's notoriety as Hollywood infidel and continental usurper. When I was old enough to understand Hitchcock's movie, I felt Cary Grant was victimising mother as much as the rest of the film public was. Later I conveniently chose to understand that film industry hostility as the same species of lust and jealousy which inflamed Grant's character, and I felt less a victim on my mother's behalf and more proud of her, and of her character, for doing what she believed in – what was only right to do. After all, how is a daughter to resent her own mother for falling in love with her father? Anyway, this movie has blurred the borders between movies and real life, and confused me in all the right ways for as long as I've lived – and, I pray, will continue to do so. It's also a really good movie, I think.

Paisà (1946)
The first film by my father, Roberto Rossellini, that I remember watching as a child. I had some girlfriends tell me afterward they were bored, so I was ashamed. Then, later, I heard some adults mumbling the same sentiments. But when I revisited this picture as a teenager I got to make up my own mind about it. I could barely handle the emotional surprise that accompanied my realisation that my father really knew what he was doing. I had been secretly and shamefully short-changing him for years, and now, without saying a word to me, he was telling me through this film that he was a force to be reckoned with, a force that for me would never go away!

Bellissima (Luchino Visconti, 1951)
Visconti, a contemporary of my father's (who shares a centennial with him this year, and who died just a year earlier than my dad), my favourite film about show business and the beauty industry. Starring Anna Magnani (father's bed was still warm from Anna when mother arrived on the scene, and both women practised the same profession – that'll never make for a solid friendship!) as the ultimate backstage mother who is willing to bankrupt her family in order to pursue her illusory dreams of success for her daughter, this film may have been as responsible as anything for my long-delayed – considering my curious pedigree – attempted entry into movies.

La Strada (1954)
I was lucky enough to meet Giulietta Masina often when I was growing up. What lightness and sadness were in her! She was literally a female Chaplin – the Littlest Tramp – both on and off the screen, it seemed. Her Gelsomina here is even a silent movie invention! By the way, did Woody Allen ever admit to stealing the plot of Fellini's *La Strada* for his *Sweet and Lowdown* – right down to the mute (played by Samantha Morton)? If it was a tribute, it was a sweet one, but if he was trying to fool the ghosts of Giulietta and Federico, there will be some strange thumpings and rattlings in Mr Allen's house for the rest of his days.

Some Like It Hot (1959)
I think Marilyn Monroe was never in sexier form than here in her third-last film playing the *über-zaftig* Sugar Kane Kowalczyk. As wonderfully as Orry-Kelly made the gowns for this doomed comic genius, I can't help but wish I could shred them off her hot body with my avid fingers, especially that number that's already half fallen off her during her wild little run with the ukulele. The darkness Marilyn constantly steps into and back out of, even during her comic scenes in this movie, never quite conceals her nakedness, and her willingness to give this much – or inability to give anything but – gave me the courage to tackle my most personally frightening work in *Blue Velvet*.

Moving picture
Holly Hunter

Actress, *Raising Arizona, Broadcast News, The Piano, Thirteen*

There are very few movies where I remember how I felt when I left the theatre – how I physically felt after it was over. Seeing *Wings of Desire* is the exception. I remember I saw it in a theatre in New York that no longer exists, on the corner of 68th and Broadway, where Broadway and Columbus split. It was playing in a small art-house cinema, and I went to an evening show by myself. It was a transcendental experience. I felt I was a different human being when I left the theatre. I remember how the sidewalk felt under my feet, walking away. I felt viscerally, sensorially changed – all of my senses were different. How things tasted, felt, smelled, how I looked and heard the world, everything had been just slightly altered like I'd taken a very subtle drug that just heightened the senses. And the world was new. It was such a delightful occurrence, and I've rarely felt that in my life. It says a lot about what a movie can do.

Moving picture
Tony Leung

Actor, *Hard Boiled, Cyclo, Chungking Express, In the Mood for Love*

I can still remember when I was little my mother took me to see a movie by Roman Polanski, *Dance of the Vampires*. And that movie really impressed me. Is it a black comedy? It's very funny – at least I think so. I can still remember how much I kept laughing – I enjoyed it so much. I don't remember what my mother thought; I was only six.

One Hundred and One Dalmations (1960)

I know Walt Disney didn't direct this (Wolfgang Reitherman and others did), but who remembers this legendary man's directors when his producer's imprint is so obvious? I think my love of animals was cemented when I saw this as a child, and hundreds of odd pets and two children of my own later, I still love this movie, and I think I'm still scared of the Cruella de Vils of this world – I'm on a number of charitable boards fighting her type to this day. I even bought a piglet for my daughter once, simply because it reminded me of one of these animated puppies, and we all had such a great time with it until it grew into a giant, furniture-raping boar. Luckily, it passed away before I had to make any Cruella decisions of my own!

Raise the Red Lantern (1991)

How the gasp-inducingly beautiful Gong Li can succeed in as many different kinds of role as she has, how she even worked up the nerve to attempt this array, is one of the awesome mysteries with which film history confronts me. People have compared Gong and director Zhang Yimou to Dietrich and Sternberg, but for me the Chinese couple is even more impressively cryptic in their design, and this movie is their best. It feels like the history of a country, a culture and even a gender are all present in any randomly chosen frame of this serene and gorgeous poem.

Let Joy be unconfined: Virginia McKenna, Bill Travers and friend in **Born Free**

JOY

Have a sense of humour!

Peter Watts wonders what the critics have against a good old laugh.

The trouble with comedy is that nobody takes it seriously. Just four of the BFI Classics and Modern Classics series of books are dedicated to comedies; only nine comedies have ever won Best Picture at the Oscars. For critics and judges, comedy just doesn't count. This is a curious oversight given that, as Andrew Horton argues in *Comedy Cinema Theory*, 'A case can be made that the first film made was a comedy – depending on whether one dates Edison's recording of Fred Ott's sneeze as having been made in 1889 or 1892.' And it's an oversight that has lead to a sort of black market in movie appreciation: while the critics debate Eastwood, Haneke and Spielberg, ticket-paying hoi polloi are conferring over much baser issues: 'Which did you prefer, *Anchorman* or *Dodgeball*?' (At this point, it should be noted that while some contemporary comedies are considered acceptable, these are normally made by Jim Jarmusch, Wes Anderson or Alexander Payne, so aren't actually funny at all. They might make you chuckle (inwardly), stroke your beard and say 'how clever', but they're not exactly *Airplane!*.)

This has lead to the rather dispiriting state of affairs in which humour is relegated to the second rank, and films that rely on humour to smuggle across otherwise serious point are all but ignored. Chris Head, a comedian and lecturer in comedy theory, says of this attitude: 'First, there's this idea that if you analyse comedy you kill it, and I simply don't agree with that – I think it gives you a richer appreciation. But I also think that people don't couple thinking and laughing: people have an idea it's just about the "ha, ha" and forget the drama and psychology comedy can have.'

Head is making two arguments here: for starters, that there is insufficient appreciation of the terrific skill it takes to produce good comedy, no matter how dumb it appears on the surface (here we should quote the critic who sniffily dismissed Ben Stiller's fashion spoof *Zoolander* by complaining that 'humour based on moronic behaviour quickly grows thin', thus spectacularly missing the point of 90 per cent of great comedy, from Keaton through Strangelove to Will Ferrell). Secondly, comedy can say quite as much as drama – indeed Socrates believed the genius of comedy was equal to that of tragedy – but people are too busy laughing to pay much attention.

And here we're not just talking about the great works of the established canon – be it Woody Allen or Charlie Chaplin – but contemporary comedy as well. *Zoolander* might be dressing down an easy subject,

Nick Broomfield on Comedy

I think the people who interested me most in film when I was growing up were Charlie Chaplin, the Marx Brothers and Peter Sellers. I was always very interested in the way brilliant films like *Modern Times* or *Dr Strangelove* were a mixture of comedy and something more. Those are certainly the films that I admire the most, that I would choose to watch. my father had this old Bell and Howell projector and I remember, as a birthday treat, he'd hire a Chaplin film from the British Film Institute and we'd screen it.

Humour is such a weird thing, really, but it's about something that's in us all, it's about the mistakes that we all make and our own stupidity – and the lunacy of the world we live in, which is why *Modern Times* and *Dr Strangelove* seem more and more relevant.

I think my early films were too earnest, too serious – *Tattooed Tears*, say. I think an audience needs many levels to react to. We've all heard about gallows humour; if you go into a prison, see people on death row, they are very light. I remember Aileen Wuornos telling us jokes (they weren't all particularly great), and she laughed a lot in our interviews, and with her friend Dawn – a lot of mucking around.

The films of Ken Loach I like most, like *Kes*, all have quite a lot of humour to them. The way you reach a bigger audience is with humour – you probably can make a stronger political statement than you could without it.

'The answer is Marx': the irrepressible Harpo in **Duck Soup**

JOY

but it's still a necessary satire of the vapidity, vanity, corruption and downright ludicrousness of the fashion industry. At one point, Stiller's character is asked to model the new fashion line Derelicte, based on the clothing of the homeless. From the notion of tramp chic to the affected gallicism of its name, the line is a wonderful jab at the amorality of the industry, and so a whole lot more telling than the worthy barbs of, say, *Prêt-à-Porter* or *Darling*. Broad comedy gives Stiller freedom to attack fashion without looking like a snob, and this is something that Altman and Schlesinger's conventional dramatic instincts are simply ill-equipped to pull off. 'Superficiality has rarely been treated with such comic depth,' noted *Rolling Stone*'s Peter Travers, one of the few critics happy to give comedy its due; but what even he fails to appreciate is that this is the only way to treat superficiality, and that Stiller's comedic sensibility innately grasped when Altman and Schlesinger could not.

Comedy is not just at its best when it confronts superficiality, however, as the Greeks, the founders of the comedy tradition, fully realised. For them, comedy was any drama that exacted laughter by holding up a mirror to all that was characteristic of Athenian social and political life. Greek dramatic theatre followed strict rules and comedy allowed writers to step outside of that (*à la* Groucho Marx or Charlie Kaufman), or to parody it. To the Greeks we can also attribute our supposedly modern fondness for 'gross-out humour': Greek comedy featured grossness and licentiousness that was in keeping with the sentiment of the Dionysian festivals at which they were performed. Writes one scholar, 'To omit these features from comedy would be to deprive it of its most popular element.'

Critics' choice
Let's dance!

The Company
(2003, US) d Robert Altman. *cast* Neve Campbell, The Joffrey Ballet of Chicago. Altman hangs out with a dance troupe and creates the best ballet movie ever.

Dirty Dancing
(1987, US) d Emile Ardolino. *cast* Jennifer Gray, Patrick Swayze, Jerry Orbach, Cynthia Rhodes. Sex and rock 'n' roll in a '60s setting. Sleazy Swayze and 'Baby' have the time of their lives.

42nd Street
(1933, US) d Lloyd Bacon. Warner Baxter, Ruby Keeler, Bebe Daniels, Dick Powell. The Bacon and Busby Berkeley backstage saga that revived the fortunes of the musical.

French Cancan
(1955, Fr) d Jean Renoir. *cast* Jean Gabin, Françoise Arnoul, Maria Félix, Gianni Esposito. Renoir's riot of colour and high kicks backstage at the Moulin Rouge is a love letter to Paris.

Guys and Dolls
(1955, US) d Joseph L Mankiewicz. *cast* Marlon Brando, Jean Simmons, Frank Sinatra. A musical with emotional depth that glitters with intelligence... and a singing and dancing Brando.

Saturday Night Fever
(1977, US) d John Badham. *cast* John Travolta, Karen Lynn Gorney, Barry Miller, Joseph Cali. Glitter balls, bell-bottoms and the Bee Gees. It's a disco inferno.

Singin' in the Rain
(1952, US) d Stanley Donen. *cast* Gene Kelly, Donald O'Connor, Debbie Reynolds, Jean Hagen. What a glorious feeling, as the prince of fancy footwork spins round that lamppost again.

Strictly Ballroom
(1992, Aust) d Baz Luhrmann. *cast* Paul Mercurio, Tara Morice, Bill Hunter, Pat Thomson. Where the bizarre rituals of the ballroom world were first exposed – for all to snigger at.

Top Hat
(1935, US) d Mark Sandrich. *cast* Fred Astaire, Ginger Rogers, Edward Everett Horton. Fred 'n' Ginger get togged up, dance cheek-to-cheek and hoof to a superb Irving Berlin score.

West Side Story
(1961, US) d Robert Wise, Jerome Robbins. *cast* Natalie Wood, George Chakiris, Rita Moreno. Wise brings *Romeo & Juliet* to the gang-ridden streets of New York.

Probably the funniest talkie comedy ever: Rosalind Russell and Cary Grant in **His Girl Friday**

So the Farrelly brothers – creators of *There's Something About Mary, Dumb & Dumber* and *Stuck On You* – are following a noble tradition with their excessive interest in bodily fluids, but it should also be noted that their films are about breaking taboos as well as breaking wind. Indeed, the subject matters of Farrelly films – obesity or conjoined twins – could just as easily be fodder for iconoclastic, abrasive directors like Lars von Trier or Todd Solondz. Another unexpected taboo-breaker was Judd Apatow's excellent *The 40 Year Old Virgin*, a subtle and rewarding comedy of genuine emotional depth that dared to take issue with one of Hollywood's uncontested maxims: sex matters. In a rare moment of comedic appreciation, the American Film Institute named it one of their ten best films of 2005.

The greatest taboo-breaker of recent times, though, was Trey Parker and Matt Stone's extraordinary *Team America: World Police*, so uninterested in convention that it dispensed with actors entirely, preferring to use puppets

in scenes involving copious vomit and patriotic gay sex. The film – a satire of the War on Terror – also tackled the complexities of the current geopolitical situation with an even-handedness designed to piss off conservatives and liberals alike, and in so doing emphasised that independent-minded comedy is the one theatrical and cinematic tradition that it would be impossible to make under any form of government other than a democracy. *Team America* got nowhere in the Oscars, which probably had something to do with the way Parker and Stone lampooned the kneejerk politics of both liberal actors and gung-ho producers, but also because its essential message was one that Hollywood and critics really aren't too comfortable with – that some ideas are too complicated for cinema to handle. Like most great art forms, cinema hates to be reminded of its own limitations, but isn't that what comedy, from Aristophanes to today, has always been best at – mocking the pretensions of the elite?

Through a child's eyes

Some films you see as a child leave lasting traces, as **Malena Janson** explains.

I carry with me three exceptionally vivid memories of cinematic experiences from early childhood, each connected to an emotion so strong I can feel it again and again at any time. First: sadness, triggered by French director Albert Lamorisse's *The Red Balloon* (1956). Second: fear, courtesy of Martin Rosen's *Watership Down* (1978). Third: happiness, from Swedish director Kjell Grede's *Hugo and Josefin* (1967).

These three arthouse children's films seem very different at first glance, but a closer look exposes at least one common feature of great importance. Unlike the vast majority of mainstream family films, they tell their stories entirely from a child's point of view. And this, I think, is the reason why they still have a strong impact on young audiences today – and why I think they should be considered timeless children's classics and made accessible to every new generation of film-goers.

In film at least, a child's point of view means more than, say, the low camera angles offered in John Lasseter's *Toy Story* (1995). There's a whole range of devices that, taken together, create a kind of children's film aesthetic, characterised by its power to address a young audience directly, on its own terms. In other words, they can make a film spark a child's emotions without making a detour via his or her intellect.

Lamorisse's *The Red Balloon* is the story of a small boy living with his severe grandmother in a shabby quarter of Paris. On the way to school one morning, he finds a magic red balloon. The two of them become friends, the balloon following the boy everywhere. This arouses the other kids' violent envy, and they don't stop hunting the odd couple until the balloon is burst. The devastated boy, though, gets his revenge and comfort when all the balloons of Paris come to his rescue and carry him away, high above the rooftops, to, one imagines, a better and more beautiful world.

JOY

Moving picture
Antoine de Caunes

Actor; broadcaster; director, *Monsieur N*

There was this place in Paris, the Cinémathèque Française, at the Palais de Chaillot [since relocated to premises in the city's Bercy quarter], where I spent part of my life as a teenager. There, for a very cheap price, you could see classic films from all over the world. That's where I discovered all the people who gave me the will and desire to work some day in the movies: Welles, Chaplin, Ford, Walsh, Minnelli, Mankiewicz, Lubitsch, Wilder, Visconti, Polanski, Renoir, Kazan. The Cinémathèque was a hot spot for young movie freaks. Just being there was already making a statement. You had to show up with *Le Monde* under your arm – no need to open it – and with a book as strong and deep as Bataille's *Ma Mère* rising from your pocket, so that the young female movie freaks could instantly understand what kind of guy you were. After the screenings, we had passionate talks about the films, where we developed our own individual theories about the way these films were done or should have been done – this is still, even today, considered a national sport in France. One particular night pops to mind: the film was Tarkovsky's *Andrei Rublev*, a long, slow and depressed Russian movie, and still one of the most powerful films ever. It was certainly not a teenage movie, even for a post-existentalist teenager from the '70s. But we all knew that here was a masterpiece. All we could possibly do when the film ended was to agree silently with its complex metaphors. Of course, this was an exception. Usually we would argue endlessly while smoking cigarettes like Humphrey Bogart to impress the girls. I don't smoke any more, I don't try as hard to flirt, but I can see that all these directors remain a major influence. God bless the Cinémathèque.

Glorious, classic sci-fi: **Forbidden Planet**

For a grown-up, *The Red Balloon* is, in intellectual terms, quite easily deciphered: it's a film about hope, trust and faith. However grey and harsh life may seem, there's always the possibility of change, of unexpected encounters and the presence of something higher than daily life. A child doesn't have an adult's capacity to explain his or her experience of the film, but since *The Red Balloon* uses non-verbal and non-intellectual devices to get its message across, I think that's why a young audience understands its meaning. And that's why I, aged five or six, was so strongly affected by one of the final scenes, when the balloon is 'tortured' by a bunch of bullying, screaming kids: hit by a slingshot once, then twice, sinking towards the dirty ground, shrinking, becoming wrinkled and ugly, until a boy delivers the final blow

Moving picture
Takeshi Kitano

**Actor; stand-up comic; director, *Boiling Point, Sonatine, Hana-Bi, Dolls, Zatoichi, Takeshis*';
TV presenter; writer**

There are actually two nights I remember especially vividly. The first was when I was a kid, and my brother took me into Tokyo to see a movie. For some reason, it was an Italian movie, Pietro Germi's *Il Ferroviere*. Foreign movies were just beginning to appear at that time and I remember feeling very depressed by it. Or maybe it wasn't the movie, which I couldn't understand a word of anyway – maybe it was because on the way home, my brother and I got beaten up by some older kids. Whatever, I don't have happy memories of it. The other memory isn't much better. I was in junior high, and some friends and I decided to go and see a film with lots of hot sex. We chose something called *The Virgin Spring*, not knowing it was by Ingmar Bergman. All that black and white angst and misery and religious questioning! We were so bored and frustrated. So much for our hopes of hardcore!

with his boot. This would not have been such a sad moment for me, had I not been emotionally drawn into the film from its first minute.

The Red Balloon is almost entirely wordless, communicating (like the boy and his new friend, the balloon) with pictures and sounds that pleasure the senses. The city's prevailing greyish colours make a striking contrast to the shimmering red of the balloon. Sounds of traffic are harsh and loud, and counterpoint the light, melodious music accompanying the boy's games with the balloon. The long shots of a seemingly endless, incomprehensible and unfriendly city are contrasted with extreme close-ups of the happy little boy and his beautiful friend.

Together, these devices create a magic universe that pulls young viewers right in – a small yet unconstrained cinematic world of their own, where borders between reality and fantasy don't exist, where balloons are as alive as you or me and the language of emotions is more important than the spoken word.

The same goes for *Watership Down* and *Hugo and Josefin*, the two other films that affected me so strongly as a kid. Martin Rosen's adaptation of Richard Adams' book a tale of rabbits fleeing an endangered warren and founding a new one on their own terms, and fulfiling their dreams of a good life – is a visually and aurally strong cinematic affair. Its distinct and multi-faceted animation style shows the world entirely from the minuscule, yet emotionally and intellectually capable, rabbits' point of view – a view a child can easily identify with.

Similarly, *Hugo and Josefin* is the story of a boy and a girl who find their own world within the larger, visible one, as a survival strategy when life gets unbearable. Together they conquer magic universes in places generally considered dangerous by adults: the woods, a refuse dump, a sandpit. This groundbreaking and much loved Swedish children's film is unconventionally couched in a fragmentary style slightly reminiscent of an Impressionist painting. It's the narration of a child's subjective experiences, rather than a more conventionally coherent, straightforward story.

What, then, does all this come down to? That arthouse children's cinema is better than mainstream family films? Yes and no. I really enjoy a well-made Disney. But I believe that the films I've mentioned here can give children something that mainstream cinema cannot:

Moving picture
William Friedkin

Director, *The Exorcist*, *The French Connection*, *The Hunted*

As a kid I'd go with my friends to see movies – cartoons, adventure films. Nothing serious, just Saturday afternoon movies. I didn't realise there was such a thing as cinema until I saw *Citizen Kane*. It was 1956, I was 20. Someone had told me that I should see this movie, which wasn't playing a lot at that time. It was showing at the Surf Theatre in the North Side of Chicago. I was working in television then, hoping for a career in live television. It was a Saturday afternoon, about noon. I stayed in the theatre for the rest of the day. I couldn't believe it. It was a revelation. I saw it four times and went back the next day and every day for a while. *Citizen Kane* is to cinema what James Joyce's *Ulysses* is to literature. I was conscious almost immediately of the incredible use of image, sound, performance, editing, music and lighting to tell a unique story. I guess I thought, 'Somebody actually did this and had the guts to do it.' That's how I turned my attention to cinema, and I still continue to do it in the hope that someday I can make a film that will impress me as much as *Citizen Kane* did then. And I certainly haven't done that yet.

JGY

strong emotional impact – memories that last a lifetime. Mainstream children's films today are driven by the commercial requirement to appeal to as many as possible. Everybody likes *Shrek*, but its purpose is to tell a story – not to supply an emotional experience. And since it has to appeal to the grown-ups who pay for the tickets, *Shrek*, *Finding Nemo* and countless recent box office hits are stuffed with verbal gags beyond the ken of children.

And that's why I doubt that any five-year-old girl of today will, 30 years from now, carry with her a vivid memory of a 2006 screening of *Madagascar*. Which is fine, as long as there are other films to provide strong emotional experiences. But are there? I do wonder if, in thrall to the widespread fear of upsetting children in any possible way, we deny them the true magic of cinema. Perhaps, with the best of intentions, we confiscate their red balloon.

Funny particular

Playwright **Conor McPherson** explains his debt to film's most famous neurotic.

For as long I can remember, Woody Allen's movies have been a cinematic touchstone for me. He's one of the very few film-makers who combine rare technical innovation with a disarming ability to dramatise the deep inner states that cause human beings so much perplexity. Allen's personality seems to shine through every aspect of his storytelling and exposes the insecure existentialist in us all.

Perhaps it was his early career as a joke writer and stand-up comedian that equipped him with an ability to roam at will through such a detailed gallery of human observation in his movies. A wonderful example is *Annie*

Hall, which leaps with the stand-up's natural flow from one metaphysical meditation to the next, each one conveyed with great visual inventiveness: Annie (Diane Keaton) showing Alvy (Allen) around her life as they roam through long-ago parties, checking out her past self in action; Annie having a literal out-of-body experience while Alvy makes love to her; Marshall McLuhan stepping in from the abyss at the edge of frame to adjudicate in a petty dispute about his theories in a cinema queue. It won Academy Awards for Best Screenplay, Best Director and Best Picture in 1977 (beating off competition from the mega hits *Star Wars*,

Critics' choice
Grub, grub, glorious grub

Babette's Feast
(1987, Den) *d* Gabriel Axel. *cast* Stéphane Audran, Jean-Philipe Lafont, Gudmar Wivesson. Gastronomic wizardry in a magical last supper.

The Cook, the Thief, His Wife & Her Lover
(1989, GB/Fr) *d* Peter Greenaway. *cast* Richard Bohringer, Michael Gambon, Helen Mirren. The cannibalism might be hard to stomach, but there's plenty of food for thought here.

Delicatessen
(1990, Fr) *d* Jean-Pierre Jeunet, Marc Caro. *cast* Dominique Pinon, Marie-Laure Dougnac. Comedy tale of a butcher dealing in human flesh, and an undergroud group of veggie fanatics.

Dinner Rush
(2000, US) *d* Bob Giraldi. *cast* Danny Aiello, Edoardo Ballerini, Vivian Wu, Mike McGlone. Mobster thriller with revenge on the menu.

The Discreet Charm of the Bourgeoisie
(1972, Fr) *d* Luis Buñuel. *cast* Fernando Rey, Delphine Seyrig, Stéphane Audran, Bulle Ogier.
Six characters search for a meal they never eat.

La Grande Bouffe
(1973, Fr) *d* Marco Ferreri. *cast* Marcello Mastroianni, Ugo Tognazzi, Michel Piccoli. A reworking of Sade's *120 Days of Sodom*, with protracted orgies of eating and screwing.

Like Water for Chocolate
(1991, Mex) *d* Alfonso Arau. *cast* Marco Leonardi, Lumi Cavozos, Regina Torne. Characters boil and bubble over as the women-folk of Mexico eat, fantasise and crave.

Partie de Campagne
(1936, Fr) *d* Jean Renoir. *cast* Sylvia Bataille, Georges Darnoux, Jane Marken, André Gabriello. Masterly adaptation of Maupassant's tale of an all-to-brief romance during a country picnic.

The Scent of Green Papaya
(1993, Fr) *d* Tran Anh Hung. *cast* Yen-Khe Tran Nu, Man San Lu, Thi Loc Truong.
A peasant girl's cooking chores take on a more fulfilling purpose as she reaches womanhood.

Tampopo
(1986, Japan) *d* Juzo Itami. *cast* Tsutomu Yamazaki, Nobuko Miyamoto, Koji Yakusho. Noodle-meister gives Zen lesson in enhancing your love life with salt, lemon and cream.

Close Encounters of the Third Kind and *Saturday Night Fever*), and lots of Allen's later themes are introduced in the movie.

Among his many preoccupations, a favourite of mine is man's inability to accept love and beauty in his life – as to do so is to welcome the attendant notions of responsibility and mortality. Just as Alvy in *Annie Hall* claims to live by Groucho Marx's adage – 'I don't want to belong to any club that will accept me as a member' – so Isaac (Allen) turns his back on Tracy (Mariel Hemingway) in *Manhattan*. He's 42, she's 17. She's beautiful and smart, but he cannot accept her unconditional love. Instead, he pursues neurotic, insecure Mary (Keaton) who's closer to him in age. In perhaps the most heartbreaking scene of any Allen movie, Isaac ineptly breaks with Tracy, apparently unable to think that his rejection could make such a young girl feel unhappy. It's one of the director's most surprising performances, as truthful in its awkwardness as it's accomplished in its execution.

Where *Annie Hall* dazzled audiences with its range of philosophical questions and manipulation of cinematic grammar, *Manhattan* cast a colder eye on its subjects. Working with his *Annie Hall* cinematographer, the talented Gordon Willis, Allen chose to shoot *Manhattan* in black and white. Its timeless, almost gothic feel is balanced by Allen's usual innovation of this period. Shooting most scenes in one long take, Willis finds wonderful compositions again and again. The characters wander in and out of shot, and sometimes there's no one in the shot at all – we just hear them. All of which adds appropriately to the mood of a film which turns out, in a strange way, to be about faith: faith in ourselves and our choices, and faith in the ability of others to see and accept us as we are.

Faith underpins perhaps my favourite Woody Allen movie, *Crimes and Misdemeanors*. Judah (Martin Landau) is racked by guilt after arranging the death of his unstable mistress (Anjelica Huston), having been stricken with terror that she would expose his infidelity to his wife. Landau's doom-laden eyes stare into his inner darkness in a moving portrayal of the hopelessness of the human condition. This is mirrored comically by Allen himself, playing Clifford, the film-maker who can only watch in horror as the corrupt subject of his

documentary, TV mogul Lester (Alan Alda), triumphs in every area of his sleazy life. In a characteristically apposite metaphor, Landau is an eye specialist whose rabbi and spiritual guide is losing his sight. In a sustained and highly satisfying manner, the film forcefully asks the question 'If there's no God, are not free to do as we please?' Of course, there's no answer – and the silence is deafening.

These three movies, *Annie Hall*, *Manhattan* and *Crimes and Misdemeanors* are, for me, cornerstones of Woody Allen's status as a great artist. In this limited space one can only hint at the appreciation and pleasure they have given. But let's not ignore what Allen deprecatingly calls his 'early, funny' movies, such as *Take the Money and Run*, *Play It Again, Sam* (directed by Herbert Ross, starring Allen in his own script) and *Sleeper*, any of which will stand up as hilarious and deeply original. And many fans will list later ones as favourites: the stylish, tragicomic and oddly affecting *Broadway Danny Rose*, the gorgeous autumnal poise of *Hannah and Her Sisters*; or perhaps *Husbands and Wives*, with its fly-on-the-wall jumpiness that unleashes a vicious roar from the depths of disappointment and anger born of broken relationships.

And then there's the extraordinary number of career-best performances given by the stars of his films. Oscar winners from his work include Mira Sorvino, Diane Weist and Diane Keaton; Oscar-nominated actors include Jennifer Tilly, Chazz Palminteri, Mariel Hemingway, Maureen Stapleton, Geraldine Page, and Judy Davis.

In his finest moments, Allen somehow has the ability to tap into and articulate the very feeling of being alive. I know there are critics who lament some of his recent films compared to past glories, but we must remember that this is only because he has created such an enormously high standard to live up to. He has single-handedly created and mastered a mini genre – and one that's very risky to imitate, as it requires such skill at so many levels. He's been as innovative with the camera and lighting as he has been in his screenwriting. He's drawn great, memorable performances from fellow actors while remaining a movie star who only ever seems to be playing himself – which, rather ironically, is the true accomplishment of any Hollywood immortal.

Cracked icon

James Christopher maps the highs and lows of Hollywood icon Elizabeth Taylor.

Dame Elizabeth Taylor announced her retirement from acting on 20 March 2003, having failed to make a memorable film for over 25 years. Very few people have taken her at all seriously as an actress since the 1970s. Yet the 74-year-old icon exerts a grip on the public imagination that belies anything she ever achieved on screen. Her greatest role has always been her own life, and it's a story of preposterous excess. The famous love affairs, the eight hysterical marriages, the ritzy diamonds and the long list of addictions are the stuff of lore. If an inventory of her physical ailments were compiled, it be as thick as a respectable medical dictionary. Heaven knows why we idolise her. Perhaps it's plain envy, or a pious sense of 'there but for the grace of God'.

Since the 1950s, Taylor has epitomised the tabloid glamour of the Hollywood juggernaut at its frothy best and frightful worst. Women wanted to look like the scarlet star and men dreamed of sleeping with her. She was the Queen of Hearts long before Diana was born. The studio system – notably as practised by MGM – cynically manipulated her sultry, forbidden fruit image as early as *National Velvet*. And for long periods of Taylor's career she didn't seem to know where her films ended and the scandals began. (A similar confusion tipped her fellow stable mate, Vivien Leigh, into madness.) Taylor thrived on the unhealthy game, despite the fact that it made her one of the most haunted people on the planet.

Even now, after incarnations as perfume tycoon, Republican senator's wife, official best friend of Michael Jackson, bride of Larry 'the oaf' Fortensky, and latterly dedicated AIDS campaigner, Taylor can still mint a bizarre headline. An example is the court battle she fought in 2005 over a Van Gogh painting. She bought *View of the Asylum and Chapel at Saint-Rémy* at auction in 1963, but relatives of a German Jewish woman claimed in 2004 that the painting was stolen from its rightful owners by the Nazis. Taylor won her case, but it's a measure of the supernatural sticking power of her celebrity that she keeps popping up in these unexpected corners.

'Her propensity for accidents and overdoses made her virtually uninsurable by the early 1980s'

JOY

The crushing irony is the scant respect she once commanded as 'the world's most famous actress'. Taylor was so much a creature of the mighty Hollywood studio system that few modish directors and critics ever really took her talent seriously. It pains her to this day. But frankly the actress herself is partly to blame. She was remarkably undiscriminating about some of the roles that came her way, to the point where she was routinely cast for who she was rather than what she could play. The most notorious example is Joseph L Mankiewicz's *Cleopatra*, a fiasco that cost $40 million (which today equates to the stupendous sum of $300 million).

Cleopatra took two and a half years to make, and brought Twentieth Century Fox to its knees. Taylor nearly died when her respiratory system collapsed in March 1961 while the film was still flapping pointlessly around foggy Pinewood sets unconvincingly dressed like sunny Imperial Rome. In some of the publicity stills you can see the tracheotomy scar snaking down one side of her windpipe. Thanks to Richard Burton's torrid affair with Taylor, the film is rather better known for what was happening off screen than for the sludgy historical epic that eventually recouped its cost, just.

Yet a handful of pictures among the 65 or so that fill her CV illustrate what a terrific actress she could be if pushed into the right part. *A Place in the Sun*, directed by George Stevens when Liz was barely nineteen, gave her a blisteringly febrile role as a society girl who tempts Montgomery Clift to thoughts of murder. Stevens directed her again in *Giant*, a soap opera of an epic that charts the oil boom in Texas from the early 1900s to the 1950s; she was Oscar-nominated for her performance as a young virgin who ages into the most glamorous grandmother in film history. Rock Hudson

plays her flinty husband; his tough-as-nails rival, James Dean, died in a car crash just days after the movie wrapped.

Creatively, it was a golden decade for Taylor, even if her friends were dropping dead around her. Her third husband and producer, Mike Todd, died in a freak plane crash as Richard Brooks began shooting *Cat on a Hot Tin Roof*. The grieving Taylor should have won an Oscar for her performance as the neurotic, frustrated wife of Paul Newman's repressed gay husband. It was amazing she was able to pull herself together long enough to act the part. The following year her best friend, Montgomery Clift, nearly died in a car accident during the making of *Suddenly Last Summer*, a deeply spooky film by Joseph L Mankiewicz (based on another Tennessee Williams play) where Liz is used as bait to lure young boys for her predatory homosexual cousin.

She finally won an Oscar for *BUtterfield 8*, in which she plays a free-wheeling, nymphomaniac call-girl. Taylor hated the film, dubbing it cheap and sleazy, and has never shaken the suspicion that she won the Academy sympathy vote on the back of her near-fatal collapse shortly after while on set for *Cleopatra*. Her second Oscar for her portrayal of a drunken, rampaging wife in Mike Nichols' *Who's Afraid of Virginia Woolf?* gave her far greater pleasure. Based on Edward Albee's stage play, and co-starring Richard Burton as her manipulative history professor husband, it proved to be Taylor's finest moment – and a portent of things to come.

The magic evaporated from her acting as surely as it did from her two volatile and exhausting marriages to Burton. Taylor's career unravelled in much the same fashion as her private life: into histrionic romances, camp thrillers, and marital comedies. Her propensity for accidents and overdoses made her virtually uninsurable by the early 1980s. Her bride of Frankenstein hairstyles, trips to the Betty Ford Clinic and yo-yoing waistline have been analysed ad nauseam. The wonder is that she remains an international shrine.

Andy Warhol once said, when quizzed about the afterlife, 'It would be very glamorous to be reincarnated as a giant ring on Elizabeth Taylor's finger.' Sadly, we'll never know if he now regrets it. But I suspect the view from her middle digit is, indeed, fascinating.

Anger

'Come on! Fancy taking a poke at me? Come on, big man.' *Scum*

Anger strike

Sukhdev Sandhu loses it at the movies – his temper, that is.

Anger has to be, today, the most common emotion that any regular film-goer is likely to feel. One stumbles out of *Charlie's Angels Full Throttle* or *2 Fast 2 Furious* in a state of incensed discombobulation. The money assembled to make these militantly brainless blockbusters would feed villages in developing countries for decades; their promotional budgets alone are the size of some countries' entire movie industries. And to think of all the technical and creative talent that has been squandered – well, it's enough to make you want to hit someone: the director, maybe; perhaps the actors. Someone, surely, should suffer for the nausea and rage you feel.

But perhaps this is just a cinecidal fantasy. For the reality is that most film-goers aren't angry. Or at least, not angry enough. We still queue up or hang around on-line in the hope of snagging returned tickets for the latest FX-heavy, sound-and-CGI-vision, dolbyed-up extravaganza that's been furiously hyped in every listings magazine, radio programme and cable-telly talk show. If, having managed to get in, we emerge a couple of hours later feeling rather disappointed, it's rare for us to froth or rage. As more and more technically competent, adequately spliced-together movies get made, our responses to them are similarly equivocal. 'It was okay', we'll mumble, when asked for our reactions. It seems we no longer go to the movies expecting to stagger out incredulous at their transcendent brilliance or abject awfulness.

Perhaps it was always thus. Perhaps, barring a few film crazies and obsessive cinephiles, most people have always gone to the pictures hoping to be calmed and reassured rather than tattered and transformed. Life is stressful and taxing enough, thankyou; maybe what most film-goers hanker after is actually gentle pacification. Even committed fright fans who crave shocks on a regular basis do so knowing that their regularity has fostered a genre – and

ANGER

Calm between storms: **Ladybird Ladybird**

standard recipes for effects – that by and large insulates them from the possibility of being truly shocked.

Speaking personally, I never went to the cinema as a child, and the chief reason was my suspicion that the form itself was incapable of sufficiently moving me. Like a lot of bookish teenagers, I was weaned on Modernist *littérateurs* who harboured deeply ambivalent responses to the advent of the movies. In particular, I was a herd follower of DH Lawrence, and agreed with his invective, articulated in such novels as *The Lost Girl*, that cinema was at best a branch of semi-vernacular mechanics. How could this medium ever rival the blood-and-sweat physicality of theatre? How could it stir the passions or succeed in catalysing its audiences when it lacked the face-to-face of soapbox orators, circus barkers and travelling showmen?

For sure, somewhere in the back of my mind was a trace memory of archive footage showing scared Parisians fleeing from a cinémathèque in fear of being mowed down by steam trains. I envied them their naivety: would that more movies could be engines of extreme emotion. Would that they were always capable of generating such shock and awe and distress. But growing up in the mid-1980s, a particularly enervated period in the history of cinema, a time when there seemed to be no escape from the crinolined and carefully suppressed emotions of Merchant Ivory productions, it seemed impossible that film could ever give voice to the idealism and tangled passions that raged in my teenage heart.

And then, luckily (it being the days when subtitled films were still shown on the main television channels), I happened to see Vittorio De Sica's *Bicycle Thieves*. A simple story at heart, it charts the struggles of proud but unemployed father Antonio Ricci (played by Lamberto Maggiorani) to find a job in post-war Italy that will let him feed his wife and child. One does finally turn up – pasting film posters across the city – but he has to lie and pretend he has the requisite bicycle. His wife pawns their bed sheets so he can get one, but it is stolen almost immediately. For the rest of the film he wanders up and down the city, often with his young son in tow, trying to track down the thief and resume his attempts to live a normal life.

The film is a classic of the neo-realist movement, and has influenced directors as various as Satyajit Ray, François Truffaut, Ken Loach and Lukas Moodysson. It indicates the intimate relationship between realism and anger (sci-fi cinema may contain scathing critiques of contemporary society, but that venom is usually subordinated to the task of creating future landscapes on screen). It also shows that cinema can act as a kind of bulletin board, a platform for highlighting all the stories that are excluded from mainstream media. Unlike news and current-affairs broadcasts, which are increasingly brief blipverts of pre-packaged pathos, movies can dispense with the pretence of neutrality as well as maintain a sustained focus on those stories.

Bicycle Thieves is a long, desperate howl of rage by a man who is in danger of losing his dignity and self-respect. It is the howl of millions of other Italians who struggled to make ends meet after the end of World War II. But the anger he reveals, both in the words that he yells to the apparent thief and to the people who shield him from capture, as well as in every mute but eloquent close-up of his face, are assertions, not merely of victimhood, but of an ennobling resistance. Anger, as John Lydon would later sing, is an energy. It's an assertion of humanity. It's a refusal to bow and be conquered.

And in Maggiorani's defiance lie the seeds of eventual reconstruction. It declares: this is not the way society should be. That simple idea is the first and most important stage in encouraging viewers to imagine what a better society would look like. That act of imagining is, of course, not confined to the late 1940s; it's one that has been proposed since time immemorial, and is almost as important as it is to drink water or eat food.

The genius of *Bicycle Thieves* is to make the father's plight both local and universal. To show us not just the extent of his particular ill-fortune, but the way so many people spend their waking lives on the thin line between poverty and meagre subsistence, dignity and degradation. We wish Ricci well, but we're also fully, painfully aware that all those smudged figures on the edge of the screen, the grey hordes he rushes past while trying to get hold of the thief – they are, in all likelihood, people as impoverished and as deserving as him.

ANGER

Film directors often produce some of their most effective work when dealing with true stories. The authenticity of the subject matter, and their own commitment to representing their subjects' lives, galvanises them in a way that dramatising fictional screenplays doesn't always do. Phillip Noyce has certainly never made a better film than *Rabbit-Proof Fence*, his chronicle of Australia's 'stolen generation', the mixed-race children who, between 1910 and 1971, were seized from their Aboriginal parents and transported to resettlement camps to be trained as domestic servants.

The challenge he faced was to balance the need for historical context – to give due weight to the social, political and philosophical foundations of such barbarous legislation – without turning the film into an educational video. Helped by Christopher Doyle, one of the greatest cameramen in the world today, he largely dispenses with dialogue and lets the desert landscape express the pain of the two Aborigine girls who decide to run away from one of the camps; it is, by turns, a ruined ancient kingdom, a lunar colony, a bleached-out Arctic hell.

The film works – that is, it appals and enrages us – because, like *Bicycle Thieves*, it's a convincingly local drama that also succeeds as a hymn to the human longing for freedom. International audiences will be unfamiliar with the story and will therefore feel free to respond to it primarily at an emotional level; if they knew more about the policy, their response would likely be more interpretative and analytical. Most of all, the silence of the film lets us hear our own fury mount, so much so in fact that timorous governments in Australia, still blind to the scale and depth of the suffering they have inflicted on their Aboriginal populations, have spent millions of dollars urging audiences to boycott the movie.

Anger tends to be most effective as a one-time blast. Repeated outbursts, as parents of young children know, tend to be less potent. Even a film as fine as *Rabbit-Proof Fence* loses some of its revelatory, if not its aesthetic, force the second time round. Rage works – and wears – best on the screen when it is embodied: the likes of *Taxi Driver*, *Falling Down*, *Naked*, *I Stand Alone* and *Crimson Gold*. In all of these dramas, the line between lunatic hysteria and righteous ire is porous in the extreme. The

'De Sica's The Bicycle Thieves *is a long, desperate howl of rage by a man who is in danger of losing his dignity and self-respect.*'

characters soak up all the tensions, pressures and malaise of the societies they inhabit: their personal struggles are also social portraits. Their anger, even though it may be nauseatingly expressed (and in the case of the racist horse-butcher of Gaspar Noé's *I Stand Alone* come from nauseating characters), always carries with it the suggestion that it is a deeper truth. Bile, as Greil Marcus suggested in his book *Lipstick Traces*, part of which traces the link between the mendicant seers of the Middle Ages and the will-to-rage of the punk era, can also be a form of premonition. Even the most feral characters, perhaps strangely linked to their madness or moral blindness, may provide a portal to some perverse lucidity.

For me, one of the most extraordinary, and most extraordinarily enraged pieces of cinema is *Punishment Park* by Peter Watkins. Dismissed by critics on its release and yanked from American screens after just four days, its sensibility is unlike that of almost any other English film of its period. It is a Kaddish, a Ginsberg howl, a Patty Waters threnody, a counter-cultural update of Edvard Munch's *The Scream*, Marlow's 'The horror' mixed with Public Enemy's exhortation to 'Bring the Noise' mixed with Billie Whitelaw blabbing and yelping in Samuel Beckett's *Not I*.

Set in late 1960s California and featuring a motley cast of mainly non-professional actors, the film is a political drama-cum-faux documentary that intercuts between two different cabals of refuseniks and hippy agitators. One of them, Group 638, is to be found in a tribunal tent defending, before a round table of hostile attorneys and politicos, their decision not to fight in Vietnam. Those found guilty are given the chance to serve lengthy prison sentences or to go to Bear Mountain Punishment Park. Here, in desert conditions so bleak and torturous they would try the hardiest camel, Group 637 has been given three days in which to reach an American flag that lies 53 miles away.

It's a perverse scenario, albeit one that anticipates recent abuses at Guantanamo Bay. But the film is best thought of in auditory terms. The courtroom debates about citizenship and loyalty, about the legality of the war in Vietnam and the war against America's own black population, are conducted at a charged, necessarily hysterical level. Group 637's wretched odyssey is narrated by a fruity-voiced English reporter who begins by trying to maintain neutrality, but ends screaming profanities at the city cops and Home Guards whose brutalities he has seen at first hand.

Punishment Park, as much as Hendrix's incendiary version of 'The Star-Spangled Banner', is about the liberating power of noise. It announces that the time for irony or polite calls for reform is over; what's needed is an infernal noise of mass rage, the human riposte to the roar of helicopters napalming East Asian villages. The force and desperation with which it does so runs counter to even the most partisan agit-prop art of the period, and has lost none of its force over the years.

Indeed, it may even have gained force. For cinema today, in common with so many other art forms, rarely features anger as a guiding principle. We live in an age when many fêted American directors, from Wes Anderson to Spike Jonze, prefer to deal in irony and archness. Slowness, drift and boredom, long seen as dominant characteristics of gallery-based movie-making, have been adopted as an aesthetic strategy by directors such as Bruno Dumont, Hou Hsiao-Hsien and even Abbas Kiarostami. Rage is visited retrospectively: from Moodysson's *Together* to Bertolucci's *The Dreamers* and Wolfgang Becker's *Good Bye, Lenin!*, a kind of nostalgia has developed for the forms of passionate

idealism and collectivised outrage that characterise today's neo-liberal consensus.

Perhaps because of this, the baton has tacitly been passed to documentary makers. Cheap, lightweight technologies; popular enthusiasm for varieties of realism (everything from the popularity of life- and confessional writing to the emergence of Blogger, LiveJournal and Flickr); the apparent uninterest of network schedulers in programming the kinds of vérité serials that used to be common a generation ago: all these developments have encouraged film-makers to use the long-form documentary to disseminate their polemics and harangues.

The best, even better than more commercially successful barnstormers by Michael Moore, such as *Bowling for Columbine* and *Fahrenheit 9/11*, remains *Hoop Dreams*. A three-hour portrait of two boys who want to use their basketball skills to escape the poverty of their inner-city Chicago homes, it's a remarkably edited (from over 250 hours of footage) and empathetically constructed critique of a wretched society that shrugs off most of its black population and leaves them with just the most minuscule chance of salvation – not via education, but though sport. The boys' families, individually defiant, strain under these circumstances, and the boys themselves fare less well than they – and we – devoutly wish.

It's a heroic story, but also a desperately sad one. Director Steve James rarely polemicises, but nor does he pull any punches. Made over ten years ago, the film, recently re-released on DVD by Criterion, is as powerful and topical as it ever was. The anger that animates it, that makes it possible, acts as a lifeline. It's a refusal to accept the apartheid of American society and its wilful blindness to the inequities of class and geography. It says, as the cinema of rage, must always say: No.

Anger in 20 films

The Birth of a Nation (1915)
DW Griffiths' visually fantastic but morally nauseating US foundation myth about a South overrun by black people, of particular appeal to members of the Ku Klux Klan – sympathetically portrayed throughout.

Battleship Potemkin (1925)
Editing is a form of violence – for good as well as for bad. Sergei Eisenstein's breathless tribute to anti-Tsarist revolutionaries also serves as a sublimely edited and lyrically composed praise-song to the concept of necessary violence.

The Cloud-Capped Star (1960)
Watching Ritwik Ghatak's film, it's hard not to be appalled, as well as saddened, by the fate of a refugee girl living in Calcutta who sacrifices her personal happiness to help her family.

Soy Cuba! (1964)
The Russian trio behind this stirring revolutionary drama (directed by Mikhail Kalatozov) makes you want to join hands with the peasants and radicals fighting Batista's evil forces.

The War Game (1965)
Peter Watkins' terrifying docu-drama about the aftermath of a nuclear attack in England. That it shows a country singularly unprepared for such a disaster is one thing, but that the BBC banned the film is unforgivable.

Space is the Place (1974)
Barking mad concert-film and intergalactic duel between good and evil, this obscure feature by John Coney, starring out-there jazz musician Sun Ra, drapes a cloak of comic mystification over anti-apartheid fury.

Downtown 81 (1981)
Rubble-strewn NYC is the star of this film, directed by Edo Bertoglio and starring Jean-Michel Basquiat, more or less playing himself. No-Wave robotniks jerk out in basements. Coati Mundi kicks up a storm on stage. Street tramps turn out to be Debbie Harry.

Britannia Hospital (1982)
One of old grouch Lindsay Anderson's last films, full of crooked doctors, cannibal African dictators and arsey painters, this is a fascinatingly messy and ill-focused rant against Thatcherite Britain.

The Cyclist (1987)
More upsetting than enraging, perhaps, Mohsen Makhmalbaf's story about an Afghan immigrant who has to ride in a circle for three days to raise money for his sick wife is so awful it could be a Greek myth.

Roger and Me (1989)
With less me-me swagger than in his later films, this Michael Moore film is an impassioned and often funny howl against the culture of 'downsizing'.

Hoop Dreams (1994)
The dreams – that basketball might rescue inner-city black Americans from poverty – turn out to be lies propagated by university admissions officer, sports coaches and politicians.

Ladybird Ladybird (1994)
Ken Loach is the cussed conscience of British cinema and its prime exponent of a social realism. This agonising film is his best, a story of a mother, branded 'unfit' by social workers, trying to win back her children.

La Haine (1995)
Pumped-up and angry, Matthieu Kassovitz's searing expose of 24 hours in the life of three Parisian estate-dwellers was a wake-up call to French politicians. Ten years on, in the wake of the 2005 riots, it seemed almost prophetic.

Life and Debt (2001)
A feel-bad poetic documentary by Stephanie Black, narrated by Jamaica Kincaid, about the transformation of the Caribbean into a privatised fiefdom for foreign tourists, agro-business tyrants and industrial free-zone barons.

American Beauty (1999)
Stagy direction, clunky symbolism and madly histrionic performances from Kevin Spacey and Annette Bening, all in the service of a hackneyed message: suburbia is for hypocrites. Thank you, Sam Mendes.

An Injury To One (2002)
Quality agit-prop doc from Travis Wilkerson about the role of corporate capitalism in poisoning half of Butte, Montana, and in subverting its anti-toxic-waste unions.

S-21 (2003)
In this documentary, director Rithy Panh brings two survivors back to a notorious Cambodian killing camp to confront their former captors. Unbelievably, the latter show no contrition.

Vera Drake (2004)
Cheap sentiment always gets the blood boiling. Mike Leigh's one-note, semi-skimmed melodrama about a well-meaning nurse who sidelines as a local abortionist garnered unfathomably florid praise.

The Life Aquatic with Steve Zissou (2004)
The studied whimsy. The pukey colours. The inability to be sincere. Wes Anderson is the most annoying American film-maker of his generation.

Basic Instinct 2 (2006)
The first *Basic Instinct*, masturbation fodder masquerading as an upmarket thriller, was bad enough. That Hollywood is so out of ideas that it has now made a follow-up beggars belief.

Telling it like it is

Hannah Patterson assesses the recent rise of documentary.

A measure of just how high the documentary bar has been raised in the cinema in recent years is the category's increased profile at the Oscars. At one time, few film-goers would have been able to name the winner, let alone the nominees. Now, films as diverse as *Spellbound*, *Super Size Me*, *Capturing the Friedmans* and *The Fog of War* regularly jostle for public attention, column space and awards. So what's changed? Are documentary-makers suddenly better than ever before? Or has a new, previously non-existent, audience emerged?

The truth, one suspects, may be more prosaic. As the success of reality TV, documentary's wayward child, has proved, the real word can be as exciting (if not more so) than the fictional one, offering gripping storylines that cover the gamut of human emotions. No longer perceived as just serious, objective or educational, documentaries have had a marketing makeover.

Incorporating the conventions of any genre, they can entertain and, crucially, attract an enthusiastic audience.

Miramax boss Harvey Weinstein understood this back in 1988 when he bought *The Thin Blue Line*, Errol Morris's Texas-set docudrama about a man falsely imprisoned, and marketed it as a murder mystery. More recently, director Alex Gibney has cleverly adopted *noir* style to unsettling effect in *Enron: The Smartest Guys in the Room*, opening with an eerie reconstruction of the suicide of executive Cliff Baxter, and delivering an engrossing rise-and-fall story of corporate greed.

Although film-makers such as Frederick Wiseman and the Maysles Brothers continue to employ distinct observational styles, one of the more popular shifts in the last two decades has been towards author-led documentaries, subjective takes on contemporary situations

Anger in Palestine, as felt by the children: award-winning documentary **Promises**

Critics' choice
Power and corruption

All the President's Men
(1976, US) d Alan J Pakula. cast Dustin Hoffman, Robert Redford, Jack Warden. Meticulous re-creation of the slow gathering of incriminating facts that led to Watergate.

The Candidate
(1972, US) d Michael Ritchie. cast Robert Redford, Peter Boyle, Don Porter. Running in the California Senate race erodes Redford's integrity and morality.

Chinatown
(1974, US) d Roman Polanski. cast Jack Nicholson, Faye Dunaway, John Huston. The point is, that at the right time and the right place, people are capable of anything.

City Hall
(1976, US) d Harold Becker. cast Al Pacino, John Cusack, Bridget Fonda, Danny Aiello. Al Pacino as the best Mayor New York never had. Or maybe not.

The Constant Gardener
(2004, US/GB/Ger/Can) d Fernando Meirelles. cast Ralph Fiennes, Rachel Weisz, Bill Nighy. Murder in Africa as a by-product of big business and hopelessly compromised global politics.

Erin Brockovich
(2000, US) d Steven Soderbergh. cast Julia Roberts, Albert Finney, Aaron Eckhart. Being the true story of a single mother's exposé of an industry water poisoning case.

Hoffa
(1992, US) d Danny DeVito. cast Jack Nicholson, Danny DeVito, Armand Assante. From trucking through union organisation into full-scale corruption and an anonymous grave.

Le Mani sulla Città
(1963, It) d Francesco Rosi. cast Rod Steiger, Guido Alberti, Carlo Fermariello. Property development rackets and political profiteering in the Naples city council.

Wag the Dog
(1997, US) d Barry Levinson. cast Dustin Hoffman, Robert De Niro, Anne Heche. A sex scandal is about to tar the Pres, so the White House diverts attention with a phoney war.

Z
(1968, Fr/Alg) d Costa-Gavras. cast Yves Montand, Jean-Louis Trintignant. Investigation into an 'accidental' death uncovers police and government corruption.

that often cast the film-maker as protagonist. The most notorious purveyor of the type is journalist-turned-film-maker Michael Moore, and although critical opinion of his methods varies wildly, he can certainly pick a tricky topic and make it play like fiction. Whether taking on the chairman of General Motors in *Roger & Me*, the powerful gun industry in *Bowling for Columbine* or the Bush administration in *Fahrenheit 9/11*, he concocts an old-fashioned tale of good versus evil and casts himself as the Capra-style underdog, yapping away at the heels of political and corporate giants. When *Fahrenheit* won Cannes' prestigious Palme d'Or in 2004, not only did it become one of the mostly eagerly anticipated releases of the year, it subsequently went on to become the highest-grossing feature documentary of all time. A seemingly astonishing feat for a movie about politics.

Morgan Spurlock, director and star of *Super Size Me*, is in many ways a natural successor to Moore, an 'everyman' figure and thorn in the corporations' sides. Plucky and self-effacing though less overtly political, his month-long diet of Big Macs and cola struck fear into the heart of McDonald's. Though the majority of Americans weren't dissuaded by Moore from returning Bush to the White House, the burger chain removed supersize meals from its menus – denying Spurlock's influence all the way. Proof, if any was needed, that documentaries can simultaneously entertain audiences and effect significant social change.

Earlier 'name' documentary directors – the Nick Broomfields (*Driving Me Crazy*) and the Ross McElwees (*Sherman's March*) – continue to mine this rich seam today, exposing their most intimate relationships and idiosyncrasies for the delight or indignation of viewers. In

ANGER

ANGER

Moving picture
Barbara Hershey

**Actress, *The Last Temptation of Christ,
A World Apart, Paris Trout, Lantana***

The first time I saw *The Last Temptation of
Christ* was in a theatre, and I remember there
was this incredible controversy surrounding it.
I was so shocked that at the end of the film,
after Christ dies, there is this ecstatic music,
with Moroccan women doing this wild keening
thing they do and then this triumphant music
that was so primitive, so primal. On the
screen it looks like fireworks, little rainbows.
I thought, 'It's heaven. He did it. Marty made
heaven.' And what it was, Marty later told me,
was film burning. They'd shot the little sparks
given off as film runs through the projector
and then just spliced it in. It was so perfect:
Marty had actually managed to create heaven
from celluloid.

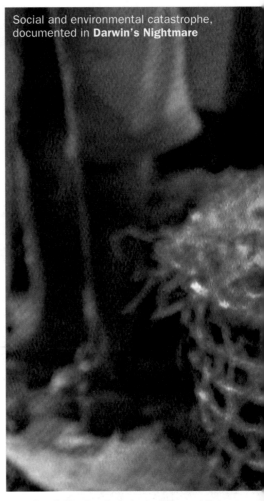

Social and environmental catastrophe,
documented in **Darwin's Nightmare**

Bright Leaves McElwee, the Woody Allen of the
documentary world, disarms his way through
the Deep South and his tobacco heritage.
Broomfield, by contrast, vents his anger at the
unjust treatment of prostitute-murderer Aileen
Wuornos to sobering effect in *Aileen: Life
and Death of a Serial Killer*. Once witnessed,
the sight of her staring eyes and bullish jaw,
so perfectly replicated by Charlize Theron in
the bio-pic *Monster*, is hard to erase.

Of course, some of the best-loved
documentaries haven't featured any people at
all. Nature, once the mainstay of television, is
increasingly finding a new home in the cinema.
The astonishing technological achievements
of films such as *Microcosmos* and *Winged
Migration* have introduced a hitherto unseen
cornucopia of insects, invertebrates and birds.
March of the Penguins, with its syrupy
Morgan Freeman voice-over, is already
the second biggest-earning documentary.

Microcosmos showed that non-fiction films
can be visually stunning, and one of the
greatest technical achievements of the last few
years, *Touching the Void*, positively demands
to be seen on the big screen. A nail-biting clash
between mankind and the natural environment,
its retelling of the disaster that befell British
climbers Joe Simpson and Simon Yates in the

Peruvian Andes is a fine piece of film-making.
Director Kevin Macdonald expertly combines
talking-heads with breathtakingly shot
reconstructions of the accident to create an
extraordinary story of endurance and an
account of tested friendship.

Indeed, the best sporting documentaries
are always about something else. *Hoop
Dreams* is as much an insight into the life of
disadvantaged black American youth as it is a
film about basketball. *When We Were Kings*
places the 1974 heavyweight championship
between Muhammad Ali and George Foreman
within the context of race, history, politics and
religion. Like *Spellbound* before it, *Mad Hot
Ballroom*, which follows a group of New York

City kids and their attempts to win a ballroom dancing contest, focuses on competition and the pressures on children to be the best. Stacy Peralta's adventure sports films, similar to such music documentaries as Ondi Timoner's *Dig!*, record alternative ways of life or forms of expression, from the birth of skateboard culture in southern California in *Dogtown and Z-Boys* to the salute to obsessive surfing cliques in *Riding Giants*.

Ultimately, though, whatever the motivation of documentary makers, it is their subjects, the diverse characters, that are their most compelling and unforgettable aspect: gentle teacher Georges Lopez in *Etre et avoir* (whose saintly image was severely degraded when he made a claim in the French courts for a share of the film's significant profits) or Jojo, his mischievous pupil; big bear enthusiast and myth-maker Timothy Treadwell in Werner Herzog's *Grizzly Man*; forthright but elusive former US Secretary of Defense Robert S McNamara in *The Fog of War*; inspirational Tommy the Clown in *Rize*; *My Architect*'s mysterious Nathaniel Kahn; indefatigably ambitious Kaleil in *Startup.com*; the sartorially challenged therapist in *Metallica: Some Kind of Monster*; and the mawkish Jonathan Caouette in *Tarnation*. A mass of contradictions, disturbing tendencies and charming eccentricities, they all prove that truth can indeed be stranger than fiction.

Unforgettable, unforgivable

Documentarist **Peter Whitehead** recalls a searing film of the Warsaw ghetto.

The University Cinema Club met in the Cambridge Arts Cinema to watch independent films. In 1960, an evening of 'political' documentary films included footage shot inside the Warsaw ghetto. An official state film, well photographed, well edited, aimed at conveying a simple enough message: this is what happened when we built an impenetrable concrete wall around the Jewish quarter of the city and starved a thousand or more inhabitants to death. It shows their degradation and their dying. This is what it looked like. Or at least, up to a point: in the film, there's not a single shot of a Nazi soldier. Necessarily absent, the authors of this atrocity are safely hidden behind the camera. Afterwards, I collapsed emotionally, had difficulty staving off a breakdown. There was one particular image a cameraman had dwelt on as if he found it especially powerful, significant, plangent with the true meaning of the film: a skinny young girl in rags, alone, filthy, digging with a stick in the mud, looking for food. The soundtrack a dispassionate description of her odd behaviour.

The images recurred in violent nightmares that woke me up (and reminded me of the nightmares of Thomas de Quincey). They would sear into my daylight mind as I worked in the Cavendish laboratory, a student crystallographer helping Crick and Watson unravel the structure of DNA using X-rays and crystals. A few years later I gave up a science career and went to the Slade School of Art to study film.

Soon after seeing the Nazi film I'd seen *Rashomon* and the two films seemed to merge in my mind, a painfully bitter, cold fusion. I'd discovered I couldn't find a single reading of the ghetto film that would offer me detachment from its inhuman truths; the planned, state-sanctioned murder; the hatred; rape. And something else was haunting me, my inability to 'enter into' the state of mind of the cameraman. I thought of him continuously. In watching the film, I must be inside his head, behind his eyes. I wasn't able to feel the necessary death-in-life detachment without which he could not stand there, camera on tripod, focusing the lens, changing to close up. Oops, film finished, pop in a new one. Or later, more hidden gods, lab technicians deciding what were the 'best' settings to convey their message. For me it was not film, not celluloid passing through a projector, I had no 'persona' with which to protect myself. I had been there. It was a young girl, the girl next door at the point of starvation digging in stinking mud for food. I'd discovered a 'flaw' in myself. Through some quirk in my own fatherless upbringing, my personal myth, I would never see film with the detachment necessary to make objective documentary or 'convincing' fiction films. 'No,

---

Moving picture
Laurent Cantet

Director, writer, *Ressources Humaines*, *Time Out*, *Vers le Sud*

When I was very young, my parents were primary school teachers in a small village, and they organised a film club a couple of times a month. They held it in the classroom that was adjacent to my house and usually I would go and see the films. I was six or so. One evening they said I couldn't go that night. Of course I was unhappy, and when I heard the projector starting up – it was in the corridor, which was just below my room – I sneaked down the stairs in my pyjamas, and into the classroom. I found myself face to face with pictures of the Warsaw ghetto. Those terrible images remain inscribed on my brain. For a moment I was shocked, then I started howling, and my mother picked me up and held me.

The photojournalist as watchdog: **Salvador**

darling, bend over more, push your bottom out, push the stick in the mud with a slower rhythm. Perfect. Print!' Was it possible that all film was rape? Of the subjects and audience? For me, irreparably wounded by the ghetto film, it was.

Arriving at the Slade on a painting scholarship, I discovered a nascent film department, a Bolex camera idle on a shelf. Within a month I'd made a documentary film of the sculpture students; sticky fingers, mud, plaster, moulds of dismembered bodies. Within six months I was a newsreel cameraman for Italian TV; filmed Aldo Moro in London with our Prime Minister. Moro soon to be assassinated by university students.

Within seven years, I'd made a film in America about a documentary maker (myself) who decides to film an act of assassination at a peace rally as the ultimate act of protest. I was inside the university during the student rebellion, filmed the police violence, the wounded students, ambulances. I gave a guy $75 for a gun, I knew whom I must kill: a soldier in uniform. The Kent State massacre was months away. I filmed Robert Kennedy, some film was wiped by the CIA at a US lab, I decided to leave before I became my fiction; an assassin. Arrived at Heathrow with forty hours of film of the counter-culture collapse into anarchy. Newspaper Headline: 'Robert Kennedy Shot Dead'.

Through five years of making documentary films about '60s socio-political events, I tried to write fiction: scripts, novels. I was losing myself, where was I in all this chaos? I loved Godard, Bergman, Fellini; the last thing I needed to express myself was documentary. But I couldn't write a script for transformation into the 'lie', the contrived untruth of a fiction film. I was trapped by the paradox: I needed

Critics' choice
Controversies

Bandit Queen
(1994, Ind/GB) d Shekhar Kapur. cast Seema Biswas, Nirmal Pandey, Manjoj Bajpai. Caused outrage in India for its graphic violence, sexuality and attacks on the caste system.

Birth of a Nation
(1915, US) d DW Griffith. cast Lillian Gish, Mae Marsh, Henry Walthall, Miriam Cooper. Hugely influential but politically reprehensible in its explicit glorification of the Ku Klux Clan.

Crash
(1996, Can) d David Cronenberg. cast James Spader, Holly Hunter, Elias Koteas. Divided UK local councils – some allowed its screening, others (notably Westminster) didn't.

The Devils
(1971, GB) d Ken Russell. cast Oliver Reed, Vanessa Redgrave, Dudley Sutton. It's not blasphemy, said Russell, but a depiction of blasphemy – a distinction lost on many.

The Last Temptation of Christ
(1988, US/Can) d Martin Scorsese. cast Willem Dafoe, Harvey Keitel, Paul Greco. Some Church officials predicted California would sink into the ocean if this film was shown.

Monty Python's Life of Brian
(1979, GB) d Terry Jones. cast Graham Chapman, Terry Jones, Eric Idle, Michael Palin. Python fans had to brave pickets of hymn-singing demonstrators outside cinemas.

Natural Born Killers
(1994, US) d Oliver Stone. cast Woody Harrelson, Juliette Lewis, Robert Downey Jr. No fewer than eight murders have been blamed on the film that the Daily Mail termed 'evil'.

Pretty Baby
(1977, US) d Louis Malle. cast Brooke Shields, Keith Carradine, Susan Sarandon. A tale of child prostitution, the film was vilified for scenes of a naked 12-year-old Shields.

Saló
(1975, It/Fr) d Pier Paolo Pasolini. cast Paolo Bonicelli, Giorgio Cataldi, Umberto Quintavalle. Sexual violence and coprophagia: fearless film-making or just exploitative and plain nasty?

Straw Dogs
(1971, GB) d Sam Peckinpah. cast Dustin Hoffman, Susan George, David Warner. According to film journal of record Variety, 'An orgy of unparalleled violence and nastiness.'

Corruption, racism and short tempers in New Jersey: **City of Hope**

to film documentary to reach the inner truth of the ghetto film; yet, if there was one thing I hated, it was the 'lie' of the so-called documentary film. Defeated, I gave up films and writing, escaped to Africa, the Arctic, the Arabian deserts, trapped and bred falcons for twenty years. Undeniable truth in that!

But bad dreams recur, ghosts that cling; the images of the ghetto film had not been exorcised, even with my films about protest, Vietnam, student rebellion, Howling Beat Poets! The young girl was like Thomas de Quincey's Ann, the girl he searched for forever, knowing she was dead, probably murdered in a mud-ridden alley behind Soho Square. Starving. Was I not hoping she had not died, not been murdered by the Nazis? If I could find her alive, would that wipe away the palpable fear the images provoked in me? Of man at his most bestial? Forever haunted by those few feet of film, unable not to do so, I had to find a way to tell her story; if not in film, in words. Always so comfortable, 'at one remove'? So I wrote a novel: Nora and… about that girl. She had survived, worked with Freud, became a successful psychoanalyst, married a handsome Aryan doctor. Was happy!

Life, so full of irony!

Master in the margins

Gareth Evans examines the work of an undervalued British film-maker.

Even leaving aside the form and content of his singularly powerful body of work, the remarkable films of committed British film-maker Peter Watkins are a fine record of the inspirational qualities he's displayed over four decades and in the face of concerted institutional and media hostility. Standing as a model of intense authorial focus and genuinely democratic, collective creativity, as well as a vital example of how uncompromising projects can be made at a certain scale outside all normal funding channels, his achievement has been to embed radical critiques of society and the media into narratives of great sophistication, engagement and energy. No viewing of his 14 films can fail to trace the larger political and philosophical concerns that Watkins has tried to tackle throughout his life.

From his earliest shorts, *The Diary of an Unknown Soldier* and *The Forgotten Faces*, it was clear that Watkins was a talent to watch, already developing a formidable visual and thematic language. But they did little to prepare the viewer for the revolutionary impact of his two longer films for the BBC, *Culloden* and *The War Game*. With these works, he virtually invented a genre – one might call it dramatic *vérité* – using the device of a television crew documenting the action within the narrative itself. This was a strategy he would employ with modifications for many of his subsequent films. In the first the notorious battle and the subsequent assault on Scottish cultural and social identity is shown with a visceral immediacy that startles and takes the breath. This is only heightened by the clipped voiceover tones of the offscreen 'TV journalist'

Moving picture
Andy Bichlbaum

Political provocateur and half of satirical double act The Yes Men (with Mike Bonanno)

Mike and I recently had a chance to see a lot of great documentaries at the Amsterdam Documentary Film Festival. One morning we decided to take a break and walk around the city. We both used to know the place. I spent six weeks there some years ago, and Mike's mother is from Amsterdam. A guy at our hotel had already told us how phone conversations had become more expensive since privatisation, and how they were lining up the same with the electricity, and the train system, and we started noticing numerous chain stores opening up – things that make the place less quirky, less distinct, more like everywhere else.

So there we were indulging this bourgeois melancholy about globalisation, and then we went to see *Darwin's Nightmare*. This is a portrait of globalisation's real victims. It focuses on the fish industry around Lake Victoria, and by the end of the film you understand how the fish trade depends on the arms trade, and that without war in Africa there wouldn't be cheap fish in England! The film also shows the on-the-ground effect of the fish industry, the workers subsisting on maggot-covered fish skeletons, the AIDS that spreads with the crowded work camps – devastating stuff. And it shows how commonplace and banal war has become, thanks to our arms dealers.

So that put our bourgeois qualms about globalisation's impact on the Netherlands in perspective. And then we saw *The Take* by Avi Lewis and Naomi Klein, which shows how laid-off workers in Argentina are reopening their old abandoned factories and making them work again, with everyone paid the same salary, and you can see the difference in the workers' happiness levels. It was heartening and amazing to see.

We came out of that film and tried to imagine what it would mean if we all took control of our lives here in the West to that degree. For one thing, we surely wouldn't sell any more arms to Africa.

Banned by the BBC, remade as a movie: Alan Clarke's Borstal docudrama **Scum**

(Watkins himself), who calmly relays, in the film's present tense but with, of course, the benefit of hindsight, the scale of the destruction.

The War Game takes this approach and projects it into the palpably possible immediate future, imagining the effects of a nuclear strike on a town in Kent. Statistics of damage and social collapse alternate with talking-head interviews about the scale of suffering and dramatised scenes of post-bang repression. A chilling vision of Cold War geopolitics taken to their logical conclusion, it was suppressed by the BBC for two decades, so potent was its feared impact on the viewing public.

With these films, Watkins made both his social intentions and aesthetic agenda clear.

Refusing to make work to fit ordained televisual moulds, he made a cinema feature, *Privilege*, that imagined the burgeoning pop culture as a zone of explicit political manipulation. Tackling the signs of American cultural dominance head on, he sought to unsettle those filmic forms that reproduced existing political and cultural hierarchies.

In 2005, 35 years after its original, brief and then suppressed release, *Punishment Park*, his most startlingly prescient film, a challenging parable of US authoritarianism, was once again made available in the UK and abroad. Charting, in his trademark style, the brutal eradication of dissidents in the desert landscape of the title, it has, despite

Bearing witness: the nine-hour documentary meditation on the Holocaust, **Shoah**

its ongoing relevance, been among his least visible features, and yet is also one of his most accessible and disturbing statements on the violence at the heart of modern Western society and its power structures.

Brilliantly filmed on one camera by Nick Broomfield's regular collaborator Joan Churchill,

it imagines a 1960s in which, the Vietnam War escalating, President Nixon declares a state of national emergency and Federal authorities are given the power to detain persons judged to be a 'risk to national security'. In a wilderness region in California, a civilian tribunal passes penal sentences on

Moving picture
Siddiq Barmak

Director, writer, *Osama*

The film I remember is De Sica's *Bicycle Thieves*. I've never forgotten one shot of this film. I remember every piece of dialogue, every camera movement. The first time I saw it was in 1982 in Moscow. It was showing as part of a course at the Moscow Film Institute. I was shocked by the film, and asked my teachers again and again to repeat the screening. I was particularly impressed by the last scene when the little boy sees the people hitting his father. This shocked me – it was very close to our

society in Afghanistan, how my people behaved during, or maybe after, the wars. I became aware of the similarities between our two societies. And it influenced me in making *Osama* because I was looking for a simple way to put across what are essentially very complicated things – with a low budget, without too much decoration or fantastic lighting, and using non-professional actors. Italian neo-realist cinema was created in response to the economic and social problems in that country, and now we are living in the same conditions ourselves.

groups of activists but offers the alternative of three days in Punishment Park. Granted freedom if they can reach an American flag, planted 53 miles away across scorching desert, and without water, the activists are pursued in increasingly bloody fashion by police and National Guards determined to stop them completing the 'course'.

The parallels with state abuses in the US and further afield today are obvious. However, the film, one of the most articulate statements of political dissent in cinema, is also a compelling and profoundly unsettling drama of terrifying immediacy and resonance.

The hostile response to *Punishment Park* in its original release led Watkins to a significant change of direction. Relocating to Scandinavia, he continued to work with non-professional actors and in ways that fully involved the community in question, but he began to move away from conventional funding and production channels. His first film in northern Europe, *Edvard Munch*, is perhaps his masterpiece, an astonishing imagination of the psychology and soul of the greatly troubled artist that achieves complete authenticity and no overwhelming sense of identification with the young painter. One of the most striking films made about the creative process, it deploys an exemplary dual approach, using Watkins' established documentary distance alongside a tremendous emotional immersion, making it utterly compelling.

Watkins made three further features in Scandinavia in the 1970s (all seldom seen), but in the 1980s he returned to the concerns of *The War Game* with his most ambitious film to date, *The Journey*, a 14-hour global exploration of the full costs, in all senses, of nuclear weapons. Rarely screened, it's on a par with Claude Lanzmann's *Shoah*.

Watkin's career has not come without cost. Disillusioned by the values of the industry and medium in which he works, and fiercely critical of its political bias and anti-democratic processes, Watkins has concentrated in recent years on making his films more widely available, a huge task, given the unusual nature of their production. His most recent work, *La Commune (de Paris, 1871)*, a six-hour re-creation of the popular uprising, shows how a revolution is made and sustained. Featuring people living in the districts from

---

Moving picture
Jonathan Demme

Director, *Caged Heat*, *Melvin and Howard*, *The Silence of the Lambs*, *The Manchurian Candidate*

Well, here's one of my most memorable movie experiences. New York Film Festival, 1966: I go see a film called *Far From Vietnam*, a French portmanteau by five directors offering perspectives on the American war in Vietnam, which by this time was really starting to heat up like crazy. I went to see it out of interest, going in as a very naïve, unpolitical and 'patriotic' young man who, despite his passions, was afraid to go to war. And I emerged from the Alain Resnais segment radicalised.

It's Eve Montand and Simone Signoret in a small room, she's on a couch watching him pace around, and he's desperately trying to come to terms with this feeling: he's grown up loving America and Americans because he remembers France under the Nazis, and the Americans coming to help free the French – but now in 1965 or 1966, he sees that America and Americans have become the occupiers of Vietnam.

Before that, had I been drafted, I would have gone and, with great fear, done what I understood was my duty. I came out of *Far From Vietnam* and a week later was down in Washington DC protesting against the war.

---

which the original Communards came, it created a kind of living historical tableau that spoke with affecting immediacy. Alongside his other astonishing achievements, it should speak to, and be seen by anyone keen to experience work that integrates its intentions, means of making and film language so completely that it stands as a vision of its time – but also as an enduring document of freethinking resistance. For these reasons, and given the historical moment in which we find ourselves, one could argue that he is Britain's most relevant and resonant living film-maker, whose importance is only now beginning to be fully realised.

Peter Watkins welcomes active and constructive engagement about his work and the issues it raises. He can be reached by email via his website, www.mnsi.net/~pwatkins.

Real to reel

Geoff Andrew considers why the movies have come back to reality.

When I was first finding my feet as a film critic, 'realism' seemed to be something of a dirty word in British cinema circles. The very mention of it almost inevitably brought to mind 'kitchen sink drama': grey-and-off-white images of steep streets containing cramped terraced houses and the odd Morris Minor, disaffected folk traipsing along towpaths and disused railway lines, chimneystacks belching smoke in the distance. Up North, in short – or at least the industrial, working-class milieu so beloved of the middle-class perpetrators of Free Cinema in the early '60s. Hadn't those people seen the error of their early ways, abandoning documentary-style naturalism for surrealism, satire, even Hollywood? So 'realism' couldn't be much cop, could it? Sure, Ken Loach was okay, but wasn't television his real home? Compared to the true greats of British cinema – Hitchcock, of course, but also Powell and Pressburger, recently (re)discovered in a really big way – Loach and others like him were merely inheritors of the somewhat stuffy British

documentary tradition of the Griersonians (whom Powell, particularly, still took great glee in disparaging). When it came to the crunch, how could films made for institutions like the GPO Film Unit and the Coal Board possibly measure up to flights of the imagination like *The 39 Steps*, *A Matter of Life and Death*, or even *Witchfinder General*?

So 'realism' was deemed to be somehow uncinematic. The big screen should be the province of fantasy and genre; not of everyday life as experienced by most of the audience, but of extraordinary events involving extraordinary characters. *Jubilee*, *The Long Good Friday*, *The Draughtsman's Contract*, *The Company of Wolves* were the work of visionaries, whereas *Kes*, in the end, had been nothing special, simply a well-observed tale of a boy and his bird...

The above may exaggerate the value placed on 'realism' and whatever its opposite was a quarter-century ago, but not so very much. It's strange now to recall how unfashionable realism was – as a cinematic mode, at least.

Ken Loach on **Political cinema**

The anger in *Ladybird Ladybird* wasn't so much about an 'issue' – here are the bad social services doing something wicked – because we didn't believe that; it was about the tragedy of someone who was caught in her own stereotype: the more events pressed down on her the more she became who they thought she was, and the more she put herself in a situation where she would be destroyed. We felt it was more tragic than a social issue, as it were.

The films that have made me angry are mostly documentaries: some of the films written by John Pilger – *Death of a Nation: The Timor Conspiracy*, for example – and some of the documentaries about Rwanda. I'm not sure fictional cinema can match up to that sort of film, because I think cinema deals in things that are retrospective. Political films *can* make an impact – take *The Battle of Algiers* – but you don't leave the cinema raging, you reflect

on what imperialism is and that strengthens your position; it's not a rage against something you weren't aware of. A film like *Bicycle Thieves* makes you feel deep anger – but it's enforced by the film, it's not like somebody dropping a bit of news on you. It feeds an existing anger.

A similar case is *Fahrenheit 9/11*, which I know some people were rather snooty about. But I thought it was good that it was made, and it had a very good effect. It was familiar territory but it was told in a kind of tabloid way that would connect with a big audience. And *Super Size Me* isn't telling you anything you're unaware of, but you cheer it on because it's carrying the discussion into areas that it otherwise wouldn't reach.

I think, at its best, cinema – like *Bicycle Thieves*, or *The Battle of Algiers*, or Chris Menges' film *A World Apart* – deepens your anger through reflection and understanding.

ANGER

Moving picture
Jeff Blitz

Director, *Spellbound*

For a reason that has since been lost to me, in 1990, during my last year of college, I volunteered to write a thesis on something called 'reader response' criticism. Stanley Fish was probably the most fun author on my bibliography and, if you know Dr Fish, you can imagine that my honours thesis was not much fun at all. To make a long and painful story short, I toiled on the project for months. I spent whole days weighing whether to include the word 'tractus' in my title. I decided abruptly that I needed to learn French before I could continue and then, two weeks later, abandoned that pursuit. On long breaks from fruitless writing, I would wander down to the Charles Theatre, Baltimore's seedy arthouse and, if I didn't like what was playing there, I'd go on to campus to see what the handful of film classes were running. It was then that I happened on *Sherman's March*, directed by Ross McElwee. I saw it against the advice of my pals – 'It's almost three hours of documentary,' they said. 'Remember how f–ing long *Shoah* was!' – and it only goes to prove that even good friends can't be trusted when it comes to movie advice. It became a seminal experience for me.

In a world where film-makers like Jean-Pierre and Luc Dardenne, Abbas Kiarostami, Nanni Moretti, Eric Rohmer, Hou Hsiao-Hsien and Edward Yang are rightly regarded as masters, it seems unthinkable that we once paid so little attention to what someone like Loach was actually up to. (He too, of course, like Mike Leigh – another Brit who regards himself as something of a realist – is now very often included in the pantheon populated by the aforementioned international auteurs.) After all, it's not as if we were unaware of the achievements of Stroheim, Renoir, Rossellini or Cassavetes. Maybe the problem was that the kind of lives dealt with by our homegrown realists were so familiar; if they were 'just' reflecting life as it was lived, how could it possibly be art?

So why the change in attitude? Are we more sophisticated now, so that we actually realise how much hard work and sheer artifice are involved in creating any 'reality' revealed on screen? Though movies like Kiarostami's *Close-Up* have shown that we should question much more rigorously the veracity of what we see and hear, that's unlikely; after all, it still comes as a something of a shock to learn just how many outright 'lies' are involved in making even a film like the Dardennes' *Rosetta* or Cristi Puiu's *The Death of Mr Lazarescu*. We get so caught up in stories, however slight, and so empathetically involved with characters, that we accept the fictions before us as somehow 'real', forgetting that, at the very least, the temporal and spatial dimensions of a film – even if it's populated entirely by people playing themselves – are wholly created, wholly artificial.

Perhaps one reason for our new welcoming approach to realism in film is that television – once regarded as the proper home of realist drama – has turned more and more to the mindless escapism of chat shows, quiz shows, makeover shows and the like. Even TV documentaries tend these days to be tarted up with computer-generated images evoking vanished or imagined worlds, or with dazzling design, cutting and camera trickery suggestive of a wannabe Scorsese. As for 'reality TV'… Only the most naive viewer is unaware that people, objects and events are transformed by the camera's gaze (one only has to see how *Big Brother* contestants act up for the audience) – especially when those objects and people are assembled in order to be goggled at by the camera, and wouldn't even be in the same room together if it weren't for the camera being there in the first place. 'Reality TV' is as artificial as anything else on television, and has only the most tenuous relationship to life as it's lived away from the gaze of a large audience.

If we can no longer get our requisite dose of realism from the small screen, we have to go back to the movies. (By 'movies', of course,

ANGER

Moving picture
Johannes Schonherr

Film curator; writer

I was at the Korea Film Show in 1999 to select a programme of North Korean titles for touring in Europe. Sitting in the screening room of the Film Export & Import Corporation, I was watching yet another heroic drama about how the Juche (self-reliance) policy of Great Leader Kim Jong Il saves the country. It was the brand-new *Forever in Our Memory*, an epic work about the recent floods where soldiers and farmers plant rice together in the middle of the night, carrying water to the paddies in buckets. At the end, when a big flood is threatening the harvest, a couple of thousand of them stand on top of a dam and keep the angry ocean away with their bodies, while screaming 'Long live Kim Il-Sung!'

When I arrived in Pyongyang, I had expected to be one guest among many. But to my surprise, my North Korean minder asked me on the way from the airport to the city, 'Don't you feel especially honoured that this festival is taking place only for you?' So there I was, watching incredible heroes doing incredible deeds for a week, all by myself. Later, I showed the weirdest of those wacky propaganda flicks to European audiences who didn't really know whether to be shocked or laugh.

ANGER

I don't just mean the cinema, in the sense of specifically built auditoria where films are projected on to big screens, but other forms of cinematic consumption, be it on a TV monitor or a laptop.) Just as there's recently been more interest in watching documentaries made for the cinema, so people no longer seem deterred by the prospect of realism. Fantasy, escapism, exoticism and genre will always take the lion's share of box office revenue, of course, but at least there now appear to be more punters prepared to pay to see a realist work than there were in the '80s and '90s.

Still, all this begs one question: what do we mean by 'realism'? It's a tough one, almost as unanswerable as what we mean by 'reality'. A realist work, surely, is one that gives the appearance of reproducing or depicting reality. But that doesn't get us too far. At the 2005 London Film Festival, I chaired a debate on realism in film; the panellists were Cristi Puiu, Isabelle Stever (writer/director of *Gisela*) and Michael Caton-Jones (director of *Shooting Dogs*), each of whom, in their different ways, had tried in their films to provide as authentic a picture of human experience as possible. But the range and flexibility of 'realism' were apparent also when in my opening remarks I listed some films in the Festival which I felt might feasibly be regarded as

inflected, to one degree or another, by this basic tenet of realist film-making. They included the Dardennes' *The Child*; Michael Haneke's *Hidden*; Steven Soderbergh's *Bubble*; Fernando Meirelles' *The Constant Gardener*; Bent Hamer's *Factotum*; Lodge Kerrigan's *Keane*; Steve Buscemi's *Lonesome Jim*; Dominic Savage's *Love + Hate*; Fabienne Godet's *Burnt Out*; Fred Kelemen's *Fallen*; Hou Hsiao-Hsien's *Three Times*; Tsai Ming-Liang's *The Wayward Cloud*; Hong Sang-Soo's *Tale of Cinema*; Gu Changwei's *Peacock*; Liu Jiayin's *Ox Hide*; Sergio Machado's *Lower City*; Marcelo Gomes' *Cinema, Aspirins and Vultures*; Ramin Bahrani's *Man Push Cart*; Amar Escalante's *Sangre*; and, presumably, other movies I hadn't seen.

What this suggested was that realism probably rests, like beauty, in the eye of the beholder; certainly, that proposition was given support when Isabelle Stever – whose *Gisela* is an admirably rigorous observation of working class mores reminiscent of some of the early films of Fassbinder – declared that she considered her favourite film, Jacques Demy's *The Umbrellas of Cherbourg*, a realist movie because, for all its pastel colour coding and sung dialogue, it was absolutely spot-on in its emotional authenticity. In the end, then, perhaps realism is no more and no less than whatever it takes to make us believe its own lies.

Food for thought

'To begin... To begin... How to start? I'm hungry. I should get coffee. Coffee would help me think.'
Adaptation

Let's get cerebral

Jonathan Romney knows that movies aren't *all* brainless.

For *Spellbound*, an exhibition at London's Hayward Gallery exhibition in 1996, a collection of artists and film-makers came together to contemplate the parallels and crossovers between their two fields. One memorable contribution was *Love Story*, a short film by artist Boyd Webb in which cinema was personified by an animated piece of popcorn. Of all the cultural items that could have become common currency to represent the pleasures of film, it's not a little worrying that a little piece of puffed corn – with optional candy coating – should have taken pride of place. It's an equation that's been made in countless adverts: cinema as a purely ephemeral delight, an air-light fancy that melts into nothing on the tongue.

The association does disservice both to a perfectly nutritious foodstuff and to an art form that – even when not at its intellectual peak – generally demands a more sustained and discerning process of consumption than it is sometimes given credit for. Cinema is not always to be bolted down and forgotten, but sometimes calls for an extended digestion process that only properly begins after the end credits.

Consider Michael Haneke's *Hidden*, a film that – like all the works of this glacial Austrian provocateur – refuses wholly to reveal either its immediate meaning or its latent implications on first viewing. The film's seemingly innocuous final shot has been so variously interpreted and misinterpreted that *Hidden* offers the perfect example of a film that only fully starts to signify once we leave the cinema and start puzzling over it. *Hidden* belongs to that privileged class of films – of which Jean-Luc Godard is perhaps the great specialist – that are made for both the auditorium and the café afterwards.

It is sometimes taken as read that any film with an intellect will tend to bypass the more immediate emotional responses, or to reject the

Chew on this: **Super Size Me**

very idea of entertainment. This is clearly a misconception: even films that are not primarily or obviously cerebral often yield deep wells of conceptual complexity, once the Dolby sound effects have stopped ringing in your ears (think of the mass of critical theory devoted in the 1980s and '90s to James Cameron's *Terminator* films). But think also of Alfred Hitchcock, who remains one of the most intellectually complex of film-makers, eliciting volumes of theoretical exegesis with such supposedly throwaway amusements as *North by Northwest, Rear Window* and *Vertigo*. And even the most austerely cerebral films – those of Marguerite Duras or Michael Snow, say – cannot be conceived without the emotional or sensual pleasures that attach to them.

There are many types of thinking cinema: films designed to make the viewer think, films that represent thought processes, films that in their complexity and inexhaustibility are themselves akin to thinking organisms. Some are obviously films by intellectuals, concerned not with the usual narratives of emotional gratification, but focused on specific interrogations of the state of things. Some films explicitly highlight specialised fields of study: an extreme, and eccentric, example is Alain Resnais's overtly sociological *Mon Oncle d'Amérique*, ostensibly a fiction narrative which intermittently wheels on real-life behavoural scientist Henri Laborit to draw parallels between human society and that of lab rats. Bernardo Bertolucci's career was for many years an exemplary case of the European leftist intellectual asking theoretically inflected questions about history, sexuality, identity and political allegiance: notably in *Before the Revolution, The Conformist* and *The Spider's Stratagem*, a many-layered parable about the deceptive ways in which history is made and remembered.

Political films – which may also be polemical ones – set out to make us see the world anew and more lucidly (although much agitprop cinema is patently at war with lucidity). Political cinema began to theorise its own methods with the Soviets, with Eisenstein and his agitprop epics – *October, Strike* and *Battleship Potemkin* – but Eisenstein's great insight was the electric effect of montage, a technique that seeks both to bypass the

critical faculties (by producing a galvanic shock to the perceptions) and to re-boot them by making them question the customary logic of how images and ideas hang together. Ideally, the uncoupling and subversion of habitual connections will bring the viewer's own intellectual response into play, and may even change an audience's political or social thought.

We see examples of this in, variously: an apparently detached, uneditorialised re-enactment of events (Pontecorvo's *The Battle of Algiers*); in those documentaries that

Complex world: **Koyaanisqatsi**

bombard us with conflicting facts and flatter us with a 'you decide' challenge (Andrew Jarecki's *Capturing the Friedmans*); in films that, without explicit commentary, dramatise extreme states of political being (Alan Clarke's *Elephant*, which questions militant violence by means of crushing repetition); mosaic narratives such as Stephen Gaghan's sprawling oil-industry drama *Syriana*; even Oliver Stone's tendentiously garbled *JFK*, a paranoid inquiry into political history that is itself paranoid in its inscrutably scrambled thought processes.

Another class of film is more concerned with the condition of the mind: less immediately with the world itself than with the ways we perceive it. The classic example – notoriously over-cited by Hollywood execs as a model for stories about the challenge of complexity – is Kurosawa's *Rashomon*, which reminds us that there's no such a thing as a fixed narrative, only a choice of angles on the same data. Some films are primarily about the problem of how to choose the appropriate viewpoint. Antonioni's *Blowup* – itself adapted from a literary master of indeterminacy, Julio Cortázar – is a drama

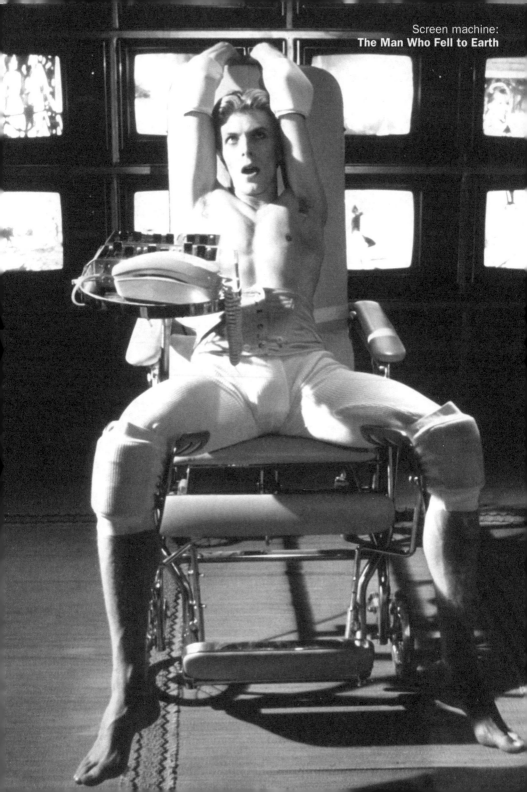

about how the eye and the mind project meaning on to the screen of the world: the detective story as phenomenological riddle. Francis Coppola's *The Conversation* tells a similar story in a sonic as well as visual mode: it was emblematic of a '70s strain of political paranoid cinema, which made it clear that to perceive the world was, invariably, to be paranoid (especially in Nixon's America).

Another strain of enigma film worries over first principles, examining the way we perceive time, live through time, make sense of linear and non-linear experience. A classic musing on time – all the more cogent for being squeezed into 28 minutes – is Chris Marker's *La Jetée*, an eloquent and starkly beautiful short story about stasis, memory and, inevitably, on the nature of film time, with its contemplation of the series of still frames of which film's deceptive movement is comprised.

Then there are all the styles of 'jigsaw-puzzle cinema' that shuffle time, confounding the habitual logic of reading narratives, and contriving to lose the viewer in labyrinthine structures from which our entrance ticket doesn't guarantee us an easy exit. The classic film of this type – a story about making sense of the world, and of a life, by a stage director for the first time trying to make sense of cinema – is *Citizen Kane*. In the '60s, the temporal labyrinth – and often, the spatial one too – became the favoured haunt of Alain Resnais, notably in the peerlessly inscrutable *Last Year in Marienbad* (written by the novelist Alain Robbe-Grillet, whose own films, including *Trans-Europ-Express*, are all-out free-for-alls of narrative uncertainty). Resnais remains the arch-explorer of temporal fragmentation, his cinema continuing to be a template for such explorations as *Eternal Sunshine of the Spotless Mind*, *Primer* and Wong Kar-Wai's *2046*.

However, another approach to the mind in time is to make us acutely (sometimes painfully) aware of our own apprehension of the world by slowing down the passage of minutes. Slow cinema – a form in which 'longueurs' is not a dirty word – throws us back on our own thought processes, sometimes even deliberately bores us so that we are obliged to keep thinking if we want to stay conscious. Never underestimate a film-maker's recourse to the oppressive effects of duration

'Cinema is not always to be bolted down and forgotten, but sometimes calls for an extended digestion that only properly begins after the end credits.'

and repetition, as with Chantal Akerman's icily analytical *Jeanne Dielman, 23 Quai du Commerce, 1080 Bruxelles*, a 225-minute account of domestic drudgery that sets out to prove that a woman's work is never done until the viewer's mind is done in.

Other devotees of duration (either over an entire film or within a single extended shot) are Jacques Rivette, many of whose films (including the original 13-hour cut of *Out 1*) make us experience the real duration of film so that the act of sitting in a cinema becomes akin to an extended theatrical experience. Also theatrical, in a more pageant-like sense, are the works of Hungary's Miklós Jancsó and Greece's Theo Angelopoulos, both of whom represent modern history as a series of stately and complex dance moves to be executed by individuals and crowds on large landscapes in long takes (Jancsó's *The Red and the White*, Angelopoulos's four-hour *The Travelling Players*). There's also a film that might be called the ultimate 'documentary' about the viewer's relationship to vision: Michael Snow's majestically incommunicative *Wavelength*, a single (or apparently single) 45-minute zoom in which the viewer's mind becomes aware of its own forward thrust, straining to detect whatever the certain hidden something is that the camera obstinately refuses to disclose.

Some film-makers are expressly concerned with their own thought processes, and strive to make cinema itself into a thinking machine.

Foremost among them – and arguably the person singly most responsible for creating an image of modern cinema as an intellectual pursuit – is Jean-Luc Godard, whose autodidact passion is an all-devouring mill into which every kind of thought and image must sooner or later be ground up. His career is, you might say, an endless process of digestion of the most heteroclite food for thought: painting, literature, political theory, history, cinema high and low, as well as slogans, movie-business gossip, transatlantic pop culture, adverts, TV. That popular culture ever became a field of academic study is surely in no small part due to films such as *Une Femme Mariée*, with its deconstruction of lingerie ads, or the omnivorous hybrid *Pierrot le Fou*, which conflates car culture, the MGM musical and Vietnam. Godard's more recent work, merging video and film, has become a representation of the free-ranging thought process itself, often using the video mixing desk as a prosthesis for the film-maker's brain, and as an analogue of Godard's cinephile memory as a sampling tool, in the encyclopedic series *Histoire(s) du cinéma*.

Godard's work is just one extreme example of cinema that thinks aloud. There are simpler, more diaristic examples of this tendency: Nanni Moretti (*Dear Diary*, *Aprile*), with his self-portraits of the intellectual funnyman in an Italy where leftist values have crashed; or Ross McElwee, whose wry first-person essays on the state of America and the bewildered independent film-maker's place in it (*The Six O'Clock News*, *Bright Leaves*) create a vivid impression of thoughts in search of their subject. Similarly, France's Agnès Varda underwent a late-flowering renaissance in *The Gleaners and I*, setting out armed with a DV camcorder and discovering afresh the possibilities of looking at the world.

Some films present themselves as luxuriating in ideas, yet actually purvey thought as some sort of top-of-the-range consumer item: notably, Godfrey Reggio's 'revelatory' *Koyaanisqatsi* trilogy, with its Discovery Channel mysticism. Yet there are films that seek to popularise abstraction and yet manage to take wing: witness the imagistic stoner fugue of Richard Linklater's *Waking Life*, with its dreamlike interface between live action and animation. For that matter, let's not

'Some films present themselves as luxuriating in ideas, yet actually purvey thought as some sort of top-of-the-range consumer item.'

discount the authentically provocative mind-bending of the first episode (but the first only) of the *Matrix* trilogy.

However, it's an entirely different business for a film actually to try to represent thought processes, especially those of artists: such films are too often committed to seeing things from the outside, to watching pens scratch, fingers type, brushes daub. Radical approaches – sometimes just a radical degree of patience – are required to draw us into the business of creation. Victor Erice's *The Quince Tree Sun* is a fictionalised pseudo-documentary portrait of a still-life painter that wonderfully vindicates the phrase 'watching paint dry'. One of the few authentically complex works about both a literary work and its creator is Raoul Ruiz's reverie on Proust, *Time Regained* – not an adaptation of the book so much as a digressive and languorous evocation of what it might feel like to read that book, or to experience time as its author did.

Another intellectual approach to film lies in the militant rejection of traditional film forms. Peter Greenaway's elaborate artifices increasingly stand apart from the history of even the most complex and demanding cinema, and align themselves instead with a tradition of experimental visual arts (from Tom Philips' painted-over books to interactive art DVDs) and non-linear literary games, as practised by the likes of Georges Perec and BS Johnson. Other film-makers speculatively challenge the limits of film language by measuring it against, or even bringing it confrontationally face to face with, other art forms: theatre (Portugal's João César Monteiro, whose dizzyingly eccentric *The Hips of John Wayne* includes an extended Strindberg performance), music (Straub and Huillet's *The Diary of Anna Magdalena Bach*) or painting (Jacques Rivette's *La Belle Noiseuse*).

There is, of course, a thoughtful cinema that also fulfils the dietary requirements of the popcorn movie: films that work as genre entertainment, that offer immediate pop-culture pleasures, while leaving enough narrative and theoretical loose ends to chew on long afterwards. *The Usual Suspects* is crime cinema's shaggy-dog story par excellence, in which nothing we see on screen may be any more reliable than our own flawed preconceptions. There are boffinish teasers such as Shane Carruth's hyper-low-budget *Primer*, in which riddles of time, identity and the ethics of technological research are couched in the form of a teasingly fractured weird-science drama. And there are ludic jugglings with time and consciousness, such as Christopher Nolan's gimmicky but satisfying *Memento*, an amnesia thriller with a backward structure resulting in a deconstructionist's dream: a story that at once writes and erases itself.

Such films wear their conceptual credentials on their sleeve: it remains for the viewer to argue whether they are truly smart or just playing smart. But at the opposite end of the spectrum are those films that may or may not explictly invoke intellectual concepts, but which, in their lucid attentiveness to the minutiae of everyday existence, its microscopic pains and dignities, its flurries and (more often) silences, can be said to have a genuinely philosophical take on the world: these include the films of Ozu, Dreyer, Korea's Hong Sang-Soo, Vietnam's Tran Anh Hung, and, above all, Robert Bresson, for whom every gesture – even the handling of a spoon, or the exchange of a banknote – becomes both the object and the subject of thought.

Thought food in 20 films

La Passion de Jeanne d'Arc (1928)
By concentrating on close-ups of faces at their most extremely expressive, from ecstatic to agonised, Carl

Theodor Dreyer produces a sort of phenomenology of the human face, while dismantling all the preconceptions that already surrounded the historical epic in the silent era.

I Confess (1953)
Traditionally regarded as the least entertaining of Hitchcock's films, this story of a priest (Montgomery Clift) facing the death penalty in an oppressively doomy Quebec because of his refusal to break the secrecy of the confessional is the master's most explicitly theological and ethical treatise, and as such sheds its sombre light on the philosophical ramifications of the entire oeuvre.

Un condamné à mort s'est échappé (1956)
Robert Bresson's portrait of a Resistance fighter trying to escape from a cell. Minimalist cinema in which every gesture takes on maximum weight – an essay on the phenomenology of things, but also a tribute to the human mind's capacity for patience, sanity and lucidity.

L'Avventura (1960)
A film that loses one of its principal characters and, apparently, its plot – and nearly lost its audience when first shown to hostile crowds in Cannes. Antonioni's narrative subversions certainly made his audience rethink their cinematic expectations, while creating a wholly new way of conceiving urban space on the cinema screen.

Persona (1966)
An actress suffers a breakdown in which she refuses to speak, and recuperates in a country cottage in the charge of a nurse. Ingmar Bergman's enduringly elusive essay on identity, memory and the way people sustain and destroy each other is still cinema's most sustained philosophical investigation into the mysteries of the human face.

Jeder für sich und Gott gegen alle (1974)
A 19th-century *cause célèbre* provides Werner Herzog with the basis for a poetic inquiry – better known in the English-speaking world as *The Enigma of Kaspar Hauser* – into the nature of the self, consciousness and language. That the life of lead actor Bruno S was in many ways not dissimilar to that of the mysterious foundling Kaspar adds to the film's resonance.

F for Fake (1974)
Orson Welles plays the magus one last time in this documentary *jeu d'esprit* about fakery and forgery. Mixing scabrous gossip, dinner-table philosophy and shaggy-dog storytelling, Welles's last piece of hocus pocus is all the richer in insight for its insouciant swagger.

The Hypothesis of the Stolen Painting (1978)

Raoul Ruiz 'adapts' a Pierre Klossowski narrative about a mysterious series of tableaux vivants, each one based on an equally mysterious painting. Their meaning, and the film's, might elude us; but this deliriously tantalising parable is also a fascinating essay on the way that cinematic craft forges (in both senses of the word) meaning.

Shoah (1985)

The facts, and nothing but. Claude Lanzmann's monumentally provocative documentary on the Holocaust assembles over nine hours of testimonials and eye-witness accounts, eschewing editorialising rhetoric: an ethically rigorous approach that sets out to give the survivors' testimony its true historical weight and clarity.

The Green Ray (1986)

One of the simplest and most direct moral comedies by Eric Rohmer, an anatomist of French social mores at their most delicately absurd. A seemingly banal anecdote about a woman trying to go on holiday, *The Green Ray* really looks into bigger questions – what people want, whether they know what they want, and the role of language as a help and a hindrance in the pursuit of happiness.

Uncommon Senses (1987)

Maverick US independent Jon Jost's ten-part documentary on the meaning and the shapes of America – politically, geographically, mythically, financially – culminates in the director's own profession of faith as a go-it-alone US dissident.

Close-Up (1989)

Not nearly as documentary as it first appears, Abbas Kiarostami's film is an investigation into the way that we invest our dreams in cinema. Following up the true case of a man who masqueraded as film-maker Mohsen Makhmalbaf, Kiarostami creates a complex panorama of gullibility, social difference and reconciliation.

Crimes and Misdemeanors (1989)

Of all Woody Allen's 'serious' (or half-serious) films, this is the most substantial – the Dostoevskian story of a man who commits a crime and gets away with it. Allen 'remade' it, after a fashion, in his glib *Match Point*, but it took older actors with the gravitas of Martin Landau and Anjelica Huston to give it the heft that this uncomfortable moral drama demands.

Notebook on Cities and Clothes (1989)

Very much a film of its moment, Wim Wenders' first-person essay is ostensibly about his own jet-setting status as global film-maker and the cerebral style of fashion designer Yohji Yamamoto. But – with the camcorder as his 'notebook' – it's also an anxious contemplation on the advent of video technology and the lure of electronic immediacy.

Calendar (1993)

A fascinating hybrid from Atom Egoyan, part fiction about a marriage cracking up, part video essay on tourism, displacement, language, memory and the film-maker's own identity (he casts himself in the central role) as a member of the Armenian diaspora. Rich in theory, but also moving and at times trenchantly funny.

Suture (1993)

A witty, dazzling treatise on race and perception from duo Scott McGehee and David Siegel. A pulp-ish psychological thriller involves a man transformed into his identical twin through a process of plastic surgery and mistaken identity. But somehow no one – except the viewer – seems aware that one twin is white, the other black. It's around this blind spot that *Suture*'s dizzying logic revolves.

Funny Games (1997)

Michael Haneke's cruelly analytical examination of the voyeuristic motivations of screen violence, and particularly of the 'home invasion' thriller sub-genre. Forcing us to occupy the position of a terrorised family, Haneke turns cinema into an intellectual equivalent of aversion therapy.

21 Grams (2003)

Several characters cross paths and exchange fates in a mosaic concocted by director Alejandro González Iñàrritu and writer Guillermo Arriaga, upping the complexity ante on their previous *Amores perros*. Mathematical and metaphysical preoccupations combine in a theological narrative of American crossed destinies.

The Five Obstructions (2003)

A ping-pong match between Lars von Trier and veteran Danish director Jørgen Leth. Trier challenges Leth to remake his own 1967 film *The Perfect Human* five times over, but Big Brother-style, insists on setting the rules. Leth's sang-froid in rising to the challenge raises questions about will, the director-producer relationship and the flexible nature of film language.

Eternal Sunshine of the Spotless Mind (2004)

Screenwriter Charlie Kaufman muses on love and memory, with director Michel Gondry using visual effects both simple and tricksy to portray a mind unravelling backwards. The inner life of the mind has never been portrayed in such sublimely direct, yet visually punning terms.

I have a film theory...

Geoff (K)andrew gets alphabetical.

Back in the halcyon days of the '70s, when I first became a certified movie obsessive and took my first tentative steps into the business as manager and programmer of the then renowned west London repertory fleapit known as the Electric Cinema Club, it wasn't just good American pictures that were plentiful – in comparison, at least, to the paltry crop of more recent years. There was also a lot of good, serious thought, talk and writing about film, far more perceptive, provocative and linguistically obscure than the money-, celebrity- and gossip-obsessed fluff that's generally passed off as an interest in 'film culture' today. And this healthy situation was reflected not, as today, in the number of rainforests pulped in order to satisfy an apparently worldwide desire to see photos illustrating the party-going habits of the latest starlet, but in the number, variety and vicious rivalry of the intellectual disciplines all purporting to be the most useful, aesthetically sophisticated, ethically right-on and socio-politically relevant critical and analytical approach needed to understand The Cinema.

There was, of course, auteurism – or, as those of us with a more precise bent and a French O-Level pedantically called it, *la politique des auteurs*. There was humanism. There was the easily graspable synthetic theory advanced by VF Perkins in his book *Film as Film*. There were variations on the montage theories of the Soviets and the reality-centred theories of Kracauer and Bazin. There was the poetic theorising of Pasolini and a modified form of Leavisite theory. There was Marxist theory; feminist theory; psychoanalytical theory (Freudian, Jungian, Lacanian); ideogrammatic theory; linguistic theory; genre theory; historical, sociological and industrial theories. There were also, of course, semiology and structuralism. And there were probably many more disciplines that I never heard of, or that I long ago forgot in my quietly persistent efforts to come up with a ground-breaking, all-encompassing theory of my own. It's taken a while; ironic, then, that I'm finally able to present it to a world wholly uninterested in such crucially important intellectual practices as the pursuit of a viable film theory. No matter; visionaries are seldom appreciated in their own time.

But first, how did I come to the theory? Why had no one previously noticed its worth, applicability, searing truth? I confess I was

---

Moving picture
Seijun Suzuki

Director, *Branded to Kill*, *Tokyo Drifter*, *Pistol Opera*

There was no particular movie I saw which made me want to make movies myself. Before the Pacific War I used to go to the movies, like everyone else. I particularly remember *Daibosatsu Toge* (*The Great Buddha Pass*) and, of course, *Tanuki Goten* (*Princess Raccoon*), which was made by Kimura Keigo. [Suzuki's latest film, *Operetta Tanuki Goten* (*Princess Raccoon*), is a musical fantasia distantly inspired by Kimura's film.]

After the war ended, I was discharged from the army and went back to high school. I took the entrance exam for Tokyo University, but failed it. My father had been expecting me to take over his business (a factory making bells for bicycles), but it went bankrupt in the economic chaos after the war. While I was wondering what to do next, a friend took me along to the scriptwriting class at Kamakura Academy. That's where I learned how to write scripts, and so that was my starting-point in the film world.

Looking back at my career, I think the job of 'movie director' fitted me quite well. But when I chose this line of work, I wasn't looking for a way to express myself. I was just looking to earn a living.

Plenty to think about in DW Griffith's **Intolerance**

lucky, having had the good fortune to write, over the years, not one but two 'critical dictionaries' outlining the artistic achievements of two hundred or more film-makers from the silent era to the present. As a thinker who takes justifiable pride in being both methodologically meticulous and entirely unimaginative, I wrote these books by starting at the very beginning – a very good place to start, as Julie Andrews once so wisely pointed out in one of the very first films I remember going to see several times – and working my critical way, entry by miraculously perceptive entry, from Aldrich to Zinnemann.

With the first book, written in the late 1980s, I was struck, when I got to 'S', by how many fine directors there were whose name began with that letter: Saura, Sayles, Schlöndorff, Schrader, Scorsese, Siegel, Siodmak, Sirk, Sjöström, Skolimowski, Spielberg (this was some time ago), Sturges, Syberberg. But aware that 'S' was a common letter, and alert to the possibility that I might have been influenced in this observation by the foreword having been provided by the director of *Taxi Driver* and *Raging Bull*, I gave the matter little thought, and forgot about it entirely until I was halfway through writing the second book a decade later. This time, the eureka moment came when I reached 'K', a far less common letter but one which included Kaufman, Kaurismäki, Kaplan (Nelly), Kazan, Keaton, Kelly, Kiarostami, Kieslowski, King, Kinugasa, Kitano, Klimov, Kluge, Kobayashi, Konchalovsky, Kozintsev, Kramer (Robert, of course), Kubelka, Kubrick, Kurosawa, Kusturica… These were only the best, and there was room for only 11 in the book, but the starting point of a theory was clear to see; if your surname begins with 'K', you're at a distinct advantage should you choose to take up film directing.

Critics' choice
Big ideas

The Corporation
(2003, Can) *d* Mark Achbar, Jennifer Abbott. Corporations rule, but do they rule wisely? Quite an eye-opener: this film means business.

Dawn of the Dead
(1978, US) *d* George A Romero. *cast* David Emge, Ken Foree, Scott H Reininger. When there's no more room in Hell the dead will walk the Earth. It's a theory.

Groundhog Day
(1993, US) *d* Harold Ramis. *cast* Bill Murray, Andie MacDowell, Chris Elliott. How would it feel to wake up to the same day every day? And face Andie MacDowell?

The Handmaid's Tale
(1990, US/Ger) *d* Volker Schlöndorff. *cast* Natasha Richardson, Faye Dunaway. A vision of America so obsessed with moral pollution it returns to Calvinism.

The Hitchhiker's Guide to the Galaxy
(2005, US/GB) *d* Garth Jennings. *cast* Sam Rockwell, Mos Def, Martin Freeman. The earth is an experiment run by white mice.

Insignificance
(1985, GB) *d* Nic Roeg. *cast* Michael Emil, Theresa Russell, Tony Curtis, Gary Busey. Marilyn Monroe explains relativity to Einstein with the help of clockwork trains and balloons.

π [Pi]
(1997, US) *d* Darren Aronofsky. *cast* Sean Gullette, Mark Margolis, Ben Shenkman. A man is obsessed with finding the numerical pattern behind the global stock market.

Primer
(2004, US) *d* Shane Carruth. *cast* Shane Carruth, David Sullivan, Casey Gooden. A movie that treats your brain like Play-Doh.

2001: A Space Odyssey
(1968, GB) *d* Stanley Kubrick. *cast* Keir Dullea, Gary Lockwood, William Sylvester. Seminal sci-fi that posits alien intervention as the catalyst for human evolution.

What the #$*! Do We Know!?
(2005, US) *d* William Arntz. *cast* Marlee Matlin, Elaine Hedrix, Robert Bailey Jr. Dude! A trip down the rabbit hole to question the nature of reality and human experience.

Moving picture
Richard Eyre

Director, *Iris*, *Stage Beauty*

The most affecting experience I've ever had with a film was when I first went to Romania on a cultural exchange in the early 1970s, at the height of the Ceausescu regime. I'd heard of Andrei Tarkovsky's *Andrei Rublev*, and I asked my translator if she would take me to see it. Her entire family had been killed by the Soviets, and so she was violently anti-Russian and said she wouldn't go. But she knew that if I went, she had to go. It was her job. I told her she had to go. We were halfway through this incredible, epic anthem to humanity and I noticed her sobbing beside me. By the end, she had experienced a conversion: for the first time, she was able to see Russians as human beings.

However strong the evidence for this premise, I must admit it seemed odd. Could an initial really be closely connected to cinematic expertise, even – given this range of Ks – genius? I therefore took the opportunity to test the premise when, just after the book's publication, I met Abbas Kiarostami, the already much-garlanded Iranian director who had only weeks before received a Cannes Palme d'Or for *A Taste of Cherry*. I liked his work a lot and so, apparently, did much of the rest of the movie-going world, so he was obviously the right person to ask. Did he feel lucky (rest assured I didn't address him as 'punk') having a name beginning with 'K'? I tentatively explained my theory. With a smile, he confessed that perhaps he did, citing an admiration for Kurosawa, Kieslowski and – very greatest of all film-makers – Keaton. Since I too had long believed Buster to be the best ever, I accepted this as unquestionable proof of my startlingly original and perceptive proposition.

But how to take the premise and inflate it into a full-blown film theory? There are various options. We might proceed along the lines of Andrew Sarris' auteurist text *The American Cinema*, ordering the letters of the alphabet and the directors listed thereby in order of merit. For example, Ks would come at the top of the pantheon, closely followed by the Ss,

As (Aldrich, Allen, Almodóvar, Altman, Angelopoulos, Antonioni, Avery), Bs (Becker, Bergman, Berkeley, Bertolucci, Boetticher, Borzage, Bresson, Browning, Buñuel), Hs (Hamer, Haneke, Hawks, Haynes, Herzog, Hitchcock, Hou, Hu, Huston), Ms (Mackendrick, Makavejev, Malick, Malle, Mamoulian, Mankiewicz, Mann, Mann, Marker, McLaren, Méliès, Melville, Meyer, Minnelli, Mizoguchi, Moretti, Morris, Murnau) and Rs (Ray, Ray, Reed, Renoir, Resnais, Rivette, Roeg, Rohmer, Romero, Rosi, Rossellini, Rossen, Ruiz). But in which order? Should the Bs take a lower position due to Besson, Brooks and Brooks, or is the might of Bergman, Bresson and Buñuel invulnerable to such irritations? How are the Ms affected by the combined power of the house of Makhmalbaf? Of the Manns, are Anthony and Michael counterbalanced by Delbert? Are the Hs seriously damaged by the failure of Hill and Hopper to live up to early promise? What of the Ds? Do the relatively minor Allan Dwan's 400 or more films compensate for the fact that the superb Dardennes, Davies, Douglas, Dovzhenko and Dreyer have all, for different reasons, been less than prolific? Then there's Disney: does Walt count as a director, and if so, is being included in a serious philosophico-critical survey like this consistent with the promotion of simple family values? Maybe he'd prefer, from his cryogenic position, to opt out, but would that leave his fellow Ds also out in the cold?

But it's not just a matter of evaluating or ordering the various letters and their 'members' or 'adherents'. (Clearly some such term needs to be found and taken up for the directors listed under each letter, though prior to selecting one, we should investigate the precise nature of the existential connection between the letter and the auteurs: is 'A-ness' somehow 'present' in Aldrich, Allen, Altman et al, or do they somehow 'participate' in 'that-which-is-A'?) We should also investigate whether different letters signify or reflect different qualities. Is there one thing distinguishing the Ms, another denoting the Ss? If so, might the relevant factors begin with that letter? Are the Ms more macho, methodical, manic, melancholy, or what? If so, where does that leave the all-conquering Ks? The letter's problematic – maybe they just share the essence of film-making talent, and are simply kinematographic.

FOOD FOR THOUGHT

If it came to this: **The War Game**

The last thing a theory should be, of course, is facile or dogmatic; complexity, subtlety and absurdity must be fully embraced, even if the theory unworkable as a result. Allowances must be made for the use of different alphabets; for the fact that first names might have some bearing on an auteur's credentials; for people known by an assumed name rather than their birth name (should Michael Curtiz be ranked among the Ks as Miháli Kertész?); for the fact that some auteur groups – most notably the Qs, Us, Xs, Ys and Zs – are so underrepresented that they should perhaps be treated as

vulnerable or disadvantaged minorities; and for the very significant fact that the poor Ws, even the late, great Orson, must cope with being lumbered not only with Ed Wood but Michael Winner, surely the most radical, damning argument yet made against *Citizen Kane*'s enduring status as the finest film ever. Even Pauline Kael, in her famous attack on Welles, missed out on that deadly indictment. But then she was never that serious a thinker. Indeed, why would she be? How could the fact that her surname began with K possibly reflect her qualities as a critic? I rest my case.

'Heavy, very heavy': **Eraserhead**

Take me where I haven't been

Andrew Kötting lines up 20 films that took him on journeys of the mind.

Un Chien Andalou and *L'Age d'Or* – Luis Buñuel and Salvador Dali. And all because of David Bowie at the Wembley Empire Pool. It was 1976, and the 'Station to Station' tour I think. During the intermission he played the two films and cinema, for me, was never the same again.

The Colour of Pomegranates – Sergo Paradjanov. His stream of religious iconography wrapped up in symbolic, locked-off tomfoolery beguiled me. I blame it on Simon Field, who screened it for us in the bowels of Slade University.

The Moon and the Sledgehammer – Philip Trevelyan. The camera makes its way into the forest and the company of a 'real family'. It's full to overflowing with eccentricity, humanity and hybrid activity. Eventually the instigator of my own muddy, bovine soap opera.

The Land of Silence and Darkness – Werner Herzog. Him and his ecstatic journeying to that place of physical and spiritual necessity. A world of the deaf-blind, a world where touch becomes the sole means of communication.

Aguirre, Wrath of God – Werner Herzog again. Him and his weightlessness of dreams versus the heaviness of reality. It moved me to my very foundations.

Associations, *The Girl Chewing Gum* and *Blight* – John Smith. Post-structuralist comedy and insightful genius.

Eraserhead and *Twin Peaks* – David Lynch. In the former, Henry's life is heavy, very heavy, and the world in which he lives is funny, very funny; in the latter an exercise in 'automatic film-making' becomes its very being.

A Zed and Two Noughts – Peter Greenaway. The codification and ceaseless collating of ideas driven along by Michael Nyman's music left me transfixed – and Jim Davidson's apparition left me befuddled.

Time of the Gypsies – Emir Kusturica. Although anchored in a world of Eastern European reality, the transcendant music of Goran Bregovic and unkempt performances help it soar up and away into the realms of magical reality.

Blue – Derek Jarman. Televisual history; the BBC provided the sound, Channel 4 provided the pictures and Derek Jarman provided the vision. Yves Klein meets Anish Kapoor and what's more it serves as his own obituary. Autobiography hand in hand with poetry.

The Cremaster Cycle – Matthew Barney. He drank from Paradjanov's chalice and spewed forth his own textural iconography that made me want to touch the screen.

Breaking the Waves, *The Idiots* and *Dogville* – Lars von Trier. Where to begin? The Beuysian Picasso of modern cinema?

Funny Games – Michael Haneke. The violence meted out, outside the frame, leaves images burnt onto the retina all the same; and the taste in the mouth might stay forever.

Songs from the Second Floor – Roy Anderson. Metaphorical meanderings and dark, dark shenanigans that remind me of the deep blue-black nights of the Scandinavian winters.

Critics' choice
Unanswerable questions

The Big Sleep
(1946, US) *d* Howard Hawks. *cast* Humphrey Bogart, Lauren Bacall.
Hawks claimed that neither he nor the screen-writer knew who killed who. It doesn't matter.

Blade Runner – The Director's Cut
(1982/1991, US) *d* Ridley Scott. *cast* Harrison Ford, Rutger Hauer, Sean Young, Daryl Hannah.
The 'unicorn dream' echoed later by the origami figure – so is Deckard a replicant, then?

King Kong
(2005, US/NZ) *d* Peter Jackson. *cast* Naomi Watts, Jack Black, Adrien Brody.
How'd they transport Kong from Skull Island to New York on a boat not much larger than him?

The Lord of the Rings trilogy
(2001-2003, US/NZ/Ger) *d* Peter Jackson. *cast* Elijah Wood, Ian McKellen, Liv Tyler.
Why didn't Gandalf just fly that great big eagle over Mount Doom and drop the ring in?

The Matrix trilogy
(1999-2003, US/Aust) *d* Andy Wachowski, Larry Wachowski. *cast* Keanu Reeves, Hugo Weaving.
What the hell were the Wachowski Bros thinking?

Pulp Fiction
(1994, US) *d* Quentin Tarantino. *cast* John Travolta, Samuel L Jackson, Uma Thurman.
What was in the suitcase? And while we're at it, *Reservoir Dogs* – who shot Nice Guy Eddie?

Star Wars
(1977, US) *d* George Lucas. *cast* Harrison Ford, Carrie Fisher, Mark Hamill, Alec Guinness.
Why didn't Darth Vader sense that the 'force was strong' in his daughter, Princess Leia?

Taxi Driver
(1976, US) *d* Martin Scorsese. *cast* Robert De Niro, Harvey Keitel, Jodie Foster, Cybill Shepherd.
'You talkin' to me?'

Titanic
(1997, US) *d* James Cameron. *cast* Leonardo DiCaprio, Kate Winslet, Billy Zane.
Did it hit the iceberg because the lookout was distracted by Rose and Jack snogging?

War of the Worlds
(2005, US) *d* Steven Spielberg. *cast* Tom Cruise, Dakota Fanning, Tim Robbins, Miranda Otto.
Why didn't the aliens do *any* research before invading earth?

Life, the universe and everything:
2001: A Space Odyssey

System failure

Ben Walters follows a thread through the films of Stanley Kubrick.

During the shooting of *A Clockwork Orange*, Malcolm McDowell found Stanley Kubrick wearing headphones, lost in thought. 'I was listening to the air traffic control at Heathrow,' the director confided, 'and you know what, Malc? There was just a near miss.'

Electronic eavesdropping is a pastime entirely in keeping with Kubrick's thematic obsessions. His work offers a catalogue of complex systems, devised by people to serve their needs, but which turn out to offer profound threats to personal identity at best – and to the survival of the planet at worst. In Kubrick's world, a near miss is the best you can hope for.

He liked puns and ironies, and a double notion of 'execution' lingers around his films: it's often hard to distinguish between the implementation of a process and the destruction of those engaged in it (as in chess, of which Kubrick was famously fond and whose motifs recur throughout his work). Once the first move is made, it can only end in mate – which means death. As well as a consistent thematic concern, however, the shrinking of the self is also at the crux of Kubrick's technique; that he is so often accused of being cold or unwilling to court an audience's sympathies is a measure of how effectively he provokes the very alienation he seeks to describe.

In hindsight, it seems telling that the working title for his first feature, 1953's *Fear and Desire*, was *The Trap*. Kubrick later dismissed the film, in which a handful of soldiers lost behind enemy lines descend into killing and rape, as juvenile and pretentious, but it declared one of his enduring interests: the dehumanising effects of combat. At its climax, the soldiers about to murder their opposite numbers realise that they literally share their faces; it's hard to imagine a more obvious rebuttal to the notion of the unique self.

The lead characters of *Killer's Kiss*, a boxer and a nightclub dame, also find themselves living a lie to save their skins, while the mannequin-filled warehouse where the final showdown takes place is hardly an advert for individuality. The title of *The Killing* refers to both the outcome anticipated by the planners of a racetrack heist and that which actually befalls them. Its first line is also a pun: the commentator's breathless 'And they're off!' might as well refer to the plotters, whose decision to implement their plan triggers a chain reaction of betrayal and murder that's given a helping hand by sardonic serendipity.

Kubrick returned to the barbaric absurdity of war in the World War I drama *Paths of Glory*, a film whose bitterly ironic title connotes

---

Moving picture
Nuri Bilge Ceylan

Cinematographer, director, producer, writer,
Uzak, The Small Town, Clouds in May

You know I have a clip from *Stalker* in *Uzak*? Well, the first time I saw a Tarkovsky film was when I was at university in Turkey. It was *Solaris*, and I left in the middle of the film. I thought: 'What is this?' But later, I came across the same film when I was in London. I was alone here, hanging out in bookshops and going to the NFT a lot; that's where I saw the film again. And I couldn't believe it – I was so impressed by it this time.

For three days the film was constantly with me. This shows that if something is different from what we are accustomed to, it first seems almost like an alien; but with time, if you have the chance to go into it, it can open new windows. *Solaris* was so strange for me the first time; but the second time, it was almost as if it made me a new person. It shows something else, too: if you're alone, you are very receptive. You tend to look more deeply into things, and that's important. Maybe that's one reason I was able to connect the second time around. The film helped me to understand myself better.

---

the hypocrisy with which French soldiers reluctant to embark on a futile suicide mission could be fired upon by their own superiors, first in the field and then in the name of military justice. To take on the machine is seen to be futile – General Broulard (Adolphe Menjou) is never more hateful or realistic than when he tells Colonel Dax (Kirk Douglas), 'You are an idealist and I pity you as I would the village idiot' – yet Kubrick leaves the film with a humanist touch worthy of Renoir. There's a similarly hopeful ending to *Spartacus*, a project Kubrick inherited rather than initiated, and which offers an atypically upbeat spin on the loss of individuality: the climactic dissolution of the lead's identity into the revolutionary mass ('I'm Spartacus!' 'No! I'm Spartacus!') denotes nobility and courage, as well as ensuring total defeat in the form of mass crucifixion. You still can't beat the system, but you can go down fighting.

The individual unselfed is also at the heart of *Lolita*, though without Kubrick's usual institutional context. James Mason's Humbert gradually has his being reduced and refined until it consists solely of the desire for his stepdaughter; once this is finally frustrated, he dies of a broken heart. *Lolita* offered another play on the notion of self through the multiple personae adopted by Peter Sellers' Quilty;

Moving picture
Jet Li

Actor, *The Shaolin Temple, Once Upon a Time in China, Lethal Weapon 4, Hero*

At different ages I liked different kinds of films. People always change. A lot of people ask, Jet, what's your favourite movie? Favourite actor, favourite director, favourite food? Favourite everything. But in Eastern philosophy, we don't believe you have a favourite. Because the favourite always changes – you grow up, your situation changes. Every moment you change yourself. So I always say about something I like it, but not that it's my favourite; I will change, I know. Like at the moment I love one woman the best; two years later, who knows? You come together with another woman and say, 'Oh, you're the one!' So listen, I believe, no favourite.

Kubrick again exploited the comedian's chameleon qualities by giving him several roles in 1964's *Dr Strangelove*, which upped the comic and tragic stakes in the director's treatment of war. Mutually assured destruction is the ultimate instance of the human-devised system whose operation brings annihilation; despite – or perhaps because of – the film's backdrop of nuclear Armageddon, it marked the director's most successful foray into farce.

In *2001: A Space Odyssey*, Kubrick moved beyond the purely human for the first time – but even though the film posits extraterrestrial intervention as the catalyst for human evolution, the causes of the collapse of the mission to Jupiter lie with HAL, a man-made machine whose murder of the crew seems to result from an attempt to reconcile conflicting commands rather than evil motives. At the same time, HAL is more rounded and sympathetic than any of the human characters, and the end – in which astronaut Dave Bowman (Keir Dullea) passes through the psychedelic 'Stargate' to be reborn as the next stage of human evolution – suggests that man's hope of survival lies in the shucking of individual identity. *The Shining* also has a backdrop that is more than human, but just as we see no aliens in *2001*, the supernatural evil of the Overlook Hotel is experienced purely in human terms: like the monolith, it seems to unleash savage potential embedded in the human – Jack Torrance (Jack Nicholson) is merely a conduit for its power.

A Clockwork Orange, like *Lolita*, is about an individual's destructive appetites – but Malcolm McDowell's Alex, lacking Humbert's self-repression, must have his rough edges smoothed away by behavioural conditioning sponsored by the state. Kubrick would offer the flipside to this in *Full Metal Jacket*. His final examination of the military machine probed the ways the state could programme adolescents for homicide as well as against it, once again through the repression of individuality: after the ritual head-shaving which opens the film, the Gunnery Sergeant makes a point of renaming his recruits – 'Private Joker', 'Private Cowboy' and so on. In *Barry Lyndon*, the lead character actively pursues the abnegation of his character through his desire for material advancement – Barry Lyndon is the name that Irish rogue Redmond Barry (Ryan O'Neal)

What happens when we die?
After Life

assumes during his prolonged social climb through the 18th-century English class system, to which end he suppresses everything that initially makes him charming and distinctive.

Social superstructures, sophisticated technology, the appetites of the id… Left to run unchecked, all can overrun and obliterate the individual. Yet there is one mechanical process without which Kubrick could never have conveyed his investigations of systems: cinema itself. Like Alex strapped to his chair as he undergoes the Ludovico technique, eyes pinned open before the screen, we are submissive and selfless before the execution of Kubrick's plans. For maximum impact, his films must be seen on the big screen, and preferably near the front of the auditorium, where we have no pretence of control (as in home viewing) and the films' calculated rejection of the conventional appeals of sympathetic characterisation and pacy narrative is often balanced by a quiet humbling visual monumentalism. From the vast Bavarian palace of *Paths of Glory* to the cavernous War Room in *Dr Strangelove*, the silent vacuum of *2001* to the echoing interiors of *The Shining*,

the painterly tableaux of *Barry Lyndon* to the bewildering masked ball of *Eyes Wide Shut*, Kubrick's films regularly make insignificant interlopers of their viewers, barely deigning to acknowledge, let alone court us.

Indeed, *Eyes Wide Shut*, Kubrick's last completed feature, is a prolonged exercise in alienation for the audience as much as for Bill Hartford (Tom Cruise), as he ignorantly ricochets from one bafflingly portentous encounter to another. It's plain that wheels are in motion but their purpose remains hidden: something's happening, but we don't know what. In what counts among Kubrick's films as a happy ending, Bill survives his trauma, no stronger or wiser, merely grateful for having had a near miss; compare this to the Cruise characters who emerge reinvigorated at the end of *Minority Report* or *War of the Worlds*. One reason to have been surprised that Steven Spielberg inherited Kubrick's final project, *A.I. Artificial Intelligence*, was that Spielberg makes films in which, through ordeal, men find themselves. Kubrick made films in which, through ordeal, their selves are lost.

Adapt (or try)

Peter Paphides quizzes the makers of a film that aims to tie the brain in knots.

There can't be many people in the world right now who spend much time discussing Gene Wilder's contribution to cinema, but in Room 208 at the Savoy, a rather animated exchange was developing. 'We all love Gene', said Nicolas Cage, decanting a small bottle of orange juice into a glass. 'We've been talking about him a lot lately. What do I like about him? I like it when he loses control.' Cage, dressed all in black, smiles to himself. 'No one loses control like Gene Wilder.' 'I loved him in *The Producers*', says Charlie Kaufman. 'For me, that was the best.'

Does he still make movies?

Cage: 'Yeah, he does, actually. He was in a production of *Alice in Wonderland*. He played the Mock Turtle, which was actually very amusing. And Willy Wonka, of course, is one of the great performances.'

Spike Jonze makes a rare interjection. 'He had a real dark side to him in that film. So loveable and charismatic and alluring, and yet there was this this danger.'

Cage: 'Just like Candy does. Candy can be a spooky thing sometimes. I think it was David Lynch who said that sugar was granulated happiness. But if you have too much it'll drive you crazy'.

We didn't convene to talk about Gene Wilder, of course. That was just an unexpected bonus arising from the curly Wilder-style wig that Cage had to don in *Adaptation*, a slightly thinner version of the barnet sported by Kaufman. In the film, Cage plays a screen-writer called, yes, Charlie Kaufman, who finds himself under intense pressure to follow up his surprise hit *Being John Malkovich*. Saddled with a commission to turn Susan Orlean's book *The Orchid Thief* into a screenplay, the self-conscious, over-analytical, crap-with-women Kaufman seems unable to find a way to adapt the story. How, after all, do you turn a book about the obsessive nature of orchid poachers in to a bankable film?

His plight is made worse by the fact that his simple, happy-go-lucky, great-with-women twin brother Donald (also played by Cage) has just returned from a New York film-writing course with a dynamite idea in his head: a thriller about a serial killer with a multiple personality disorder who also turns out to be the cop who's chasing him. No such crass whoring for Charlie. He eventually realises that his film needs to be all about someone who can only overcome his writer's block by writing a film all about his attempts to overcome his writer's block. What we talking about is the movie equivalent of standing in a room of mirrors.

If you enjoyed *Adaptation*, you probably enjoyed it for the same reasons that others might volubly exclaim, 'Oh, purlease!' These being: that it's the real (and the fictional) Kaufman's outrageous attempt to escape his own predicament through a portal in which he turns into – no, not John Malkovich, but his fictional self; and that the final third of the film turns into exactly the kind of action movie that so repels the fictional Charlie (and the real Charlie?) involving, among others, Orlean (Meryl Streep).

For a couple of self-referential, reality-blurring mischief-makers, Kaufman and Jonze were cautiously happy to shed further light on a plot that several US critics deemed something of a cop-out. Yes, Kaufman did originally set out to write a simple adaptation of Orlean's book. Regarding the action-packed ending: 'If you look at the credits, you'll see that the movie is written by me and my brother Donald'. Your fictional brother Donald? 'Um, yes'. Jonze elucidates: 'We spent a lot of time trying to create a movie that doesn't exist on one plane. We were playing with several themes'. For 39-year-old Cage, the biggest of those themes was plain old insecurity, both in the film and as it relates to his own life. The twins' differing personalities mirrored a dilemma that the actor has wrestled with in his own life: 'I definitely identified more with Charlie', he explains. 'I have my own machinations that I go through before I start a movie.' In the past, these 'machinations' have resulted in some pretty extreme behaviour. Playing a homicidal gangster in *The Cotton Club* for what was only his second major role, the 20 year-old Cage would routinely smash up his trailer in order to summon the necessary anger. On one occasion, fearing that he wasn't sufficiently angry to do a good day's work, he smashed an LA street vendor's remote-control car.

'Thankfully', he says, 'that period stopped. I think I realised that you don't have to live the part. But, you know, I had no training, so I was probably trying to compensate. I was the boy in *Birdy* who pulled out one of his teeth to try to get some concept of physical pain.'

That would do it.

'Well, yeah', he says, momentarily transfixed by his huge, long legs, 'I didn't know how to play these parts. It was my way of figuring them out. And then I think it became clear to me that I learned publicly. I learned to act through experience as opposed to learning in a classroom. But now I've been acting for almost 22 or 23 years, and I think what happens is that you cultivate, through osmosis or something, a process where you don't have to destroy yourself – although the insecurity never quite goes away. In the lead-up to any film I have grave doubts as to if I even know how to act at all. And it happens every time. I don't know if it's sort of a self-

Robert McKee on *Adaptation*

In *Adaptation*, severely blocked scripter Charlie Kaufman signs up for the famous seminar given by screenwriting sage Robert McKee (played in the flm by by Brian Cox). The real-life McKee, whose TV writing credits include *Quincy MD* and *Columbo* (several of his movie screenplays have been optioned but none flmed), has been giving three-day courses on story structure since 1984. We asked McKee to analyse *Adaptation*'s screenplay and discussed his role within it.

Does *Adaptation* adhere to the McKee commandments?
I think it's pretty classically structured. It has the inciting incident, progressive complications, crisis, climax and resolution.

Would you say the film falls into a genre?
It's autobiography. Have you read my book? In the chapter on genres, I talk about the education story: the character comes into it with a negative attitude towards life and himself. Over the course of the story, he ends up with a positive attitude towards life and himself. That's the Charlie Kaufman story. Now, the counterpoint is what's called the disillusionment story, which starts with a character who has a positive attitude towards life and himself, and by the end is in disillusionment, with a negative attitude. That's the Susan Orlean story. What Charlie has done is, he's criss-crossed an education plot with a disillusionment plot, but in the broad category of autobiography.

How would you have advised a student if they'd told you they wanted to adapt *The Orchid Thief*?
I would have told them it's unadaptable. It is genuine literature, which means that the heart and soul of that book are in the mind of Susan Orlean. You cannot drive a camera lens through an actor's forehead and photograph thought.

Are you happy with how you're portrayed?
Oh, very much so. I cast Brian Cox as myself. They brought me a list of ten of the greatest English actors alive today: Michael Caine, Terence Stamp and so on. They were all wonderful actors. But I said, I see what you want to do, but there's one name that's not on this list, and that's Brian Cox. Other actors, there's a certain subtext to their acting which says, no matter what they're doing, 'Love me.' Brian Cox does not do that.

Your character cautions Charlie against using a deus ex machina in his screenplay, but the film positions you as the *deus ex machina* – your appearance triggers the crazy 'resolutions' of the third act. Did you appreciate the irony?
I'm not the deus ex machina. The only *deus ex machina* is the alligator.

What function do you fulfill in the film, then?
In the education plot, there's a teacher character. In *American Beauty*, there's an education plot for the Kevin Spacey character, and the teacher character is Teenage Drug Dealer. In *The Accidental Tourist*, Geena Davis is a teacher character for William Hurt. In *Harold and Maude*, it's Maude. In the education story, there will be this teacher character who gives guidance somehow to get the negative-minded protagonist looking positive. That's the role I play. I'm a teacher character, in an education story.

Moving picture
Stacy Peralta

Director, writer, *Dogtown and Z-Boys*, *Riding Giants*

I saw a movie that I absolutely loved – the friends I was with and I had to go out and talk about it all through supper afterwards. It was *The Barbarian Invasions*. I thought it was so well done. It's very difficult to tackle intelligent ideas the way that Denys Arcand dealt with them, and make them palatable without being heavy-handed. And he did it in such a fabulous way, because the movie's very smart, very provocative. It's also absurd and very funny, because while his characters are discussing all these heavy intellectual problems, they're also speaking in the most graphic terms about sexual behaviour.

The father is stuck in a hospital, there's no city money to keep the hospital up, so construction's going on while the father's in his bed. There's a wing downstairs that's not even being used because they can't afford to use it, so his wealthy son gets his father a private room downstairs with private nurses. It's a commentary on how dislocating our capitalistic society has become there's the have-nots and the haves, and it's becoming very difficult.

It's an ensemble piece, so you're seeing all these different impressions and interpretations of the same experience. At the same time you're seeing how important the simple act of friendship is, and how it takes a life-and-death situation to bring everyone together, to realise how important they are to each other.

inflicted means to get pressure on myself so I can get creative. I just don't know'.

How do those doubts announce themselves?

'Oh, it's like, "You don't know what you're doing. How are you ever going to do this? You've forgotten. You have to get back to work and you don't know what you're doing." And so you're pacing back and forth until you're literally banging your head against the wall and then you go, "Oh, wait a minute! Okay! That's an idea! Let's get serious." So, I think it's more or less like a pressure to motivate me to get to work. Now, I think there's a way to get to that point without having to do that. I think there's a way to just sort of emanate the work from a place of joy and having a song in your heart that you're thrilled do be doing this.'

Do you know any other actors who are like that?

'Do I know actors who are like that? Not a lot. Hahaha! I'm not sure I've met one yet! I've read articles about Jack Nicholson and he says the same thing. He never relaxes. And you think: "Well, if that's Jack…" In fact, I think it was Francis (Ford Coppola – Cage's uncle and Jonze's father-in-law) who said to me: "A good actor never relaxes until "Action". But up to that point it's just constant head-banging, you know?'

There's a point in *Adaptation* where the twin brothers are just beginning to understand each other. Charlie remembers a childhood incident when Donald was scornfully rejected by his high-school sweetheart, and yet his euphoria seemed undimmed. When Charlie asks him why the rejection didn't bother him, Donald merely explains: 'You are what you love, not what loves you'. Cage makes a link between that line and his own life. 'Yeah, I think so, definitely. I really felt a lot of truth and simple beauty in that And even if you don't quite always practise it, it's something to aspire to'.

We were saying our goodbyes when news came through that Cage had earned an Oscar nomination for his performance – his first since his winning turn in Mike Figgis's 1995 film, *Leaving Las Vegas*.

'I don't know how many months I spent emoting to a tennis ball on a stick', he says, alluding to the price to pay of being one's own co-lead, 'but I guess it was worth it. Not that I'll be playing twins again in a hurry.'

'Are you sure about that?' asks Kaufman.

'Quite sure', confirms Cage.

'How about female twins?'

'Now *that* maybe I would do'.

'See? I'm always thinking.'

'You're always thinking.'

FOOD FOR THOUGHT

Desire

'People fall in love because they respond to a certain hair colouring, or vocal tones, or mannerisms'
Spellbound

Desire
in the dark

We've all fallen in love at the movies – **Chris Peachment** more than once.

Desire in the cinema manifests itself in as many different ways as there are lonely viewers in the dark. One friend of mine once revealed that as a youth he had secretly wished he could be shrunk to six inches and be allowed to abseil into Sophia Loren's cleavage. Another otherwise sophisticated author once wrote in *Sight & Sound* that his heart's desire was to run barefoot along the filtrum of the Swedish boy who played Tadzio in *Death in Venice*. (The filtrum, also called the infranasal depression, is the groove between the nose and upper lip.)

Everyone experiences desire at the movies – indeed, there would never have been a movie industry without it. The phrase common among Hollywood producers, when casting a female lead, is 'Yes, but does the audience want to sleep with her?' It is base reductionism perhaps, but that's always the target to aim for, when talking about desire. For all the other errant joys that cinema can provide, desire is the bottom line. It's what you get down to, finally, *au fond*. And I don't think it admits of very much analysis. Better by far for me to point a finger at a few objects of desire and mutter something out of the side of my mouth.

As François Truffaut said, 'The film director's task consists of getting pretty women to do pretty things.'

Objects of desire

Catherine Deneuve, in anything, but especially in *Tristana*, on a balcony, lifting her skirt for a peasant boy, and still not cracking that façade. An author and film director friend of mine and I once spoke to her for about 20 minutes at a British Film Institute function. When we came away, we were still so overawed that neither of us could remember a single thing that had been said. A third party who had seen us did report, however, that Deneuve had smiled occasionally, which made us happy.

Wearing it well:
In the Mood for Love

DESIRE

Kim Novak, wearing a green dress to fuel James Stewart's necrophiliac fantasies, and looking bewildered by the silliness of it all.

Drew Barrymore, scion of the great Barrymore actor clan, in *The Wedding Singer*. Her smile makes you want to put her in your pocket and take her home.

Rebecca De Mornay. A flawless bottom revealed when the wind swept up her skirt in *Risky Business*.

(Whatever happened to Molly Ringwald? So horrible in pink, and so obviously dying for a tomboy role.)

Debra Winger. Everyone said she was 'difficult', which only underlines how lazy most directors are and how inattentive to why a woman of no obvious beauty can still be desirable. On the one occasion I interviewed her, she was wearing a petticoat that kept slipping down and that she kept trying to pin up with a safety pin, to no avail. She was a farmgirl sort of dresser, and looked uncomfortable in her best clothes.

The young Sandrine Bonnaire, alone on the prow of a boat in her bikini, while Purcell's 'Cold Song' played on the soundtrack of Maurice Pialat's *To Our Loves*.

Fanny Ardant. Succumbing to *amour fou* and breakdown in *The Woman Next Door*. And then being given a get-well present from Truffaut (who loved her and had a daughter with her) as a private eye in *Vivement Dimanche!*

When I interviewed her on the set of the remake of *Sabrina*, she wanted to know how to pronounce 'floors'. It took a while before I discovered that the word in the script was 'flaws', and even longer to describe the minute difference in pronunciation between the two words. (The line is actually 'Illusions have no flaws', and it still sounds odd in the finished film.) I have never seen eyes so dark.

When she was 19, she came to work at the BBC in London as a tea lady, wheeling a trolley from which she sold beverages and buns. It would be nice to think that a producer or director then working at the BBC might have spotted her presence, her sophistication and her beauty, and cast her in the latest Jane Austen adaptation. But no one did; it took a Frenchman to see her potential. Which is why France has a thriving film culture, and Britain never will.

Kristin Scott Thomas. So highly strung that if she were a horse I would think twice before getting on her. When she declared her love to Hugh Grant in *Four Weddings and a Funeral* ('It's you, Charlie. Always has been.') the film should have stopped there. The fact that he did not throw himself to his knees, beg forgiveness and offer a lifetime's devotion, but instead settled for that patently fake American, is another reason why British film will never get it right.

Edith Scob (whose name always looked like it was spelled backwards, though it doesn't work when you try to put it right), in *Les Yeux sans Visage*. If ever a woman was in no need of a face transplant it was her. What she was dying of was a broken heart.

FBI agent Jennifer Lopez, who finds herself locked in the boot of a getaway car with felon George Clooney in *Out of Sight*. And what do they do? They discuss the movies and fall in love.

Frances McDormand, who made throwing up loveable in *Fargo* – and I never thought I would write that sentence.

From *Le Silence de la mer*, by Jean-Pierre Melville. The Nazi officer, and the French girl, Nicole Stéphane, both out for a walk, pass each other silently in the snow. You can't see their faces but you know for the first time that they are in love.

Bogart and Bacall. I'm getting tired of this pair, we all know them so well, until… the very next time I see them, for they never fail. The horse racing conversation in the night club in *The Big Sleep* is a great example of flirting with outrageous double entendre. ('You look like a man who likes to come from behind…', 'strong finish…' and so on.) You can keep the scene in *To Have and Have Not* when she tells him to put his lips together and blow, though that check suit sets her off to a T.

Smoking. What a loss to flirtation has been the decline in smoking. The first offering of the cigarette, the initial acceptance, the ritual with the cigarette lighter, the proximity of the burning flame of desire, the cool, steadying hand, the sensual inhalation, the glance, the long sigh of exhaling smoke, the exchange of breath, the fragrance of Turkish tobacco, the shared intimacy. Bogart and Bacall were especially adroit with all of that. What she

That bob! Louise Brooks in **Pandora's Box**

does with the matchbox and cigarette in that night club scene in *The Big Sleep* ought to have an adult rating. It is profoundly wicked in thought, word and deed. (I suspect that everything connected with smoking will soon be lost to us, even forbidden. And prostitutes will specialise in allowing men to sit and watch them light up.)

Anouk Aimée, imprisoned by windscreen wipers, in *Un Homme et une Femme*. Even a bad film can provoke desire, and it's strange that no other bad work of art can do that.

Renée Zellweger, who proves that being likeable can be sexy, too.

Ingrid Bergman, looking at the bodies of the victims of Pompeii, in *Viaggio in Italia*, and knowing that life was too short.

Rita Hayworth in *Gilda*. As a young man, I could always see why that dress stayed up, but not how. 'Every man I knew has fallen in love with Gilda and woken up with me.' A line repeated by Julia Roberts in *Notting Hill*, to no good effect.

Natalie Portman as the knowing 12-year-old next door in *Beautiful Girls*. It wasn't that she was so young, it was that she was so old.

Sharon Stone. 'If you have a vagina and an attitude in this town, then that's a lethal combination.' She has shown us the first, but not the second, and that is the wrong way round if you wish to be an object of desire.

Julie Andrews. Out of sheer perversity, and because it would be like jumping on your nanny.

Jane Greer in *Out of the Past*. Not for any one moment in particular, though heaven knows there are plenty, but for the feeling that, when off-screen, she and Robert Mitchum got down to something really dirty.

Melanie Griffiths, proving that big can be beautiful in black underwear in Mike Nichols' *Working Girl*, and the first time I thought a thong looked something more than just uncomfortable.

Barbara Stanwyck. Wearing an ankle chain in *Double Indemnity*. When she crosses her legs, I swear you can hear the nylons sigh. In all cinema, I never saw a woman so on heat.

Jessica Lange. The original 'big-boned' girl, getting her white knickers mashed by Jack Nicholson in *The Postman Always Rings Twice*.

An actress whose name I never managed to catch as the titles rolled in *Mulholland Falls*.

'The proximity of the burning flame of desire, the cool, steadying hand, the sensual inhalation, the glance, the long sigh of exhaling smoke.'

She was the one in the motel that Nick Nolte loved and who was having other affairs. No doubt she had integrity and talent, but she also had prodigious breasts.

Sophie Marceau, the daughter of D'Artagnan, swordfighting in a pair of thigh-high boots.

A lonely Holly Hunter gently grasping her masseur's buttocks in *Living Out Loud*.

Kim Hunter's shade of lipstick in *A Matter of Life and Death*. And the way David Niven and she fall in love before they have even met. Their first kiss occurs because her bicycle falls over.

Jeanne Moreau, in a false moustache and large sweater, running over the railway bridge, in *Jules and Jim*. And for showing, over a long career, that the most plain of faces can flash into beauty when in the mood.

Eva Marie Saint on the train in *North by Northwest*, pushing Cary Grant so far as to say: 'You could tease a man to death.'

Anjelica Huston, as Mae Rose, heiress to a thousand years of Sicilian witchcraft, in her father's *Prizzi's Honor*. 'Come on Charley. You wanna do it? Let's do it right here, on the Oriental. With the lights on.' I met her once. She was tall and very funny. That film also contained another object of desire in the shape of hit-woman Kathleen Turner. It strikes me that the movies have never properly harnessed her scathing contempt, with the exception of one line in *Body Heat*, spoken to the thick

lawyer William Hurt: 'You're not too smart, are you? I like that in a man.'

Gena Rowlands, proving that 66 can be sexy, in her son Nick Cassavetes's *Unhook the Stars*.

Rosalind Russell, the only woman to match Cary Grant's insolence in *His Girl Friday*.

Julianne Moore, red-haired, red hot in Altman's *Short Cuts*, half naked (the lower half) but carrying on anyway.

Mrs Danvers. Gliding around on castors and so obviously a lesbian.

Marlene Dietrich, in full tuxedo, kissing a woman in her audience and tipping her hat.

Cyd Charisse. The best legs in the movies and the only one who could give Astaire a run for his money. Their best film together, *Silk Stockings*, is the only time I would like to be in his shoes.

Louise Brooks. For letting us know, early on, that being the sexiest woman ever to appear on celluloid is not about acting, but about revealing thought. And for the rueful shrug she gives when caught *in flagrante* in a cupboard with another woman.

Obstacles to desire

Finally, I offer the following as proof that acting too hard at being desirable will kill desire stone dead.

Raquel Welch in a fur bikini.

Demi Moore. Robert Redford offered $1 million for a night with her, in *Indecent Proposal*. Which suggests the sort of raging frustration that will overlook a grating voice and unpleasant attitude.

Julia Roberts as *Pretty Woman*. Pretty enough, but the least likely-looking hooker in the history of Sunset Boulevard.

Glenn Close, who still managed to look wholesome while boiling a live rabbit. Her recent outing as a chief of police in *The Shield* TV series may prove me wrong.

One exception is the Swiss actress Ursula Andress. Honeychile Rider's emergence from the waves, wearing a white bikini, in *Dr No* happened in parallel with my own emergence into adolescence. She has no claims to greatness as an actress, but I will always remain grateful to her, in the way that Benjamin should have remained grateful to Mrs Robinson – if only he had understood her.

Modest, *moi*? Bardot in **En Cas de Malheur**

DESIRE

The thrust of the idea

Sex on screen: how much can you show? **Atom Egoyan** tests the boundaries.

When I promised my producer, Robert Lantos, that I would deliver an R-rated version of my latest film, *Where the Truth Lies*, I signed the contract confident that this wouldn't be much of a problem. Even though the script had several scenes that seemed sexually explicit, I also realised that careful framing and editing could solve any obstacles.

Or so I thought.

I hadn't realised – and this is the big problem – that it wasn't necessarily the depiction of thrusting that would be the basis for the MPAA (Motion Picture Association of America) rating, but rather the actual number of thrusts seen. A few thrusts would be allowed, but anything more might land the picture in the dreaded NC-17 category. The challenge became how to choreograph extended scenes of sexual activity without seeing the prolonged thrusting associated with the act.

The obvious solution, used by countless films, is to frame the actors' heads and shoulders as their lower bodies thrust. This efficient method effectively frames out the offending area, allowing the viewer to concentrate on the faces as they stare at each other, blissfully thinking about the nice feelings their unseen groins are producing.

Lust in a hot climate: **Ai no Corrida**

DESIRE

Moving picture
Nagisa Oshima

Director, writer, *Ai No Corrida*, *Merry Christmas Mr Lawrence*, *Taboo*

In everyone's life, there's a moment when one particular film becomes unforgettable. In effect, that film becomes the film in your life, the cinematic experience that means most to you. In that sense, the one film in my life is *Onna No Sono* (*Garden of Women*), made in the 1950s by Keisuke Kinoshita.

I saw *Garden of Women* with my then-girlfriend in Kyoto, just one week before I moved to Tokyo to take up a job as an assistant director with the Shochiku Company. The previous November there had been a student rebellion in Kyoto University, which had ended after a pitched battle with the police. I'd been one of the instigators of the rebellion. The whole thing had been seriously misjudged and it represented a big failure for the nascent student movement. I felt responsible, and consequently guilty.

In the film Takamine Hideko plays a university student, and there's a scene where she tells her boyfriend about that rebellion in Kyoto University. She also stresses the difference between the reactions of female students and male students. Watching this with my girlfriend, I found it speaking directly to me. I don't admire the film that much, but because of the situation in which I saw it, it became absolutely unforgettable.

DESIRE

'Peel me a grape!' Mae West in **I'm No Angel**

Moving picture
Michel Reilhac

....

Director/editor, *The Good Old Naughty Days*

My best cinematic memory is actually a London screening of *The Good Old Naughty Days* – with apologies.

It was a little over a year ago at the Chelsea Arts Club, a wonderful old town house that mostly hosts writers and painters. They put on an early British screening, invited a porn actress and producer and advertised it as a 'naughty evening'. It was packed.

The lights went up for the Q&A session and this lady stood up and started screaming outrage at the scene with a dog. She was so over the top I thought it was a put-on and burst out laughing. But she was genuinely enraged, even though the scene was 80, 90 years old.

The whole discussion came close to a fight, people were shoving tables and shouting insults. I thought it was wonderful that these films made by our grandparents could still provoke uproar.

We went for dinner, and the discussion kept on returning to the subject of dogs and porn. It has never been raised elsewhere.

It's been interesting to see how cultural values vary: in Japan they fixed on the body hair in the film, in Spain the nuns and priests, in France the school teacher. But that was definitely the liveliest screening. It certainly changed my perspective on the British audience, which I now consider the most Mediterranean of all.

Occasionally the director will then cut to a wider shot, but this is never more than a few thrusts, and it usually finds the actors' bodies covered by a sheet.

The problem with this solution was that it didn't convey the feeling that the sex scenes in the movie were supposed to express.

One of the lead characters in the film – a hugely popular entertainer, played by Kevin Bacon – recounts his sexual exploits as though he was an actor in a porn film. I needed these scenes to feel lurid and unbridled, even though my intention wasn't to be particularly graphic. The traditional 'head and shoulders' framing wouldn't work.

I'm convinced that the best way to shoot a sex scene and make it seem real is to use a master shot – an uninterrupted sequence with no cuts. I wanted to see the bodies. The overwhelming challenge was how to show two (and in this case even more) people having sex without depicting the act of thrusting.

By its very nature, sex needs thrusting. More specifically, one part of the body must be in some form of friction with another. This isn't a very romantic way of thinking about it, but then again the MPAA isn't a very romantic organisation. Their job is to count thrusts, and then decide – depending on the number – who should see the film. Nice work if you can get it.

The two male leads are popular entertainers in the '50s. The idea of tantric sex, or anything involving sexual activity in a semi-comatose position was not a possibility. As the deadline approached for filming these scenes, I began to panic. I resorted to playing with dolls, trying to figure out angles and configurations. Finally, in total defeat, I approached Robert with the news. It was impossible to show a sexual act of longer than a minute (one scene involved two pages of dialogue) without resorting to some form of thrusting.

And with this decision, we veered our film into NC-17 territory. To this day, I sometimes wake up in a sweat, thinking of other ways the scenes might have been filmed.

Errant pieces of furniture, masking piston-like body parts. Tasteful cut-aways to trains, tunnels, and collapsing chimney stacks. A lamp toppling and smashing at the beginning of the scene, making the screen black. All of these solutions fell somewhere between the coy and the ridiculous.

The sex scenes in *Where the Truth Lies* are essential to the dramatic and psychological construction of the film. They are playful, transgressive and even traumatic. Like most sex scenes, they involve issues of intimacy, love, power, desire, escape, anger, ambition and a thousand other emotional configurations.

They also involve thrusting.

Swede sensation

Ingrid Bergman's life and art marched in step, as **Ed Buscombe** explains.

In Ingrid Bergman's first big success, *Intermezzo*, made in her native Sweden, she plays a young pianist who has an affair with a married man. In her best-known Hollywood film, *Casablanca*, she's married while having a romance with Humphrey Bogart. And in *Notorious*, the greatest film she ever made, she's again a scarlet woman, having a love affair with Cary Grant but marrying Claude Rains (though for the best of motives). Perhaps not surprising, then, that life should imitate art when in 1949 she fell in love with Italian director Roberto Rossellini. Both deserted their spouses, in the process sparking one of Hollywood's biggest ever scandals. The world went through one of its regular fits of high-minded morality, as all and sundry vied to denounce the adulterous pair. Even Pandit Nehru, Prime Minister of India, got involved, calling Rossellini a scoundrel, more or less about the time he was conducting his own affair with Lady Mountbatten.

Again, perhaps it shouldn't surprise us, given Hollywood's fixation on the madonna/whore syndrome, that Ingrid also played saintly roles, including a nun in *The Bells of St Mary's*, the Maid in *Joan of Arc* and missionary Gladys Aylward in *Inn of the Sixth Happiness*. But it's in the films where she suffers for love that her real talents are displayed.

Swedes have a contradictory image: rational, enlightened, even a little bit cold – yet Sweden has produced a long list of actresses whose erotic allure is matched only by their acting ability. First in that line was, of course, the immortal Garbo, enticed to Hollywood in 1925. Later would come the radiant leading ladies of Ingmar Bergman, including Bibi Andersson and Gunnel Lindblom. In between was Ingrid.

Autumn Sonata, her only film for namesake Ingmar (no relation) was to come late in her career. In the beginning, in Sweden in the 1930s, she had been the protégée of director Gustav Molander, and it was his film *Intermezzo* that

'She's again a
scarlet woman,
having a love affair
with Cary Grant
but marrying
Claude Rains.'

DESIRE

brought her to the attention of David O Selznick. Although Selznick signed her up and put her into a remake of the film, he had little direct involvement in her Hollywood career, preferring to loan her out to other studios at considerable profit to himself. But just about the time that he signed Bergman, he also signed Alfred Hitchcock, and in 1945 Hitch directed Bergman in *Spellbound*, with Selznick producing. The two European exiles hit it off, sympathising with each other over the way their careers were held in a vice-like grip by Selznick's contracts.

Spellbound is a convoluted story about psychoanalysis, chiefly remembered now for the dream sequences designed by Salvador Dalí. It hardly prepares one for Bergman's next collaboration with the 'master of suspense'. Fortunately *Notorious* was another loan-out, this time to RKO, so Selznick was less directly involved once the script was settled. Hitchcock had wanted Cary Grant for *Spellbound*; he got the dull Gregory Peck instead. But this time Grant was on board.

The story of *Notorious* is easily told. World War II has just ended. Bergman plays Alicia, whose father has been jailed as a Nazi. In reaction she falls into a life of dissipation, before being approached by Devlin (Cary Grant), a US government agent, to spy on some Nazi sympathisers in Brazil. Reluctantly she agrees, and then, after she has fallen in love with Devlin, Alicia is pressured into marrying one of the Nazis, Sebastian (Claude Rains), so she can penetrate his spy-ring.

In the key sequence Alicia and Devlin have a long embrace (the longest in all Hitchcock's films, a single take lasting two minutes and

40 seconds), and she opens her heart to him. But despite the intimacy he holds back somewhat, still influenced by her 'notorious' reputation. He's called away by phone and told of the plan to have her marry Sebastian. Devlin tries to resist it, wanting to believe she could never do such a thing, but orders are orders. When he's told that Sebastian was once in love with Alicia, this only seems to confirm his suspicions of her dissolute past. Back at her apartment he tells Alicia what they want her to do. She desperately wants him to show his love by forbidding her to prostitute herself, even for reasons of state; but, standing in the shadows, the emotion on his face hidden from her, he refuses, saying the decision is hers. He'd protested to his superior, 'She's not that type of woman,' but now that it comes down to it, he can't be sure.

Hitchcock shows himself the master of mise-en-scène, the earlier intimate clinch contrasting now with the couple's placing in different spaces on the screen, half the time not even looking at each other as the mood of happiness turns to resentment and even hostility. Bergman gives a heartbreaking performance as Alicia, deeply hurt by Devlin's refusal to commit to his feelings for her, and by the way he throws her reputation in her face. She keeps saying the same thing to him, in different ways, imploring Devlin to 'tell me what you didn't tell them,' that he loves her and can't let her marry another man. But he stubbornly refuses; instead, he expects her to prove her love by saying that she can't possibly go through with the marriage. He persuades himself that if she really loves him, she would surely do this without him having to ask her. Both, in their obstinacy, make it impossible for the other to pull back from the plan, and this almost leads to Alicia's death.

Hitchcock isn't usually thought of as a political film-maker, but what the film says about the capacity of realpolitik to corrupt personal feelings anticipates all the Cold-War spy dramas that came after. *Notorious* is also modern in its sexual politics, in its critique of Devlin's commitment phobia and his readiness to dismiss Alicia as a slut, which is what the word 'notorious' implies. Too bad that the third and final Hitchcock collaboration with Bergman, *Under Capricorn*, was a turgid melodrama set in 18th-century Australia. After that, she was off to Italy and Rossellini.

Skin chic

Tod Davies was so taken by the *Emmanuelle* franchise, she made a film about it.

Emmanuelle was the first softcore movie I ever saw. I was a teenager then, in San Francisco in the early '70s: a wonderful time and place to be a teenage girl.

I went to see *Emmanuelle* by myself, in the little cinema in Ghirardelli Square, and I thought it was just the sexiest movie I'd ever seen except for *The Moonspinners* – and that had Hayley Mills in it.

But Sylvia Kristel was another case entirely. Sure, the movie was spectacularly stupid, and the character of Mario was one of the creepiest since Maurice Chevalier in *Gigi*. But she fascinated me. She held that drek together. She was so pure and graceful, and she looked so great without a bra, and even if the character of her husband was not one that any sane teenage girl would consider marrying.

And indeed it wasn't. *Emmanuelle* became not just a genre, but an absolute franchise. Like the Spaghetti Westerns of around the same time, the basic concept – heroine bonking in various ways in exotic locales – developed and spun off into all manner of imitations. There was *Emmanuelle 2* and then 3 and then 4 and then 5. There were the *Black Emanuelle* spin-offs (so cheap they could only afford one 'm'), starring the even more devastatingly gorgeous Laura Gemser. There was *Carry On, Emmanuelle*.

Critics' choice
Voyeurs

DESIRE

Ai No Corrida
(1976, Fr/Japan) *d* Nagisa Oshima. *cast* Tatsuya Fuji, Eiko Matsuda, Aoi Nakajima, Meika Seri. Oshima's erotic masterpiece. The most involving (hence disturbing) film about voyeurism.

American Beauty
(1999, US) *d* Sam Mendes. *cast* Kevin Spacey, Annette Bening, Thora Birch, Mena Suvari. Spacey 'turns on, tunes in and drops out' in this polished and acerbic social satire.

American Pie
(1999, US) *d* Paul Weitz. *cast* Jason Biggs, Chris Klein, Natasha Lyonne, Thomas Ian Nicholas. Famous for a ludicrous masturbation scene and plenty of webcam hilarity.

Atlantic City
(1980, Can/Fr) *d* Louis Malle. *cast* Burt Lancaster, Susan Sarandon, Michel Piccoli. Part thriller, part love story… and Lancaster sees topless Sarandon rub herself down with a lemon.

Back to the Future
(1985, US) *d* Robert Zemeckis. *cast* Michael J Fox, Christopher Lloyd, Lea Thompson. Travel back to a time when your mum fancies you and your dad's a peeping tom.

Monsieur Hire
(1989, Fr) *d* Patrice Leconte. *cast* Michel Blanc, Sandrine Bonnaire, Luc Thullier, André Wilms. Prime suspect in a murder, Hire secretly gazes at Alice, who lives opposite.

One Hour Photo
(2002, US) *d* Mark Romanek. *cast* Robin Williams, Connie Neilsen, Michael Vartan. Photo booth op makes the *Peeping Tom* movie journey from spectator to participant.

Peeping Tom
(1960, GB) *d* Michael Powell. *cast* Karl Böhm, Anna Massey, Maxine Audley. A film about scoptophila (the morbid desire to watch). Its protagonist works in the movies!

Rear Window
(1954, US) *d* Alfred Hitchcock. *cast* James Stewart, Grace Kelly, Wendell Corey. Immobilised Stewart watches everyone else's dirty linen while designer-clad Kelly's away.

Sur mes Lèvres
(2001, Fr) *d* Jacques Audiard. *cast* Vincent Cassel, Emmanuelle Devos, Olivier Gourmet. Exquisitely elegant thriller with voyeurism, power shifts and an understated sexual-romantic side.

I liked all of them, even the unwatchable ones – and there were a lot of unwatchable ones. Why did I like them? At first because I just liked watching people have various kinds of sex; and then because I'd crack up watching the loony ways the film-makers hit on to make people have sex, or something that by the end of the franchise only vaguely resembled it. (My favourite character in a later *Emmanuelle* carries an aeroplane propeller around with him. Everywhere. This is, unsurprisingly, never explained.)

And, finally, I liked them from a kind of teenage girl defiance, long after I ceased to be a teenage girl. Because it pissed me off that the Spaghetti Westerns, which were just a bunch of boys shooting at and torturing each other in various manly ways, got a fanatical cinephile following, with a sort of hushed semi-academic respect paid to their ridiculous plots and even more ridiculous characters. The actors in Spaghetti Westerns were invited to film festivals and panels, and generally made much of.

But what of the poor *Emmanuelle* films? What of their ridiculous plots and ridiculous characters?

And what about the actresses?

Well, they were treated like something to be sniggered about and to be denigrated and to be felt superior to. No self-respecting person was supposed to enjoy them. Not only that, but they were supposed to be dangerous in some way – censors censored the *Emmanuelle* movies. (Presumably the feared that somebody watching might feel a sudden urge to don a dinner jacket, speak in a French accent and entice a beautiful Dutch girl into kinky sex.) But mostly they were supposed to be sort of… well, sort of disgusting, really, like something you picked up on your shoe in a Tenderloin porn cinema.

But they weren't. They weren't any more disgusting than a Spaghetti Western. They were silly, sure. They were incoherent, definitely. They were just an excuse to show people copulating in as many unreal situations as possible. But then what were Spaghetti Westerns? Just an excuse to show as many manly men torturing and being tortured in as many unreal situations as possible.

But what both had in common was a kind of weird innocence. Spaghetti Western movies are not about real violence – they are about the kind of violence a normal teenage boy fantasises about, so unreal as to be almost

Moving picture
Petr Zelenka

Director, writer, *Buttoners*, *Year of the Devil*

It was the first film festival I'd ever been to. I went to Montecatini in Italy with a student film that I'd written and a friend had directed. It was a 15-minute film about an interpreter who ends up dubbing porn films into German, but develops a very special psychosis: he has to have his own intercourse dubbed by somebody else. So his psychiatrist is hired to dub what he and his wife get up to.

'There were two screenings: indoors in the late afternoon, then outdoors at night. The indoor was very improvised, it was a gymnastics hall, and they screened it on a sheet, but it wasn't properly attached to the wall, so everybody had wrinkles on their faces and elsewhere. And the interpreters would sit in small booths, and translate into Italian but they didn't have any idea how it should be done. They simply took the dialogue sheet and started reading it, regardless of what was happening on screen and when they'd finished they left the booth, halfway through the movie. The fact that it was a film about interpreters made it even more funny.

When I complained, they said: 'Okay, we apologise, and the outdoor screening tonight will be much better.' But it turned out even more bizarre, because there weren't any interpreters at all. And those showing the film had miscalculated – the screening began at nine o'clock, when it was still light, so we couldn't see anything. The Italian audience would just hear some Czech words out of nowhere while the sun shone. Only later did we understand that the whole festival had been organised by the Mafia and that films were not actually that important at all.

The fairest of them all? **Emmanuelle**

DESIRE

innocent. And the *Emmanuelle* movies are not about real sex. They're about the kind of sex a normal teenage girl fantasises about, so unreal as to be almost innocent. You can look at both of them as cinematic wet dreams. One set for boys, one set for girls. As is usual these days, the wet dreams for boys get a lot more positive press.

And, as is too depressingly usual as well, violence gets a lot more positive press than sex.

Moving picture
Todd Haynes

Director, writer, *Poison*, *Safe*, *Velvet Goldmine*, *Far from Heaven*

I virtually lived in the repertory cinemas of LA when I was a teenager: places like the NuArt and the Fox Venice. It was that era when every night there was a double-bill, and I'd go three or four times a week to sit through the Bergman night or the Fellini night, or *O Lucky Man!* with *If...*. But then there was another interesting,

more lurid thing that almost coincided with that film obsession: people groping you! So it was as if the beginnings of sexual aspiration became fused in my mind with great films and dark theatres all kinds of possibilities there! A whole other world of silent communication going on! It just seemed a more perverse time, but also a richer one in terms of all the movies you could still see on the screen. What a gift that would be today!

Critics' choice
Repression and obsession

A Streetcar Named Desire
(1951, US) *d* Elia Kazan. *cast* Vivien Leigh, Marlon Brando, Kim Hunter, Karl Malden.
Brando mumbles and scratches his way through a tale of neuroses and passion.

Black Narcissus
(1946, GB) *d* Michael Powell, Emeric Pressburger. *cast* Deborah Kerr, Sabu, David Farrar.
Heady melodrama, with a group of nuns in the Himalayas falling prey to doubt, jealousy and madness.

Cat on a Hot Tin Roof
(1958, US) *d* Richard Brooks. *cast* Elizabeth Taylor, Paul Newman, Burl Ives, Judith Anderson.
Frustration, greed, lust and impotence, in the screen adaptation of Tennessee Williams's play.

Death in Venice
(1971, It) *d* Luchino Visconti. *cast* Dirk Bogarde, Björn Andresen, Silvana Mangano.
Bogarde's mannered pederast is obsessed with a beautiful boy in a plague-ridden city.

Far from Heaven
(2002, US/Fr) *d* Todd Haynes. *cast* Julianne Moore, Dennis Quaid, Dennis Haysbert.
An immaculate confection of taboos, confusions, prejudices and double standards.

In the Mood for Love
(2000, HK/Fr) *d* Wong Kar-Wai. *cast* Maggie Cheung, Tony Leung, Rebecca Pan, Lai Chan.
Wong's paean to the agony and ecstasy of buttoned-up emotions.

Lolita
(1961, GB) *d* Stanley Kubrick. *cast* James Mason, Sue Lyon, Shelley Winters, Peter Sellers.
In this tale of unlawful obsession, Mason is all repressed passion and furrowed brow.

Paris, Texas
(1984, WGer/Fr/GB) *d* Wim Wenders. *cast* Harry Dean Stanton, Dean Stockwell, Nastassja Kinski.
Having 'lost' his family, Stanton's character begins an obsessive quest to find them again.

Play Misty for Me
(1971, US) *d* Clint Eastwood. *cast* Clint Eastwood, Jessica Walter, Donna Mills, lonesome Californian DJ gets involved with a suicidal hysteric who won't take no for an answer.

The Remains of the Day
(1993, US) *d* James Ivory. *cast* Anthony Hopkins, Emma Thompson, Peter Vaughan, James Fox.
Hopkins plays a fanatically devoted butler who falls, in an uptight way, for the housekeeper.

DESIRE

Why is that? This is something I really want to know. If you get a choice between a silly movie about sex and a silly movie about violence, why is the silly movie about sex the one that sends everybody nuts? (I would really like a sensible answer to this question. Anyone possessing such a thing should send it on to me, care of the editors of this book.)

When my partner Alex Cox and I made *Emmanuelle: A Hard Look* for Channel 4 TV in 2000, we got to interview Sylvia Kristel and Laura Gemser ('Black Emanuelle'). They were beautiful women with an innate sense of grace. They had been doing a job, and you got the feeling from both of them that they'd had to put up with a lot of slimy putdowns and indignities that they might have been spared if they'd been in some other kind of films. But why? It's fun watching them both.

And heaven knows they worked hard.

As Laura Gemser so memorably put it: 'It's not easy making love to the women. But, you know, you get paid, you just do it.' (I would have loved to have heard something like that from Franco Nero. 'It's not easy maiming, torturing, and killing people, or being staked to a desert mound in the sun with toothpicks propping open your eyes. But you know, you get paid, you just do it.')

As for me, I'm still, at heart, the same teenage girl who went to watch the first *Emmanuelle* in San Francisco all those years ago. Give me a choice between watching a man staked out in the sun with ants crawling all over him, and watching a beautiful nude body cutting through the blue of a swimming pool, and I'll take the sex over the violence any day. Any day at all.

Getting animated

Ten UK-based animators and experimental film-makers, all part of the animate! project, write about the films that have fired them up.

Perpetual Motion in the Land of Milk and Honey

AL & AL

Derek Jarman's *Blue*. We watched this the day after meeting in Derek's garden in 1997. It marks the beginning of our own journey into the blue void. The film is an extraordinary visionless piece about going blind with AIDS. And Kubrick's *2001: A Space Odyssey*. Every time we see this we end up discussing Heidegger's *The Question Concerning Technology*, the evolution of lip reading, the effect of minimalism on monkeys and how the 'Blue Danube' waltz orchestrates the German rocket research aspect.

Run Wrake

Snow White, by Dave Fleischer. I'm a huge fan of the early Fleischer Brothers cartoons, and was heavily influenced by their 'loops'. This is a classic: Betty Boop, Cab Calloway singing 'St James Infirmary Blues', and some wonderfully surreal animation. And *Brazil*, by Terry Gilliam. His animation for Monty Python had been a massive inspiration, and this film perfectly fitted my angry student view of the world – it's as relevant today as it was then. And *Dimensions of Dialogue*, by Jan Svankmajer. Dark and wonderful animation from the Czech master.

Rabbit

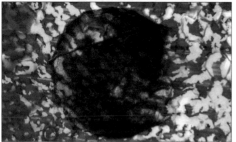

Sunset Strip

Kayla Parker

Looking back, I can see how my childhood memory of Disney's *Snow White* surfaced in my own animated films: *Cage of Flame*, based on dreams around the time of menstruation, creates an internal landscape with emotional sweeps of image and sound, and is resonant with poisoned fruit, magic mirrors, suspense, longing and transformation. I watched the DVD recently: Snow White's squeaky, saccharine simper got on my nerves, and I was struck by the age gap between her and the dodgy prince. Most of all, though, I love the evil queen, the magic and the shadows.

Dryden Goodwin

A blip, a momentary stumble, a double take, the short shots in the last few seconds before the end titles of Taxi Driver. They're disquieting and strangely complex, punctuated by a sharp musical sting, a reversed reverberating note. My senses are shocked and sharpened, in tune with Travis Bickle's adrenaline start, suddenly noticing something unseen to me in the rear view mirror of his taxi. Bickle's eyes, bouncing off the mirror, seem to look straight at me: I am his passenger, I'm accompanying him back into his self-perpetuating loneliness.

Flight

3 Ways to Go

Sarah Cox

At college in Liverpool, it was Robert Breer films that set me on the path of experimental and graphic animation, and to Michael Snow, Kurt Kren and Stan Brakhage. I liked the authenticity in a kind of 'film is film' way, and for me Len Lye's *Free Radicals* was never bettered. But eventually I missed the drama and headed back to narrative. It was Lynne Ramsay's *Ratcatcher* that did it – I knew I loved it from the opening shot of the boy twirling himself up in the net curtain and his friendship with the girl with the scabby knee.

Richard Wright

In 1991, along came David Blair's *Wax, or the Discovery of Television Among the Bees* and blew us all out of the water. Using the simplest of means – a one-person cast, old archive footage and cheap, low-res computer graphics (animated by Blair's wife Florence Ormezzano and media theorist Lev Manovich), Blair showed how you could construct a hallucinatory narrative that tied together the Gulf War, flight simulators, psychic research and bee keeping. Blair gave the film just enough coherence to make you think you've found its true meaning every time you watch it.

LMX Spiral

DESIRE

Matt Hulse

You've got a life to spend. What do you do with it? It's over before you know it. My impetus has always been 'Hey, look at this', and 'Wow, did you hear that?' If I can catch a little of the things that excite me and articulate them, I have purpose. Influences? Poets: Ivor Cutler, McGonagall, Stevie Smith, Lear. Photographers: Ansel Adams, John Hinde, August Sander. Film-makers: Tati, Kötting, Campion, Kubrick, Svankmajer, Lynch. Writers: Ishiguro, Carson McCullers, Bachelard, Spike Milligan. Music: Wire, Gang of Four, Joy Division, Microdisney, The Who.

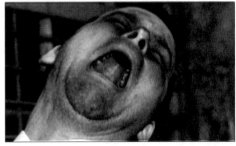

Half Life

End of Restriction

Robert Bradbrook

As the irritatingly catchy 'Midnight at the Oasis' emanates from the hotel bathroom, your heart sinks: Bob (Bill Murray) has given into loneliness and spent the night with the hotel's cabaret singer. Like much of Sofia Coppola's wonderful *Lost in Translation*, the use of such a simple device removes the need for dialogue. Similarly, Bob's growing rapport with Charlotte (Scarlett Johansson) is so beautifully portrayed, a hesitant touch of her foot during a conversation says much more than words. I've always been inspired by films that are visual in their storytelling.

Oliver Harrison

Cocteau talks about the 'poetry' of film – a quality caught between sound and image. At the moment the camera in *Eraserhead* disappeared through the bars of the radiator to reveal the singing girl, I realised it was possible to portray the imagination on screen – that a dream could be captured on film, and things crepuscular, minutiae and sub-worlds could be the subject matter of film. David Lynch also uniquely prised the soundtrack out of the domain of post-production and made it totally his own. He made it inextricable from the visual world.

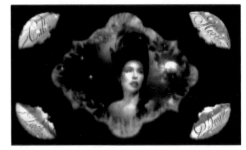

Love is All

Who I Am and What I Want

David Shrigley & Chris Shepherd

A film I like very much is *The Big Lebowski*. Its plot is like that of a Raymond Chandler novel but without closure or revelation. My favourite moment is when the central character, the Dude (played by Jeff Bridges), is trying to get information from pornographer Jackie Treehorn. Treehorn writes on a notepad, tears off the page and leaves the room. In a moment of sleuthful inspiration, the Dude dashes to the pad and rubs a pencil over the page to reveal the embossed text. It is a crude drawing of a man with a giant cock.

DESIRE

Fear

'It's in the trees! It's coming'
Night of the Demon

What a scream

Christopher Frayling steels his nerves to look at how films can scare us.

In July 1935, the novelist and critic Graham Greene wrote a review of the Hollywood version of *The Bride of Frankenstein* – sequel to *Frankenstein* – for *The Spectator*. The Bride was the one where Elsa Lanchester as Mary Shelley creates a mate for Boris Karloff's 'monster' in the from of Elsa Lanchester, but this time with an extreme Nefertiti hairdo. 'Poor harmless Mary Shelley, when she dreamed that she was watched by pale, yellow, speculative eyes between the curtains of her bed, set in motion a vast machinery of actors, of sound systems and trick shots and yes-men. It rolls on indefinitely… presently, I have no doubt, it will be colour-shot and televised; later in the Brave New World to become a smelly.'

Greene's point was that the journey from Gothic text to Hollywood film involved a steep decline, and one that was likely to get steeper in the future. For him, the richness and the horror – the pleasurable fear – of the original had been lost on the way, and Mary Shelley's personal nightmare of June 1816 had turned into the anonymous product of a modern assembly line. Part of the problem, Greene concluded, was that film-makers had to be so very *literal* in their visualisations of the horror. The most pleasurable horror stories were about suggestion and obscurity rather than shock-horror. They were also about the personal rather than the industrial. But the old stories were proving to be surprisingly resilient.

It's true that in the three foundation texts of the literary horror genre – *Frankenstein* (1818), *Strange Case of Dr Jekyll and Mr Hyde* (1886) and *Dracula* (1897) – the horror tends to be seen from the edge of the retina. Much of the anxiety they created was about what they didn't reveal. As a result, there was remarkably little for dramatists and screenwriters to work with. As late as 1928, Universal was despairing of ever being able to turn Frankenstein into an acceptable movie, even after it had been successfully dramatised on stage.

How did Mary Shelley describe Doctor Frankenstein's first view of the creature, in the

The horror! **An American Werewolf in London**

One of the most dramatic entrances in movie history: **Alien**

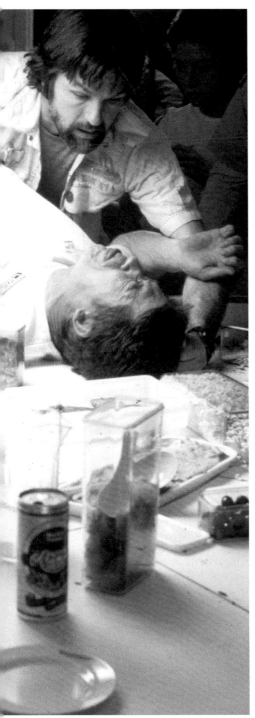

original novel? 'His limbs were in proportion, and I had selected his features as beautiful. Beautiful! – Great God! His yellow skin scarcely covered the work of muscles and arteries beneath; his hair was of a lustrous black, and flowing; his teeth of a pearly whiteness; but these luxuriances only formed a more horrid contrast with his watery eyes…'

And how did Robert Louis Stevenson describe Mr Hyde? 'I had taken a loathing to my gentleman at first sight'; 'And still the figure had no face by which he might know it; even in his dreams it had no face…'

And how did Bram Stoker describe Jonathan Harker's first view of Dracula? 'His face was a strong – a very strong – aquiline, with high bridge of the thin nose and peculiarly arched nostrils; with lofty domed forehead, and hair growing scantily round the temples, but profusely elsewhere. His eyebrows were very massive… The mouth, so far as I could see it under the heavy moustache, was fixed and rather cruel-looking, with peculiarly sharp white teeth…'

In the process of turning these vague descriptions into the cinema of fear, various changes took place. Frankenstein's creature was to become not a new Adam, but a thing of scars and stitches and skewers. His huge dome-like forehead and big feet made him resemble someone with an acromegalic condition and a serious pituitary problem: an image of disability (like many 'monsters' in film) rather than of beauty. It simultaneously made him resemble a well-built working man.

Mary Shelley had never once mentioned the exaggerated forehead, the big feet, the stitches or the steel bolt through Karloff's neck. When describing the nightmare which gave birth to her story, she referred casually – maybe too casually – to 'the working of some powerful engine' that made the creature 'show signs of life and stir within an uneasy, half vital motion'. And that was all. Hollywood, in 1931, was more than ready to fill the gap (films do indeed have to be literal about these things) with pieces of technology that had not been invented by 1816: lightning-arc generators, bakelite dials and an adjustable metal hospital bed. And some pieces that had: among them, a huge voltaic battery. Result: *'It's alive.'* The main influence here was not *Frankenstein* at all, but Fritz Lang's film *Metropolis*, with its climactic transformation of a human being into a soft machine with the aid of arcs and sparks at the hands of the evil inventor/necromancer Dr Rotwang.

At about the same time, the faceless Mr Hyde turned into a crouching, ape-like creature who enacted Dr Jekyll's secret desires on the streets of the East End of London (rather than the Soho of the original novella): an immature lout and a throwback to an earlier, less repressed, stage of evolution. The cinematic Hyde was always, following theatrical tradition, from John Barrymore (1920) onwards – including Fredric March (1932), Spencer Tracy (1941) and Boris Karloff (1953) – played by the same actor as Dr Jekyll. Stevenson insisted that 'Hyde was the younger of the two', that Jekyll was 'not good looking' in the first place and that Hyde was not 'a mere voluptuary' who was jealous of Jekyll's attraction for his girlfriend. But the films forgot about all that, and even decided to fuse the story with the Whitechapel murders while they were about it. The transformation of Count Dracula from elderly military commander with massive eyebrows and a breath problem into a red-eyed lounge-lizard in evening dress was less straightforward.

The first cinematic Dracula, *Nosferatu*, arguably the most influential horror film of all time, was cursed from the start, because it was made illegally without clearing copyright on the literary property. The Count still had massive eyebrows and a lofty, domed forehead. There were a few changes of name (Orlok for Dracula, Hutter for Harker) but that didn't fool anyone. Production sketches, graphics and poster designs were by Expressionist painter, devout spiritualist and amateur film producer Albin Grau, and the Count turned into a creature of folklore with pointy ears, rodent teeth and a bald head. A German court eventually ruled that all positive and negative copies of *Nosferatu* had to be destroyed. But then a print surfaced in London... and so on. There was no stopping the circulation of the vampire. He just went on rising again from his legal grave – which was just as well, because *Nosferatu* contains one of the most beautiful intertitles of the whole silent era: 'And when he had crossed the bridge, the phantoms came to meet him.' The film also led inexorably to the first Hollywood *Dracula*, in 1931. No longer a repulsive folkloric Count, Dracula here became utterly irresistible to the female characters and,

it was hoped, to the paying customers as well. Bela Lugosi rolled his *r*s too much, his castle staircase was infested with armadillos for some reason, and all the interesting action took place off-screen; but despite all this, Dracula was a box-office sensation.

So Graham Greene was right when he wrote that the journey from literary text to Hollywood film had involved a series of elaborate transformation scenes. But it was not a question of decline. It was, and is, a question of an even more important transformation – from the 19th-century literature of fear to 20th-century popular myth. The narratives have been made linear; the missing facts in the case have been supplied; the absences have been remedied; the surface realism that was lacking in the originals has had to be invented and visualised; and the great horror stories have been re-created over and over again – as myths, as vehicles for receiving the demons and fears of successive audiences, or rather the demons and fears of audiences as interpreted by Hollywood professionals. The stories have made new sense. They have even been absorbed into everyday speech: 'Frankenstein foods', 'a Jekyll and Hyde character', 'a vampiric relationship'. Frankenstein's creature and Count Dracula are both in the list of top five 'characters most often portrayed in film' (the list is headed by Sherlock Holmes), while *Dr Jekyll and Mr Hyde* is the third 'most remade story' in film history after *Cinderella* and (surprisingly) *Hamlet*, and just ahead of *Faust*. The real creation myth these days, as a critic once said, isn't the Book of Genesis any more: it is *Frankenstein*. A creation myth for the age of genetic engineering.

But Graham Greene's criticisms of *The Bride of Frankenstein*, and concerns in 1935 about where the cinema of fear might be heading, themselves had a long backstory. The two most important attempts to understand why fear could be so very pleasurable – Edmund Burke's *A Philosophical Enquiry into the Origin of Our Ideas of the Sublime and Beautiful* and Sigmund Freud's essay *The 'Uncanny'* – had been about similar issues. Why was a deliberate, masochistic revelling in fear so enjoyable? And what were the *legitimate* ways of stimulating it? For Burke, the emotion of fear 'robs the mind of all its powers of acting and reasoning', and such a strong emotion – outside a person's control; an unwilling suspension –

was much more pleasurable than a weak one. The roots of fear lay partly in 'obscurity' – in not being too explicit – and partly in 'power'. Power in this context meant confronting extreme or hostile phenomena (dark landscapes, howling wildernesses, gloomy forests, raging storms, vicious animals); confronting death itself (ghosts, goblins, resurrections, sadistic tyrants, torture, confinement) or witnessing flagrant transgressions of various kinds. With these, the mind could be 'so utterly filled with its object, that it cannot entertain any other', and the result was an astonished kind of pleasure. Burke's Sublime was much discussed in the late 18th century: controversial aspects included the differences – if any – between legitimate 'terror' (the result of 'obscurity') and mere 'horror' or shock (the result of physical revulsion); and the question of when repetition of hostile phenomena led to diminishing returns.

Freud dated the origins of 'the Uncanny' to precisely this period, the late 18th and early 19th centuries, when the age of reason banished and simultaneously internalised 'spectral emanations' – interpreted from now on as hallucinations and projections of the mind – while introducing the idea of the Uncanny for the first time; the darker side of an era obsessed with classifying everything. His essay concluded that familiar desires and fears particularly scare us when they appear in unfamiliar guises, so that at a deep level we identify with them. The Uncanny has held up a haunted mirror to a modern rational civilization: the German word in fact means 'unfamiliar'. For Freud, particularly strong examples included 'dismembered limbs', 'the return of the dead' and being buried alive.

Graham Greene was right about how resilient the old stories have proved to be. Many of them date back, in one form or another, to Edmund Burke's time. Frankenstein is still very much around, 'colour-shot and televised'; even in Alfred Hitchcock's *Psycho*, the prototype of all subsequent slasher movies, there is still the castle on the hill; and the Dracula myth has proved so flexible since 1922 that it has even survived Francis Ford Coppola's big-budget Symbolist version, in which Van Helsing becomes the fundamentalist bad guy and the Count somehow becomes the last romantic. Charles Dickens wisely wrote of ghosts in

'The mouth was fixed and cruel-looking, with peculiarly sharp teeth.'

A Christmas Tree that 'it is worthy of remark [that they are] reducible to a very few general types and classes; for, ghosts walk in a beaten track'. They certainly do, as was predicted by Burke's disciples in the golden age of the Gothic novel. And the same could certainly be said of the cinema of fear. Which shows that the foundations of the genre – in literary and cinematic form – are of much more than antiquarian interest. Some reckon, as writer Geoffrey O'Brien has observed, that these foundations are 'crucial to a genre that seems to define itself by constantly recapitulating everything it has been ... To watch many horror movies is in some sense to watch the same movie over and over: they are drawn to their past in the same way that their characters are compelled to go back to the ancestral crypt... The rest is ornament and variations on a theme, a matter of more masks or bigger masks or more convincingly detailed masks.'

This super-movie has survived many variations in the 20th century: the German Expressionism of the 1920s that deliberately hooked into psychoanalysis and hypnotism, and the camp Hollywood expressionism of the 1930s; the drive-in triple features of the 1950s; the rise of Hammer Films, where British cinema discovered sex and the gore was presented for the first time in chocolate-box colours; the Italian pop Surrealism of the 1960s; the psycho killers and seriously dysfunctional families of the 1970s and 1980s; the shift from margin to big-budget mainstream in the 1990s; above all, the change from pre-Second World War horror (where normal society was where the heroes and heroines lived) to post-'70s horror (where the horror has become a form of liberation, and normality has itself become strange). Today, it is rare for 'normality' to resume in the last reel, though that may have as much to do with sequels as with deep significance.

FEAR

Many complicated things have been written about horror films in the last quarter of a century. But in the end, the point of the cinema of fear boils down to one simple fact: it assumes the audience wants to be pleasurably scared. Sure, it will seek new and more forceful ways of polishing up the old stories, but it still depends on the thought that we will enjoy seeing, from the relative safety of our cinema seat, the horror that normally would not dare to speak its name. Burke was right about the appeal of transgression, and about the aesthetic choices faced by artists who want to instil fear – or who will settle for mere shock instead. The Romantic poets wrote of 'desire with loathing strangely mixed' and 'the tempestuous loveliness of terror'. Dickens's fat boy in *The Pickwick Papers* expressed the thing more bluntly: 'I wants to make your flesh creep.' We believe these old stories and we don't believe them, both at the same time. We approach them as we do the carnival magician in *The Wizard of Oz*, even when we have realised he is the fairground charlatan behind the curtain. Which is one reason why the most recent chapter in Hollywood horror – scary films that depend in a self-conscious way for their effect, and their gags, on other scary films – are still frightening.

Fear in 20 films

Frankenstein (1910)
The first horror film worthy of the name, made for Thomas Edison no less, added an alchemical theme to Mary Shelley's original. The film has only recently resurfaced – and the monster still looks grotesque.

The Cabinet of Dr Caligari (1919)
A hypnotist and a white-faced somnambulist cause expressionist havoc amid exaggerated and distorted sets – or do they? The German crucible of future Hollywood horrors.

Un Chien Andalou (1928)
Shock juxtapositions include a man sharpening a razor, a wisp of cloud passing over the moon, a cut-throat razor slashing a woman's eye in two. Once seen, never, ever forgotten.

Murders in the Rue Morgue (1932)
Mad scientist Dr Mirakle seeks to prove Darwin's descent of man with help from Erik the ape. It's nothing to do with Edgar Allan Poe, but still a seriously unsettling and transgressive film.

Painted light and expressionist paranoia:
The Cabinet of Dr Caligari

Were you expecting
someone else? **Frankenstein**

The Black Cat (1934)
Again, a long distance from Poe, but its unusual Modernist setting (and obsessive contemporary architect played by Karloff) show that scary need not involve Gothic castles and Bavarian forests: it features the only Bauhaus Black Mass in film history.

Snow White and the Seven Dwarfs (1937)
The animated transformation, Jekyll and Hyde style, of the wicked stepmother into a warty old crone has probably given more nightmares to children around the world than any other film sequence. The dark forest with trees coming to life runs it a close second.

Cat People (1942)
Directed by Jacques Tourneur, this is the first, and best, of producer Val Lewton's nine low-budget *film noir* horrors for RKO. In it, a Serbian woman in 1940s New York thinks she will transform into a leopard when sexually aroused: this film contains the definitive stalking sequence.

Night of the Demon (1958)
Another Tourneur film, this time an adaptation of MR James's 'ghosts and scholars' story *Casting the Runes* that retains the original's understated creepiness and adds a medieval fire-demon for good measure. When the runes are cast, the result is memorably frightening.

Dracula (1958)
Best of the Hammer horrors, the film that transported British cinema from black and white repression into a gaudy kind of liberation: it comes complete with extreme colours, Shakespearean acting, gore and busty maidens. Dracula came of age with this movie.

Peeping Tom (1960)
A study in voyeurism, which cleverly implicates its audience in the horrors – cinematographer kills his victims with a stiletto on his tripod, in an attempt to photograph fear – and finishes with the film unspooling: still shocking half a century later.

La Maschera del Demonio (1960)
A stylish blend of subtle fairytale – big-eyed Barbara Steele as both a sorceress and her identical descendant – with Hammer-influenced gore: the mask leaves nasty traces on faces. The success of this film launched the craze for Spaghetti horrors.

The Innocents (1961)
Classic ghost story based on Henry James's *The Turn of the Screw*, in which a governess is convinced that the children of the house are possessed. The breath on the window, the spirit of Miss Jessell sitting quietly in the reeds… Such widescreen black and white images linger in the mind.

Night of the Living Dead (1968)
Seven people take shelter from undead cannibals in a remote farmhouse: the everyday setting and gross moments of violence – which happen in surprisingly matter-of-fact ways – emphasise the arbitrariness of horror. Almost as influential as *Psycho*.

Daughters of Darkness (1971)
Updated, designer-horror Countess Dracula story set in an off-season Ostend hotel, which succeeds in being both surreal and camp with tongue firmly in chic: Delphine Seyrig, as a vampiric Dietrich-figure, steals the show.

Don't Look Now (1973)
From the opening sequence – of the accidental drowning of a child – to the killer dwarf wearing a red plastic mac in the back alleys of Venice, this is full of intriguing nastiness: time-games, second sight, and flashes of memory all contribute.

The Wicker Man (1973)
A virgin policeman visits a Scottish island on a murder enquiry, only to be lured into assorted folkloric rituals: at the unhappy ending, he is burned alive inside a huge fertility symbol. This is like a horrific travelogue.

Suspiria (1977)
With his operatic visuals, choreographed camera movements and knowing references to Hollywood classics, Dario Argento is the Sergio Leone of the cinema of fear: the fairytale setting in a dance academy, primitive colours and schlock double homicide at the beginning make this his finest film.

Alien (1979)
A bio-mechanical organism reproduces itself aboard a claustrophobic spaceship: it bursts through John Hurt's chest, appears unexpectedly round corners and spits what looks like battery fluid at its victims. The ultimate 'behind you' film, and a very fine tagline to boot: 'In space no one can hear you scream'.

Ring (1998)
A cursed videotape seems to bring death to whoever views it, like an electronic version of the runes. The heroine foolishly investigates (don't they always?). For maximum impact, watch this one on video – not the Hollywood remake, the Japanese original – the one that triggered a horror renaissance.

The Blair Witch Project (1999)
Three student film-makers lose their bearings while researching the legend of the Blair Witch in a Black Hills forest. While mainstream horror was spending megabucks on special effects, this was filmed in wobblyscope – do-it-yourself camcorder footage – which helped to suspend disbelief all over again.

FEAR

'Terror rides from hell'

Alex Cox on one of the bloodiest Spaghetti Westerns ever made.

When I was a teenager I was fanatically fond of Spaghetti Westerns. I liked American Westerns, too, especially Sam Peckinpah's. But the ones that really drew my attention were the Italian ones. Filmed in the deserts of Almería, Spain and in studios in Rome, they had a weird, violent, yet familiar quality – thanks mainly to Sergio Leone, who had a lot of respect for the American model and hired American actors like Clint Eastwood and Lee Van Cleef to populate his films.

Then, one day in the late '60s, I went to the Scala Cinema in Liverpool to see another one. I wasn't even sure it was a Western: the mini poster in the *Liverpool Echo* had shown someone dragging a body, with the tagline 'Terror Rides – From the Depths of Hell!' So, uncertain whether I was about to see a horror film or a cowboy picture, but happy with either possibility, I sat down in the Scala's nicotine-reeking precincts.

Django Kill was indeed a Western. But it was a Western unlike any I had ever seen. Its plot resembled that of many Spaghetti Westerns – thieves fell out and killed each other, townspeople outdid the bandits in their corruption and rapacity for gold – but in its execution it was horribly unique. For *Django Kill* is also a catalogue of perversity. The bandits are killers and betrayers, but the townsfolk are infinitely worse. The town into which the bandits ride has no name, and it's populated with legless animals, naked urchins and the suggestion of incest and sexual exploitation behind closed doors.

Having murdered the bandits, the townsfolk steal their money and bury it in the graveyard. Unfortunately for them, outside town lives a gangster rancher – Zorro by name – who gets wind of the gold. Zorro and his gang kidnap a young man, son of one of the leading townsfolk, in an effort to get the money. But Zorro's men rape the kid, who commits suicide. Django is hired to protect Hagerman, a local grandee who has just murdered his principal rival, the saloonkeeper – but he singularly fails to do so. Instead he's captured and tortured, and Hagerman's mad wife – a pyromaniac – escapes and burns the house down. In the penultimate scene, Django escapes from Zorro's clutches and returns to town, only to see Hagerman staggering blindly through his burning mansion, covered in molten gold.

Django Kill was directed by Giulio Questi, in 1967. That same year, Questi made a strange French/Italian sex comedy/thriller, titled *A Curious Way to Love* (or *Death Laid an Egg*). The script was co-authored by Franco Arcalli, who was also the editor of both films.

A Curious Way to Love is about a power struggle, for control of a chicken ranch, between a sadistic chicken breeder, his dominatrix wife and her murderous niece. Like *Django Kill*, it has a complicated plot involving money, power, sex and grotesque killings.

Both are highly edited films. Indeed, *Django Kill* is super-edited: there are many quick cuts and obscure flashbacks – one of the shots is actually upside-down. Questi said that he didn't use the movie Western formula, only the look; he said he wanted to recount the cruelty, the comradeship and the experiences that he had had as a young partisan, fighting against the Fascists and the Nazis. His strange film certainly suggests dimensions to the anti-Nazi struggle which have yet to be fully explored.

FEAR

Moving picture
Arthur Penn

Director, *Bonnie and Clyde*, *Little Big Man*, *Night Moves*, *The Missouri Breaks*

My most memorable trip to the cinema was when I was very young. I was four or five years old, and my big brother took me to the cinema for the first time. It must have been 1927. All I remember was that I was so scared I hid under the seat for the whole movie. And I didn't see another one for ten years! As an intellectual friend pointed out to me: what a counter-phobic reaction, that I end up making the darned things!

The slow burn of menace:
Roman Polanski's **Knife in the Water**

FEAR

What comes supernaturally:
Alan Parker's **Angel Heart**

Like Nicholas Ray's *Johnny Guitar*, *Django Kill* is a gothic Western. It begins with a hand and arm emerging outstretched from a grave (a reference to Buñuel's *Los Olvidados*?). Its characters are clad in elaborate, uniform-type costumes. The bandits dress in rags; the townspeople look like refugees from an amateur version of *Dracula*; Zorro wears a white suit while his 'muchachos' dress in black mariachi outfits.

Most of the characters in the film are mad: the bandits laugh as they murder their enemies and then their friends; the townspeople conceal horrible secrets and will do anything for money; the crazed Zorro converses with his parrot (the parrot talks back), and has a torture chamber in his basement, where he stages crucifixions and ordeal by rats and bats…

Django Kill is relentless in the cruelty of its characters, their determined pursuit of mayhem, and the general atmosphere of bizarreness. At the tender age of 15 years, I had never seen the like. Indeed, at the less tender age of 51, I still haven't.

Django Kill was released in January 1967, just a few months after Sergio Corbucci's *Django*. It had nothing to do with Corbucci's famously violent Western: its title had originally been *Si sei vivo, spara!* (*If You Live, Shoot!*), and had been changed to capitalise on the success of Corbucci's film.

While the original *Django had* boasted sensational violence and cynicism, it escaped the censors. Other Westerns, made by lesser talents than Questi, copied it, becoming more arbitrarily and ingeniously violent, and calling their lead characters 'Django.' It wasn't long before the spaghetti hit the fan.

After its first week in the cinema, the Italian censors took action against *Django Kill*. All the prints were confiscated by the court. The original 117-minute version was cut down to 95 minutes, at which length the film doesn't make much sense. The version I saw at the Scala was partially restored, at 101 minutes.

All this cutting and re-cutting is unfortunate, because *Django Kill* is quite unusual, even by the standards of the genre: a baroque, philosophical, complex, Spaghetti Western killing spree. According to some reports, Questi's original cut featured explicit homo-erotic violence, people being roasted on spits, cruelty to animals and much, much more. All this is now lost.

But over the years, bits of the film have been found, mostly on different video versions, and this amazing film has been partially reconstructed. One of the censored scenes which has been saved depicts a wounded bandit, Oaks, being carried by the townspeople into the saloon. The doctor operates on him, pulling out bullets. When he finds the bullets are made of gold, everyone pounces on the operating table and gouges the remaining bullets out of the dying patient.

Which is pretty grotesque and funny, and a good metaphor for Giulio Questi's entire, extraordinary film.

Moving picture
Adam Elliot

Claymation animator, *Harvie Krumpet*

I remember the first time I saw David Lynch's *Eraserhead*. I was 16 at the time, *Twin Peaks* was just on, so I guess that's what spurred me. I was a morbid, angst-ridden teenager, and it was a very old, antiquated cinema in the darkness of a gloomy Melbourne winter. It was a period of my life when I was into dark films.

Eraserhead still haunts me. Years down the track I'll have to have some therapy to work out what impact it has had on me. I followed it up with *The Elephant Man* and became a big Lynch fan. I don't know if his stuff has influenced me directly, but part of me owes him a debt.

Critics' choice
Monsters

Alien Resurrection
(1997, US) *d* Jean-Pierre Jeunet. *cast* Sigourney Weaver, Winona Ryder, Ron Perlman. Meet a monstrous trio: the alien queen, a ghastly genetic hybrid and Ripley herself.

An American Werewolf in London
(1981, GB) *d* John Landis. *cast* David Naughton, Griffin Dunne, Jenny Agutter. In which special effects wizard Rick Baker stages a fantastic lycanthropic transformation.

The Blob
(1958, US) *d* Irwin S Yeaworth Jr. *cast* Steve McQueen, Anita Corseaut, Earl Rowe. A gigantic ball of interstellar mucus devours a small American town, with fries to go.

Creep
(2004, GB/Ger/US) *d* Christopher Smith. *cast* Franka Potente, Vas Blackwood, Ken Campbell. Something horrible lurks on the Underground, and it's not just drunks on the last tube home.

Gojira
(1954, Japan) *d* Ishiro Honda. *cast* Akira Takarada, Momoko Kochi, Akihiro Harata. US nuclear testing unleashes rampaging scaly dinosaur Godzilla – and decades of sequels.

Jason and the Argonauts
(1963, GB) *d* Don Chaffey. *cast* Todd Armstrong, Nancy Kovack, Honor Blackman. Ray Harryhausen's finest moment: bronze giants, hydras, harpies and an army of grinning skeleton warriors.

Jaws
(1975, US) *d* Steven Spielberg. *cast* Roy Schneider, Robert Shaw, Richard Dreyfuss. The movie that made fish frightening.

King Kong
(1933, US) *d* Merian C Cooper, Ernest B Schoedsack. *cast* Faye Wray, Bruce Cabot. A monster in size, but Kong is also by turns noble, sympathetic and – finally – tragic.

Starship Troopers
(1997, US) *d* Paul Verhoeven. *cast* Caspar Van Dien, Dina Meyer, Denise Richards. Humanity is threatened by armies of enormous space insects and giant brain-sucking maggots.

The Thing
(1982, US) *d* John Carpenter. *cast* Kurt Russell, Wilford Brimley, TK Carter, David Clennon. The men of a lonely Antarctic research team are menaced by a shape-changing alien.

Hitchcock in person

Director **Atom Egoyan** considers 'the master of self-consciousness'.

Twenty years ago, I directed an episode of *Alfred Hitchcock Presents*. The assignment came completely out of the blue (a producer had seen a short film of mine and 'liked the way I moved the camera'), and so – after a few manic days of preparation – I found myself lifted out of the obscurity of Toronto's independent film scene and placed in front of Martin Landau, the legendary actor who was starring in the episode.

In this episode, special-effects artists stage an emergency fire in a devious plan to make their evil boss, played by Landau, jump to his death. It was a lot of fun to shoot, but what I remember most vividly was the time I spent with Landau talking about what it was like to work with Hitchcock. I couldn't believe I was directing an actor who had appeared in *North by Northwest*, and Martin certainly didn't disappoint me. I listened enraptured to stories about everything from Hitchcock's mannerisms to his choices of lens.

Weeks later, as I was watching the studio's final version of my episode, I was stunned to find that Alfred Hitchcock *was actually in it*. All the authentic Hitchcock intros from the original series had been colorised and re-edited, so that the 'master of suspense' had been

---

FEAR

Critics' choice
Phobias

Arachnophobia
(1990, US) *d* Frank Marshall. *cast* Jeff Daniels, Harley Jan Kozak, John Goodman, Julian Sands. The film that makes it hard to believe spiders are supposed to be more scared of us.

As Good As It Gets
(1997, US) *d* James L Brooks. *cast* Jack Nicholson, Helen Hunt, Greg Kinnear. A typically charismatic performance by Nicholson as an obsessive-compulsive novelist.

The Aviator
(2004, Ger/US) *d* Martin Scorcese. *cast* Leonardo DiCaprio, Cate Blanchett. Scorcese's empathetic biopic of the King of Phobias, Howard Hughes.

The Birds
(1963, US) *d* Alfred Hitchcock. *cast* Tippi Hedren, Rod Taylor, Suzanne Pleshette. Hitchcock heaven – enough to give us all a dose of ornithophobia.

High Anxiety
(1977, US) *d* Mel Brooks. Mel Brooks, Madeline Kahn, Cloris Leachman. Themes and scenes from Hitch's thrillers, set in the Institute for the Very, Very Nervous.

Klute
(1971, US) *d* Alan J Pakula. *cast* Jane Fonda, Donald Sutherland, Charles Cioffi, Roy Scheider. Oscar-winning Fonda plays a NY call-girl in this study of claustrophobic anxiety.

Raiders of the Lost Ark
(1981, US) *d* Steven Spielberg. *cast* Harrison Ford, Karen Allen, Paul Freeman, Ronald Lacey. Hero Jones (Ford) is happy to battle it out with the Nazis – it's the snakes he can't cope with.

The Parallax View
(1974, US) *d* Alan J Pakula. *cast* Warren Beatty, Paula Prentiss, William Daniels, Walter McGinn. Journalist Beatty is drawn into a nightmarish world in this inexorably agoraphobic thriller.

Spider
(2002, Can) *d* David Cronenberg. *cast* Ralph Fiennes, Miranda Richardson, Gabriel Byrne. Out of the asylum and into the community – but Spider (Fiennes) is still a frightened man.

Vertigo
(1977, US) *d* John Badham. *cast* John Travolta, Karen Lynn Gorney, Barry Miller, Joseph Cali. Hitchcock's acclaimed study of obsession, phobia, sexual desire and identity.

Full throttle fear: **The Texas Chain Saw Massacre**

Moving picture
Neil LaBute

Director, writer, *In the Company of Men*, *Your Friends and Neighbours*, *The Shape of Things*

Okay, here's a formative trip to the cinema. I must have been ten; we were a group of kids in Spokane, Washington, dropped off with one older kid there marshalling us. I'm sure I was supposed to see some Disney movie. I used the pretext of going to the bathroom, and sneaked down the hall to see *Deliverance*.

I knew it was a film I wasn't supposed to see. I don't think I actually caught Ned Beatty getting friendly with a woodsman, but it was scary, like a horror movie. I grew up in the woods, spent a lot of time hiking. And you can see that the world of men is something that's compelled me in my writing: the muscular language men share when they get together, when they've lost as many of the trappings of society as they can and don't have to be polite in a restaurant or around women. John Boorman taps into a real paranoia.

I did a fair amount of sneaking into movies, it was the early days of multiplexes. They'd be asking, 'Why are you going upstairs?' And you'd say, 'Oh, my father's upstairs.'

of Salvador Dali', and that Hitchcock had been 'victimised in American intellectual circles because of his facetious response to interviewers and his deliberate practice of deriding their questions.' And for a long period of time, I found it upsetting that the experience of watching my favourite films was punctuated by the Hitchcockian money shot – that odd moment when the director needed to cross the frame.

For all his status as the 'master of suspense', Hitchcock was first and foremost the master of self-consciousness. He was, in the best sense of the word, all about show. He showed us how his characters wanted to present themselves, how he wanted to show them showing us who they were, and – if he could show himself off in the process, that became part of the project. These are the sequences and moments that define Hitchcock's brilliance.

Many movies have used film directors as characters, yet Hitchcock – while never referring to the actual mechanics of film production – has given us the most compelling and complex depiction of why someone would need to direct. I'm thinking of the scene in *Vertigo* where Scottie takes Judy to the dress shop and tries to costume her as Madeline. The expression on James Stewart's face as he forces this identity on the unwilling Kim Novak is one of the most astonishingly rendered depictions of obsession I have ever seen. And it is in this moment that the viewer is truly able to see Hitchcock cross the frame.

'I just want an ordinary simple grey suit,' Scottie says, as he rejects a pale imitation of his beloved's garments.

'The gentleman seems to know what he wants,' the shopkeeper responds.

Later, as Kim Novak's new shoes click seductively towards the camera lens, the viewer gets to know exactly what Hitchcock wants. No other director has ever put his audience in the direct line of fetishistic pursuit, made them want to see something so badly that it can tear apart all reason and sensibility. We are all implicated in this mad chase of the true Madeline, enraptured by the sheer thrill of the elaborate psychological reconstruction. Hitchcock, through his creative genius, is illustrating the perverse core of the creative act – making something happen that isn't really there, and making us all believe in the process.

re-cycled for the remake. Somehow, through the weird alchemy of imagination and digital effects, it seemed as though Hitch was indeed drolly referring to a show he had absolutely nothing to do with.

And this, of course, is one of the most enduring legacies of this extraordinary film artist. After countless books, essays, exhibitions, retrospectives and dialogues (the Truffaut/Hitchcock conversations are one of the most remarkable documents in film appreciation), the most disturbing artefact of Hitchcock's output may well be the image he made of himself. No other commercial film-makers have so meticulously inserted their own directorial persona into their work.

Certainly, this had its impact on the director's reputation. Responding to the indifference accorded to Hitchcock's output in the early '60s, Truffaut commented that the director's 'genius for publicity was equalled only by that

Stranger on a train

A scene from *The Love Song of Alfred J Hitchcock*, **David Rudkin**'s 'film for radio'.

[SOUND: *fade up discreet restaurant-car murmur, smooth and classy, underpinned by rhythm of swiftly gliding train: trans-Continental, New York-Chicago service, for example*]

WAITER
Yours was the sole, sir?

HITCHCOCK
Mm?

WAITER
Dover sole, sir?

HITCHCOCK
[*A grunt*]

[SOUND: *of serving*]

HITCHCOCK
Come, flat fish. Enter this great round O of flesh I am. Joke: should change my middle name. Alfred O Hitchcock. Initials on my tie, A O H. [*Raging, ugly caricature of a Washington society dragon*] 'Mr Hitchcock, what's the O for?' [*Abrupt, silencing*] 'Nothing.' [*Malevolent chuckle*] Use it somewhere.

WAITER
Potato, sir?

[SOUND: *of serving*]

HITCHCOCK
Alfred Nothing. Great round eye; bounden in a chair. Hitchcock Eye; nothing am.

WAITER
Enjoy your meal, sir.

HITCHCOCK [SOUND: *of starting to eat*]
Fatten this nothing. Fodder this loathsome eating and excreting flesh, I hate my flesh! Oh flay it from me! Dangle it all, a shrivelled hide, downscreen right in signature's corner and daub on it my doleful face: There's Hitchcock, there he goes! Fat, round Hitchcock on a slimming ad, fat, round outline on a neon sign, fatso struggling with a double-bass to board a train – [*Pause*]
Once I was only half my back framed off screen left: they knew me. Once, in the back of a bus, framed off screen right, a glimpse of my ear alone, and the tribes of men shrieked out as one: 'Heetch! Heetch!'
Hitch indeed. What's in a name. William may shake his spear: a hitch in my cock, no joking.
[*Sudden rage*] I'll rend my name asunder on that screen one day! Frame by frame I'll crumble it apart: to nothing. Directed by Alfred Hitchcock… direct Fred itch cock, 'rect red cock, fine bird. Private joke, no one'll see. Oh they see: but they don't see. Good.
Hitchcock invisible, and all his Hell pellucid. All they see, a fat round goblin leering out of it – there's Hitchcock, there he is!

WAITER
Something the trouble, sir?

Moving picture
Ian McKellen

Actor, *Richard III, Gods and Monsters, X-Men, The Lord of the Rings, Emile*

Going to the cinema can be a lonely experience, embraced by larger than life images and louder than life sound, separated from others, privately guzzling and slurping in the dark. Most memorable are those moments when an audience is suddenly bound together, shocked out of its separation by a moment of horror or humour and there's a collective shriek or howl of laughter. It was like that seeing *Psycho* first time round as an undergraduate in Cambridge, over 30 years ago, not knowing the story and revelling in the shock of sudden violence and menace.

FEAR

Terror in the shower: **Psycho**

FEAR

HITCHCOCK
Nothing.
Eat on. Food, be the solace of my love. Open,
mouth. Bite, champ and masticate. Grind,
mandicate, congurgitate and intrasume.
Ingest and transubstantiate, fish into
Hitchcock, feed my face. [*Wretched*] And this
same mouth would do the kissing too?

[SOUND: *loathsome eating*]

All kissing's but a parody of eating. The love
act, but a picayune excreting. And food's a
parody of…
Oh look… She, there…
Standing from table, dinner done…

[SOUND: *subtly softening texture and train-
rhythm. A music, gentle, spare, a melancholy
yearning* – Vertigo *'love music', his first
glimpse of Madeleine*]

With the blonde hair… She's turning…
To face this way, to come this way…
Oh, she is… Oh… [*Breath fails him*]

Hitch, hang your head.
You don't exist in her creation. A beauty like
that… She comes toward you from your
dream… Toward you…
Oh, feel the essence of her: close.

The husband's signed the bill.
He's coming after.
Draping the costly stole he's bought her
about the yoke of those shoulders he's bought
too, so milky smooth…
Gone, now.
She and he… Passed now… Gone…

[SOUND: *music receding. Discreet restaurant-
car murmur again*]

How shoot that?
Wide single on me, seeing…
Long shot, she coming…

[SOUND: *now the music of yearning again,
obsessional, as far back within* – Vertigo *art-
gallery scene*]

Close on me, turning screen-rightward away,
eyes down, away.

Close on she not seeing: pausing… passing…
Cross the line now, cut to my opposite profile,
turning leftward now onscreen… gazing up
after… Head turned indeed.
Gazing after…
Long shot: far doors there, closing on the two
of them.
She gone. The vision, gone.

[SOUND: *music recedes; background
restaurant-murmur as before*]

Change that dress, though. Should be deep sea
green; blue in it. And the hair, almost platinum
white.
Location… 21 Club, New York – no, need red
décor: deep red, burgundy… Ernie's, San
Francisco. Like Ernie's. Any old excuse to
film there…

[SOUND: *train, muted*]

Moving picture
Robert Englund

**Actor, *A Nightmare on Elm Street*,
*Freddy vs. Jason***

I was quite young, about nine, when I saw the
movie that damaged and scarred me. I had
been dropped off with three of my compadres
by a young mother in a station wagon, to see
what we thought was going to be an Anthony
Quinn Western, *Man from Del Rio* or something
like that. As kids in the '50s, we liked cowboy
movies. So we went in with our popcorn and
our Cheeko bonbons, completely oblivious to
the fact that the matinee had been switched
to adult fare, and we found ourselves prisoners
of *The Bad Seed*, starring Patty McCormack as
a child killer. I mean literally a child who kills.
We watched, horrified, as the little blonde girl
with her hair in braids murdered someone in
the first reel. I remember the neurotic parents,
the chain- smoking, alcoholic aunt, the little
ditty she sang, the scene with the janitor: 'I
know about you! I know about you! We have
a little blue electric chair for boys, and a little
pink electric chair for girls.' Then she burned
him alive. This movie traumatised me. We
walked out at the end, and never told anyone
about it. But knew we'd been changed forever.

FEAR

Peer of the dark

Michael Eaton extols the pioneering, shiver-making films of Louis Feuillade.

Less than two decades after cinema shocked its first audience with its vision of a train pulling into a station, a scarily enticing poster appeared in Paris. A man in full evening dress, starched shirt, shiny top hat, left hand in white glove against his chin as if he's deep in thought. His eyes are covered by a black mask and, in his right hand, he conceals a flashing dagger, and he straddles the city.

'Who is he?' 'Fantômas!'

'What does that mean?'

'Something... Nothing...'

'What does he do?' 'He spreads terror!'

These days the yarn industry insists upon the 'three act drama': 'Put your hero up a tree; throw some rocks at him; get him off the tree.' But what if you don't know who the hero is? And what if he enjoys being pelted? Isn't the real problem with narrative that we never want our stories to end? Thus began, in cinema's very infancy, the eternal arm-wrestle between the feature and the serial.

In December 1911, a daring bank robbery took place on rue Ordener in Montmartre, the first bloody action of a bunch of anarchists who came to be known as the Bonnot Gang, the original 'band apart'. Their destabilising reign of terror coincided with the Fantômas novels (by Marcel Allain and Pierre Souvestre; 'more words than there are in the Bible' was their boast). And a few months later, the first of Louis Feuillade's five Fantômas films appeared, pure cinematic delirium.

The method of film-going advocated by the surrealists was to flit between fleapits watching only a few minutes of whatever film happened to be on the screen at the time, forcing the inner eye to create some sort of continuity from the disjointed fragments – a story which might turn out to be far less bogus, more psychologically meaningful, than the tales highly paid professionals had struggled to make coherent. The beauty (which must be convulsive or not at all) of the Feuillade serials is that these bizarre pleasures construct themselves without the spectator having to shift seats or pay more than one price of admission. A few short years after *The Interpretation of Dreams,* Freudian cinema was realised. The camera seemed to turn its implacable eye on the subconscious.

It's not simply that the master villain is a master of disguise, but that the righteous detective who pursues him might suddenly metamorphose into the criminal himself; the intrepid young journalist in whom we've invested our desire for truth might turn out to be a member of the gang. The uniqueness of the self is a temporary construct at best. Any

Roman Polanski on **Safety in numbers**

I'd rather watch a film in a movie theatre. It's much more fun. I have all the kit you need at home, but it's not the same. I don't think that the fear of cinema being obsolete has any reason to exist, because it's not the big screen that makes a cinema superior to your home theatre – it's the fact that you're watching it with an audience, and particularly that you're watching with people who you don't know. That gives you a different feeling from watching it with your wife in your living room.

It's something that has existed since the dawn of humanity: from Greek theatre to Roman circuses to medieval passion plays, people just loved seeing, witnessing an event in an anonymous crowd. I remember that when cassettes came into general use, people began to say that there'd be no concerts, but during the same period, rock concerts drew more people than ever – take Woodstock! – because it's an entirely different experience. It's a question of experience, not so much of the quality of the projection.

That's why, if I have a choice, I always prefer to see a film in the cinema. If it's something that I'm just curious to know what it's about then I watch it at home, but if I want to have fun I'd rather see it with an audience.

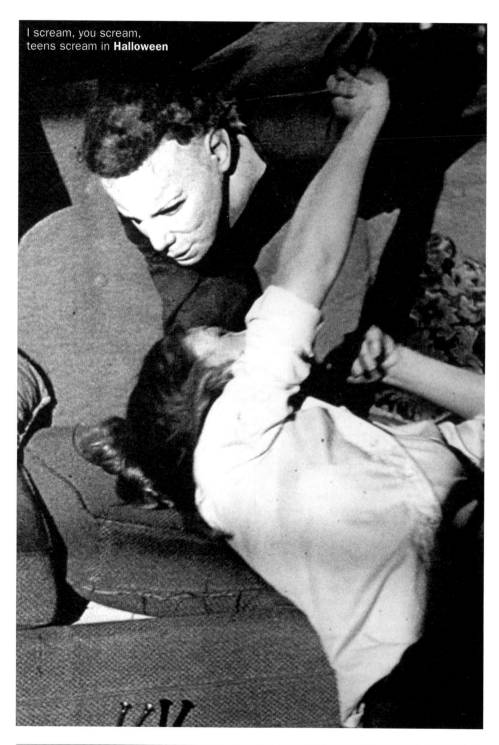

I scream, you scream, teens scream in **Halloween**

FEAR

pretence at psychological consistency is a joke. Fantômas might be played by the actor René Navarre, but he can transform into anyone. The most terrifying nightmare: the unknown creature who has committed the most villainous crimes might turn out to be none other than ourselves. In *Les Vampires* it is a feminine icon who personifies the great question mark, Musidora in a black body stocking playing the anagrammatical enigma, Irma Vep. '*Qui? Quoi? Quand? Où?*' – questions never fully answered at any time in the ten-part series. Though she's the mysterious emissary of a clandestine criminal society, her 'leader', Satanas, changes personae continually. It is as if this gang is at war not just with respectable, law-abiding society but identity itself.

As is so often the case, works which at first sight seem so off-centred, so demented, provide a much sharper depiction of a world than any documentary. The teeming streets of Paris that supplied the backdrop to so much of the action in the Fantômas series seem completely deserted in *Les Vampires*. For now, in 1915, France is at war and the capital's inhabitants dread defeat and occupation. The director snatched performances from some of his players when they were on leave from military service; some of them never returned. In the next serial, *Judex*, made in 1916, the year of Verdun, Feuillade not only decamped to the safety of the Côte d'Azur, but bowed to censorial pressure from the authorities. The narrative is no less contorted, but the images are softer, the morality is less ambiguous, expressing perhaps a longing for a world where it is possible to tell good from evil. Judex is still masked and cloaked, but now he is the avenger, the righter of wrongs – though his wrath is initially directed at an immoral banker, personification of all that was rotten in the ancien régime.

The pursuit of these films seems to have determined the course of my life. I was a teenager struggling to get an adolescent handle on the stern aesthetics of European art house movies when I first saw Georges Franju's 1963 remake of *Judex*. The sou finally dropped: you can actually wallow in a film rather than having to interpret it. Subsequently, I'd hitchhike to film societies whenever poor prints of any of the Fantômas films were projected. Many years later, under the auspices of the Shots in the Dark mystery and thriller festival, I fulfilled a fantasy of screening all the original *Judex* in one day. In the sparse Nottingham audience was a bright young Angelino; it was the first time Quentin T had been exposed to the wonders of Feuillade. And accompanying all 12 episodes on various keyboards was maestro Neil Brand, whose improvisations fitted the music like a glove. When the day was over I was disturbed to learn that he had never seen the serial before, either.

These days *Fantômas*, *Vampires* and *Judex* are genuinely new films again, recently restored and available on DVD in a condition far more pristine than André Breton or Guillaume Apollinaire ever knew. But I've still had to travel to Italy to see Feuillade's other secret society serial, *Barrabas*, and the one Jacques Rivette considers his masterpiece, *Tih Minh*. The other week, in a second-hand bookshop, I came across an old French film mag edited by Franju before he made his own *Judex*. He'd written: 'It's not mystery that creates anxiety. It's anxiety that creates mystery. Mytsery expresses itself through style. The unique style of Louis Feuillade.'

Let us rediscover our beginnings. Let there be no more endings.

Moving picture
Steven Soderbergh

Cinematographer, director, editor, producer, writer, *sex, lies, and videotape*, The Limey, Traffic, Ocean's Eleven, Ocean's Twelve

I remember the summer of '75, and having my head taken off. I was 12, and I went to see *Jaws*. I was so affected that I really thought to myself, for the first time, 'How did this happen to me? Who did this?' It was the first time I became conscious that someone actually made movies. I wanted to know more about that so I went out and bought what turned out to be an excellent book, Carl Gottlieb's *The Jaws Log*, which I kept by me all through my teen years. I got through several dog-eared copies, because it became my Bible of film-making for a long time. Seeing *Jaws*, finding out who Steven Spielberg was and what he did was very formative for me.

Sadness

'Life isn't fair, then, is it?
Somebody always draws
the short straw.'
Secrets & Lies

Celluloid sorrow

Tom Charity looks on the far-from-bright side.

Joy and jolly japes are all very well but the truth of the matter is this: the world is going to hell and we're all just collateral damage. Like Ed Norton in the opening moments of *Fight Club*, we're staring down the barrel of imminent extinction, wondering how we got here and whether this is the beginning or The End.

And if that doesn't open your tear ducts, dear film lover, try this: for cinema itself the writing is on the wall – and has been for some time. From this vantage point there is every likelihood that within 15 years the celluloid experience will be relegated to museums; at any rate, we know that ever since the video revolution the circuit of repertory houses which kept cinema history kicking has been in terminal decline. With the advent of DVD, even cash-strapped colleges and film schools have routinely cut back on expensive 35mm projection facilities and refocused their programming on digital kit. Like it or not, it's time to bid adieu to the shimmering projector beam, the lustrous black and white shadows of our youth. Make no mistake, the ribbon of dreams is unspooling fast. Soon (it's already the case) digital reproductions will be the only way future generations will experience the 20th century's liveliest art.

As I write this paragraph, the latest casualty is my own neighbourhood cinema, the Ridge, opened in 1950, and a rep house since the 1970s. Its modest claim to fame is the 'crying room', a glassed-in booth on the balcony designed to accommodate mothers and babies – though its most famous guest was Katharine Hepburn, who was neither. In two weeks the current management hands over the reins and the Ridge will revert to first-run programming. In the interim, with a certain savage wit, it offers a last chance to watch Nicholas Ray's *In a Lonely Place* on its big screen. 'I was born when she kissed me. I died when she left me. I lived a few weeks while she loved me.' There's no word yet on the fate of the crying room.

Leave a message after the weep: **Secrets & Lies**

SADNESS

Young romance under death's shadow: **Love Story**

At such a juncture – only the coming of sound compares with such a momentous formal transition in the relatively brief history of the movies – it's surely more pressing than ever to determine the value of our cinematic heritage, to sift what is essential from what is merely amusing or attractive, so that we may pass on what is truly worthwhile to our own sons and daughters. And if that's what we're doing here, I can't be the only one who finds Woody Allen's supposedly life-affirming epiphany at the end of *Hannah and Her Sisters* just a little depressing. Is *Duck Soup* really the best we can hope for? Even speaking as a Marx Brothers fan, hand on heart I ask: is inspired lunacy the sum of a century's artistic endeavour? To be clear: *Interiors* is not the answer. Solemnity is not in itself a virtue. Give me the sublime effrontery of *The Palm Beach Story* over the preachy-keen *Sullivan's Travels* any day of the week.

'Tragedy is a close up, comedy a long shot,' declared Buster Keaton. Our lives invariably oscillate between joy and sorrow, tragedy and comedy, as Woody Allen attempted to demonstrate in *Melinda and Melinda*. But try as we might to keep them apart, life rarely conforms to generic convention. Which is why the movies that reflect pain as well as pleasure are usually the ones that stay with us.

For instance Allen's best films – let's say *The Purple Rose of Cairo* and *Broadway Danny Rose* – tread more delicately between humour and melancholy, and incline towards the latter. These two heartworn valentines find solace in romance and movies, but fleetingly. Like Mickey Sachs (Allen himself) in *Hannah and Her Sisters*, at the end of *The Purple Rose of Cairo* Cecilia (Mia Farrow) finds herself alone in a movie theatre, but this time it's apparent that the cinema offers only cold comfort, its vision of hope and happiness an illusion which makes the real world seem more cruel in comparison.

Not coincidentally some of the most heartening films are also the most heartrending: does

'Could it be that the movies' greatest gift is the expression of our repressed emotions, our secret anguish and silent sorrow?'

It's a Wonderful Life move us so deeply because we believe in miracles, or because we know the claustrophobia and frustration of dreams unrealised? If it's the latter, could it be that the movies' greatest gift is just this: the expression of our repressed emotions, our secret anguish and silent sorrows? Further, that films operate on identification and empathy, and that this empathy is – in a cinema – a shared experience, a recognition that we are all in this together? (Preston Sturges put it very eloquently: 'I like the movies. You get to hold hands.')

What a debasement then, what a travesty, when this empathy machine – the cinema – is disposed only to flatter and deceive; when our blemishes are nipped and tucked out of sight – the lines of experience erased; when pain is overrun by numbing action overkill; when complication and ambiguity are processed out; when endings are happified and everything always feels good. Too often, now, the screen is a mirror that reflects nothing but light. Let us propose, in this barren time, that one true measure of a film-maker's artistic stature might be precisely his ability to express feel-bad: mortality, suffering, anguish, disappointment, despair (let's wrap them all up in a bundle and call it 'pathos'); that pathos must be woven deep into any meaningful poetics of cinema.

And so to map this cosmology of sorrow…

At bedrock, the Tearjerkers. The sons of DW Griffith. Purveyors of neo-Victorian sanctimony through suffering, and a thoroughly middle-class crowd (though a lover might occasionally scramble in from the other side of the tracks), they specialise in domestic trial and tribulation especially of the female persuasion. Renunciation and self-sacrifice are the central themes. Careers are sacrificed. Or lovers. Or children. For the sake of propriety, or family, or for the child's own sake. In such stories, happiness cannot – must not – be pursued without a reckoning. Almost invariably the cost is too high. Such scenarios are redeemed only in part by the privileged emoting of grandes dames Bette Davis, Joan Crawford, Greta Garbo or Greer Garson.

Key directors include Michael Curtiz, Mervyn LeRoy, Edmund Goulding, and (higher up the scale) Frank Borzage, William Wyler and George Cukor. Key movies: *Camille*; *Dark Victory*; *Now, Voyager*; *Casablanca*; *Mrs Miniver*; *Random Harvest*; *Mildred Pierce*; *Gone With the Wind*; *Washington Square*; *The Best Years of Our Lives*; *Brief Encounter*; *A Place in the Sun*; *Love Story*; *Titanic*. A veritable tidal wave of tears.

To their right, and closely associated with the Tearjerkers, the Sentimentalists: Charlie Chaplin, Walt Disney, Steven Spielberg and their legions of imitators. Fake religiosity, feigned innocence, separation anxiety and bleeding hearts on sleeves: a US army general blubs in his seat at the death of Bambi's mom. On their off-days, John Ford and Frank Capra fall in here, too. The films: *The Kid*; *City Lights*; *Sleeping Beauty*; *Pinocchio*; *Dumbo*; *E.T. The Extra-Terrestrial*; *The Color Purple*; *Always*; *Hook*.

To the left, the Fatalists. This clique has its roots in late 1930s France after the failure of the Popular Front. The prime exponent was Marcel Carné, who constructed a decorative poetic realism from artfully quotidian studio sets, atmospheric shadows, and glamorous but naturalistic actors (Jean Gabin, Arletty) floundering in romantic *désespoir*. The mood was taken up first by Jean Renoir in his more pessimistic moments, then the European émigrés who smuggled *film noir* through Hollywood's subterranean channels: moody Jacques Tourneur, gloomy Robert Siodmak, cynical Billy Wilder, the exacting Fritz Lang. Films to watch with an eye in the back of your head: *Le Jour se lève*; *Le Quai des Brumes*; *La Bête Humaine*; *Out of the Past*; *Phantom Lady*; *The Killers*; *Criss Cross*; *Double Indemnity*; *Fury*; *You Only Live Once*; *The Big Heat*.

You might sketch an arrow from here across to the Objectivists (Otto Preminger), the

SADNESS

SADNESS

Rationalists (Stanley Kubrick), the Nihilists (Henri Georges Clouzot), and the Alienationists (Ingmar Bergman and Michelangelo Antonioni). God is a spider, and disappears without a trace.

Then there are the Hysterics (Douglas Sirk, Maurice Pialat, John Cassavetes), the Manic Depressives (Jean Eustache, Rainer Werner Fassbinder, Ritwik Ghatak), the Melancholics (Max Ophuls, Wong Kar-Wai, Jacques Demy), the Sadists (Lars von Trier) and the Masochists (Lars von Trier).

Off to the side – as far from the Sentimentalists as they can get – the Stoics: Buster Keaton and Howard Hawks. Above them, the Memorialists: Theo Angelopoulos, Sam Peckinpah, Sergio Leone, John Ford to the west. Hou Hsiao-Hsien to the east. Photographing time past.

Still rising, the Penitents: Dreyer and Bresson.

And finally – above and beyond – the Philosopher Kings: Welles, Kieslowski, Rossellini, Ray, Renoir, Mizoguchi, Ozu.

Partial and sketchy as this putative pantheon must be, at least it evokes something of the emotional breadth today's film-makers studiously avoid (honourable exceptions: the Andersons, PT and Wes).

'Endings are hard. There is only one honest ending, and that's death,' Robert Altman said. Supposedly anathema to the general public (who stayed away from *Titanic, The Godfather, Casablanca, The English Patient, Love Story* and *Gone With the Wind* in their droves!), the unhappy ending is consequently a rare and precious item – something to be treasured, savoured, contemplated and replayed.

Think of a gunfighter collapsing in the snow… a retired soldier watching the parade and reflecting on his life… a lady carried away from her lover, his cries drowned out by surging crowds… a fat old man rejected by his best friend, the King of England… a couple smoking on the stairs, and the tired resumption of an exhausted marriage… Think of Bonnie's wistful, dying smile a half-second before the bullets hit… Ethan Edwards returning to the wilderness… Scotty Ferguson looking down on what he has wrought at San Juan Batista… and a gangster blissing out in an opiate haze… Emotional rehearsals for death and separation, these parting shots and slow fades may be as close to a raison d'être as the movies are likely to get.

Kyoko: Isn't life disappointing?

Noriko [*smiles*]: Yes, it is.

Sadness in 20 films

The Crowd (1928)
King Vidor's great silent film is a naturalistic slice of life: Johnny is born on the Fourth of July, but his American Dream goes nowhere and he ends up just another face in the crowd.

The Magnificent Ambersons (1942)
Truffaut said that Welles made film with his right hand and his left hand; in the right-hand films there was always snow, and in the left-hand films, always gunfire. Like *Chimes at Midnight* and *Citizen Kane*, this is a snow movie, and quite sublime.

The Life and Death of Colonel Blimp (1943)
The poignance of an honourable man who has outlived all that he stood for and believed in. Powell and Pressburger's most profound collaboration.

Letter from an Unknown Woman (1948)
Love unreciprocated. Joan Fontaine throws everything away for the unworthy Louis Jourdan in Ophuls's graceful but clear-eyed melodrama.

Tokyo Story (1953)
Ozu accepts sadness with a serenity that is itself enormously moving. He gives us life and nothing but, yet the simplicity resonates loud and long.

Sansho Dayu (1954)
'Without mercy, man is like a beast'. The motto speaks to the compassion and despair invested in Mizoguchi's remarkable retelling of an ancient Japanese folk tale.

The Man Who Shot Liberty Valance (1962)
John Wayne dukes it out with James Stewart in Ford's reverie about youth, freedom, the frontier, and the ideals which civilised it. His most meditative and mature movie.

Subarnarekha (1963)
Ritwik Ghatak's overwhelming family tragedy is one of most unjustly neglected films in cinema. When an educated Bengali puts family above principle, he curses everyone and everything he cares about.

Au Hasard, Balthazar (1966)
A donkey with a soul is the improbable index for human kindness and cruelty in Bresson's masterly ascetic fable.

Sea of tears: **Titanic**

The Umbrellas of Cherbourg (1964)
An entirely sung musical from Jacques Demy and Michel Legrand, and a love story that will end in tears. Catherine Deneuve stars.

Fat City (1972)
John Huston's unremittingly downbeat – but tremendously moving – portrait of the bottom rung of the boxing circuit, where perennial losers slug it out for chump change. Stacy Keach is Tully, over the hill but still plodding on; Jeff Bridges is his discovery, the not-so-great white hope, Ernie.

Pat Garrett & Billy the Kid (1973)
How the West was lost. Peckinpah in elegiac mood, with Chill Wills knockin' on heaven's door.

Fear Eats the Soul (1974)
Fassbinder does Sirk (*All That Heaven Allows*) with an ageing German cleaning lady and a Turkish *gastarbeiter*. Shot in two weeks, the film takes no prisoners, but it remains a genuine love story.

A Nos Amours (1983)
Pialat's raw, ragged dramas are all about capturing or liberating emotion. *To Our Loves* is a devastating film about different kinds of love – if love exists at all.

Once Upon a Time in America (1984)
A requiem for the American dream, Sergio Leone's gangster epic reverberates with the longing of betrayed love and dashed hope.

Twin Peaks (1990)
There has probably never been a more harrowing TV show than the feature-length pilot episode for David Lynch's cult series. Laura Palmer is dead, the whole town is stunned.

A Brighter Summer Day (1991)
Edward Yang's measured remembrance of growing up in Taipei in the early 1960s is dense, panoramic, and unforgettable.

The Age of Innocence (1993)
Newland Archer lives according to his society's expectations, and comes to rue his folly in Scorsese's exquisite Edith Wharton adaptation.

Happy Together (1997)
Asked to record a message to take to the end of the world, Tony Leung sits with the tape recorder and breaks down into uncontrollable sobbing. Wong Kar-Wai is cinema's most melancholy poet; even more than the rest, this is a film of separation and heartache.

Magnolia (1999)
Talking of melancholia… Paul Thomas Anderson's multi-layered mosaic of the misguided, misunderstood middle-classes is the best misery fest in years.

'Peculiarly poignant':
Shakespeare Wallah

Terms of India

John Pym remembers Ismail Merchant and the start of an illustrious partnership.

First love. Lizzie (Felicity Kendal), an English girl brought up in India, falls for Sanju (Shashi Kapoor), a wealthy, aimless, impossibly handsome young Indian. He has a notion that he'd like to produce an arty abstract film about the Rhythm of Life – featuring icicles and herons. At the key moment, Sanju fails to ask Lizzie to give up the stage and the unrooted life she endures (she beds down on railway platforms among pye-dogs). Lizzie's parents, Carla and Tony Buckingham, seasoned actors who wander the subcontinent with their little Shakespearean troupe, acknowledge at last that there's no future for their daughter at that time in this place, and send her back home to England on an ocean liner. The curtains close.

Across North India in the mid 1950s, the Buckingham Players (half-English, half-Indian, everyone cash-strapped) revisit yet again scenes of former glories. In an echoing palace on the plain, a maharaja in a boiler suit fixes his own car for no better reason, perhaps, than simply to while away the time. At a boys' school in the hills, the deputy head, a suave 'bandleader' in heavy shades, fiddles with a ping pong ball as he tries to think of an excuse not to book the actors for their customary second performance.

Shakespeare Wallah – the film that fixed the early reputation of its American director James Ivory ('It became my calling card') – echoes with a tone of singularly ironic regret. It isn't only the heat and dust of the new India, a few years after Independence, that saps the players' determination to keep performing their Sheridan and their Shakespeare; waiting in the wings is the spectre of Bollywood (if not film-making in general) in all its thoughtless, vulgar glory.

On a pine-covered hill in the sunshine near the rain-sodden garrison town where, at one point, the travelling actors find themselves marooned, the songstress Manjula (Madhur Jaffrey) dances and mimes to a playback track, barely able to contain her petulant boredom. Her filmy veil and birdlike movements are in vivid contrast to the tattered props and heavy, overstuffed costumes of the Shakespeareans. Her work ethic ('Pack up, finished for today!' – the producer looks aghast) is a slap across the face of the self-protective rituals of the stage players: the voice exercises before breakfast, the sacredness of the dressing room one hour before curtain up. To make matters worse, Manjula – shocking though she is – is clearly much more alive and in the world than the poor, washed-up Anglo-Indian thespians fighting a losing battle against indifference.

I saw *Shakespeare Wallah* for the first time during its opening run at the Academy cinema, that cavernous, dark-panelled place of pilgrimage on Oxford Street in the West End of London. The magnificent, now-vanished arthouse had a unique waxy smell of dusty antiquity (an odour, almost, of the Austro-Hungarian empire), hard red-plush seats and a screen just a little too high for comfort. Before the main feature – and here Londoners

were introduced to such exotic delights as Mizoguchi's *Ugetsu Monogatari*, and if you missed it one year it always played the next – the crick-necked spectator encountered not a screaming pop video or senseless advertisement, but more often than not a gem from the Canadian Film Board or a homemade Czech cartoon on a pacifist theme.

Shakespeare Wallah fitted the Academy – a canny enterprise that saved money on its posters by employing a master (refugee) lino-cut artist – in much the same way that the film's Buckingham Players, who mended their own ruffs and painted their own flats, fitted the maharaja's palace on the plain – the three arches of its courtyard stage unconsciously echoing Philo's famous description of Antony ('the triple pillar of the world transform'd into a strumpet's fool'). The audience for the players' after-dinner *Antony and Cleopatra* was five, not counting the servants; the audience for *Shakespeare Wallah* – in its own way as rough-edged as one of the troupe's makeshift get-in-get-out productions grew and grew. Word spread. Londoners became affectionately attached to this unheralded movie, partly, I suspect, because not since Renoir's *The River* had another Western director caught the tone of India (and particularly the tone of slightly woebegone English people mixed up in India)

Moving picture
Craig Armstrong

Composer, *Moulin Rouge, The Magdalene Sisters, Love Actually, Must Love Dogs*
Visconti's *Death in Venice* is one of the great films. I remember clearly the first time I saw it. It was the late 1970s and I was 21, studying at the Royal Academy of Music in London. It was a rainy Friday evening at a cinema near Leicester Square. It's such a beautiful film, so well shot – the opening frame of the boat slowly crossing the lagoon in Venice remains one of cinema's most sublime moments. Dirk Bogarde has to be my favourite actor, and his performance in this is legendary. And the music, by Gustav Mahler, is incredible.

The film stopped me in my tracks. Everything about it was perfect. All the elements came

together to form something that I found moving beyond words. But the film's impact was more than aesthetic – *Death in Venice* was the first film I saw that made me realise that cinema could go beyond entertainment and also be a work of art. When I left the cinema that evening something had changed. To create a film that so totally consumes the viewer like Visconti did is immensely difficult. There are so many elements that could go wrong for a director – the actors, the costumes, the music. When it actually does all come together, it's a wonder. It takes a film-maker of rare vision and daring to make it all work. Beautiful art makes people aspire to what is best in life. It might sound trite, but it really does make the world a better place.

with quite such melancholy assurance. Satyajit Ray's cameraman, Subrata Mitra, who shot the picture in widescreen black and white, knew his business; and Ray himself supplied a captivating Indian-Western score that offset Ruth Jhabvala's script with a sometimes jaunty, tip-tapping lightness.

Felicity Kendal, with her oval face and quizzical eyes, caught everyone's attention and perhaps surprised herself in the process. 'Why do you do that? Lizzie! Stop biting your hair. It's such an odd habit.' One sympathised with Carla, the girl's concerned mother, but equally one felt for the teenager in her boredom – the boredom of trapped youth eager to be up and doing, not the spoilt boredom of a songstress who had only to open her mouth for her mute servant to pop in a snack. When the ocean liner docked at Southampton and a little later Lizzie stepped out on the stage at Stratford (as her mother intimated she might), one just knew – as art faded into actuality – that Felicity was going to be a star. Well, in real life, the young actress did become a star, though one who turned out to be too knowingly impish for the high seriousness of the Royal Shakespeare Company.

Almost exactly 40 years after the premiere of *Shakespeare Wallah* at the Berlin festival in the summer of 1965, its producer, Ismail Merchant, died suddenly in London, aged 68. 'He enjoyed', James Ivory wrote, '– or would have enjoyed – the vast, celebrity funeral he had in Bombay, the chief mourner being Shashi, who led the cortege.' Thinking again, a few months after this funeral, of *Shakespeare Wallah* (the real starting point of Merchant's long unbroken partnership with James Ivory, the first of their films to set off a firework display), one fugitive moment hangs in the air and seems now, for anyone who subsequently felt the heat of Ismail's enthusiasm for his profession and for life in general, peculiarly poignant.

At the Gaiety Theatre in Simla, Desdemona (Lizzie) lies innocent on her bed. The Moor (played by her father Tony) unsheathes his scimitar. Into the principal box at the rear of the auditorium bustles Manjula, her mute servant, Sanju and the theatre manager, a dapper young man in a dinner jacket with wavy hair and a neat moustache. Manjula has no intention of losing her boyfriend – her cousin Sanju – to this pretty little English girl, brazenly displaying herself in a nightdress. She whips up a splendidly melodramatic scene, ostentatiously consumes a sweetmeat, will not be silenced by the polite stage manager. Finally, she can abide the nonsense no longer

---

Moving picture
Malgorzata Szumowska

Director, writer, *Happy Man*

It was my second year at the Lodz Film Academy, in the middle of winter. Our year – which comprised five directors-to-be, including myself – was preparing for exams. At the same time, there was a festival of cinematography taking place in Torun, 200km north of Lodz. The festival was showing films too artistic to be distributed in Poland, and as we were studying directing, not cinematography, we were not allowed to go to the festival. This, together with the imminent exams and the weather, made us all feel discouraged, frustrated and deeply depressed, so instead we discussed life's problems and consumed gallons of vodka.

Then we got a message from Torun about an unmissable Danish film. Despite the drink, or because of it, we jumped into a car, drove the 200km and arrived five minutes before the screening began. We didn't even know the film's title. But with each passing minute we became more involved, and after an hour we were in a kind of trance. We felt as if Fate had made us drive through snow and ice to see this film. One friend cried so loudly that after the screening other people stared at him, suspicious or worried.

It was Lars von Trier's *Breaking the Waves* that had such an effect on us. We drove back to Lodz in silence. At dawn, with morning returning as if by magic, we burst into tears again. I will never forget the feeling of being so small, weak and helpless in this world. Our lives changed that night. I myself never got so emotional again watching the film. But that cold, winter night created a memory that will always stay with me.

It ain't easy: **Days of Being Wild**

SADNESS

Emotional firepower: **Land and Freedom**

Moving picture
Rob Green

Director, *The Bunker*

My most memorable film experience didn't happen at a cinema, but at a Butlins holiday camp in the early '70s. The main hall was the stage for all their entertainments: Tarzan yelling contests, wrestling matches, cheesy comedians and the big movie, which that night was *Butch Cassidy and the Sundance Kid*. Even at the age of six or seven I'd heard of these legendary outlaws. The hall was packed. Everyone was sat on plastic seats, talking loudly and spoiling my anticipation. The Star Comedian came on to perform his chicken walk, and then he introduced the movie. No curtains to draw back, just the loud click of the projector and the first sounds from the screen.

I remember Butch and Sundance jumping off the cliff and feeling terrified. I remember the bull chasing Butch on his bike, and how Sundance seemed mean. And I remember with absolute clarity how I felt when Butch and Sundance came running towards the camera, guns blazing, to meet their certain death. I was stunned: heroes die! That was the moment when I absolutely grasped the true power of movies, and my love affair with sad endings began. You never forget a sad ending.

and sweeps out, entourage in tow, to sign some autographs in the corridor behind the box. The manager, still mindful of the paying customers, lifts a tentative finger to his lips to try to quell the hullabaloo.

Who played the anxious non-speaking manager? None other than Ismail Merchant: young, good-looking, uncharacteristically restrained, a man on the cusp (off-screen) of a memorable life in the movies. There at the Gaiety Theatre, in that moment rescued from the past, you wouldn't have guessed he had a care in the world; but whirring through Ismail's head even at that moment, perhaps, was a foolproof scheme, a plan to nail down, once and for all, the mere $80,000 needed to complete this wonderful film about some penniless, no-hope, itinerants – a film that was, without a doubt, absolutely certain to make Merchant Ivory's fortune.

The *bigger*
picture

Hollywood
dynamite

Dave Calhoun talks to one of Tinseltown's most celebrated living actors.

It's 4.25 on a dark November afternoon in London, and I am talking to Al Pacino. On the other end of the phone line I can hear the unmistakable voice, deep and resonant, immediately familiar, quietly paternal. Pacino is sitting in the departure lounge at New York's JFK airport, waiting for a flight to Los Angeles. I can hear announcements on the PA and I imagine how he might be sitting: hunched, head bowed, body squeezed into a plastic bucket seat, hands cupping a vending-machine coffee and his back smothered, perhaps, in his trademark full-length, black leather coat. But whatever he's doing at the other end of the line, he is undisturbed and alive. He wanted to start our discussion by explaining his role as Shylock in the 2004 film *The Merchant of Venice*; while I wanted to steer him back to the past, to the 1970s when he was cinema's most gloriously singular, iconic actor. A true star.

Film stardom fully seized Pacino at 33, in 1972, when he played the ever-hardening mafia scion Michael Corleone in *The Godfather*. But the role almost eluded him. The film's director, Francis Ford Coppola, had to fight to hire him. Robert Evans, the producer of *The Godfather*, tagged Pacino 'that little dwarf', and remained keen to fire him even as the cameras rolled. 'They told me Al was too scruffy and looked too much like a gutter rat to play a college boy', Coppola says, recalling that if he hadn't fought to cast both Pacino and Brando, he 'would have made a movie with Ernest Borgnine and Ryan O'Neal set in the '70s.' How did Pacino, by his own admission an unsure and nervy young man, cope with this kind of hostility? 'I got through it with prayer!' he says, laughing. 'And the idea that it was all going to be over and I was going to quit. But Marlon Brando was so helpful to me. He was very generous to a very young actor who was in the middle of a big movie and didn't know where the hell he was. You don't forget those kindnesses, especially when they come at these points of your life.'

World-weary: **The Merchant of Venice**

By the time he tackled the sequel in 1974, Pacino had two further hits, *Serpico* and *Scarecrow*, under his belt. *The Godfather* had swept the Oscars in 1973. He was hot property. But it didn't make much difference, he says.

'I'm sorry to say it, but it was all a drag doing those things. The reason it wasn't more pleasant was because of my state of being. It had nothing to do with Francis, or the ambience on the sets or anything. When I was younger, making films, I would try to stay in the role and be in a state of isolation, both on and off set.'

So when did he start to enjoy making films?

'I can't really say that I enjoy any of them', he says, declaring that, even now he finds film-making something of a chore.

Pacino exorcised many of his demons during a four-year break in the late '80s, a hiatus that followed the poor reception of Hugh Hudson's historical drama *Revolution*. He returned in 1989 alongside Ellen Barkin in *Sea of Love*, and *The Godfather, Part III* soon after, and he has worked almost ceaselessly since, amassing over 20 roles since *Sea of Love*, and finally winning a Best Actor Oscar for *Scent of a Woman* in 1992. 'The break was probably the most helpful thing I've ever done', he says. 'I didn't even know I was doing it. I sort of felt that I wanted to go back to stuff I was familiar with, and

develop a little in some way. Then four years had gone by and I was broke!'

I mention to Pacino that on the night before our interview I watched for the first time his 1971 film, *The Panic in Needle Park*, in which he plays a mouthy, streetwise junkie. He was 31 and it was his second film. His trademark fireball energy – Pacino in his prime always seems to be twirling, spinning, looking for something over his shoulder – is on show for the first time, and the actor who fills the screen is a world away from the bearded, world-weary Shylock in *The Merchant of Venice*.

'That's one of the horrors of film', he says. 'You see yourself ageing before your eyes. We all think of ourselves at a certain age. Then, as you get older, you catch your image in a mirror and you're shocked. You think: "Who the hell is that? My father's here!" Or, in my case: "My grandfather's here!"' Age might have withered some of Pacino's matinee idol looks, but he's happier now than he ever was in his 30s and 40s, during the peak of his career, when anxiety, depression and drink closed in around him.

His first movie role was in *Me, Natalie* in 1969, but, before that, in the late '50s and '60s, the South Bronx boy who had moved to the Village at 16 spent much of his time carving a hand-to-mouth existence on the nascent Off-Off

Broadway theatre scene. He trained and performed with Lee Strasberg at his famous Actors Studio, where Brando, Robert De Niro, James Dean and others all learned the Method, and later joined the Living Theatre: 'We did 16 shows a week passing the hat around, passing the straw basket around', he recalls. 'That's how we ate!'

When it came, the move into film was a painful one. Pacino was a wreck, insecure, miserable. Fame troubled him and the rigid mechanics of film-making left him cold. 'I didn't like being away from what I knew, my home: New York and the theatre. I felt I was in a strange world, in a strange land. I found cinema impossible. That's why I did fewer movies back then than I'm doing now.' Today, theatre remains a refuge for Pacino, a place where he can recharge his creative batteries. In 1996 he made the engaging *Looking for Richard*, a meditation on the relevance of Shakespeare today and a document of Pacino's own staging of *Richard III* for the film.

And it's this basic love of the stage that brought Pacino back to Shakespeare in 2004. I suggest that he was born to play Shylock, the complex, domineering, damaged Jew. Did he always have his eye on the part? 'No, actually,' he says without hesitation, 'I mean there were a couple of times when the thought passed through my head, but I never really saw how I would do it, not before I read Michael Radford's script.' It must be comforting to tackle a role to which he is so obviously well-suited… 'Absolutely. If you're going to count the perks of getting old, and you probably can't even count them on one hand, that would be one of them. But it's also a part that could be played by an actor at any age. With Shakespeare, it's like playing great music; it doesn't matter how old you are if you're playing the cello.'

There's a commotion in the background at the airport. Someone is calling out Pacino's name. 'Oh, we're moving', he says. 'We're going.' He asks if I can call him again tonight. I tell him of course, no problem.

After hanging up, I consider his voice a little longer. It has barely changed. Indeed, it's what links the Pacino of today with the Pacino of the early '70s. A little more worn now, a little rougher, the voice sounds so New York, so, well, Al Pacino. It has a truly disarming quality, a life of its own, like the sidewalks of the Bronx

come alive. It is the very essence of the man. It's the voice, too, that conjures up some of the late twentieth century most iconic and enduring film characters: Michael Corleone in *The Godfather*, Tony Montana in *Scarface*, the fast-talking salesman Ricky Roma in *Glengarry Glen Ross*, the blind lothario Frank Slade in *Scent of a Woman*, Lieutenant Vincent Hanna in *Heat*…

When we speak again eight hours later, it's the early hours of the morning in London and Pacino is in LA. Does he like it there? 'It's okay, it's just not my home. Two of my children are here. I have one on the East Coast, too, so I try as much as I can to straddle both coasts.' I can hear his children down the line, clamouring for their father's attention. I ask about his children. He has three: twins by his last partner, the actress Beverly D'Angelo, and a teenage daughter, Julie Marie, from an earlier relationship with an acting teacher, Janet Tarrant. He has never married.

Would he let his children watch *Scarface*, the blisteringly violent, coke- and ego-fuelled movie he made with Brian de Palma in 1983? 'No!' he screams, laughing. 'My oldest has sworn to me she hasn't seen it, but I'm pretty sure she has.' He's not keen on picking highs and lows from his career, but says he's happy with the cult following that *Scarface* has attracted. 'When it first came out, it wasn't fully celebrated. It was always a controversial film and always will be. I feel good about it because even at the time I thought it had a certain appeal: Oliver Stone wrote it, Brian de Palma directed. I think there was a real energy there.'

The last decade or so has been good to Pacino. If you think of his peers – Robert De Niro, say, or Dustin Hoffman – it's Pacino time seems to have been kinder to. A director who worked with both De Niro and Pacino in the mid '90s has said that it was the latter who exuded true passion on set. It's impossible to imagine Pacino joining De Niro and Hoffman in the comedy *Meet the Fockers*. There have been some misses, of course, *The Devil's Advocate* among them. But there have been more hits too: *Donnie Brasco* and *Heat* stand out as two of the best movies of his career. But can he see a point when it will be time to give it all up?

'Totally, yes.', he says. 'I don't know why I haven't seen it yet. Sometimes, I just sit around thinking: Why am I still doing this, why am I here? I do feel that from time to time.'

Things fall apart

Guy Maddin selects five entries for a personal history of sadness in film.

Footlight Parade (1933)

Footlight Parade, directed by Lloyd Bacon in 1933, is the third and the greatest of the big Warner Bros Depression-era musical extravaganzas. It reminds me of a Western, except the landscape has been turned into women – as far as the eye can see. The way they photograph women in these musicals – it's a cattle call. And there are things to be taken in the same spirit as the pioneers did in Westerns: 'It's mine because I took it.'

The Warner Bros musicals are always down and dirty – you feel like you have to wash your hands after watching one – and this is particularly true with *Footlight Parade*. The art direction is always interested in breaking scenes down. People are already broken down, you can really feel the desperation of the Depression. You can feel that the film is full of poor women desperate for stardom. There's something deeply disturbing, something very white slavery, about this film.

Footlight Parade is the zenith of the Busby Berkeley cycle. From here on, it's all downhill, you can start to feel the exhaustion and overstraining for ideas. Although the budgets were massive in the 1950s musicals, the hysteria of it all was at its last gasp. But in these early

How the west was glum: **Heaven's Gate**

SADNESS

Depression musicals, the feeling of discovery is palpable, like a first love.

The Face Behind the Mask (1941)

Robert Florey's *The Face Behind the Mask* is a strange, haunting disfigurement parable starring Peter Lorre as a happy-go-lucky immigrant in America. It represents the best combination of elements in the poetic allegory fairy tale film, best done in silent films with actors like Lon Chaney. It feels like a Hans Christian Andersen fairy tale photographed as a *film noir*, which gives it its poetic and painful heart and soul. You really feel you've caught a whiff of the poetry of a life.

The film is a singular expression of the multi-genre B movie. It's a disfigurement melodrama, a pure gangster film that becomes a revenge film, a tearjerker, a fairy tale – and there's even a love story with a dog. Yet it never lingers on any one genre. It keeps on turning corners and ending up in unexpected places. It stands astride these genres in a balancing act that makes it a work of art, and it shows how liberating low budget movies can be.

The Chase (1946)

Arthur Ripley's wondrously delirious film *The Chase* shows, perhaps more than any other film, the extraordinary proximity of films to dreams. It's full of wonderful set pieces that lead in a strange and dreamlike non sequitur fashion into one another. It's an amazingly Wagnerian story showing how love can win

---

Critics' choice
Tearjerker deaths

Ghost
(1990, US) *d* Jerry Zucker. *cast* Demi Moore, Patrick Swayze, Whoopi Goldberg.
The murdered Swayze enjoys his last embrace, kiss and goodbye ('See ya') with Moore. Sniff.

Hana-Bi
(1997, Japan) *d* Takeshi Kitano. *cast* 'Beat' Takeshi, Kayoko Kishimoto, Ren Osugi.
Beleaguered ex-Inspector Takeshi and his terminally ill wife are cornered on the beach – and there are just two rounds in the revolver…

Les Invasions Barbares
(2003, Can/Fr) *d* Denys Arcand. *cast* Rémy Giraud, Stéphane Rousseau, Marina Hands.
An estranged wife calls an even more estranged son to the terminally ill husband's bedside…

Knute Rockne: All American
(1940, US) *d* Lloyd Bacon. *cast* Pat O'Brian, Gale Page, Ronald Reagan, Donald Crisp.
Reagan, as dying football star George Gipp, croaks, 'Win just one for the Gipper'. (The scene is riotously lampooned in *Airplane!*)

Kes
(1969, GB) *d* Kenneth Loach. *cast* David Bradley, Lynne Perrie, Freddie Fletcher, Colin Welland.
Unsentimental tale of a boy and his bird – but with a tearjerking avian death at the end.

Love Story
(1070, US) *d* Arthur Hiller. *cast* Ali MacGraw, Ryan O'Neal, John Marley, Ray Milland.
One big blub-fest, particularly when the dying MacGraw says her final farewell to O'Neal from a hospital bed.

My Girl 2
(1991, US) *d* Howard Zieff. *cast* Macaulay Culkin, Anna Chlumsky, Dan Ackroyd, Jamie Lee Curtis.
Who'd ever have thought we'd get upset by Macaulay Culkin being stung to death by bees?

Old Yeller
(1957, US) *d* Robert Stephenson. *cast* Tommy Kirk, Dorothy McGuire, Fess Parker, Jeff York.
A young kid has to pull the trigger on his infected and dying canine companion.

Terms of Endearment
(1983, US) *d* James L Brooks. *cast* Shirley MacLaine, Debra Winger, Jack Nicholson.
Winger's goodbye to her kids is possibly one of the best-acted and most moving of all death-bed scenes.

21 Grams
(2003, Ger/US) *d* Alejandro González Iñárritu. *cast* Sean Penn, Benicio del Toro, Naomi Watts.
Three figures pulled together by a tragic accident – but Watts's wracked sobs linger longest.

SADNESS

through war, shellshock and even wakefulness, and how love's roots are in dreams.

The logic of *The Chase* is like the free-flowing logic of a piece of music. And it achieves what all film-makers are trying to do no matter what the genre: it totally creates its own world. To a certain extent it's a B movie whose plot elements are a bit mysterious; nothing seems to makes sense. But if you give in to it, it's as inexplicable as a dream, and the plot twists feel exactly the same.

The Chase goes to the heart of the dream state, releasing little narcotic trickles into the body; yet it doesn't set out to say that its thesis is dreams. And it's an inspiration to see someone able, with primitive means, to create such a masterpiece.

Possessed (1947)

Curtis Bernhardt's *Possessed* is an expressionist melodrama, with Greek tragedy ancestry, and at the same time a star vehicle for Joan Crawford, the all-time queen of melodrama. The film is about the extraordinary highs and lows we experience in romance. Crawford really knows how to suffer, how to do these primary emotions we experience when we're really stripped naked by sleep.

Possessed is one of the first episodes in Hollywood's love affair with psychoanalysis. The psychoanalysis functions like the Greek chorus in Euripides, letting the film cover acres of story in a few medically explanatory vignettes. It's great storytelling.

Possessed really seizes on the emotion of jealousy and hyperbolises it, sends you on an emotional roller coaster before concluding with a cathartic blast of steam. You can really feel the Furies emanating from it. At the same time, it's packaged as a thriller with all the loose ends neatly tied together, a nice Hollywood star vehicle for a mass audience.

Critics' choice
Melodramas

All About My Mother
(1999, Sp/Fr) *d* Pedro Almodóvar. *cast* Cecilia Roth, Marisa Paredes, Penelope Cruz.
A beautifully crafted melodrama chock-full of coincidences, contrivances and twists.

All That Heaven Allows
(1955, US) *d* Douglas Sirk. *cast* Jane Wyman, Rock Hudson, Agnes Moorehead.
Wyman gives up her affair to protect her children – and gets a TV as a replacement.

Camille
(1936, US) *d* George Cukor. *cast* Greta Garbo, Robert Taylor, Lionel Barrymore.
The camera's love of 'the Face' was never more obvious than during Camille's demise.

Dark Victory
(1939, US) *d* Bette Davis, George Brent, Humphrey Bogart, Geraldine Fitzgerald.
Petulant heiress Davis has just months to live!

In a Lonely Place
(1950, US) *d* Nicholas Ray. *cast* Humphrey Bogart, Gloria Grahame, Frank Lovejoy.
Despair and solitude: Bogart is suspected of murder, the girl-next-door gives him an alibi.

Letter from an Unknown Woman
(1948, US) *d* Max Ophuls. *cast* Joan Fontaine, Louis Jourdan, Mady Christians.
Classic unrequited love. Fontaine has an secret crush on Jourdan; he loves her, then forgets her.

Limelight
(1952, US) *d* Charles Chaplin. *cast* Charles Chaplin, Claire Bloom, Sydney Chaplin Jr.
Tears outweight the titters in Chaplin's most personal film. Spot the cameo by Buster Keaton.

Mildred Pierce
(1945, US) *d* Michael Curtiz. *cast* Joan Crawford, Jack Carson, Zachary Scott.
Hard-working, self-sacrificing Joanie carries the can for spoiled, murderous daughter (Ann Blyth)

Written on the Wind
(1956, US) *d* Douglas Sirk. *cast* Lauren Bacall, Robert Stack, Dorothy Malone, Rock Hudson.
A fierce critique of a disintegrating middle class.

Wuthering Heights
(1939, US) *d* William Wyler. *cast* Merle Oberon, Laurence Olivier, David Niven.
The much-filmed tale of Cathy's passion for Heathcliff makes fulsome melodrama.

It all gets too much: **Le Jour se lève**

Bring Me the Head of Alfred Garcia (1974)

Sam Peckinpah's *Bring Me the Head of Alfred Garcia* is one of the great films about male sexual rivalry: each male character seems to be bristling with his own erect gun barrel throughout the film. It's a solipsistic trek into a jealousy fever, that takes you into a timeless state of mind and shows how immortal jealousy is.

It's a revenge picture loosely framed as a Western, embedded in a sweaty, immoral and abysmal Mexican landscape. It brilliantly portrays the strange, obsessive relationship between the two male rivals and shows how the cuckold desperately needs to recover his honour, but also the utter hopelessness of his ambition. Yet it's not at all comic book – it's not like the *Death Wish* revenge films – it deals with specific feelings that everyone goes through.

Bring Me the Head of Alfred Garcia is the zenith of what you might call the 'mad cuckold' genre, which usually needs to piggyback on a host genre, normally a gangster movie or a musical; but in this film it stands alone. It's as if it has finally learned to walk on its on own two feet.

Moving picture
Samantha Morton

Actress, *Under the Skin, Morvern Callar, Minority Report, The Libertine*

I couldn't afford to go to the cinema – I grew up in a very working-class area of Nottingham, so the cinema was something you sneaked into to skive off school. I do remember watching *2001: A Space Odyssey*, though, with my brother and sister, and having this image of a baby floating in space. I didn't know what it was called until years later. I suppose when you're little you don't know you're watching a film – you know you're watching something, but you don't know what film is, you don't really know the difference between film on television and in a cinema. All you know is how you feel, you have the innocence of youth.

The first film I remember ever affecting me was a film I watched in school, and that was *Kes*. I don't think the teachers would have thought, 'We're showing a Ken Loach film', it was just a film about a kid, one a lot of children in the north can relate to – a child from a very poor area who didn't want to go to school, who felt he didn't fit in at school, who had to put up with fighting in the home but still fell in love with an animal and spent time nurturing this animal.

I was eleven when I joined the UK's Central Junior Television Workshop. But even though I was involved in drama, I still couldn't afford to go to the cinema for quite a long time, and I didn't have an interest in film. I hadn't caught the bug of sitting in a cinema in the dark, having a shared emotional experience with strangers. The films I was able to see then were, again, films on the telly – like *Cathy Come Home, Ladybird Ladybird*. I was 17 or 18 when I saw that. I also remember walking past the Broadway cinema in Nottingham and seeing advertisements for *La Reine Margot* and thinking, 'Wow, that looks amazing.'

But when I lived in New York, I started to go to the cinema in my spare time, buy secondhand videos or DVDs, and ask people – like, say, cinematographers I worked with – to tell me who had inspired them, and why. 'Why are you doing this, why are you sitting behind the camera, who inspired you, what films would you want to watch?' I'd get little lists that I'd put in my pocket. That's the only way I've been able to learn my craft: by working in front of a camera, and by working with very diverse people and watching the films that influenced them – films by Werner Herzog, say, or Cocteau, or Vigo or Tarkovsky. I was recently introduced to Ozu, and now *Tokyo Story* has to be up there as one of my most influential films. There are certain films you can watch over and over again, that continually inspire you with your craft, their technical brilliance – and ones that can take you back a little bit, like a perfume can do.

I've been incredibly lucky, because I believe I care so much about getting better at what I do, and because I've worked with brilliant people. I want to be around people who love what they do so much that they're willing to push a little bit, go against the grain. And I'm not just talking about being quirky for quirky's sake, I'm talking about being talented.

Exhilaration

'You – you've got me?
Who's got you?' Superman

Foot on the
exhilarator

Jessica Winter measures the cardiac effect of a cinema ticket.

In the film critic's array of enthusiastic adjectives, there's a small but dependable stable of cheerleaders for feather-brained action pulp. Alongside interchangeable terms such as 'taut', 'gripping' and 'thrill-a-minute', 'exhilarating' soldiers on through poster quote after poster quote, conscripted to sell *The Matrix Reloaded* or *2 Fast 2 Furious* or whatever monster-truck-rally-cum-PlayStation-sequel happens to slam into the multiplex that week. An exhilarating, roller-coaster ride of a white-knuckle epic. The edge of your seat will be exhilarated.

The word's etymology doesn't necessarily foreshadow a career selling car chases. 'Exhilaration' also crops up in blurbs for film comedies, even if fraternal twin 'hilarity' is more frequently used. The Latin *exhilaratus* is a development of *hilarare*, 'to gladden' (*hilarus* means 'cheerful'); today's 'exhilarate' variously means 'to make cheerful', 'to enliven, excite' or 'to 'refresh, stimulate'.

All these meanings could conceivably apply to an exhilarating action-adventure, where the hero escapes from a ganglord's Uzi-wielding henchmen in a death-defying leap from an 80-storey skyscraper, landing on a jet-ski fastened to a radio-controlled crane that plucks the ticking bomb from the speeding bus, mere seconds before the non-lethal but still dazzling detonation propels him into the arms of the sultry, bikini-clad CIA operative who awaits on a perfectly positioned yacht. But movie exhilaration could also describe the sensory jolts of horror and porn, the cerebral massage of Tarkovsky and Godard, the humanist warmth of Lubitsch and Sturges – and the bracing, astringent work (movies as cold showers) of Bresson and the Dardenne brothers.

Of course, the most obvious outlet of gladdened excitement available to humans is laughter, so the average person's list of exhilarating film experiences would probably include many a ribcage-rattler: the sublime

Keaton's immortal, unimprovable **The General**

choreographies of Harold Lloyd and Buster Keaton; the anxiety-driven, anything-goes zaniness of early Woody Allen; the historically exacting hilarity of *Monty Python and the Holy Grail* and *This Is Spinal Tap*; or the baby-craving headlong rush of *Raising Arizona*. Or something starring Will Ferrell, a galvanising force of nature, macho-suave yet thrumming with reserves of sugar-smacked hysteria, hairy of chest and manner yet unafraid to cry like a girl or scream like a woman. I first watched *Anchorman: The Legend of Ron Burgundy* in a double bill with *Bad Santa* on a transatlantic flight, and I'm surprised that no one alerted flight attendants to my protracted sobbing convulsions as a matter for medical attention (or maybe an prologue to air rage). In high concentrations, movie exhilaration provokes nothing less than a seizure.

My examples are highly subjective (funny is in the eye of the beholder), but exhilaration is a bona fide organic phenomenon, focus of its own scientific sub-discipline: gelatology, the physical and physiological study of 'rhythmic,

Adrenalin rush: **Speed**

a belly laugh can achieve the effects of a love buzz or a runner's high: the delighted brain exudes endorphins and neuropeptides, raising pain thresholds and mood levels. (The American School of Laughter Yoga, which claims 250,000 members worldwide, uses laughter as group therapy to decrease stress and social tension, strengthen the immune system and alleviate symptoms of insomnia, hypertension and arthritis.)

This salubrious sense of belonging, whereby the individual experience heightens and deepens as I becomes We, is especially potent in films that embody the very effects they produce. It's not just the dizzying, ping-pong verbal wit of Howard Hawks' comedies that satisfies so completely; for all the pop and crackle of the overlapping zingers, the movies often radiate a fireside glow of rough-and-ready solidarity, a group cohesion forged through practical problem-solving. The ensemble wish-fulfilment of Depression-era screwball escapism also applies, as does the cross-class alliance in *Caddyshack* between the old-money ironist, the slobby arriviste and the working-class kid.

In Peter and Bobby Farrelly's unhinged comedies, the spectacle of boundless body horror is also weirdly reassuring in its frank acknowledgment of the filthy, secret indignities of everyday existence; the brother directors mine a visceral laughter of identification from the many ways our bodies can shock, embarrass and betray us. I fondly remember watching the Farrellys' underrated *Me, Myself & Irene* at a packed Times Square preview, and hearing knowing guffaws from the men in the audience, followed by the women who were understandably slower to catch on, when Jim Carrey gives an uproarious lesson in the mechanical defects of the post-coital urethra.

vocalised expiratory and involuntary actions' (says the *Encyclopaedia Britannica*) – in other words, laughter. We laugh when a negatively charged electrical impulse whizzes through our cerebral cortex, and we have multiple, mostly complementary explanations for how and why laughter evolved. Group laughter – in a darkened movie theatre, for example – is a comforting, confidence-building, and highly contagious mode of social bonding, one that scientists liken to grooming among chimpanzees. Properly shared and sustained,

EXHILARATION

Apart from preparing a versatile remedy of soothing togetherness, laughter can also express literal relief. Reporting from the Fifth International Summer School on Humour and Laughter in Tübingen, Germany, a writer for *The Economist* explained that 'laughter, incapacitating as it is, is a convincing signal that the danger has passed.' The danger might take form simply as a joke that goes exactly too far, resulting in a moment of vertiginous suspense between signal and response. Another midtown-Manhattan memory: the sound of an entire audience drawing a startled intake of air, as if socked in the gut, when a character in *South Park: Bigger Longer & Uncut* observes of a female associate, 'I don't trust anything that bleeds for five days and doesn't die,' and then the gradually accumulating wave of laughter rippling through the theatre. Or the danger might be more straightforward: hence the laughter that typically bubbles up at a horror flick after the initial, heart-seizing appearance of the knife-wielding maniac.

The broadest explanation of the giggles is the 'incongruity theory', to be found in the writings of Blaise Pascal and Arthur Schopenhauer (the latter proposed what's known as the 'theory of the ludicrous'). The incongruity theory suggests that laughter is a reaction to a dissonance between our expectations of a scenario and its actual outcome; the laugh conveys surprise at an illogical or contradictory state of affairs, but also understanding of the situation, which is in itself pleasing. Accordingly, the movies that enliven and excite are those that make it new, confound expectations, mis-fit their constituent parts – whether or not they extract laughs per se. The exhilarating mindfuck to end all

'Just a little torture': Takashi Miike's horribly funny **Ichi the Killer**

exhilarating mindfucks is arguably *Being John Malkovich*, wherein the impeccably controlled lunacy comprises a slapstick comedy, a transsexual love story by proxy, and a serious philosophical investigation, all presented so matter-of-factly that the confusion and pain of the characters is never in doubt or belittled, even at the hysterical peak of the film's gleefully contorted metaphysics. Just as unpredictable and unapologetically emotional, *Punch-Drunk Love* locates its crowning incongruity in harnessing Adam Sandler's soulful-autist persona to a shaggy, irresistible romance of opposites, shot in lush widescreen colour like the most sumptuous MGM musical.

Speaking of which, the golden age of the musical assembled its own evidence for a theory of the ludicrous: preposterous beauty, promiscuous intercourse between workaday,

dream and nightmare, not to mention people spontaneously breaking into song and dance. In Vincente Minnelli's wistful and nostalgic *Meet Me in St Louis*, incongruity takes the shape of seven-year-old Margaret O'Brien as the cheerfully morbid Tootie, flinging a chair on the flames of the Halloween bonfire and shrieking, 'I'm the most horrible!' In Stanley Donen and Gene Kelly's *Singin' in the Rain*, Donald O'Connor back-flips the bird at the laws of physics and Kelly breathes underwater. In Minnelli's *An American in Paris*, café culture and baroque fantasy realms meet in starbursts of song, dance, and design: in Oscar Levant's daydream of orchestral megalomania, in the flabbergasting Dionysiac black-and-white ball, and when Kelly's starving artist lifts Leslie Caron into his arms only to open his eyes and see a clutch of flowers, slipping from his grasp. Across the ocean, Powell and Pressburger had already achieved an equally orgiastic fusion in *The Red Shoes*, where anything is possible: naked carbons conjure Moira Shearer's shadow dance partner, the orchestra pit becomes a teeming sea, the camera becomes a spinning ballerina.

Given its historical context, *The Red Shoes* is also gloriously presumptuous, a Total Art of cinema pirouetting brazenly through the cooling wreckage of total war. There's nothing like a dose of subversion to get the neurotransmitters doing jumping-jacks, from James Mason's overmedicated suburban dad roaring 'God was wrong!' in Nicholas Ray's *Bigger Than Life*, to James Stewart raging against type as he manipulates and terrorises Kim Novak in *Vertigo*, to Buñuel's devoutly irreverent dream factory in its entirety. Victor Erice's *The Spirit of the Beehive* is a grave political allegory of Franco's barren, ghost-haunted Spain, necessarily embedded in a child's quest – in this case, to summon the spirit of Frankenstein's monster after she sees the 1931 film. Illuminated by the oneiric light of the cinema, the movie makes the fears and mysteries of childhood unsettlingly tangible, and erases any line between movie-life and life itself. Its child's-eye view descends from Charles Laughton's *The Night of the Hunter*, a film that, whenever I've seen it in repertory houses, always inspires a communal outpouring of terrorised mirth – perhaps a telltale sign of exhilaration in progress.

Subversive in his very tirelessness, Werner Herzog is a man who gives every indication of having the physical and psychological fortitude of an ironman triathlete, and has built his exhilarating oeuvre by doing things that just aren't done: you don't hypnotise your entire cast, or hire a disturbed man who's spent most of life in institutions as your star, or write a sequence requiring that a steamboat be dragged over a mountain in the Amazon, or collaborate with a highly flammable egomaniac like the late Klaus Kinski. One of Herzog's richest achievements, *Aguirre, Wrath of God* descends into febrile madness in tandem with its doomed 16th-century explorers in search of El Dorado, ending with wild-eyed Kinski bewildered amid a hallucinatory rain of monkeys.

Movies exhilarate when, as *Aguirre* does, they court frenzy and ecstasy at risk of catching the fugue themselves, and when they dare to embrace unlikely second chances and magical thinking. The climactic breakout of Bresson's *Un Condamné à mort s'est échappé* and the explosive disco-dance coda of Claire Denis's *Beau Travail* both imply a soul reborn, here on earth or elsewhere. At the miraculous ending of Dreyer's *Ordet*, the resurrected Inger awakes so hungry for life that she all but devours her stunned husband with her kiss. Frank Borzage's films pitch love as a secular religion that enables a spiritual continuity between this realm and the next, his lovers glowing with a sensuous, mysterious purity that's not quite of this world. In his Hemingway adaptation *A Farewell to Arms*, starring Helen Hayes and the young, touchingly awkward Gary Cooper, vehement melodrama builds into visionary delirium, a vivid testament to love everlasting even unto death.

Such an ethereal ideal is twisted and warped almost beyond recognition in David Lynch's *Mulholland Dr.*, the who's-dreaming-who Möbius strip of dual identities, sublimated desires, and skewed Hollywood satire so invigoratingly off-kilter that I wanted to cartwheel out of the theatre where I first saw it. After the decade of false starts and half-great films that followed Lynch's television programme *Twin Peaks*, *Mulholland Dr.* marked the director's masterful return to form. It's at once a revision of Lynch themes and fixations and something entirely new – its tonic powers ensured by the presence of

the astonishing Naomi Watts in her first major role, pulling double duty as the naive, perky aspiring actress Betty and the abject, crazed Hollywood casualty Diane. One woman is the fever dream of another, and here Lynch both indulges his obsession with martyred blondes and amends it – he puts the doomed celestial fantasy into the hands of the fallen angel herself. In so doing, he also handed an extraordinary unknown actress the chance to deliver the performance of two lifetimes. The thrill of new talent discovered, the operatic abandon in seeking out emotional extremes, the mind-altering vortex of dream logic, the restorative joy of singular film-making – now *that's* exhilaration.

Exhilaration in 20 films

Sunrise (1927)
The late silent era was a wellspring of exhilarating dreamscapes, including FW Murnau's elemental melodrama, sweepingly subtitled *A Song of Two Humans*. The romantic plot is built on solid binary oppositions – wife versus mistress, city versus countryside – but the nimble camera is constantly in dizzying motion.

Twentieth Century (1934)
In his first comic talkie, Howard Hawks was already perfecting his knack for overlapping, rapid-fire dialogue and delightful sight gags, aided no end by John Barrymore as a director on the slide and Carole Lombard as an ascendant starlet.

Gold Diggers of 1935 (1935)
There's a plot, but it's mere filler between Busby Berkeley's heady musical numbers: 'The Words Are in My Heart' cues a flotilla of dancing, white pianos, and the mini-masterpiece 'The Lullaby of Broadway' chronicles 24 hectic hours in the life of a nocturnal party girl who plummets to her death from a skyscraper.

Bride of Frankenstein (1935)
'We belong dead!' Karloff's creature speaks, eludes a mob, makes a friend, and gets a mate in this wickedly funny sequel. Crowned with electro-shock hair and hissing like an angry swan, Elsa Lanchester creates an icon out of mere minutes of screen time.

The Philadelphia Story (1940)
Sly, sexy, brimming with frothy dialogue and swimming in champagne, this most beloved of Hollywood movies deploys the fantasy-league triple threat of Katharine Hepburn, Cary Grant and James

Stewart in a soulful comedy of remarriage – of second chances, self-recognition and subtle inner transformation.

Cat People (1942)
Sinuous and splendidly underlit, the first of producer Val Lewton's horror films is a mesmerising Freudian psychodrama, in which the return of the repressed comprises erotic desire, sexual jealousy and historical atrocity.

Black Narcissus (1947)
Powell and Pressburger used painted backdrops to transform Pinewood sets into a Himalayan palace convent still thick with the fumes of its bordello past, where a beleaguered order of nuns begins to unravel – dizzied by the heat, wind, and high altitude, and seduced by their own memories and latent desires.

Kind Hearts and Coronets (1949)
Many an Ealing affair would deserve a spot on this list, but one could start with this elegant, pitch-black comedy, wherein plebeian Dennis Price clears a path to nobility by murdering eight members of an aristocratic family – each of them embodied by Alec Guinness in a tour de force set of performances.

The Exterminating Angel (1962)
An elegant dinner party spirals into sordid chaos when the guests develop a mass neurosis whereby they can't bring themselves to leave the room. Buñuel's delicious masterpiece ridicules mob mentality as expressed in the arbitrary and binding codes of 'polite society'.

Woman of the Dunes (1964)
An urbane man of science wakes up a powerless detainee in a deep sandpit, reduced to his most basic desires as landscape and body alike become defamiliarised under the camera's magnifying glass. Hiroshi Teshigahara's unnerving nightmare nods stoically to humankind's adaptive powers while letting rip an existential primal scream.

Pierrot le Fou (1965)
Love and lust go up in flames when Godard's most iconic stars, Jean-Paul Belmondo and Anna Karina, run away for a doomed interlude on the French Riviera, filmed by Raoul Coutard in feverish hues.

Sleeper (1973)
Woody Allen enjoyed a superb run in the '70s, but measuring purely by laughs, nothing beats this futurist farrago, wherein Allen reworks the Rip Van Winkle yarn and introduces an immortal piece of machinery known as the Orgasmatron.

Zardoz (1973)
Starring Sean Connery, resplendent in a red loincloth, John Boorman's unfairly maligned class-warfare

dystopia dares to envision the opiate of the masses as a levitating godhead that vomits up guns and ammo and intones, 'The gun is good, the penis is evil!' Need we say more?

Suspiria (1977)
A gruesome Grimm fairy tale painted in storybook primary colours, Dario Argento's masterpiece pulses with arterial gushings, lurid crimson backlighting and blood-thick wine, while the controlled cacophony of the Goblin soundtrack keeps the delirium high.

Videodrome (1982)
Expanding the director's perennial interest in viral transmission and the body as a social and biological battleground, this is David Cronenberg's most ingeniously choreographed collision of the provocations of horror and the consolations of philosophy (and vice-versa).

Archangel (1990)
Befogged by mustard gas, amnesia and the loss of his leg in World War I, a Canadian lieutenant mistakes his nurse for his dead girlfriend – the first of many romantic mix-ups in the oneiric haze of Guy Maddin's hypnotic movie, which features both strangulation by intestines and a rainstorm of bunny rabbits.

Chungking Express (1994)
Shot quickly, and radiating all the more energy and improvisational thrill for it, Wong Kar-Wai's paean to the most beautiful broken hearts in Hong Kong is hilarious, wistful and endlessly inventive, as characters project their lovelorn aches and pains on to the song 'California Dreamin', miscellaneous household objects or canned pineapple.

Schizopolis (1996)
Steven Soderbergh dismantles narrative, identity, language and his own dead marriage in this shape-shifting experiment in maximum narrative fragmentation, wherein the writer-director-star plays both an office drone for a Scientology-like corporation and a dentist who's having an affair with the drone's wife.

Pola X (1999)
Derived from Herman Melville's self-defeating attempt at a profit-turning sentimental novel (*Pierre, or the Ambiguities*), Leos Carax's thrillingly ludicrous melodrama is almost kaleidoscopic in its visual range, and heedlessly pushes tragedy into the domain of deranged comedy.

Esther Kahn (2000)
At once cerebral and ridiculous, and often hugely moving, Arnaud Desplechin's incomparably strange chronicle of a sullen East End girl's unlikely success on the London stage is – like cinema itself – an experiment in consensual illusion.

Great escapism:
The Great Escape

Flickers

In the editing room of his own head, **Chris Petit** splices a lifetime of film memories.

Lee Marvin walking, low angle, through LAX in *Point Blank*; footsteps like gunshots. The sound of wind in the trees in *Blowup*. Driving shots through the windscreen in *Vertigo*. Kim Novak asking Kirk Douglas about shaving the dimple in his chin in *Strangers When We Meet*. The woman's blink in *La Jetée*. Robert Mitchum's walk across the rodeo ground in *The Lusty Men*. The number of fucks in the history of cinema (on and off screen). Fritz Lang's statement: that in the end it is necessary to finish what one has started. Ray Milland's vision in *X – the Man with X-Ray Eyes*. Orson Welles's hair in *The Third Man*, his overcoat and his shoes. Manny

Farber's observation on a great moment of cinematic space: Bogart crossing the street to the bookstore in *The Big Sleep* and looking up at the sky. The plughole in *Psycho*. Warren Oates' bemused grin; his wretched singing of 'Guantalamera' in *Bring Me the Head of Alfredo Garcia*. Magwitch in the graveyard of *Great Expectations*. Clu Gulager flipping aside his jacket to show his gun in *The Killers*; the gesture repeated in *Thief* as James Caan sees off a man cutting in on Tuesday Weld in a bar. The gaucheness of Anna Karina in *Le Petit Soldat*. The way Lee Marvin holds a gun. Christopher Walken in the credits for *King* of *New York* – the face of a revenant – later confirmed by the line 'Back from the dead'. Walken in just about anything (gut-punching Rupert Everett in *The Comfort of Strangers*). The loneliness of Diane Keaton in *The Godfather*. 'All work and no play makes Jack a dull boy' in *The Shining*. Doorways (thresholds) in the films of Fritz Lang. The way Harvey Keitel's head hits the pillow as the Ronettes start 'Be My Baby' in *Mean Streets*. Dean Martin's hat in *Some Come Running*. Clint Eastwood's chipped tooth. Genevieve Bujold's eyes. The tree-house in *Swiss Family Robinson*. The eaves of the attic room where Mitchum kills Shelley Winters in *The Night of the Hunter*. Death in cinema: palace of dreams versus mausoleum. Ingrid Bergman cooking eggs in *Viaggio in Italia*; George

Sanders's boredom and his tweed jacket in the same. *Pick-Up on South Street*. Bad early Jack Nicholson performances. Bresson's note on the ejaculatory force of the eye. Jeanne Moreau's shoes in *The Diary of a Chambermaid*. The last walk in *The Wild Bunch*. (The sound of a pump-action gun being worked.) Karina's wobbly cycling in *Bande à part*. Peter Lorre's oyster eyes in *M*. A shot of a plane passing over Powis Square in *Performance*. Three young girls walking down an Icelandic road in Marker's *Sans Soleil*. Ralph Meeker on being asked who he is in *Kiss Me Deadly*: 'Who am I? Who are you?' The deathly quiet suburban streets at the beginning of *Badlands*. The awfulness of Alan Parker. Ray Durgnat's writing (*A Mirror for England*). The slyness of the actress's look in *Un*

Critics' choice
Superheroes

EXHILARATION

Akira
(1988, Japan) *d* Katsuhiro Otomo. *cast* voices: Mitsuo Iwata, Nozomu Sasaki, Mami Koyama. Biker gangs wage war in an outlandish future Tokyo that awaits a second coming by the legendary Akira.

Barbarella
(1967, Fr/It) *d* Roger Vadim. *cast* Jane Fonda, John Phillip Law, Anita Pallenberg. Camp classic with future radical feminist Fonda, off to Planet Sorgo to battle vampire dolls.

Batman
(1989, US) *d* Tim Burton. *cast* Michael Keaton, Jack Nicholson, Kim Basinger. Keaton's nicely broody and the set's dark and moody, but Nicholson's Joker steals the show.

Flash Gordon
(1980, GB) *d* Michael Hodges. *cast* Sam J Jones, Melody Anderson, Chaim Topol, Brian Blessed. 'Flash, Flash, I love you, but we only have 14 hours to save the Earth!' Terrific.

Hellboy
(2004, US) *d* Guillermo del Toro. *cast* Ron Perlman, Selma Blair, Jeffrey Tambor. A grouchy, 60-year-old, seven-foot adolescent half-human devil with a giant right arm and girl problems. How could this not be fun?

The Mask
(1994, US) *d* Charles Russell. *cast* Jim Carrey, Cameron Diaz, Peter Riegert, Peter Greene. Part man, part Looney Tune and totally Jim Carrey's best ever turn.

Sin City
(2005, US) *d* Frank Miller, Robert Rodriguez. *cast* Jessica Alba, Bruce Willis, Mickey Rourke. Some very dodgy sexual politics and appallingly gratuitous violence, but boy, does it look good.

Spider-Man
(2002, US) *d* Sam Raimi. *cast* Tobey Maguire, Willem Dafoe, Kirsten Dunst, James Franco. 'With great power comes great responsibility. This is my gift, my curse. Who am I? I'm Spider-Man.'

Superman
(1978, GB) *d* Richard Donner. *cast* Christopher Reeve, Margot Kidder, Gene Hackman. For a moment there in the pre-CGI 1970s, we really did believe a man could fly.

X2
(2003, US) *d* Bryan Singer. *cast* Patrick Stewart, Hugh Jackman, Ian McKellen, Halle Berry. The first X-Men was polished and punchy, but the sequel offers even more *Bam!* for your buck.

Chien Andalou. The house on Narrow Street in *The Passenger*. Windows in *A Short Film About Love*. The terror of the mountains in Wellman's *Track of the Cat*. A country gas station in *Two-Lane Blacktop*. The eroticism of *Woman of the Dunes*. Extreme long shots. The tenderness of the pickpocketing sequences in *Pickpocket*. A Jancsó travelling shot. James Stewart having to act with Dion. Dan Duryea. A brief close-up of an unknown actress in Loach's TV version of *Up the Junction*, looking fed up in the street. Nuns in films. Noise of a chainsaw. Claudia Cardinale's voice. Alain Delon's isolation. Any face in a crowd. Rainer Werner Fassbinder. The assassination on the steps in the rain in *Foreign Correspondent* (umbrellas in films). Anton Walbrook's alien speech in *The Life and Death of Colonel Blimp*. Timothy Evans's hanging in *10 Rillington Place*. Morricone's music in *Once Upon a Time in the West*. All the drinks and drugs ever taken by all the people who worked in movies (cinema as narcotic). Charles Bronson's fear of tunnelling in *The Great Escape* (Donald Pleasance's blindness in the same). The train arriving in the station by the brothers Lumière. Jane Birkin looking through the keyhole in

Look, Ma, no wires: **Superman**

Moving picture
John Cusack

Actor, *Bullets Over Broadway*, *Grosse Point Blank*, *High Fidelity*, *Runaway Jury*

Apocalypse Now came out originally in 1978, I think. It came and went, and then in 1982 or '83 it started playing in these revival houses, which was when I saw it. My parents were out of town, a friend was staying with me, and a friend of the family took us to the 10 o'clock show. I didn't know anything about it, I was just a kid of fourteen. I remember having my head blown off and staggering out of the theatre. It was then I realised the power cinema has. The commitment Coppola had to making it, and to what he was trying to say and explore, was incredible. And the emotional impact it has on you! I think on some level, when it comes down to it, all criticism is bullshit; a piece of art just makes you feel something. It makes you realise something about yourself – you have an emotional connection with it, it taps into stuff.

Rivette's *L'Amour par terre*. Lou Castel and Jean-Pierre Léaud washed up in *Irma Vep*. The fevered eroticism of Clara Calami's hands in *Ossessione*. Robert Vaughn catching flies in *The Magnificent Seven*. The young Belmondo's torso. The emptiness of Handke's *The Left-Handed Woman*. Burton's drunken driving in *Who's Afraid of Virginia Woolf?* Steve McQueen's haircut in *The Cincinnati Kid*. The insecurity of Rita Hayworth. Lino Ventura crossing a railway track in *Le Deuxième Souffle*. Straub and Huillet's framing. Sue Lloyd's line to Michael Caine in *The Ipcress File*: 'Do you always wear glasses?' 'Yes, except when I'm in bed.' Sleet and a roadside café

in *Le Cercle Rouge*. The gaunt officer in *The Battle of Algiers*. Graham Greene's cameo in *Day for Night*. Edith Scob's bandages in *Les Yeux sans visage*. The vulnerability of Kurt Raab's serial killer in *Tenderness of the Wolves*. The nervy camera in *Festen*. The quizzical narcissism of Warren Beatty. The boisterous laughter of Ava Gardner in *The Night of the Iguana*. Dreyer's *Vampyr*. The blonde Russian actress in *Ballad of a Soldier*. A still of Lee J Cobb's cliff-top death in *Man of the West*, hand thrown high, back arched. *You Only Live Once*, 'the story of the last romantic couple' (Godard). The predatoriness of Connery's James Bond.

The restlessness of Cassavetes's camera in *The Killing of a Chinese Bookie*. The way Woody Allen ripped off Eric Rohmer (the shirt Zouzou buys the man in *Love in the Afternoon*). Busted careers. Delon's line in *Nouvelle Vague*: 'I inspire derision.' The increasingly desolate look of James Mason ('The saddest eyes in cinema', according to Greene.) The failure of British cinema. Sam Shepard and Bob Dylan's song 'Brownsville Girl': 'Well, I'm standing in line in the rain to see a movie starring Gregory Peck.' Trams in *The Man with a Movie Camera*. The direct gaze of women in the films of Ingmar Bergman. Lang's *Spione*. Orson Welles' remark that most directors are not

Moving picture
Peter Sollett

Writer, director, *Raising Victor Vargas*

I think it was sometime in 1996 or '97. There was a retrospective of Cassavetes' films at the Paris Theatre in New York, across the street from Central Park – it's a very beautiful theatre in a beautiful spot. They were doing double features, or maybe I bought a ticket for the first and they screened another after and I stayed. I think it was *Faces* and *Husbands*.

I was in film school at the time, dying to see Cassavetes' films. I'd read a bunch about them, but at NYU they don't like to use Cassavetes as any part of their methods. There are no Cassavetes films screened; none discussed, neither structurally or technically; no conversation about his use of or direction of actors. They just lecture to you about structure – like how to build a house or something – and it was just stifling.

I finally got to see these films, and they just flew in the face of everything I was being taught. They were, in a way, rigidly structured, but in such a subtle way that they could also adopt all of the emotional truths and spontaneous moments that structure always seemed to prevent. And it was incredibly liberating. That afternoon and evening at the movies taught me a completely new way of thinking about how those two things, structure and spontaneity, could co-exist and how movies could have both a moment-to-moment truth, and also a literary narrative truth.

EXHILARATION

found out. 'The wasted life of Louise Brooks. Food on Dirk Bogarde's chin in *Accident*. Nigel Green in The *Face of Fu Manchu* (actors' suicides: Green and George Sanders). Chris Doyle's nocturnal camera. The bizarre cinematic journey of Walerian Borowcyk. Gene Hackman eating ice-cream after cold turkey in *French Connection II*. The foolhardiness of Werner Herzog. The missing tiles in the floor at the beginning of *Rosemary's Baby* (cracks in the wall in *Repulsion*). The desire to see again films I hated at the time (*Le Bonheur*, *Céline et Julie Go Boating*). *Manhunter* versus *The Silence of the Lambs*. Robby Müller's camera for Wim Wenders; ditto Raoul Coutard's for Godard. The derangement of Klaus Kinski. Sleeping Japanese ferry passengers in *Sans Soleil*. The exemplary career of Raúl Ruiz. The 13-year gap in Buñuel's film-making. Photographs in cinema. Fredi Murer's only feature, *Alpine Fire* (1984) – Buñuel's Mexican *Wuthering Heights* relocated to Switzerland and contained within a single family – and the fact that he hasn't made a feature since. The speed of Paul Greengrass's direction in *The Bourne Supremacy*. The magnificence of Delphine Seyrig in *Daughters of Darkness*. Still lives in *Hana-Bi*. The Wednesday in *Big Wednesday*. The tracking shots in Michael Snow's *Wavelength*. The critical writings of Godard, Manny Farber and David Thomson. Silk stockings on screen

(*Silk Stockings*). Jerry-built French architecture and an out-of-season coastal resort in *Les Valseuses*. The nostalgia of German expatriates in Hollywood for European weather: hence *film noir*. Lisa Eichhorn in *Cutter's Way* (a film of lost careers – Passer, Heard, Eichhorn). Kenneth Anger's mapping of the other Hollywood. David Niven's smirk. Zapruder's 8mm film of the Dallas assassination. (Costner's line, 'Back, and to the left', in *JFK*.) The greatness of Don Siegel. *The Switchboard Operator* and her cat. Richard Boone (the unsuccessful Lee Marvin) in The *Night of the Following Day*. Snow in *McCabe and Mrs Miller* and Leonard Cohen's soundtrack. The black and white grading in *Eloge de l'amour*. The lines 'Baby, I don't care,' and 'I think I'm in a frame,' in *Out of the Past*. The belief by dull practitioners that cinema cannot be transcended. Michael Klier's *The Giant*, a feature-length film of back-to-back video surveillance images (diaries recorded by machines). Credits that are the best thing about the film: *JFK*, *Seven*, *Mean Streets*. TV as cinema: *The Sopranos* credit sequence; *Homicide: Life on the Street*; *The Shield*. The frequently unadventurous use of music in film (the dominance of picture over sound). The dreariness of critical orthodoxy. Godard's *Histoire(s) du cinéma*, the ultimate desert island/cul-de-sac film: the director as Prospero. Video. DVD. The fact that films don't say The End any more.

Play it again, samurai

The movies won't let the warriors of feudal Japan sleep, as **Ben Slater** reveals.

In 1960, director/producer John Sturges released *The Magnificent Seven*, a remake of a successful 1954 Japanese movie, Akira Kurosawa's *Seven Samurai*. The plot – about a gang of itinerant swordsmen in feudal Japan hired by a village to protect them from a gang of marauding bandits – transplanted to the American West so smoothly it barely needed adaptation. Slicker and shorter, the Sturges version cannily reproduced the pleasures of the Japanese film, such as the section where each member of the gang is recruited, and the poignant, post-climactic realisation by the mercenaries that they were the losers, the villagers the winners. This cultural exchange wasn't one-way, of course: Kurosawa admitted frequently over the years that *Seven Samurai* was heavily influenced by Western guru John Ford. The figure of the wandering warrior, unable to adjust to modernity and bound by a deeply felt moral code, was straight out of *Stagecoach*.

A year later, Kurosawa produced a film that could have been the antithesis of *Seven Samurai*: *Yojimbo*, a violent comedy of power and factionalism in which an absurdly laid back swordsman exploits the struggle between two gangs in a small town entirely for his own ends. Surely this was way too dark to be remade as a Western? Five years later, though, it was remade – in Spain, where it was directed and produced by Italians and starred a young American TV actor, Clint Eastwood. The film was *Fistful of Dollars*, and it transformed the personality of the action hero in world cinema. He didn't have to be a nice guy any more – and he didn't have to give a damn.

One more year passed, and in France, thriller specialist and one-man film factory Jean-Pierre Melville released *Le Samouraï*, which pared the genre right to the bone, distilling the essence of 30 years of gangster flicks, *film noir* and cops and robbers capers into 100 minutes of taut, existential atmospherics. Alain Delon, as the icily distant, virtually silent killer Jef, was a continental cousin of Clint, Toshiro Mifune and Yul Brynner. Now it was the criminal's turn to be the samurai. The landscape shifted again.

Then came 1968, a year of massive escalation in the war in Vietnam and radical civil disobedience all over the world. Back in the fictional West, Sam Peckinpah's *The Wild Bunch* revisited bushido as a covertly critical 'remake' of Sturges remake, with a strong sense of the Japanese original's sombre grace. This time the 'professionals' are an antic gang of middle-aged desperadoes, but deep underneath, the ancient code of 'doing it right' is waiting to be excavated. The group is sacrificed and sanctified in a dazzling series of slow-motion falls and freeze-frames.

Many more samurai materialised, in film industries all over the world. There's even an unacknowledged remake of Melville's movie, Walter Hill's *The Driver* (1978), with Ryan O'Neal eschewing guns for cars but remaining impassive. Gradually the swordsman loses his edge in the '80s, superseded by muscular freaks like Schwarzenegger and Stallone, whose moral codes were merely a pantomine – an excuse to smash heads and empty gun chambers rather than a basis for acting in a chaotic universe. Less existential or mystical, and more self-righteous and vengeance-seeking. The remote coolness of the samurai had been reduced to a lame, post-kill quip.

Unexpectedly, the next wave of ronin would hail from Hong Kong. Like feudal Japan or the American West, the Hong Kong of the '80s was living on borrowed time. The handover to China was just around the corner, and this precipitated an enormous rush of energy – not least in the film industry, which was partially bankrolled by Triads. Hong Kong had its own equivalent to the the samurai movie or the Western: the martial arts film, which had its origins in Chinese opera, legends, circus, pulp fiction stories set in medieval China, genuine fighting traditions and legendary proponents like Wong Fei Hung. But the glory days of the Shaw Brothers hit-machinery were over.

EXHILARATION

Moving picture
Michael Mann

Director, *Heat, The Insider, Ali, Collateral*

I remember seeing the 1946 version of *The Last of the Mohicans* when I was about five, in the basement of a church a block away from where I lived in Humble Park in Chicago. It was very much post-war – bear in mind that there'd been virtually no building in the States between 1929 and 1939, because of the Depression. So my mum had taken me to see this movie; it was 16mm and it made a real impression on me, especially the haircuts and the people running. So in 1991, when I was wondering what to make next, I thought, 'Wow, what about *The Last of the Mohicans*?'

Another memorable experience was when I first saw *Dr Strangelove*. I remember being fearful, thinking, 'Shit, this thing's going to end soon.' I remember vividly watching every minute of that movie. It was in 1963, at a cinema called the Orpheum in Madison, Wisconsin – a big old theatre on State Street at the University of Wisconsin. The film was so good, I didn't want it to end; I was worried it might only last 90 minutes! It was so bold. And mainstream cinema, too! It wasn't French New Wave or from the third world or anything like that, but it showed you could do something audacious and have all the benefits of the system to work with. Soon after that I saw Murnau's *Faust* and something by Pabst, and that's when I had this illumination, that I wanted to work in filmmaking.

John Woo, apprentice of Shaw's straight-up action man Chang Cheh, and part of the city's avant-garde underground, recast TV star Chow Yun-Fat in a genre-busting series of contemporary thrillers. Chow's persona – which combined Delon's Jef with some of that old samurai magic and more than a twinkle of Cary Grant, was persuasively iconic from the off. In *A Better Tomorrow, Hardboiled* and *The Killer*, Woo choreographed Chow in an ecstatic, exaggerated, gun-in-each-fist reworking of Peckinpah's style, against the rain-slicked haze of a city on the brink of extinction. This borderline homoerotic parody of 'action', where every cop had a criminal reflection, would filter straight back to Tinseltown – echoing all through Michael Mann's *Heat* (for which Hong Kong queen Maggie Cheung auditioned), then ripped off and plagiarised in a vast range of high-concept action/buddy films directed by hack Michael Bay and many others. So much so, that Woo's own entry into Hollywood would prove superfluous.

It was the geeks who first freaked out over second-generation VHS dubs of John Woo and Shaw Brothers mayhem who made the next set of moves. The Wachowski Brothers blended Japanese sci-fi anime and the orientalist sheen of 1980s cyberpunk in *The Matrix*, and hired Yuen Woo-Ping, a veteran fight choreographer who was a legend in Hong Kong, but little known in the West. His work on Ang Lee's retro-period piece *Crouching Tiger, Hidden Dragon* had radically rewired the way Western film audiences viewed martial arts. No longer about Bruce Lee, bad dubbing and wah-wah guitars, it was suddenly seen as a thing of brutal elegance. Since Yuen worked on *The Matrix* his LA phone hasn't stopped ringing. It's been a while since characters in any American film flailed at each other clumsily with fists (Western style); now everyone knows kung fu.

The paths of influence are complex and slippery, but there are no dead ends in sight. Quentin Tarantino's pop art take on Japanese avengers and Shaw Brothers tea-house showdowns in *Kill Bill* was trumped by Stephen Chow's disco-dancing, top-hatted axemen in *Kung Fu Hustle* – a surprise hit in the States (both worked with Yuen). There's a ceaseless process of images, ideas and characters, all passed along and changing through repetition and altered contexts.

These days the focus is on South Korea, and Park Chan-Wook, adored and despised by critics, is pumping a shocking vitality back into the thriller genre, which will surely have an impact on American and European film-makers in the coming years. The journey continues. Genres are revived and refreshed. Old samurai learn new tricks.

How the West was fun: **Butch Cassidy and the Sundance Kid**

Barrel of laughs: **The General**

To Buster, with love

Ex-Python **Terry Jones** describes his affection for the greatest silent comedian.

The odd thing is that the first time I saw one of Buster Keaton's feature films it didn't actually grab me. I say it's odd because I'm such a huge fan now, but it's even odder since the film in question was *The General* – regarded by many as Keaton's greatest masterpiece.

I think the print of *The General* that I saw back then had a big orchestral soundtrack, and that may have been the problem. I think comedy is a fragile construct that can be overwhelmed by too much sound. For example, when we first screened *Monty Python and the Holy Grail*, the film was received in almost total silence, hardly a laugh – not even for the Black Knight or the Knights Who Say Ni!

Eventually, we discovered that we'd made the soundtrack too rich: we'd jammed it with birdsong, atmosphere, wind, effects, music, clothing rustles (it's true, I'm afraid most films have added clothing rustle!) and footsteps. Every second of the soundtrack was filled to the last decibel, and this wasn't allowing the comedy to breathe. The comedy and the laughs often lie in the pauses and silences. A continuous soundtrack tends to disrupt the natural rhythms of the dialogue.

So I didn't really get into Keaton until 1967, when the NFT screened a season of his films with a piano accompaniment by Florence de Jong. Florence, I have since read on the internet, was the first woman ever to play an organ in the cinema (that is, I suppose, officially). At all events, her playing seemed to me to be right, and Keaton's films started to come alive for me. I didn't miss a single screening, and it was during that season that I fell in love with Keaton. Yes, it seems odd to write that, but that, I think, is the truth. I fell in love with Keaton. I love his presence. I love his sense of humour. I love his stillness. I love the way he moves. I love the places he takes me to.

For me, the love affair all started with a film called *Seven Chances*. You know how sometimes a relationship can start in unpropitious circumstances? It was like that with me and Buster. *Seven Chances* isn't reckoned as one of the great Keaton features. It was made in 1925, after a run of three wonderful movies: *Our Hospitality*, *Sherlock Junior* and *The Navigator*. By comparison, *Seven Chances* is a lesser offering, but it was the moment I fell in love with Buster, and for me it holds a special place.

In *Seven Chances*, a young man (Keaton as Jimmy Shannon) receives notice that he is due to come into a large inheritance, but only on condition that he is married by 5pm that

Critics' choice
Heist highlights

The Asphalt Jungle
(1950, US) *d* John Huston. *cast* Sterling Hayden, Louis Calhern, Jean Hagen, Sam Jaffe.
One of Huston's finest, and a classic that has spawned countless imitations.

Le Cercle Rouge
(1970, Fr/It) *d* Jean-Pierre Melville. *cast* Alain Delon, André Bourvil, Yves Montand.
Dark, desolate and moody, with a superbly executed silent robbery in the Place Vendôme.

The First Great Train Robbery
(1978, GB) *d* Michael Crichton. *cast* Sean Connery, Donald Sutherland, Lesley-Anne Down.
Freewheeling Victorian criminals in the Butch and Sundance mould try to rob a bullion train.

The Italian Job
(1969, GB) *d* Peter Collinson. *cast* Michael Caine, Noël Coward, Benny Hill, Raf Vallone.
More famous for the stunt-riddled getaway than the heist itself... and eminently quotable.

Nine Queens
(2000, Arg) *d* Fabián Bielinsky. *cast* Ricardo Darín, Gastón Pauls, Leticia Brédice.
A craftily impressive thriller working on the premise that there's no honour among thieves.

Ocean's Eleven
(2001, US/Aust) *d* Steven Soderbergh. *cast* George Clooney, Matt Damon, Andy Garcia.

Soderbergh's hi-tech robbery makes wholly enjoyable entertainment in this much improved remake.

Palookaville
(1995, US) *d* Alan Taylor. *cast* William Forsythe, Vincent Gallo, Adam Trese, Gareth Williams.
Chaos ensues when the robbers overshoot the jewellery shop and hit the pastry shop next door.

Reservoir Dogs
(1991, US) *d* Quentin Tarantino. *cast* Harvey Keitel, Tim Roth, Michael Madsen, Chris Penn.
This powerful homage to the heist-gone-wrong thriller might be the last word on the subject.

Rififi
(1955, Fr) *d* Jules Dassin. *cast* Jean Servais, Carl Möhner, Robert Manuel, Perlo Vito.
Highly acclaimed for the 35-minute robbery sequence, carried out in total silence.

The Thomas Crown Affair
(1999, US) *d* John McTiernan. *cast* Pierce Brosnan, Rene Russo, Denis Leary.
First-class remake with a deft robbery sequence, and a sexy awayday in Martinique.

Welcome to Collinwood
(2002, US) *d* Anthony Russo, Joe Russo. *cast* William H Macy, Isaiah Washington.
Low-rent criminal dunderheads attempt to finesse a 'Bellini'.

EXHILARATION

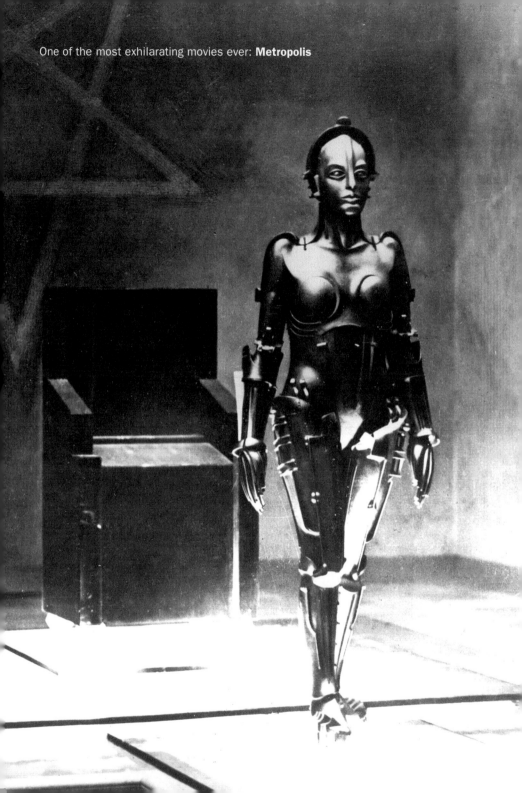

One of the most exhilarating movies ever: **Metropolis**

evening. He rushes round to his girlfriend and proposes. She accepts, but when he tells her the reason for his haste is that he stands to make some money, she feels insulted and turns him down. Undeterred, the hero puts an advert in the newspaper saying he will marry any girl who turns up at the church by 4pm that afternoon. His advert works. Five hundred would-be brides arrive to take up his offer.

The hero panics and races out of the church with the 500 would-be brides in pursuit. It took me several viewings to notice that the brides are all wearing hastily improvised bridal gowns, made up from tea-towels and table cloths, but then I'm not very good on costume. The brides chase our hero through the town, and then out into open country, and here the film takes on the look of a primitive Western, with Indians hollering in pursuit of the lone white man (the kind of reversal of the truth that one could get away with back in 1925).

The hero gives them the slip, however, and then it starts to get even more surreal – and this was the sequence that sold me on Keaton. He starts running down a slope and dislodges a ol gravel, then a few stones, then more and more, and the stones get bigger and bigger and eventually turn into boulders, which in turn get bigger and bigger. Our hero ends up having to turn and face the avalanche of huge boulders, dodging them as if he were in a football game.

It is still a seminal image for me: a vision that is funny and yet strangely beautiful. Seeing it for the first time convinced me that there was more to comedy than just making people laugh. And I think this is where Keaton had an influence on Monty Python – his ability to make comedy look good and at the same time stray into the realm of surrealism influenced a lot of my thinking in the Python days and so, I assume, leaked into the shows themselves. Keaton's shade was always urging both me and Terry Gilliam to try to make everything look as good as possible, while at the same time tapping into a world of incongruously juxtaposed images.

There is also another aspect of Keaton that appeals to me, and that is manifested in *Seven Chances*. There is a strain of unsentimentality in Keaton that borders on the cynical. When, at the beginning of the film, Keaton has his hero tell the girl that he wants to marry her that afternoon not because he's so in love

with her but because he stands to get a lot of money, he's taking quite a risk with his main character. There's a chance of alienating the audience.

But Keaton pushes it even further. At the end of the film, when the hero finally arrives back at the family home, where his girlfriend is ready waiting with the vicar to marry him after all, he arrives too late. The deadline has passed. He won't inherit the money. Now, at this point, any other film-maker would have had his hero accept the inevitable and marry the girl anyway, but Keaton doesn't. Jimmy turns away and starts to leave the house, and it's only when he sees that the church clock is a little slow and has not yet struck 5pm that he rushes back in and the marriage takes place. The couple live happily ever after, but the clear inference is that he wouldn't have married her if he wasn't going to get the money.

I've always liked this side of Keaton – his willingness to present his hero in an unsympathetic manner, be it cowardice or avarice or whatever. Keaton's face wasn't only straight. He also had a fierce and discerning eye that looked at the human condition with an unsentimental affection that makes him (to me, at any rate) the greatest of the silent comics.

EXHILARATION

Moving picture
Bill Nighy

Actor, *The Lawless Heart*, *Lucky Break*, *Underworld*

One of my most memorable film experiences was definitely the first time I saw Nic Roeg's *Performance* – I then went to see it another five times. I think it's one of the great films: funny, sexy, spooky and moody. I hadn't been so exhilarated by a film since those Saturday morning pictures I saw when I was a kid and used to come out and sword-fight all the way home. I felt just like that again, it got me so wired. James Fox's performance in it is one of my favourites by any actor in any medium. I can quote it almost verbatim. There's a part where he impersonates a juggler, and comes out with the immortal line 'Goodbye the Ferrari'. My friends and I used to sign letters with that line for years afterwards, we thought it was so cool.

Short *and* sweet

Nick Bradshaw sings the praises of thumbnail cinema.

The midgets of the movie world, short films somehow tend to get overlooked. Stature aside, they may not have much in common – but beyond the glare of the commercial projector, strange and wild things can grow…

Some of the following are the origin of the film species, others its far-flung mutations. Of course, this list itself is hopelessly short.

La Sortie des Usines Lumière (1895)
It all started here: the Lumière brothers' single-shot, one-minute record of their workforce emerging from the factory gates introduced the world to the breakthrough forms of the cinema, the documentary, even the movie-movie…

The Cameraman's Revenge (1912)
After beating his wife for her adultery, Mr Beetle's own illicit high-jinks with Ms Dragonfly are filmed by the jilted Mr Grasshopper and publicly screened – to the horror of all. Filmed with insect puppets, Wladyslaw Starewicz's 1912 stop-motion masterpiece is a red-blooded passion play of infidelity and double-standards; it lasts 12 minutes and is anything but cute.

Cops (1922)
Buster Keaton's early two-reelers were often as witty and exhilarating as his features. Hard to single out one, but *Cops* is to be cherished for its spectacular chase climax, with a veritable sea of cop uniforms teeming through the city streets on the tail of our hero's inadvertent anarchist bomber.

Un Chien Andalou (1929)
Buñuel and Dalí's seminal surrealist experiment, a 'public call to assassination' full of infamous images and disjunctive games with time and space. The opening shot of a sliced eyeball still has the power to shock, for all that the film-makers' attacks on social and cinematic norms have otherwise since been assimilated.

A Propos de Nice (1930)
The 25-minute maiden outing of *L'Atalante* director Jean Vigo, also shot by the great Boris Kaufman, twisted the contemporary trend of 'city symphonies' into something much more subversive and unsettling. Cocking a snook at the class-bound playground of the Côte d'Azur, the film teems with mocking camera angles, satirically associative editing and a carnivalesque energy all of its own.

The Fatal Glass of Beer (1933)
'I think I'll go out and milk the elk,' announces WC Fields midway through this gloriously offhand parody of Yukon melodrama, where his prospector Mr Snavely and his wife keep warm to sentimental thoughts of their innocent son's tribulations in the big city. 'And it ain't a fit night out for man nor beast', he points out at least a dozen times.

Meshes of the Afternoon (1942)
An essential bridge from European surrealism to the post-war American avant-garde, Maya Deren's 'trance film' broke new ground in its exploration of dream states and desire, feminist expression, and the ritual of film-making itself. It was beautifully shot by her husband Alexander Hammid, too.

Begone Dull Care (1949)
Building on Len Lye's camera-less animation breakthrough (in 1935's *A Colour Box*) of painting directly on to celluloid, Norman McLaren's 'caprice en couleurs' is pure movement incarnate, a joyous burst of abstract shape and colour dancing in time to an Oscar Peterson ragtime original.

Le Sang des Bêtes (1949)
Georges Franju's most famous short, and one of his most perfectly unflinching visions of human horror: a documentary-like tour of Paris abattoirs shot with a surrealist tenderness and terror. The workers smoke, prod and hack; the beasts spurt, shudder and die.

Duck Amuck (1953)
Daffy Duck (and cartoon 'normality') are undone as his dreams of movie star glory are punctured by a malevolent animator-creator who switches his backdrops, costumes, body-parts and frame positions at whim, until the

EXHILARATION

enraged duck is driven to join the assault on the film form.

Pas de Deux (1962)
Norman McLaren broke ground left and right, making ever-fresh connections between visual movement, music and geometry. This refraction of the dance film captures the flow of a body's movement through stroboscopic multiple exposures of two dancers' silhouettes, who in effect dance with their own trails and shadows. It's ethereally beautiful.

Les Jeux des Anges (1964)
An abstract horror film by Walerian Borowczyk, in which angels are processed through a series of hellish interiors, painted in impressionistic watercolours reminiscent of Bosch or Bacon. The sound design clearly intimates the nightmare of a train journey ferrying prisoners to a concentration camp.

The Hand (1965)
The artist versus power: puppet-master Jiří Trnka's final testament is about an unassuming would-be flower pot-maker terrorised by an imposing, white-gloved hand that demands he fashion sculptures in its image. A simple, cogent fable about totalitarianism, duly banned by the Czech Communist government.

Wavelength (1967)
Michael Snow's renowned formalist/structuralist experiment certainly doesn't feel 'short', but then the term 'featurette' seems to imply a feature-like narrative. And the only 'story'

here is that of the film's single 45-minute fixed-camera zoom, the method as subject. It's the self-reflexive movie-movie stripped to its bare essentials.

The Girl Chewing Gum (1976)
John Smith's superbly witty deconstruction of filmic 'truth' and directorial control, in which he dictates action to a clearly naturalistic East London street scene, toggles the synchronised soundtrack with that from a spatial remove, and generally makes play with the gentleman's presumptions, distinguishing live documentary and re-created fiction. A delightful study.

Powers of Ten (1977)
A simple yet fascinating essay film (by Charles and Ray Eames) on scale and the relative size of things. Like *Wavelength*, it uses the illusion of a constant zoom to widen the frame (increasing the distance by a power of ten every ten seconds) from the human level to the universal, then reverses right in to the sub-atomic particular. Like *Wavelength*, too, it leaves the human perspective on the sidelines.

Tale of Tales (1979)
Yuri Norstein's autobiographical animation is a hymn-like collage of childhood memories, a scrapbook reverie, an interrupted lullaby rich in wonder, terror, innocence and waste. A boy shares his apple with the crows and drifts into daydream... A little wolf carries a baby through the woods; men are wisked away from their women, to return from war as alcoholics;

EXHILARATION

Moving picture
Matthew Vaughn

Director, *Layer Cake*; producer, *Lock, Stock and Two Smoking Barrels*, *Snatch*

It's not a night to remember – more of an afternoon really – when I was about six years old. Until then, cinema for me had only ever been watching Disney movies on a Sunday afternoon in the basement of the old Lumière in Covent Garden. Then one day I went to a friend's house for lunch, and they announced that we were going to the movies. I was expecting *The Love Bug* again, or something similar. So, I'm sitting in the Odeon Kensington and I can clearly remember the Twentieth Century Fox logo appearing and this huge yellow text scrolling up the screen. I thought, 'What is this?' It looked very boring. Then a huge spaceship appeared: it was *Star Wars*. I've never felt so awakened: the characters, the story, the action, the light sabres, everything. I'd never even seen a Western before. When I left the cinema, I said to my friend: 'That's what I want to do.' I don't know if I meant I wanted to be George Lucas or a Jedi knight. Either would have done, really.

and the wind blows… Animation-festival panels have voted it their favourite animated film ever on more than one occasion.

Dimensions of Dialogue (1982)

The masterpiece from Czech animator Jan Svankmajer: a brutally succinct satire on the limits of human interaction, mounting three snapshots of mutually assured destruction – fruit and veg heads chomping one another into common mush; clay lovers parting messily and angrily; two wise men chewing the fat until they foam at the mouth… The logic is devastating.

Street of Crocodiles (1986)

Still the most celebrated puppet play from the inscrutable brothers Quay (Stephen and Timothy), an elusive prowl through a surreal, subliminal world of repetitive, compulsive, dead-end disorders. Based on a short story by Bruno Schulz and set to Lech Jankowski's singing-saw score, it's ravishingly imagined and almost tactile.

The Wrong Trousers (1993)

A criminal penguin casts out Wallace's faithful mutt into the street, then rewires Wallace's techno trousers to mount a daring jewel heist by proxy… Second and best of Aardman's three Wallace and Gromit claymations, this unstoppable pastiche of movies from *The Lodger* to *RoboCop* is testament to director Nick Park's ability to merge retro and modern.

Il Giorno della prima di 'Close Up' (1996)

True to the spirit of Kiarostami's cinephile semi-documentary *Close-Up*, Nanni Moretti's seven-minute short charts his fretting preparations for the opening of said film at Moretti's Nuovo Sacher arthouse cinema in Rome. Across the city – apparently everywhere across the city – *The Lion King* is also opening.

Gasman (1997)

A beautifully elliptical, resonant portrait of two Scottish children's night out with their dad, during which they encounter what seems to be his second family. It's a crisp encapsulation of themes Lynne Ramsay would elaborate on in her feature debut *Ratcatcher*: childhood curiosity, the baffling ways of adults, fractured beauty and life on Scotland's urban edge.

Moving picture
Jill Sprecher

Director/writer, *13 Conversations About One Thing*

It would be Kubrick's *The Killing* for me, a movie that influenced me a lot. It was an amazing experience, seeing that in a New York repertory theatre that also housed a Hungarian theatre troupe, which is gone now. I lost track of time and was completely absorbed in the movie, really on the edge of my seat. I was literally gripping the handles of the seat, and when the lights came up I realised some guy next to me had his hand on my knee. I hadn't even felt it. It was creepy but amazing at the time, to be so sucked into another world like that. I ran out of the theatre on my own, I should add.

Come to Daddy (1997)

The pop promo as horror freak-fest: video and special-effects wunderkind Chris Cunningham's video for Aphex Twin's hardcore techno rumble broke new ground in the world of music videos, with images as unbridled and disturbing as the gruesome street-urchins and albino pod-beastie that terrorise a little old lady around a concrete tower block.

Lifeline (2002)

Victor Erice's ten-minute, monochrome snapshot of time and stasis in a Spanish village, 1940, whose idyllic afternoon rhythms are shattered by the sound of a baby bleeding to death. The outstanding entry in the portmanteau film *Ten Minutes Older: The Trumpet*, the film condenses much of the mood of Erice's masterpiece *The Spirit of the Beehive* into ten radiant minutes.

Boundin' (2004)

A 3-D animated musical short, written, directed, composed and sung by septuagenarian Pixar animator Budd Luckey, and featuring the mythic Jackelope of his home state of Montana. Narrated in lilting rhyming couplets over camerawork that revolves like a merry-go-round, it tells a timeless fable of a bushy-tailed young ram learning to roll with life's ups and downs after being sheared of his dignity.

Regret

---

*‘You know, Billy,
we blew it.’* **Easy Rider**

What might have been

Tony Rayns has a rueful gaze at films that remind us how much we've lost.

Storytelling cinema as we know it now had its origins in the nascent film industries of the 1910s, and the earliest storytelling film-makers very quickly realised that audiences were hungry for wish-fulfilment fantasies. Hollywood pioneer DW Griffith specialised in them for a while: the cavalry rides to the rescue in the nick of time, the young woman is saved from the melting ice-floe, the lovers are reunited.

The flipside of such wish-fulfilment fantasies is regret: the more nuanced feeling that comes with the realisation that a desired outcome is not going to be achieved.

Let's admit at the start that the most common experience of feelings of regret at the movies these days takes the form of resentment that we were suckered into paying money to see something so rancid that it should never have been made, let alone distributed. But consumer satisfaction is not our subject here; we're focusing on movies that are capable of finessing reasonably complex emotional responses from

viewers. Those viewers, that is, who expect something more from their moviegoing experience than utopian solutions to the kinds of problems that remain intractable in real life.

Hollywood nowadays relies on 'happy endings' as much as it did in the 1920s, but it wasn't always so. In the 1930s, as the Great Depression affected virtually all levels of American society, film-makers (especially the ones lucky enough to work for Warner Bros) were emboldened to end their movies on notes of loss, failure and threat. One seminal example is Mervyn LeRoy's *I Am a Fugitive from a Chain Gang*, which closes with the title character, played by Paul Muni, slipping away into the darkness and whispering that he can survive only by stealing: no justice, no redemption, no hope in sight. The viewer is expected to leave the cinema alarmed, chastened and, yes, regretful. In that movie the Muni character is a victim of circumstance – essentially, an injured innocent. But around the

Life slipping away: **About Schmidt**

Domestic bliss on the surface, trouble brewing beneath it: **Far from Heaven**

same time, the studios began making biopics about Prohibition racketeers and other actual criminals, all of whom met bad ends even before the Hays Code mandated that no crime should go unpunished. However villainous the gangsters played by George Raft, James Cagney and Edward G Robinson, though, there was always a sense that they'd once had the potential to turn out better: their comeuppances were underscored by a regretful sense that their lives had been wasted. This element was conspicuously missing when Hollywood returned to the Prohibition era in such movies as Roger Corman's *The St Valentine's Day Massacre* and Brian De Palma's *Scarface*.

Ill-fated vamps and femmes fatales had been ubiquitous in Hollywood movies from the get-go, but it was also in the 1930s that movies began dealing with unrequited love and unconsummated relationships. Director Josef von Sternberg led the way. After making several 1920s classics about doomed quests for

dignity in extremely adverse circumstances (*The Salvation Hunters*, *Underworld*, *The Last Command* and others), he went to Germany to shoot *The Blue Angel* – the archetypal account of a stolid bourgeois man brought low by his uncontrollable passion for a heartless nightclub singer – and returned to Hollywood with Marlene Dietrich. The first of their six Hollywood films together was *Morocco*, which ends with Marlene kicking off her slingbacks and setting off into the Sahara in pursuit of Gary Cooper, the man with a past who has opted for the French Foreign Legion over a future in her adoring arms. None of the subsequent Sternberg-Dietrich movies ended with a conventional romantic clinch; together, they added up to a virtual catalogue of the ways that 'love' can be used to mask sadistic and masochistic impulses of all stripes. As such, they paved the way for everything from *Gone With the Wind* (in which Scarlett O'Hara's closing burst of optimism doesn't quite eclipse the fact that Rhett Butler, the man of her dreams played by Clark Gable, has just walked out of her life) to *Casablanca* (which ends with Humphrey Bogart on the arm of Claude Rains rather than Ingrid Bergman).

Regret is usually not the dominant emotion experienced by viewers of the *films noirs* of the 1940s: the procession of amoral no-hopers and ruthless schemers in such movies as *Double Indemnity*, *Out of the Past* and *Gun Crazy* tends to send audiences out in much the state that Aristotle prescribed for consumers of Greek tragedy, purged of pity and terror in a grand catharsis. But regret creeps back into the picture in the Eisenhower era of the 1950s, very noticeably in the melodramas directed by Douglas Sirk which later entranced the German director Rainer Werner Fassbinder. Writing about Sirk in the 1970s (nearly twenty years after Sirk retired from his successful Hollywood career), Fassbinder was the first to note that a romantic 'happy ending' could be unbearably poignant – precisely because viewers would perceive it as an impossible outcome. This perception went on to spawn a thousand 'film studies' theses on the bitter ironies underpinning such Sirk movies as *All That Heaven Allows*, *Imitation of Life* and *Written on the Wind*.

Fassbinder himself was always more angry than regretful, and the movies in which he tried to reinvent the Hollywood studio ethos in modernist, German terms generally focused on victim figures trapped in vicious circles of exploitation, prejudice and corruption; this is true even of the Fassbinder films that directly evoke Sirk, such as *Fear Eats the Soul*, which 'translates' the forbidden love between a middle-class widow and her gardener (from *All That Heaven Allows*) into the 'scandalous' marriage of a char-woman to a Moroccan immigrant labourer. But when this baton was later picked up by the gay indie film-maker Todd Haynes in *Far from Heaven*, in which an idyllic 1950s marriage is torn apart by the husband's homosexuality and the wife turns for solace to a lover who happens to be black, regrets make a storming comeback. Haynes' film may be an attack on the hypocrisies of the 1950s, but it's also a regretful elegy for those who suffered through years when neither open homosexuality nor miscegenation was commonly thinkable.

It goes without saying that movies have changed since the death of the studio system in the 1960s. It's arguable that the American 'blockbusters' that still dominate the global film market (everywhere, that is, except South Korea, which we'll come back to) rest on the same structural and dramatic principles that once shaped films made by the studios: but it's also indisputable that the qualities of wit, subtlety and emotional nuance found in many old studio movies have gone missing. This is true even of genre movies by first-division cinephile directors like Ridley Scott, Jonathan Demme, Martin Scorsese and Michael Mann. Nobody looks to the likes of *Blade Runner*, *The Silence of the Lambs*, *GoodFellas* or *Heat* for an emotionally nuanced experience.

But feelings of regret did resurface in a rather different form in the 'counter-cultural' movies of the late 1960s and 1970s. When the biker/drug-runner heroes of *Easy Rider* went 'looking for America', their failure to locate it was presented as poignant; the fact that they could be blown away by a shotgun blast from a redneck thug was less an indictment of the Old South than a lament for the extinction of idealism in modern times. This forlorn mood triggered a series of movies, several directed by Bob Rafelson, most starring Jack Nicholson, which mourned the fate of losers and under-achievers in post-Vietnam America: films such as *Five Easy Pieces*, *The Last Detail*, *The King of Marvin Gardens* and *Drive, He Said*. *Easy Rider* also triggered a series of road movies in which geographical journeys mapped spiritual desolation; the best examples were Monte Hellman's *Two-Lane Blacktop* and Wim Wenders' *Kings of the Road*. While these movies played like alternative 'state of the nation' reports, they found unlikely parallels in Roger Corman's exactly contemporary series of adaptations from the stories and poems of Edgar Allan Poe, in which 'the repressed' always returned to wipe out the protagonist, leaving everyone else sadder, wiser and, of course, regretful. As if recognising the secret kinship between his Gothic genre movies and the mood of the counter-culture, Corman eventually combined the two forms in *Wild Angels*, *The Trip* and *Gas-s-s-s, or it became necessary to destroy the world in order to save it.*

True to stereotype, European movies are generally less brash and more nuanced than

American movies, despite the best efforts of Luc Besson and Jean-Pierre Jeunet (among others) to reverse the trend. Regret is an emotion that was regularly conjured by the late François Truffaut and Jacques Demy (Truffaut's *Jules and Jim* and Demy's *Lola* offer bittersweet experiences of lasting intensity) and it still looms large in much of Eric Rohmer's output, albeit in the rather limited form of an ageing male's regrets for his waning appeal to young women. Many of Ingmar Bergman's films are pitched in the key of regret; the 'death of god' trilogy, comprising *Through a Glass Darkly*, *Winter Light* and *The Silence*, went further into existential-expressionist gloom than any other work of the 1960s, and Bergman's way back into the struggles to exist and relate in a godless world – via *Persona*, *Hour of the Wolf* and subsequent films – was invariably marked by regretful feelings of loss and missed opportunities. The same goes for all of Federico Fellini's best films, although in a somewhat more frivolous register; does anything evoke a mood of regret more poignantly than Nino Rota's scores for *La Dolce Vita*, *8½* and *Juliet of the Spirits*?

The history of world cinema is almost as vast as the reservoir of regrets we all carry within us, and space here is limited – and so it's time to interrupt this scattershot survey by naming a few personal favourites. For me, the highest expressions of regret anywhere in cinema appear in films by the great Japanese director Kenji Mizoguchi, who entered the film industry at the start of the 1920s and began making masterpieces in the late 1930s. His *Story of the Late Chrysanthemums*, set in Meiji Japan, centres on the illicit love of a servant girl for an aspiring kabuki actor. Her support and sacrifices eventually enable him to achieve greatness on the stage, but his new-found fame cuts off all possibility of further relations between them. This kind of poignant irony derives from a Japanese stage tradition (a genre of tragic melodrama known as *shimpa*), and Mizoguchi was consciously running counter to the spirit of the late 1930s by embracing it. In his post-war classics *Ugetsu Monogatari* and *Sansho Dayo*, though, Mizoguchi transcends literary and stage sources with endings that locate personal tragedies and losses within a larger frame in which life goes

'Ill-fated vamps had been ubiquitous from the get-go, but it was also in the 1930s that movies began dealing with unrequited love.'

on regardless. In both cases the effect is almost unbearably moving.

I also look East for some of the most potent experiences of these emotions in recent cinema. In South Korea, where the film industry has reinvented itself (with remarkable success, both at home and abroad) since the end of militarist governments, the usual battle is being fought between big-budget schlock and more personal kinds of cinema. In this context, the US-trained Hong Sang-Soo has established himself as the reigning poet of missed opportunities and alternative possibilities, with a particular focus on the absurdity of male pride. His debut feature *The Day a Pig Fell into the Well* cross-cuts through the lives of a small group of city-dwellers, emphasising (without malice) their failures, their fears and their capacities for self-delusion. This and his more recent films provoke regret in its wryest form. And in Taiwan, where the film culture is inevitably dominated by the towering figures of Hou Hsiao-Hsien, Edward Yang and Tsai Ming-Liang, I'd single out a comparatively unsung movie by Yi Zhiyan called *Lonely Hearts Club*. It looks back to the emotional dynamics of Sirk's melodramas, as filtered through the modernist variations of Fassbinder and Haynes. An unhappily married woman develops an unfeasible crush on an office boy many years her junior, never remotely suspecting the reason he's unattached is that he's gay. The film spends half its length following the boy through his rites of passage,

Bitter-sweet odyssey: **2046**

which include one disastrous wrong turn: he impulsively steals a wallet from a neighbour, and his life spirals down in consequence. I can't remember ever silently wishing a character in a movie not to make a mistake more fervently than I did when I first saw Yi's film.

Regret in 20 films

The Last Laugh (1924)
Murnau's mythically resonant tale of an aging hotel doorman, symbolically stripped of his peaked cap and epaulettes and demoted to basement lavatory attendant, is a tragic tale of status and its loss.

The Devil Is a Woman (1935)
A cigarette factory girl is loved by two men – a young revolutionary and an older military man – who both submit to the agonies of being rejected by her. It was Sternberg's last film with Dietrich.

The Loyal 47 Ronin of the Genroku Era (1941-42)
Made during the build-up to war, Mizoguchi's tragic retelling of a traditional tale – loyal feudal samurai avenge the death of their clan lord – is an elegant and technically accomplished marvel.

Portrait of Jennie (1948)
William Dieterle's tale of a love that transcends space and time, as a struggling artist meets, falls in love with and is inspired by a strangely ethereal girl – whom he eventually realises is the spirit of a woman long dead.

This Whole Life of Mine (1951)
This superbly observed adaptation of a short story by Lao She is probably the finest work of actor/director Shi Hui. An old man dying on the winter

streets of Beijing reviews a lifetime of defeats, betrayals and humiliations.

Suddenly, Last Summer (1953)
Mankiewicz's outrageous medodramatic shocker touches on madness, homosexual prostitution, incest, disease and cannibalism, with enough imagery to sustain an American Lit seminar for months.

Eaux d'Artifice (1953)
A mesmerising short film by Kenneth Anger. An 18th-century woman wanders through a water garden where the fountains appear to be moving to, and taking on the mood of, Vivaldi's *Four Seasons*.

Vertigo (1958)
Hitchcock's brilliant but despicably cynical view of human obsession and the tendency of those in love to try to manipulate each other. James Stewart's detective is a lesson in strained psychological stability.

An Autumn Afternoon (1963)
An elderly widower marries off his daughter in Ozu's poised reminder of passing time and the inevitable approach of mortality. It's all the more poignant since it was the great director's last film.

The Private Life of Sherlock Holmes (1970)
The most moving and least embittered of Billy Wilder's films. Holmes foresakes his emotional life to become a thinking machine, turning from a fallible romantic into a disillusioned one.

The Birth of a Nation (1973)
Klaus Wyborny's avant-garde landmark defines cinema as a 'nation' that has acquired rules, laws and hierarchies before it has even been physically mapped out. This is film-making of a rare wit, highlighting the redundancy of closed systems, whether social or cinematic.

The Spirit of the Beehive (1973)
Set soon after Franco's victory, Victor Erice's film sees rural Spain as a wasteland of inactivity thrown into relief by the industriousness of bees in their hives. A haunting mood piece that works its spell through patterns of sound and image.

Badlands (1974)
An impressive directorial debut, Terrence Malick's complex perspective on an otherwise simple *Bonnie and Clyde* plot focuses on the psychological motivation of his young 'innocents'.

Mirror (1974)
In this personal history of his country, Andrei Tarkovsky intercuts autobiographical episodes with startling documentary footage, lovingly building a world where the domestic expends into the political.

Rouge (1987)
A courtesan who died for love in the 1930s roams present-day Hong Kong as a wraith, because she has failed to meet her lover in the after-life. Stanley Kwan's satirical portrait of '80s Hong Kong is an elegant and deeply felt movie about the transience of things – especially love.

King of the Children (1987)
An unschooled young man, one of the countless victims of Mao's Cultural Revolution, begins to see the possibilities of a life beyond the parameters of traditional education. Chen Kaige's masterpiece.

REGRET

A steady look at life's problems: Edward Yang's masterful **A One and a Two**

Good Men, Good Women (1995)

Hou Hsiao-Hsien's look at recent Taiwanese history blends the personal with the political in a multi-layered exploration of changing cultural ideals, haunted memories, and the joys and pains of love.

Roadmovie (2002)

In Kim In-Sik's remarkable debut feature, a ruined stockbroker who has been rejected by his wife discovers a community among the winos of Seoul. After embarking on a cross-country trip with an ultra-macho, one-time celebrity mountaineer, he realises he's the focus of an all-male love story.

Bad Education (2004)

Pedro Almodóvar's tragedy is a tale of a tortuous love triangle refracted through three time periods and myriad layers of make-believe. An ever-shifting kaleidoscope in which identity, desire and power are in permanent disarray.

Brokeback Mountain (2005)

Love on a mountain top. Ang Lee's adaptation of E Annie Proulx's short story is a tale of forbidden love between a ranch-hand and a rodeo cowboy who forge a lifelong connection in the mountains of Wyoming. As visually beautiful as it is affecting.

REGRET

The humanist touch

Wally Hammond looks back in awe at the films of a true master.

Charlie Chaplin said some rum things in his time, but when answering the question of who was the greatest film director of all time, he was spot on. He said: 'He's a Frenchman. And his name is Jean Renoir'.

Renoir is co-incident with the cinema of his time. In 1897, aged two, he attended – and visited the projection room of – the free cinema in Dufayel's department store in Paris, two years after the Lumière Brothers fixed the finishing screws to their new cinematograph. Abandoning pottery, he made his first film, the Chaplin-esque 1924 silent *La Fille de l'Eau* (or so he says in his 1974 biography), simply to make a star of his beautiful young wife Catherine Hessling, model to his celebrated painter father Auguste. Having 'got the bug', he continued to make films – the co-operative *Le Crime de Monsieur Lange*, the pastoral *Partie*

de Campagne, the internationalist war film *La Grande Illusion*, the tragic-comic *La Règle du Jeu* among them – until 1971, citing the gammy leg he sustained through a German bullet in the trenches in 1915 as his reason finally to quit.

So what was special about his cinema? There are many aspects. As a very young man, Renoir had been a fan of the American 'action' film, the dynamism of Mack Sennett and, later, the formal invention and breathtaking scope of DW Griffith, and resolved to make a French cinema purged of the stale melodrama inherited from the theatreland of the 'Boulevard de Crime' and freed from the restrictions of the literary adaptation. So it's ironic that it was with a literary adaptation, of Emile Zola's scandalous tale of Nana, a Second Empire prostitute, that he found his feet. *Nana* showed up Hessling's limitations as an actress, and lacks the master's later characteristic fluency, but it shows his nascent ability to modulate between light and dark, using acute accumulation of details to flesh out character in naturalistic performance.

But it was with the beginning of sound cinema that Renoir's real, collaborative genius began to show. The story of *La Chienne*, his first great, real-location 'talkie', made in 1931, may be more familar from Fritz Lang's *Scarlet Street*. Here he continued to develop his relationship with the great actor Michel Simon – he starred in many of Renoir's early works, notably *Boudu Sauvé des Eaux* – who invests great pathos in the role of the duped bank clerk. His next film, the Simenon adapatation *La Nuit du Carrefour*, could well be the foggiest film in world cinema; it also vies with Hawks' *The Big Sleep* for the crown of the thriller most difficult to follow. But it's a beautifully atmospheric and eerie essay in mystery and character, and with Jacques Becker, the assistant director, Renoir had formed probably the most fruitful of his series of collaborations, a pairing that lasted for eight films, including many of his greatest masterpieces (*Le Crime de Monsieur Lange*, *Boudu*, his extraordinarily popular *La Grande Illusion*), ending with *La Marseillaise*, the culmination of the leftist 'popular front' movie movement, which was released on the eve of the outbreak of war and the start of Renoir's exile from France. Such was their chemistry that, in the featurette *Partie de Campagne*, they could take a little Maupassant tale of a country jaunt and magic from it one of the cinema's most supreme evocations of the presence and transience of love and life.

Renoir's films provide fascinating insights to one of the world's greatest 'humanist' directors; they also constitute a terrific case study in cinematic progression, the accomplishment of an energetic and tireless innovator and stylistic experimenter. You can feel the cinematic representation of the world grow broader and richer with each passing movie.

'The history of the cinema may be summarised as the war of the filmmaker against the industry', said Renoir. The director took his own battle for independence and a personal vision to America in 1941 to make *Swamp Water*. Ten films were to follow, ending with 1971's *Le Petit Théâtre de Jean Renoir*. Generally, the quality of the work in this second period doesn't rival his extraordinary 1930s output, but that's not to say there aren't some lovely films. Maybe it was the relative freedom Renoir experienced making his story of a family of po' sharecroppers' fight against 'nature', *The Southerner*, that enabled him to express so poignantly their reality and their specific relationship to their formative environment. I have a great liking, too, for Robert Ryan's softening coastguard in *The Woman on the Beach*, made a year later in 1946.

In 1955, Renoir celebrated his return home with the nostalgic drama *French Cancan*, set in the Montmartre theatres. Before that he made a trip to India to adapt a Rumer Godden novel, *The River* – the river itself being one of the director's central and most enduring images. It was to be his last great film: a tender, lyrical, quietly passionate meditation on life's cyclical nature. It was also his first colour film. Renoir died of a heart attack in Beverly Hills in 1979.

Moving picture
Valeria Golino

Actress, *Storia d'Amore*, *Rain Man*, *Hot Shots*, *Respiro*

It's not a huge story, but it was beautiful to be there, so I hope I can convey that. In the middle of the River Tiber, in the middle of Rome, there's a little island called Isola Latina, with old houses, and every summer they screen movies. And there, I watched a very bad copy, but big, with very bad sound, of *La Dolce Vita* – which for some reason I always thought as a minor Fellini film. 8½ is a masterpiece, but not *La Dolce Vita*. But I watched it again with all these Romans, and it was raining – so hard that the Tiber started to rise up to the island and flood the movie theatre. The water was lapping the chairs, people were crouching on their seats, there were loudspeakers saying 'You have to leave the island', but of course nobody wanted to miss the film's ending, which is gorgeous. Mastroianni, and the little girl who's like his lost innocence, calling him from the other side, and he says 'I can't hear you', because there are the waves, no? 'I can't hear you, sorry, goodbye', and he turns. And so the end of the movie, with our socks completely wet, we went off to our Vespas, and we thought: 'That's a masterpiece'. It was one of the most beautiful nights in Rome.

REGRET

The *bigger* picture

Auburn verdict

Lisa Mullen talks to Julianne Moore, one of the finest actresses working today.

Unless you count the Silver Bear she got at the Berlin Film Festival in 2003 for her role in Stephen Daldry's *The Hours* (a prize she shared, in any case, with her co-stars Meryl Streep and Nicole Kidman), or the Tribute to Independent Vision she received at the Sundance Festival in 2001, Moore has yet to win a really major award despite being hailed repeatedly as one of the most exceptional talents in the business. Still, she's walked up enough red carpets to be an old hand as a nominee. And yes, she still lets herself get a little bit excited. 'It's a different kind of experience,' she admits sagely. 'It's like, when you have your first child, everything's brand new, and when you have your second child you know what to expect, but that doesn't make the emotion any less intense.'

In person, she's as sharp as a knife, warm and friendly. She focuses on every question she's asked, possibly hoping for an interesting line of enquiry to help pass the time, and certainly not afraid to disagree with a stupid one. You get the feeling she's spent a lot of her life talking to people who are less intelligent than she is. Only when she smiles does that spooky light stream out of her the same way it does when she's on screen. Luckily, she smiles a lot.

Directors love her for this. Not only is she subtle, clever and a connoisseur of film, but she generates her own electricity as well. Bart Freundlich, who directed her in 1997's *The Myth of Fingerprints*, told her: 'There's a duality to your personality that I really like. When you smile, your face completely transforms.' He became her partner, and the father of her children; other directors have had to settle for casting her as often as possible. Paul Thomas Anderson has used her twice as the emotional anchor of an elaborate ensemble piece (in *Boogie Nights* and *Magnolia*); Todd Haynes, who gave her her first big role in *Safe*, wrote *Far from Heaven* with her specifically in mind.

In the latter film, Moore plays Cathy, a 1950s housewife undergoing a personal crisis. Cathy's

struggles to come to terms with her husband's repressed homosexuality, and her growing love for a working-class black man, clash bitterly with the social norms of the time.

Haynes set out to make a homage to the 1950s melodramas of Douglas Sirk, and as well as going for the full three hankie effect, he faithfully reproduced Sirk's peculiar colours, the old-fashioned lighting, the overwrought music and even some of the sets. Sirk used his bread-and-butter 'weepie' commissions to smuggle social commentary into American cinemas; Haynes used his film-geek homage to point up, among other things, the internal tensions of Sirk's super-real approach and the hypocrisy that can trip up even the best intentions. Still, his cerebral intentions are overtaken by the film's sheer emotional punch. In *Far from Heaven*, the plight of Cathy, her husband Frank (Dennis Quaid) and her gardener Raymond (Dennis Haysbert) may have a comic inevitability for those who know the genre that Haynes is recreating; yet ultimately these characters are even more tragic than those of the 1950s originals.

Like Sirk's films, *Far from Heaven* refers constantly to nature, and what constitutes 'natural' human behaviour – although Haynes is doubtful that these ideas hold any salvation for his characters, and shows this plainly in every scrupulously designed shot. Casting Moore was a masterstroke, because she can operate within this kind of knowing artifice, yet still convey the honest-to-goodness emotion that brings the film to life. 'The way Cathy falls in love with Raymond is interesting to me', she says, 'because it dawns on her in a really organic way.' Haynes elaborates further. 'The term 'melodrama' is used so pejoratively nowadays. We see method acting and authenticity as a superior form of narrative. But what people forget is that authenticity is just as subject to the specific codes of its time.'

Moore agrees. 'I think that method's been misrepresented, really. What method's saying basically is, create a feeling, and follow that actual emotion. It's important that there be a level of truth in what you're doing, because that's what makes it interesting for people. They're connecting with their feeling. It's about the audience, it's about representing who the audience is in the character. The personal is the most important thing; what's most intense and

personal to me is the thing that will resonate, I think, universally.'

Theorising about how to achieve this as an actor is something she associates more with drama school than real work, though. 'Since my kids have been born, I haven't really been able to indulge in that stuff', she laughs. 'Which is also kind of great. You have no time, you just have to find a way to move into something quickly. All that stuff you used to indulge in just goes out the window.' While she's immune to the frothier aspects of fame, that she dismisses as 'empty of meaning', she does have the clout to move a production to the city of her choice, and will admit that, 'the one benefit of fame that you have is access to more material, which is what you want.'

She's now 45 years old, and given that she has only a narrow window before her options close down again, it must be frustrating that full-blown success has been such a long time coming. Certainly, she's angry about the way the cynical blockbuster aesthetic has taken over the industry. 'There was a decision at some point in Hollywood that the audience for film, the broadest audience, were young, international males between 18 and 24', she says, ticking off the points on her fingers. 'So, the movie that plays in Japan, that plays in Germany, that plays in California, that plays in Australia, that goes everywhere and doesn't need to be translated, that's an action movie. And that leaves everything else in the dust. Everything that's dependent on language and nuance and anything that's difficult, that's not the easy moneymaker… But I'm interested in characters that are about who we are and how we live. I'm very drawn to ordinary characters in domestic situations, because I think that's what our lives are about generally.'

Which brings us back to Sirk's 'women's pictures'. 'One of the things that you see in this film particularly', Moore argues, 'is the ability of the men to pursue their desires somehow, and the inability of women, societally, to be able to express theirs. And I think that still does hold true to a certain degree. In terms of social mores and the rules that we follow, I think that women are more often left holding the bag than men are.' So Moore will keep taking on the little domestic dramas about housewives, the cinema of 'blood, tears, violence, hate, death and love', as Douglas Sirk put it. You know: girl stuff.

The route of the problem

Jason Wood maps the journeys of disappointment in road movies.

A road movie entails the making, by one or more characters, of a journey – a journey for adventure, redemption or escape from the constricting norms of society. As an expression of America's fascination with the road and, by extension, the mythology of freedom, the road movie ranks among US cinema's most enduring contributions to contemporary film culture.

However, on closer inspection the dream of the road is typically tarnished, a dead end in which love and dreams are dashed and hopes vanquished by deadening reality. Road movies tend to begin with the expression of a search for self by an individual or individuals disenfranchised from society on economic, racial or sexual grounds; but the journey's end rarely brings peace or contentment, and most likely further suffering or even death. As eloquently put in Hal Hartley's *Simple Men* (described by the director as 'a road movie with one flat tyre'), 'There's no such thing as adventure. There's no such thing as romance. There's only trouble and desire.'

The evolution of the road movie in US cinema runs in close convoy with the development of the motorcar itself – indeed, directors including DW Griffith used them to provide effective travelling shots. Such shots, later framed to include the car windscreen, would become one of the classic road movie motifs. Cars were also, from their invention, incorporated into film narrative as a way for couples to elope and gangsters to escape; the road theme is central to John Ford's *The Grapes of Wrath*, which deals with enforced social migration and the search for work in Depression-era America.

Built to traverse the US after it entered World War II, the freeways would come to play a fundamental role in road movies thematically, and as a central element in a distinctive iconography (all those recurrent shots of a vehicle speeding towards distant vistas). The glory of their construction was tempered by social fragmentation, as families were split by the need to travel greater distances to the munitions factories where they worked. Once the war ended, many of the GIs who came back from overseas found themselves unable to regain their place in a shifting society, and alienation and disenchantment crept into the American psyche. As a certain cultural psychosis took hold, films such as *Detour* and *They Live by Night* mined this terrain, with the pursuit of dreams becoming the stuff of nightmares. As idealism soured, so the protagonists of road movies became not just outsiders, but criminals (as in such later films as *Bonnie and Clyde* and *Badlands*) and, with a pinch of *film noir* in its fateful encounters and dead end fatalism, the road snaked its way to death and destruction.

Then came *Easy Rider*. Advancing the politically rebellious spirit of *Bonnie and Clyde*, it further crystallised what *Driving Visions'* (a book-length study of the road movie) author David Laderman calls 'a sense of postmodern anxiety and restlessness'. A major work in

Moving picture
Tareque Masud

Director, writer, *The Clay Bird*

As a boy in Bangladesh, I studied in a madrasa, an Islamic religious school, where we were forbidden to see films or draw any living being. That possibly made me more curious about cinema. But my first encounter with film was very disappointing. A roving open-air projection team came to our village to show a film, but because of a technical fault the projectors weren't working properly. So it wasn't until I was in college that I saw my first film. A friend took me to a screening in a small, ramshackle room; it was organised by one of the film societies that were very active then. They were showing Robert Flaherty's documentary *Louisiana Story*, and I was overwhelmed that film could be so interesting. I'd thought that films were only full of songs and dancing! I became an obsessive film-society member, and that eventually led me to film-making.

Happy end? Not likely: **Gloria**

American counterculture cinema that used such advances in technology as more mobile cameras, the film, for many, marked the moment when the road movie became a distinct genre. Others stop short of conferring full genre status, and in any case, road movies clearly intersect with less disputable categories. Examples include the buddy movie (*Thunderbolt and Lightfoot*), the comedy (*Planes, Trains and Automobiles*) and the horror film (*Near Dark*). With its cocktail of exterior long shots, intense interior close-ups, troubled relationships and attention to American mythology, the road movie has often been explained as the junction of *film noir* and the Western.

What's clear is that *Easy Rider*, in which a trio of anti-authoritarian bikers go in search of the real America but are unable to 'find it anywhere', cast a long shadow over the road movies that proliferated in the 1970s and '80s. Monte Hellman's *Two-Lane Blacktop* and Richard Sarafian's *Vanishing Point* are two emblematic films that trailed in the wake of *Easy Rider*'s exhaust fumes. Similarly, Hellman and Sarafian, with their off-kilter, out-of-synch heroes, were instrumental in refuelling the road

movie renaissance of the 1990s. Tapping into the genre's propensity for nihilistic cool and the iconography of cultural isolation, directors such as Jim Jarmusch and Gus Van Sant cooked up a new breed of existentialist traveller for whom the journey itself frequently outweighed the destination.

Other film-makers during the '90s gave their road movies a more political purpose, confronting the conflicting social forces bearing down on their various outsiders. Ridley Scott's *Thelma & Louise*, a rare example in what is almost exclusively male terrain of a road movie with female leads, examined sexual politics alongside automotive fetishism. Compromised by its debated denouement in which the titular heroines take their own lives, Scott's film is nonetheless an explicitly feminist Hollywood work. The following year saw Gregg Araki's remarkable *The Living End*, an important film in the New Queer cinema of the '90s, in which two HIV-positive outlaws go on the run after shooting a cop. Araki's film, which makes an instructive companion piece to the series of serial killer road movies that also unfortunately included *Kalifornia* and

Natural Born Killers, seems primarily to be influenced by Godard's *Pierrot le Fou*.

To sum up, it's vital to note that the road movie is not an exclusively American domain. It has been used by film-makers across the globe as a way to explore national identity, confront social and political issues and express disenchantment with the status quo. Examples from Europe include Fellini's *La Strada*, Alain Tanner's *Messidor* and Andrew Kotting's *Gallivant*; while on a broader international canvas, George Miller's *Mad Max*, Fernando Solanas' *El Viaje*, Kyun-Dong Yeo's *Out to the World* and Ismael Ferroukhi's *Le Grand Voyage* have all performed similar functions. Recent years have seen a notable exploration of road movie topography by Latin American film-makers, with Alfonso Cuarón's *Y tu mamá también*, Walter Salles' *The Motorcycle Diaries* and Carlos Sorin's *Bombón el perro* rolling up in quick succession.

Directors working outside the US have also frequently reformulated the American road movie as a way to sustain a dialogue with the notion of American imperialism and the pan-global export of American culture. Wim Wenders, a director so beholden to road movies that he named his production company after them, considered this fully in his *Kings of the Road*, wherein a character remarks, 'The Yanks have even colonised our unconscious.'

Critics' choice
Jiltings

The End of the Affair

(1999, US/Ger) *d* Neil Jordan. *cast* Ralph Fiennon, Julianne Moore, Stephen Rea, Ian Hart.

The rancorous diatribe of a jilted writer who loses his passionate lover to God.

Fatal Attraction

(1987, Can) *d* Adrian Lyne. *cast* Glenn Close, Michael Douglas, Anne Archer, Ellen Foley.

New York attorney enjoys illicit weekend fling, gives woman the brush off, bunny gets topped.

The First Wives Club

(1996, US) *d* Hugh Wilson. *cast* Goldie Hawn, Bette Midler, Diane Keaton, Stockard Channing, Dan Hedaya.

Three former college friends plot revenge on the husbands wholeft them for younger women.

Four Weddings and a Funeral

(1993, US) *d* Mike Newell. *cast* Hugh Grant, Andie MacDowell, Kristin Scott Thomas, James Fleet.

Hugh Grant has dumped heartbroken Anna Chancellor and ends up with Andie MacDowell – which serves him right.

The French Lieutenant's Woman

(1981, GB) *d* Karel Reisz. *cast* Meryl Streep, Jeremy Irons, Hilton McRae, Emily Morgan.

Victorian fossil hunter breaks off engagement to moneyed totty to take up with mad Meryl.

The Graduate

(1967, US) *d* Mike Nichols. *cast* Anne Bancroft, Dustin Hoffman, Katharine Ross, William Daniels.

The most parodied jilting in film history, as a frantic Dustin hammers on glass to stop the wedding of the girl he loves.

High Fidelity

(1988, US/Can) *d* Stephen Frears. *cast* John Cusack, Iben Hjejle, Jack Black, Tim Robbins.

Jilted by a lover, Rob runs us through his most memorable break-ups.

Intermission

(2003, Ire/GB/US) *d* John Crowley. *cast* Colin Farrell, Shirley Henderson, Kelly Macdonald.

A jilted fiancée lets herself go to the extent that she grows a moustache of shame.

Jane Eyre

(1995, GB/It/Fr/US) *d* Franco Zeffirelli. *cast* Charlotte Gainsbourg, William Hurt, Anna Paquin.

The wedding is interrupted by a lawyer pointing out that Rochester is already married.

Kill Bill

(2003, US) *d* Quentin Tarantino. *cast* Uma Thurman, Julie Dreyfuss, Michael Bowen.

The bride (Thurman) isn't just jilted at the altar, lover Bill initiates a bloodbath and puts her in a coma. Not very gentlemanly.

REGRET

Locked in: **The Criminal**

'See you at Mass, Johnny'

Iain Sinclair gets to grips with a gritty film by Joseph Losey.

Films, stored and edited in memory, are not the simple occasions they seem to be. Marzipan nostalgia for vanished fleapits is an ugly conceit; a sentimental attachment to a better life, an easier world. But that's not how it works, not on the ground. Not in a London where identity is never resolved and the polarities of geography and cultural influence shift by the minute. The drift out of one territory into the next, one political allegiance to an even worse alternative, is registered by skid marks left in fogged celluloid. In charity shop cassettes that shudder on exposure. In fluctuating sound levels. Memories are not accessed in cavernous, smoke-filled buildings, not any more. Viewings are private. You interrogate the favoured scene, the line of smart dialogue, the cut of a coat. What was once a seamless progression, the guilty dream somebody was having on your behalf, is now dirty evidence; the surveillance footage of pain and loss.

I came to Dalston for the first time in 1961 to track down a poorly-released feature by the exiled American leftist Joseph Losey. My own exile, from industrial South Wales, had taken me to a film school in Electric Avenue, Brixton. I relished the anonymity of pollarded avenues, makeshift chapels of exotic allegiance, street markets peddling pulp paperbacks. Navigation of the city depended on finding the places where films were shown. *Touch of Evil* as the ballast in a double-bill at the Paris Pullman, South Kensington. (A scrap of rootless London that Polanski identified for the token exteriors of *Repulsion*: Italian restaurants, hairdressers soliciting endorsement.) *Breathless* at the Academy in Oxford Street. *L'Avventura* loitering on the King's Road and looking so bleached-blonde, so enervated, even then. Remorseless

Bergman, thumbprints of the absence of god, at the top of the hill: the Everyman, Hampstead. *Rio Bravo*, a casual pick-up, walking home through Stockwell. Ritual gunshots that would, in years to come, leak into the local topography. Two, three films a day. Mostly accessed by the Northern Line. The connections between cinemas taking years to confirm.

Darkest Dalston was *The Criminal*. Typecasting, even then. This journey, my original Hackney excursion, involved a suspension of everything I thought I knew about London. The disorientation, crossing the river, affected my viewing of Losey's film. It became a screen through which I saw a city of shadows. Stanley Baker, who played the armed robber, Johnny Bannion, was of interest. He'd got away from the Rhondda and attacked the layers and potentialities of the metropolis with a physical hunger that critics called 'American': enraged, in-your-face, finding the right gesture. Losey, before he used Baker for the first time in *Blind Date*, said that he'd been aware of him for years but had resisted the pitch, leaving this emphatically working-class Welshman to another blacklisted exile, Cy Endfield. *Hell Drivers*, a cluster of egos and bad roads (conveniently close to the studio), is Home Counties *noir* at its best. Baker's heavy eyebrows, in full arch, suggest Nye Bevan.

The Criminal is so much more than it says on the label. A 'baroque realist' prison drama with a vestigial heist plot tacked on. The romance element, involving Margit Saad, is a smokescreen to disguise the overwhelming maleness, the banter and bonding of the prison seminary. The random continuity stems from the thirty-five minutes hacked out of the delivered cut. But even this works in Losey's favour: life outside prison is a hallucination, the women no more real than the sellotaped pin-ups on a trustee's wall. The budget, as David Caute points out in his exemplary book on Losey, was £60,000. (Not much more than the amount lifted in the racetrack robbery at Hurst Park.) Caute is very good on contracts, budgets, expense accounts. He understands that film production is essentially a machine for manipulating credit (very much like stolen paintings now). The old legends of Mafia money laundries are all true, but that's just the start of it.

There's so much happening off-screen that it's astonishing how well *The Criminal* coheres.

Moving picture
Jan Hrebejk

Co-writer, director, *Divided We Fall*

I saw *Billy Elliot* for the first time when it came to the Czech Republic, and it's the kind of film that is very near to me that I would like to make. I do love Tarkovsky and Bergman, but I just wouldn't know where to start trying to make films like theirs. It's a human comedy, and I like films that have a humorous quality, but a humour that contains a certain sadness. Very early on it raised an important subject, one very relevant to the Czech Republic. It's about living in some kind of situation that is limiting you. Like in the film, to know that your father or brothers will never be anything else but miners. And you come from a place where the mines are being closed one after another. The scene when the father decides to go against the strike and go to work – that was a very strong moment for me. All the characters in the film – the father, the dancing trainer, but also all the minor characters – have depth, and I like that. Watching the film, I felt that I would have given anything in the world if only it could have been me who had made it.

I remembered it as a London film: a winter park, a Soho café with posters for Tommy Steele and Cliff Richard, American cars in empty streets. Oblique prompts giving a fictional gloss to Baker's admiration for 'Italian' Albert Dimes, veteran of a notorious potato-knife duel with Jack Spot in Frith Street. Those old gangland figures were ghosts out of Gerald Kersh's novel *Night and the City*, filmed with some panache by Jules Dassin (a Losey rival). Dassin could do heists, the slow build-up, the detail. Losey couldn't be bothered. When he slummed, he wanted it known that he was slumming. The escape from the prison van, carried out by a solitary heavy (the notably long-coated Nigel Green), is so implausible that the final reel becomes a posthumous dream. The wilful suspension of disbelief, the absurdist comedy, prefigures the sorry saga of the Kray twins springing Frank 'The Mad Axeman' Mitchell from Dartmoor. Film crime and true crime are both extensions of place. They define the city as the quest for the perfect

REGRET

Critics' choice
Losers

Beijing Bicycle
(2000, Tai/China/Fr) *d* Wang Xiaoshuai.
cast Cui Lin, Li Bin, Zhuo Xun, Gao Yuanyuan, Li Shuang.
A country kid in the big city gets his bicycle stolen, recovers it and loses it again.

Boogie Nights
(1997, US) *d* Paul Thomas Anderson. *cast* Mark Wahlberg, Burt Reynolds, William H Macy.
Macy majors in losers, but few are as wretched as his humiliated cuckold in this LA porn epic.

Dog Day Afternoon
(1975, US) *d* Sidney Lumet. *cast* Al Pacino, John Cazale, Sully Boyar, Penelope Allen.
Film history's most incompetent, anxiety-ridden, homosexual bank robber – in a field of one.

Ed Wood
(1994, US) *d* Tim Burton. *cast* Johnny Depp, Martin Landau, Sarah Jessica Parker.
Biopic of a man who was talentless, naive and misguided in virtually everything he did.

Glengarry Glenn Ross
(1992, US) *d* James Foley. *cast* Al Pacino, Jack Lemmon, Alec Baldwin, Ed Harris, Kevin Spacey.
Levene 'the Machine' (Lemmon) is such an icon of loserdom he's enshrined in *The Simpsons*.

Happiness
(1998, US) *d* Todd Solondz. *cast* Jane Adams, Lara Flynn Boyle, Philip Seymour Hoffman.
Black take on New Jersey family life with a core of despair, exemplified by the paedophile father.

The King of Comedy
(1982, US) *d* Martin Scorsese. *cast* Robert De Niro, Jerry Lewis, Diahnne Abbot.
De Niro as a repellent prize nerd obsessively desperate to make it as a TV stand-up.

Midnight Cowboy
(1969, US) *d* John Schlesinger. *cast* Dustin Hoffman, Jon Voight, Sylvia Miles.
Hoffman's limping guttersnipe is almost as wretched as Voight's subsequent film career.

Night On Earth
(1991, US) *d* Jim Jarmusch. *cast* Winona Ryder, Gena Rowlands, Béatrice Dalle, Roberto Benigni.
Five taxi tales, by turns poignant, funny and, in the case of the Helsinki driver, truly pathetic.

Paris, Texas
(1984, WGer/Fr/GB) *d* Wim Wenders.
cast Harry Dean Stanton, Nastassja Kinski.
Harry Dean Stanton, sporting a red baseball cap, attempts to fit together the shards of his broken life.

---

location shot. The most convenient parking place for a rapid getaway.

Dimes came to Saffron Hill from Scotland in the '30s. The influence of the Sabinis (an inspiration for Graham Greene and *Brighton Rock*) was still felt; four streets and an ornate church. Bannion's rival in the prison is an Italian (played by Grégoire Aslan). His name is Frank Saffron. Bannion's 'B' wing is token Irish (any Celt will do). When he faces a punishment beating from the fearsome O'Hara (Neil McCarthy), the big man sarcastically enquires: 'Are you an Irishman at all?' His cellmate, Flynn (Tom Bell), bruised and battered, takes down a crucifix from the wall. When there's a bit of business to transact, Saffron gets word to Bannion. 'See you at Mass, Johnny.'

Here was a film, immaculately shot in harsh black and white by Robert Krasker, that was the culmination of a series of British realist dramas made by the likes of Endfield and Val Guest. Baker appeared in most of them, sometimes a driven copper, sometimes a villain: two sides of the same glass. *The Criminal* predicted, in its use of a specific criminal sub-culture, future projects such as *Performance* and *The Long Good Friday*. But it's always the topography that gets skewed. The notional London of Johnny Bannion that I'd extrapolated from my original Dalston viewing now felt like photographs of a winter of the soul. A scatter of locations within a few minutes of the Merton Park studios. Five men meeting at a bandstand. Distant church bells. An ugly bridge across an unseen river. The last seconds of dying consciousness in a snow-covered field. Baker, cradled by the snaky Sam Wanamaker, muttering an act of contrition.

Alun Owen's screenplay, drawing on Brendan Behan's *The Quare Fellow*, brings to life the maggot-cathedral of the prison. His mongrel Liverpool Catholicism tempering Losey's bleak and narcissistic puritanism. (Owen would return to play an Irish priest in *The Servant*, with the psychotic prison warder, Patrick Magee, as his bishop.) The faces are memorable. Many of the characters of British and Irish drama are here: Tom Bell, Brian Phelan, Kenneth J Warren, Murray Melvin.

After London, I moved to Dublin. In the pub we listened to extras who claimed to have done time in *The Criminal*. They remembered it as a Stanley Baker picture. Losey barely registered, a distant presence. The exteriors, they claimed, were shot in Ireland. So once again, as with the *Fu Manchu* series, a mythical London becomes Dublin. Anywhere is nowhere. Baker, by unsupported rumour, was fingered as the banker behind the Great Train Robbery. Ironically, he would become 'our mutual friend from Highgate'; the unseen Mr Fixit who is Bannion's nemesis. The man with the white mansion and the racehorses.

Returned to London, and lodged in Hackney, I learnt that we had a local celebrity, a writer who was working with the Beatles and Dick Lester: Alun Owen. Much of the credit for *The Criminal* should go to him. Losey's career inflated, then stalled; he made good money and bad debts. He drank too much and made peevish phone calls about pigeons and loutish behaviour in the streets. Baker moved successfully into film production. Owen, respected but largely reforgotten, got to live in De Beauvoir Town before Hackney became a satellite of Moscow, an off-shore investment as risky as an art movie in a time without culture.

Looking back: **Paris, Texas**

REGRET

Larry the man

Don Boyd remembers working with Laurence Olivier in his final, elegiac film.

It has to be dark. In East Africa the flame trees become silhouettes in the dusk before half past six in the evening. Those Africans who live away from the cities have to wait until then. But imagine their excitement. The truck ambles noisily into the village in the late afternoon. The dust-ridden driver slides out of his smelly cab, pulls the bolt out of the dropdoor at the back of the truck, clambers up and begins to hand down a long, thin tube to a couple of boys who have been promised a cold Coke if they help him. Near the lake some fishermen are fixing their nets in the water. On the parched red earth nearby, their women are washing long, beautiful, ochre coloured clothes. Ochre make-up on their faces. The sun is beginning to cast long, romantic shadows over the murram and wattle huts that pepper the landscape. The sound of a child's voice mingles with the cow bells and tall cones of dust spiral into the cloudless azure sky.

It's getting darker and the skyline is pink. The lake hovers like a huge, black ink spot on a brown canvas eiderdown. People are beginning to slope up the gradient from the village by the lake. They squat in groups around the truck. They begin to chatter animatedly: those kids, that fish, the drought and their grandfather's dreams. Facing them is a raised white sheet flanked by what looks like a broken down old gramophone. Wires everywhere. The boys are guarding what has become their Hades like a pair of Cerberus with Coke bottles between their teeth. Their eyes shine in excitement. The sun has almost disappeared. The community has gathered in its hundreds and the driver of the truck starts a generator. Within seconds there are screams and shouts. A naked white light has flickered from the back of his truck and a cockerel appears on the screen. This is not the cockerel of their initiation ceremonies. This is not the cockerel of their back yards. This is the cockerel of their new gods. The gods of Agincourt and the River Plate. The gods of Lavender Hill and Brighton. The gods of the River Kwai and dog-infested Yorkshire moors. And the goddesses of steam-laden

---

Moving picture
Simon Pummell

Director, *Bodysong*

I was 16 or just 17. She was maybe a year younger – a good Catholic girl, although in my mind she was some kind of International Gothic Beauty. (She had nightmares in which one of her aunts would visit her in Satanic guise, and on the same nights her aunt would always dream about her.) I asked her to the movies.

For me the movies were still Fred Astaire on TV on a rainy Saturday afternoon. But this film had caught my eye. From openers I was hooked. Urban lights and rain on the taxi's windshield, De Niro's voice: 'May 10th. Thank God for the rain which has helped wash away the garbage and trash off the sidewalks.' But the kicker was when Travis takes Betsy on a grotesque first date to see *Swedish Marriage Manual*.

My date didn't storm out like Betsy, and even sat through the reprise, when Travis goes back alone and we see his disappointed and lonely face to the soundtrack, 'It's getting harder baby, it's getting harder!' But she did say that seeing me was a social experiment we would not be repeating, and that I should never, ever phone her house.

As Travis says, 'I tried several times to call her, but after the first call, she wouldn't come to the phone any longer. I also sent flowers, but with no luck.'

I never saw Clare again. But that was OK, because I'd fallen in love anyway. That was the first time a movie had jumped off the screen and folded me into the way it saw the world. *Taxi Driver* had changed things for me for ever.

Laurence Olivier in **A Bridge Too Far**

stations and lavish rituals in white veils. The goddesses of fantastical dancers in taffeta tutus. The goddesses of cold dank kitchens and poor starving orphans.

Huddled next to the truck is a tiny group of paler faces. As enraptured as the others. A bespectacled boy in short trousers and his friend. Neat ties knotted into starched linen shirts. Vaseline smarmed over their hair. A naked man with a gong has appeared. Shouts and screams of excitement, and a tall, brooding man begins to talk to a ghost. Waves below the cliffs. To be or not to be. Sword fights and poison. To die, to sleep, perchance to dream among hundreds of fellow dreamers under the stars in the dark. Laurence Olivier's great film *Hamlet* was mesmerising all of us. My first sound movie – the others had been Chaplin and Mickey Mouse.

Nearly forty years later that same craggy face, bearded and lonely, glows out of a blanketed huddle as Olivier walks slowly across the devastation of another landscape. The landscape of Kent devastated by motorways and chimneys. That dark, swarthy, black and

white prince had emerged from those white sheets. He has been resurrected from the gloom of his Elsinore. The thrill of those congregations in the Africa of my youth has been matched by the thrill of small smoky rooms in Edinburgh and vast pleasure palaces in London. And I have become one of those witchdoctors of the white screen. I can conjure up gods. I can animate their goddesses. I can provide dreams and nightmares.

Laurence Olivier made his last film, *War Requiem*, for me. It was directed by Derek Jarman, who used him in a small cameo role at the beginning of his spectacular cinematic setting of Benjamin Britten's opera of the same title. On the soundtrack his unmistakable voice echoes over imagery of the Great War and images of his own cinematic valediction. When I showed the film on New Year's Eve in 1987, I thought about those Africans. They would have understood this moving masterpiece with its imagery of war and waste. They would have recognised their prince, older and wiser and alive. They would have wept and ululated as Tilda Swinton, another great goddess of the

Moving picture
Lukas Moodysson

Director, writer, *Show Me Love*, *Together*, *Lilya 4ever*, *A Hole in My Heart*

Ten years ago I saw this Russian film which I hated very much and did not even remember the name of. It was at the Gothenburg Film Festival, and I fell asleep because it was so bad, and so boring. It's called *The Chekist*, directed by *The Cuckoo*'s Aleksandr Rogozhkin. It takes place during Stalin's purges of the '30s, and it's a small story about an officer who has to kill people the whole time and someone who's cleaning up the place afterwards. But as the years went by the film continued to live inside of me. I haven't seen it again, and only saw half of it then because I fell asleep in the middle, but now it's something I think about almost every day. And this is how I want my films to work: I want them to live like a virus inside of people.

cinema, offers a wreath of white poppies to the body of a dead warrior as the sublime chorus of Britten's music dies away.

I had struck up a tiny friendship with Olivier; it started when we had first met in his Chelsea home only a couple of months before. 'Which of you is the director and which is the producer?' he had muttered with a twinkle in his eyes. Derek and I walked out of that house like a couple of cherubs in the clouds of a Tintoretto picture. But we were carrying Laurence Olivier's shoes! And he was going to be in our film.

He had telephoned me a couple of times. Long calls during which he tried out his various provincial British accents on me. I had told him about the corrected proof of Wilfred Owen's poem 'Anthem for Doomed Youth' that I'd been shown by Daniel Day-Lewis in the study of his father, who was a contemporary of Owen. Important changes to the words crossed out in the trenches of Flanders and posted to a friend. Perfectionism. Passion. Despair. Olivier was determined to provide all he could for his symbolic role. On the weekend before we began, his nurse called. I was desperate. He was over 80 and obviously ill. But she been preparing the way: 'Larry

here! I just called for a bit of an enthuse!' He chuckled and launched into a recital of Wilfred Owen's entire poem to me – a feat he repeated when we were recording his voice in the caravan laid on for him during shooting. Without the book.

One lunch break during the shooting of the film, Olivier shuffled across the bleak tarmac in front of the old hospital that served as our studio. He had promised to do some still photographs to help us with the publicity. He reached the end of a long corridor and had recognised my wife and two of my daughters; they'd eaten lunch with him a few minutes before. He stopped and with a very deliberate gesture of respect he looked them in the eye and took his hat off. As he walked into the makeshift photo studio we had rigged up, he whispered to me quietly, 'The governor's wife!'

Derek Jarman's film received the best reviews from the British critics of any film I had produced, but audiences did not want to be depressed by abstract images of the wars of our century and the film was a box office flop. The BBC ran the film on Easter Sunday and over a million people tuned in. I sent Olivier the reviews and he wrote back to me in shaky handwriting – he had inked over a pencilled draft of the letter:

Malthouse
Thur. 9 Feb '89 Ashurst
W. Sussex

My dear Don,
It was so dearly kind of you to write to me, sending the press 'Menchies'.
I must say, they aren't anything to complain about, are they?
I would be so happy if I were to find myself doing another piece of work for you, but I do realise juveniles of 85 are not all that easy to cast!
However I am going through a time of life when any age from 55 to 85(!) will do nicely, thank you!
And thank you again for your kindness – acceptable at any time!
Ever sincerely

Larry Olivier

Contempt

'Behave yourself, will ya?
Go find real work.'
Fahrenheit 9/11

Breeding contempt

Emilie Bickerton takes a forensic look at cinema's less admirable side.

You shall not enjoy, you shall endure! This seems to be the mission statement of a number of auteurs making films today. Catherine Breillat, Michael Haneke, Lukas Moodysson and Gaspar Noé, to name a handful, have all made films that seem to chastise the viewer for daring to enter the auditorium. To watch *Anatomy of Hell*, *Time of the Wolf*, *Hole in my Heart* or *Irreversible* is to feel contempt for humanity and its mores. It becomes a struggle to sit through each scene, to keep your eyes on the screen, so sexually explicit, violent or revolting are the images. Cinema has become an endurance sport.

This state of affairs is markedly different from watching merely with a sense of unease or fear. The latter emotions are produced by a compelling narrative, the result of a convincing situation or set of characters that you feel involved with. David Lynch's *Eraserhead* is hardly a laugh-a-minute, but at no point do we feel Lynch aspired, primarily, to make us feel queasy. What queasiness there is arises as a by-product of Lynch showing us the internal world of his characters and all their contorted realities. But the new ethic is different: it's rooted in a perception of the audience as a bunch of thoughtless consumers, people who expect entertainment and unthinkingly accept society's taboos and prejudices. For today's 'extreme' film-makers, as they might be called, the only way to jolt the spectator awake is to sabotage cinema's assumed aim of supplying entertainment and instead create features that test the stomach.

In their features – partly a tirade against Hollywood, and cinema as an industry – extreme film-makers convey their message with a visual language that's spare, raw or sickening. Michael Haneke's *Time of the Wolf* is a kind of anti-*War of the Worlds* (the Spielberg version, that is). Although both films fantasise about post-apocalyptic scenarios, Haneke expresses his pessimism in the images.

Familiarity: **Saraband**

Charm offensive: US Marines recruitment staff at work in **Fahrenheit 9/11**

The film has no electric light; bodies and faces are briefly lit by candle or firelight, and for two long hours we squint and struggle to make out anything at all. What justifies this? When we endure Haneke's film, do we emerge more enriched than we might after a similar period watching Tom Cruise's heroic gallivants? The difference for the viewer is the contempt he or she has been subjected to, and, to an extent, encouraged to feel – even towards cinema itself. With Haneke and company we've become aware of ourselves as spectators, prevented from losing ourselves in the picture. But this means that our visceral reactions are likely to be so strong, they defeat our capacity for

reflection. We come out of the cinema shocked or disgusted – and largely inarticulate. Does Haneke want to make us feel the poverty of a situation, not reflect on it? By making a film that's nearly impossible to watch, he provokes gut reactions in the audience, but what else?

The question arises again with Lukas Moodysson's tale of slimeball amateur pornography, *Hole in My Heart*, which includes a stomach-churning, unbearable sequence of adults vomiting into each other's mouths. And again in Gaspar Noé's *Irreversible*, which asks us to sit through a nine-minute rape; and in the film *In My Skin*, by young French director Marina de Van, which stages full-on scenes of

'For today's "extreme" film-makers, the only way to jolt the spectator awake is to sabotage cinema's assumed aim of supplying entertainment.'

Adolf Hitler, one that takes the latter's actions and tics to their absurd extremes. As we watch Chaplin's preposterous dictator feverishly gesticulate, we laugh and recognise the target of the satire – but he has been made so unreal that we momentarily forget Hitler's actual existence and the horror he unleashed. Because the figure on screen is so roundly ridiculed, the real atrocities set in motion by the real dictator are forgotten. Through Chaplin, contempt appeases the film-goer.

In the 1950s, contempt swung towards the private realm of couples and families. One particular scene springs to mind, from Nicholas Ray's *Rebel Without a Cause*. Ray was savage in his depiction of failed parenting in this film, and he set about encouraging viewers to feel complete contempt for the two culprits. The scene takes place on the stairs of the family home, as the father, effeminate in a white apron, brings his wife a tray of food. Suddenly he trips and flails around for what feels like an eternity. Witness to this pathetic fiasco is his son, played by James Dean, a son who wished for a strong figurehead, someone to look up to and be advised by. But no. 'You're tearing me apart!' Dean's character screams as his parents bicker. Watching this, our contempt wells up, as does our conviction that good families are what we must all believe in.

But by 1976, when Robert De Niro stared at us accusingly in *Taxi Driver*, his mad eyes were alight with disgust fuelled by nothing so specific as poor parenting. Instead it was an

human cannibalism. To these directors we really are what Barthes described as 'soporific', dazed and unthinking before the screen and wholly deserving their brutal, condescending tactics. The audience can't be given images to make it think, only images to make it feel. (Of course, viewers may be pushed so far that they sever their relationship with the film – by walking out. By then, contempt for the film and its makers becomes all-consuming.)

An earlier and rather different example of contempt sparked by a film is found in Charlie Chaplin's *The Great Dictator*. Here contempt for a political figure is nurtured by political satire. Chaplin's Adenoid Hynkel is a clear parody of entire sickly society. The contempt in *Taxi Driver* is all Travis Bickle's, but we watch his transformation from frustrated lonely cabbie to megalomaniac with profound unease. This is because we understand Bickle's contempt, and may even share it. At the same time, we condemn his response. While Scorsese portrays his protagonist's contempt, he also presented its catastrophic effects, and we leave the cinema with the need, finally, to question the film's conclusion. Faced with that environment, feeling Bickle's acute frustration and sadness at the route society had taken, we ask ourselves: 'What is to be done, given that complete slaughter of all those you despise is out of the question?' Contempt in this film – even a contempt you share – results in atrocity. The

audience retains the contemptuous feelings but rejects their expression, so the dilemma is: how do we differentiate ourselves from Travis Bickle?

The war films that emerged in the wake of America's intervention in Vietnam reflect that era's fraught political mood, as well as evoking another kind of contempt in the viewer and on screen. *The Deer Hunter*, *Apocalypse Now*, *Platoon*, *Full Metal Jacket*, *Casualties of War* and *Born on the Fourth of July* all typify a characteristic approach to representing war, where self-contempt is the dominant mood. Such films often have a protagonist who reflects on his experience, with extensive monologues, flash-backs and voice-overs that offer an understanding of events through

Extreme measures: **Saló**

hindsight. These characters struggle with their memories and the roles they played in the conflict, being party to some of humanity's basest actions, and the viewer's contempt for these is ever-present. However, because these films are structured by the personal view, following one character who has been absorbed by a collective group and pushed into conflict by higher forces, further reactions develop from our original contempt. Just as Stanley Kubrick opened *Full Metal Jacket* with a scene of disappearing individuality (shears cutting off men's hair to leave identical rows of heads), war films from this period presented the individual in his depleted form – full of regret and self-loathing, trying to readjust to a society in which his patriotic acts were vilified rather than glorified. The self-contempt depicted by the likes of Michael Cimino or Oliver Stone translates, for the viewer, into empathy, if not sympathy. In contrast to the character who is so crippled by self-contempt he is unable to adjust, the viewer has been invited (by the monologues and sustained individual focus) to make sense of this struggle, to see it as one forced on the individual by the state as opposed to any innate evil. Our contempt shifts from the individual to the state, and we condemn the American intervention because the politics were not shared by those forced to carry out the orders to fight.

These war films, through the depiction and evocation of contempt, use the emotion to suggest a particular interpretation of historical events, from their personal to their political connotations. Contempt may fire the cinema-goer, provoke him or her to seeking out answers. Feeling contempt for a political regime or figure may, however, be counter-productive. Take *Super Size Me*, which is likely to succeed at a personal level (by making me so sickened by junk food that I boycott McDonald's) – but is it really a powerful indictment of global business? My contempt may not lead to my grasping other issues around obesity, alienation and economics. *Life and Debt*, *The Corporation* and Michael Moore's documentaries – *Bowling for Columbine*, on the Colorado high school massacre, and *Fahrenheit 9/11,* on the invasion of Afghanistan and Iraq by the US – are further cases of spectator contempt backfiring. Moore makes the most of documentary conventions (talking heads, real footage, documentary's

potential claim to being a neutral and dispassionate account of events) to punch his points across: a critique of Big Business (Walmart), particular beliefs or groups (the freedom to carry a firearm, defended by the National Rifle Association) or political figures (notably George W Bush). How does this critique register with the viewer? Moore's cheap techniques and lack of alternatives to the status quo deflate the potential power of his work. He provokes a baseless contempt in the viewer: we are appalled by Charlton Heston's smugness, his rich isolation from the world as he spearheads the NRA's campaigns, but there is little else in Moore's documentary to move us to action. We see him place the photograph of one of the murdered children from Columbine at the foot of Heston's private swimming pool, but the scene is nothing more than manipulated poignancy.

But the problem of gun crime in the US can't be blamed entirely on the NRA, nor is it perpetuated by Heston's obnoxiousness. Why those responsible for Columbine could be so casual about human life, could stop seeing their classmates as fellow human beings – *that* is the question (and one Gus Van Sant addressed far more successfully in the elegant fiction of *Elephant*). Moore unleashes instead angry diatribes at various groups in American society, playing the blame game, littering his films with anecdotes. *Fahrenheit 9/11* was effective political satire – we scoff at Bush – but what else? Our contempt does not allow for earnest consideration of the situation in Iraq and US policy. What Moore awakens in the film-goer leads to passive resistance rather than activism, a hands-in-the-air, 'oh, what a terrible world' response that is also an admission of our powerlessness in the face of the System. Our contempt here is counter-productive to comprehending the world. Of course, we shouldn't burden film with the responsibility of getting us out on the streets – leave that to politics. The difficulty with Moore's approach is that he encourages us to feel disdain for politics itself. With him you see a single man battling against what is presented as a *fait accompli* – the contempt you feel is thus dead on arrival, there's no inspiration, no deepened understanding or insight.

Not that the audience need feel any contempt at all. When part of the narrative, an emotion within the film rather than a sought-after effect in the audience, contempt does not necessarily come unstuck from the screenplay (or the images) to be felt by the viewer. Unlike the laughing face that nearly always succeeds in bringing a smile to our own, contempt isn't infectious. Jean-Luc Godard's *Le Mépris* and Ingmar Bergman's *Saraband* are two examples of films that study the emotion without provoking it in the viewer. Instead, what Godard was able to do through his tale of love poisoned by a single seemingly banal act, was to communicate the extraordinary subtlety and festering nature of the emotion. In particular, as *Saraband* suggests, contempt can stem from love, or deep attachment. This prior existence is what differentiates contempt from hatred, anger or disgust. The dictionary definition of the word isolates a 'lack of respect' as its key characteristic, but we mustn't forget that there's often also an original loss at the root of contempt; respect must have once existed for it now to go astray. Godard's lovers and Bergman's family are appropriate subjects through which the emotion can be explored: I despise you now because once I had such hopes for you, I believed in you, loved you.

As film-goers we see this on screen and understand the process, the terrible effects an action can have, the silent, festering life of contempt. Camille, the desperately disappointed wife played by Brigitte Bardot, never voices the reason for her contempt towards Paul (Michel Piccoli) – it merely grows, expressed through her actions, her demeanour. Godard uses various techniques to communicate it – the increasingly insistent and dramatic musical score, the quick editing and flash-backs – all suggest the emotion without ever spelling it out.

The tangible impact contempt has on the viewer is extremely varied. We move from disdain to despair to scorn and resignation, but it may also push us towards greater sympathy and compassion, or – paradoxically – deepen our understanding of love.

Contempt in 20 films

M (1931)
Fritz Lang's first sound film was based on the real-life manhunt for a Düsseldorf child-murderer (an extraordinary performance by Peter Lorre). A radical, analytical film that carries Lang's own view of the arbitrariness of the Law.

Triumph of the Will (1935)
Leni Riefenstahl's record of the sixth Nazi congress at Nuremberg in 1934, a massive documentary tribute to the German concept of the Aryan super-race. Technically brilliant, and still one of the most disturbing pieces of propaganda around.

On the Waterfront (1954)
Brando struggles against gangster Cobb's hold over the New York longshoremen's union. Superb performances (none more so than from Brando as Terry Malloy, the ex-boxer unwittingly entangled in corrupt union politics), a colourful script by Budd Schulberg and a sure control of atmosphere make for electrifying drama.

Nuit et Brouillard (1955)
Cloquet's camera tracks slowly through a deserted, autumnal Auschwitz. This muted Technicolor 'now' is intercut with grainy monochrome records of 'then', as the commentary outlines the development and operation of the Nazi death camps. The achievement of Alain Resnais' film is to find a tone appropriate to the desolating enormity of what took place.

The Searchers (1956)
A marvellous Western that turns Monument Valley into an interior landscape, as Wayne pursues his five-year odyssey, a grim quest – to kill both the Indian who abducted his niece and the tainted girl herself – which is miraculously purified of its racist furies in a final moment of epiphany.

The Battle of Algiers (1965)
The prototype for all the mainstream political cinema of the '70s, from Rosi to Costa-Gavras. It relegates the actual liberation of Algeria to an epilogue, and focuses on a specific phase of the Algerian guerilla struggle against the French, the years between 1954 and 1957. Gillo Pontecorvo refuses to caricature the French or glamorise the Algerians: instead he sketches the way a guerilla movement is organised and how a colonial force sets about destroying it.

Mouchette (1966)
Adapted from a Georges Bernanos story, Robert Bresson's film describes the life and tribulations of a poor, barely mature peasant girl (played with sullen but affecting grace by non-professional Nadine Nortier). In his angry yet compassionate denunciation of a rural society's self-interest, immorality, alcoholism and spiritual bankruptcy, the director conducts you to the heart of life's paradox.

Weekend (1967)
Godard's vision of bourgeois cataclysm, a savage Swiftian satire that traces a new Gulliver's travels

through the collapsing consumer society as a married couple set out for a weekend jaunt, passing through a nightmare landscape of highways strewn with burning cars and bloody corpses.

Death in Venice (1971)
Luchino Visconti's adaptation of Thomas Mann's novella turns the writer of the original into a composer. Bogarde is more than a little mannered as the ageing pederast whose obsession with a beautiful young boy staying at the same hotel leads him to outstay his welcome in the plague-ridden city.

The Discreet Charm of the Bourgeoisie (1972)
Delightful comedy from Luis Buñuel, flitting about from frustrating situation to frustrating situation as six characters in search of a meal never manage actually to eat it. Are they prevented by their own fantasies? By their lack of purpose? By their discreet charm? Buñuel never really lets us know.

Saló, o le Centoventi Giornate di Sodoma (1975)
Pasolini's last movie before his brutal murder may now seem strangely prophetic of his death, but it is undeniably a thoroughly objectionable piece of work. Transporting Sade's novel to Mussolini's Fascist republic of 1944, Pasolini observes the systematic humiliation and torture of beautiful young boys and girls, herded into a palatial villa by various jaded, sadistic members of the upper classes. According to the director, the story was meant to be a metaphor for Fascism. It's very hard to sit through.

Carrie (1976)
Brian De Palma's film is almost an amalgam of *The Exorcist* and *American Graffiti*, with Sissy Spacek as a religious maniac's daughter whose experience of puberty is so harrowing that it develops paranormal aspects. De Palma's ability to combine the romantic and the horrific has never been so pulverising.

The Elephant Man (1980)
More accessible than his disturbing *Eraserhead*, David Lynch's *The Elephant Man* shows how the unfortunate John Merrick (John Hurt), brutalised by a childhood in which he was abused as an inhuman freak, was gradually coaxed into revealing a soul of such delicacy and refinement that he became a lion of Victorian society. A marvellous movie, shot in stunning black-and-white by Freddie Francis.

La Haine (1995)
Twenty-four hours in the Paris projects: an Arab boy is critically wounded in hospital, and a police revolver has found its way into the hands of a young Jewish skinhead, who vows to even the score if his pal dies. Matthieu Kassovitz's virtuoso, on-the-edge film is

confrontational, to say the least, but there's a maturity and depth to the characterisation that goes beyond mere agitprop. A vital, scalding piece of work.

Breaking the Waves (1996)
Lars von Trier's epic melodrama about love, faith, suffering and redemption is emotionally overwhelming. Its raw power is assured by forthright performances and the increasingly cruel, violent events of the last hour. It's a rapt movie, so wrapped up in its harrowing dynamics that it finally, perhaps, goes too far in subjecting its heroine to pain and indignity. Is this sympathy or sadism?

Funny Games (1997)
Proof of Michael Haneke's fascination with violence and its representation, his movie may be shocking, but it's also entirely serious. A couple and their young son arrive at their holiday home, only to have it invaded by two strange, ultra-polite young men who turn out to be sadistic, homicidal psychopaths. A masterpiece that is at times barely watchable.

Boys Don't Cry (1999)
The grimly compelling true story of Teena Brandon, a 21-year-old Nebraskan who chose to carry herself off as a boy, 'Brandon'. This deals in sexual transgression and retribution, but director Kimberly Peirce keeps a lid on her artier tendencies, with the focus squarely on the actors.

Lilya 4-ever (2002)
Sixteen-year-old Lilya is cruelly abandoned by her mother to post-Soviet welfare and an aunt who only wants to steal the little she has. From here, things go downhill. The third film from writer/director Lucas Moodysson is grim and gruelling, a 'feelbad' entertainment signalled by scalding blasts of cacophonous Rammstein at ear-splitting volume. A movie with heartbreaking power.

Dogville (2003)
Lars von Trier's ambitious, intriguing but fatally self-important account of how an archetypal small town in the Rockies, proud of its ethics, turns against a woman apparently on the run from a gangster. It pounds home its somewhat obvious points, and is repetitive and overlong. That said, the final scene has an infectiously wicked glee that almost redeems it.

The Return (2003)
Echoing Odysseus and Oedipus, as well as stories of imprisonment and release, while playing on paranoia about all kinds of vulnerability, Andrey Zvyagintsev's Venice prize-winner succeeds as a metaphorical fable which may be read in mythic, psychological, political or existential terms. Avoiding the predictable, it achieves a near tragic inevitability.

Exit strategy

Nick Bradshaw talks to Monica Bellucci about a film that sent them out in droves.

Gaspar Noé's film *Irreversible* provoked a storm of protest at Cannes in 2002, as critics recoiled from its extended portrayal of a brutal rape: 'sick', 'repugnant', 'stomach-churning', 'ugly, gratuitous, profoundly unsettling', 'grotesquely violent and sexually explicit', 'a repulsive masturbatory exercise', 'exists solely to be controversial', 'just a movie; people don't have to watch it'.

Tumble through this howling wind and you reach the eye of the storm: *enfant terrible* Gaspar Noé's follow-up to his rancorous *I Stand Alone*. Upping the ante, *Irreversible* serves up a lethal head-pummelling, a brutal rape and a blissful boudoir scene at unflinching length for your consideration, and drags into the fray French cinema's reigning glam couple, Vincent Cassel and Monica Bellucci.

'There are no bad deeds, only deeds.' Does *Irreversible* flirt with nihilism? Certainly it's a film that asserts the extremities of human existence; but if indeed 'Time Destroys Everything', as Noé sloganises with typically vaunting portent, then what this attempts is a

Ire-inspiring depictions of sex: **Last Tango in Paris**

CONTEMPT

Critics' choice
Prejudice

Black Hawk Down
(2001, US) d Ridley Scott. cast Josh Hartnett, Ewan McGregor, Tom Sizemore, Eric Bana. Hundreds of Somalis die in a US incursion into Africa and we're to honour the brave marines?

Cry Freedom
(1987, GB) d Richard Attenborough. cast Kevin Kline, Penelope Wilton, Denzel Washington. Powerful political drama about the brutal murder of black activist Steve Biko by white South African police.

Far from Heaven
(2002, US/Fr) d Tod Haynes. cast Julianne Moore, Dennis Quaid, Dennis Haysbert. Exploring the taboos of 1950s suburban America, with the most taboo of all being inter-racial love.

Guess Who's Coming to Dinner
(1967, US) d Stanley Kramer. cast Spencer Tracey, Katharine Hepburn, Sidney Poitier. A liberal couple suffer doubts when their daughter brings home the black man she intends to marry.

Hidden
(2005, It/Ger/Fr/Aus) d Michael Haneke. cast Juliette Binoche, Daniel Auteuil. A thriller with a compendium of strong ideas about guilt, racism and recent French history.

Hotel Rwanda
(2004, GB/US/SAf/It) d Terry George. cast Don Cheadle, Sophie Okonedo, Joaquin Phoenix. The manager of an elite hotel harbours refugees fleeing the blitzkrieg of ethnic slaughter.

In the Heat of the Night
(1967, US) d Norman Jewison. cast Sidney Poitier, Rod Steiger, Warren Oates. A bigotted Mississippi sheriff is forced against his will to work with a black partner.

I Stand Alone
(1998, Fr) d Gaspar Noé. cast Philipe Nahon, Blandine Lenoir, Frankye Pain, Martine Audrain. Racism is merely one of the traits exhibited by Nahon's misanthropic horsemeat butcher.

Rabbit-Proof Fence
(2002, Aust/GB) d Phillip Noyce. cast Everlyn Sampi, Tianna Sansbury, Ningali Lawford. True story of how three young Aboriginal girls trekked across the Outback to escape a misguided government's white supremacist policies.

To Kill a Mockingbird
(1962, US) d Robert Mulligan. cast Gregory Peck, Brock Peters, Robert Duvall. White lawyer defends black man against a charge of rape, putting his own family at risk.

perverse act of creation: not only does it batter down taboos surrounding the representation of humanity's wilder behaviour, but it turns back the clock on the most horrendous ravages of time (and man) to resurrect a lost state of grace.

In other words, beginning at the tale's endpoint, the film performs a succession of backward somersaults, retracing the route from effect to cause, from one scene to its precursor. The technique follows *Memento* (if not Jane Campion's *Two Friends*), but the aim is less a disquisition on memory than an attempt to shade what would otherwise be a banally Manichean illustration of the vagaries of good and evil. The reversal into light alleviates the experience of the film's horrors, even as their foreknowledge tempers the brighter moments.

'We are incredible, but we are monsters, too', averred Bellucci, sticking by the film after its mauling at Cannes. 'And the film shows both those sides. We don't like to touch on this horrible part we have; but the film is just saying "Look what we are. We are that." For me it's like life. In life we have moments of joy and ecstasy, moments of pain. Those characters to me are like flies lost in the universe, looking for structure for their lives. They're looking for answers, always asking about love, sex, life. But all this talk, what is it about? We don't know anything. All we know is we are born, we live, we die. In between we're kind of lost.'

There's a line in the film her character Alex utters to the effect that 'you should have sex,

CONTEMPT

not talk about it' – a dictum that could equally be applied to film-making.

But what's to be gained by asking an audience to sit through the entirety of a rape?

'That was Cassavetes' way of working,' she replied. 'A lot of improvisation, the camera keeps rolling. Also the New Wave, Godard used to improvise. Maybe not in such long scenes. But it's like Pasolini's films, *Salò*, for instance – they're hard to watch, but you learn something; when you come out, you're not the same. Also, for me as an actress, this improvisation was the most incredible freedom I have ever had. When we started, we didn't have a script, just 15 pages of synopsis. So of course I was a bit scared.

That rape scene, which is so long, we shot four or five times, and each time I had to go into the tunnel knowing what was going to happen – it was so hard. It's crazy work that we do!'

Moving picture
Tom Tykwer

Director, *Run Lola Run* and *Heaven*

When I first met my ex-girlfriend, she hated films. She was a student of philosophy and we regularly argued about the importance I attached to cinema. I remember one time, we had planned to go to the movies, and on the way we had a ferocious argument about something, shouting and screaming at each other as we walked down the street and went into the movie theatre. 'What are we going to do – watch a fucking film now?' she shouted. I said, 'You do what you want, but I'm going in.' She followed me in just to continue the fight. I'm embarrassed to think of it now, but it was a very loud fight, we were still shouting at each other: nothing was resolved and people were shushing us. The film was the four-and-a-half hour version of Lars von Trier's *The Kingdom*, subtitled, shot on video. You'd think you couldn't see a worse film at such a time, yet within ten minutes my girlfriend and I looked at each other, and we were both calm, entranced by how great this film was. It put everything in perspective, and afterwards we left the cinema as friends and lovers. It makes me think how powerful film can be.

Some put it more strongly than that. Take, for instance, the *Evening Standard*'s notorious picklepuss, the late Alexander Walker: 'Actresses are often ready to behave like whores for their living, but seeing the camera simply stand there and record Monica Bellucio (sic) spread-eagled on the dirty floor of the underpass and suffering, even in simulation, the worst degradation that a woman can incur, I felt debased and exploited.'

Bellucci disagreed. 'It's incredible how many men have said "this film degrades women". This is stupid, it means they didn't understand anything. The film shows how men are stupid, how they are weak and insecure, and that's why they abuse their power and do those kind of things to women. Alex, she's just a normal person and just because she's pretty, these men feel threatened and want to destroy her.'

But Walker thought that he's seeing you as an actress being abused.

'But I didn't fuck for real', she exclaimed. 'It's just acting. I wasn't raped. It's incredible: we see so many violent films, yet this one got everyone so angry it makes me think, God, we really did a great job. People really felt what a rape is about. You're not just a spectator, no, you're involved. It's like in the love scene, you feel like you're in bed with them. Because everything is so realistic, it gets under your skin. That's why people talk about degradation: the film makes you a victim with her.'

Schools for scoundrels

Don Boyd remembers the winning team of Richard Harris and Lindsay Anderson.

Rugby is a game invented by an elite in the Victorian era at schools designed to nurture fortitude and leadership skills among the children of the privileged classes in Britain. Memories of cold soggy afternoons on the school playing fields of the Scottish upper classes, of waiting on the sidelines for the slippery rugby ball to be passed from a mass of steamy, scrummaged humanity… The fleeting exhilaration that came from the moment when the ball was in your hands, and you were running like a hellhound towards the try line pursued by a dozen or so psychopaths, was severely diluted by the certain knowledge that within an hour of the tub room's welcoming luxury, your bum would be the object of some sadistic punishment ritual meted out by the public school hierarchy.

There are two great films directed by Lindsay Anderson that extraordinarily encapsulated the brutal rough-and-tumble of rugby and the peculiar, rarefied, equally violent environment of the British boarding school. Seeing them both at film school in 1968 was cathartic and inspirational. Ironically they chronicle brilliantly two very different social milieux:

Critics' choice
Hitmen

Collateral
(2004, US) *d* Michael Mann. *cast* Tom Cruise, Jamie Foxx, Jada Pinkett Smith.
Who'd have thought it of that nice Mr Cruise – a vicious contract killer?

Grosse Pointe Blank
(1997, US) *d* George Armitage. *cast* John Cusack, Minnie Driver, Alan Arkin, Dan Ackroyd.
A hitman attends his high school reunion: 'I killed the president of Paraguay with a fork. How've you been?'

In the Line of Fire
(1993, US) *d* Wolfgang Peterson. *cast* Clint Eastwood, John Malkovich, Rene Russo.
Clint's in it but it's Malkovich's movie as the psycho out to off the president.

Leon
(1994, Fr) *d* Luc Besson. *cast* Jean Reno, Natalie Portman, Gary Oldman.
Reno as the assassin with a soft spot for 12-year-old Madonna impersonators.

Munich
(2005, US) *d* Steven Spielberg. *cast* Eric Bana, Daniel Craig, Ciarán Hinds, Mathieu Kassovitz.
A politically-sanctioned hit squad and major issues regarding revenge and morality.

Point Blank
(1967, US) *d* John Boorman. *cast* Lee Marvin, Angie Dickinson, Keenan Wynn.
Double-crossed and left to die, Marvin returns to eliminate the unfortunates responsible.

Prizzi's Honor
(1985, US) *d* John Huston. *cast* Jack Nicholson, Kathleen Turner, Robert Loggia.
Hitman falls for girl, who turns out also to be a killer. And they're hired to kill each other.

Pulp Fiction
(1994, US) *d* Quentin Tarantino. *cast* John Travolta, Samuel L Jackson, Uma Thurman.
'And you will know my name is the Lord when I lay my vengeance upon thee.' Jackson and Travolta are the most voluble of hitmen.

Road to Perdition
(2002, US) *d* Sam Mendes. *cast* Tom Hanks, Paul Newman, Jude Law, Jennifer Jason Leigh.
Hanks is an enforcer for the Mob but the real scary killer is whacked-out loon Law.

Three Days of the Condor
(1975, US) *d* Sydney Pollack. *cast* Robert Redford, Faye Dunaway, Max Von Sydow.
Intriguing slice of neo-Hitchcock with a particularly cool Von Sydow as the hired assassin.

Anarchic: Richard Harris
in **This Sporting Life**

In *This Sporting Life* Richard Harris is an ambitious, talented professional rugby player whose anarchic spirit bucks the bourgeois sensibilities of a deeply divided community in Britain's Northern industrial wasteland of the 1960s; in *If....*, Malcolm McDowell plays a teenager whose anarchic spirit challenges the repressive and smug totalitarian hypocrisy of a famous public school. Made within five years of each other at a time when British cinema echoed the sociological changes which were part of the political landscape of post-war Europe, they were profoundly disturbing experiences for anybody who knew either phenomenon. To have had a taste of both, as I had, was bad enough; to watch poetic and provocative re-enactments in a movie gave me lifelong benchmarks for my own career in the cinema. I would never have produced *Scum*, also set in a repressive institution – Borstal, a

juvenile prison. I would never have produced *Look Back in Anger*, directed by Anderson and starring Malcolm McDowell as John Osborne's anti-hero Jimmy Porter, a young man with the same flavour of anarchic frustration as the militant hero of *If....*. And I would never have directed Richard Harris in his last great performance in *My Kingdom*, another film set in the wasteland of Britain's industrial North but made almost 40 years after *This Sporting Life*.

Harris and I agreed from the start to make a film which might provide some sort of metaphorical bookend for *This Sporting Life*. Nick Davies, who wrote the film, used the plot and characters of *King Lear* as an editorial springboard to show the desperation of a corrupt criminal society. Harris plays its doomed emperor as if the character in David Sherwin's great 1962 script had been morphed,

'You cannot change human nature':
Robert McNamara in **The Fog of War**

like some cinematic ghoul, into the brutal murderer he played in Liverpool's underworld in 2002.

Richard fell out with Lindsay during production. They were both awkward, opinionated, cantankerous men, but they also had deep respect for each other. Scurrilous, revisionist gossip from the era has it that Lindsay was in love with the spectacularly heterosexual and beautiful Irishman. But both men inspired, nay expected, powerful adoration and a corresponding, perverse hatred from their more respected collaborators and in their most vibrant creative relationships. There is no doubt that Richard's habit of fierce, daily critical analysis of a script was begun when he worked on *This Sporting Life*. Both men had explained to me that every day and night they would revisit the screenplay, revise dialogue and change scenes radically in a spirit of determined perfectionism. And they screamed at each other, too.

Lindsay came from the battleground of the Free Cinema documentary movement in the 1950s and its enlightened film criticism. His patrician Oxford education, coupled with a childhood among the embers of Britain's dying imperial bonfire in the Raj, had, ironically, fostered vibrant left-wing fervour and cynicism worthy of the post-war existential philosophers. He also adored cinema, and saw it as a great medium for popular social engagement. All his work oozes with the intellectual influences of the political spectrum of the 1950s. But he had wit and considerable charm, and he managed to balance his acerbic cynicism with generosity and affection. Watching him direct actors was a joy: he could cut to the chase by gently saying just two words – 'No, Malcolm!' – and somehow Malcolm knew what he meant. He also listened carefully to opinions. And absorbed them – sometimes without giving any indication that he might have secretly agreed with them.

Richard came to the set of *This Sporting Life* from a very different background. He had been a child of poverty in working class Catholic Ireland. He was a brilliant rugby player and would have remained one, playing for his beloved Munster, had it not been for injury and a desperate need to be the best at anything he turned his hand to. By his own admission, his early education had been truncated, but his startling good looks and rich poetic voice led him to the vanities of performance. He supplemented drama school (RADA) with a self-imposed, autodidactic education. The scars of childhood abuse and lack of privilege he turned to artistic advantage, and he combined a powerful sense of almost physical individuality with quintessential Irish artistic ambition.

When I met him, we both marvelled at the shared passions: rugby – he was fanatically informed about the nuances of the modern game; and art – he loved great poetry, paintings, literature and, of course, the performing arts with the kind of fervour of an adolescent amateur. Unlike Lindsay, he was also very good at spotting what might take the public fancy, and his shrewd commercial judgment had made him a massive fortune. He had owned the rights to the musical *Camelot*, for example, which had given him a lifelong annuity.

Richard also had a warm and generous heart, and that Irish propensity for exaggeration and irony. His lifelong hatred of that peculiar eccentricity, English cricket, was tempered on his death bed: his great friend, an incredulous

Peter O'Toole, caught him watching the game only hours before he died. 'O'Toole! I am preparing for Death!' he bellowed. 'There can be nothing worse than watching a game of cricket!'

Apart from the social impact of *This Sporting Life* and the beautiful depiction of an awkward and doomed love affair between the Harris character and his landlady Rachel Roberts, Lindsay managed to draw out of Richard a performance that ranks as one of British cinema's greatest. It is consistent, accurately observed from the character's point of view, moving and – sadly unlike Harris's later work in the same vein – restrained.

When I met Richard at the Savoy a few months before we began to shoot *My Kingdom*, I told him a story about Lindsay. He had been rehearsing Chekhov's *The Cherry Orchard* for the Royal Court Theatre in London, with a great cast that included Irene Worth, then a grande dame of British theatre. During the sessions in a small, smoke-filled rehearsal room, Irene had been quiet and almost mouselike in her delivery. The company transferred to the stage at the Court where Lindsay would sit on his own in the darkened auditorium to deliver his directions to the actors as they blocked their movements on the stage. The moment arrived for Irene's entrance, she breezed in from the wings and boomed out her lines as if she were in an open-air opera house. The rest of the cast battled on, somewhat exasperated, until there was a strange, unrehearsed pause. During the embarrassed silence, three succinct words echoed around the theatre from the darkness of the auditorium. 'Steady, Irene! Steady!' The great actress paused for another moment, burst into a shy giggle, returned to the wings and came back on stage in the same restrained manner she had displayed in the rehearsal rooms. She gave one of her great performances in that production.

When I had finished this story Richard laughed out loud. I smiled back and said to him by way of a gentle warning: 'Steady, Richard! Steady!' That simple economic utterance characterised the great love and respect for Lindsay Anderson and his great work in *This Sporting Life* and *If....* – two films that certainly changed my life, influenced my work in the cinema and were the catalyst for several later British films.

Moving picture
Markku Peltola

Actor, *Drifting Clouds*, *The Man Without a Past*

When I was in my teens I went to see Tarkosvky's *Andrei Rublev* with a girlfriend, who'd recommended we see it. But after a while I was so angry with the film that I walked out and told her, 'If that's the kind of movie you think I'd like, you can take your things and move out!' So we went home and I was in a pretty grim mood with her, until suddenly I burst into tears! And I cried the whole night; I couldn't sleep, and couldn't understand why. But the next day I calmed down, and we even went to see the movie again, and this time I felt it was the best movie I'd ever seen! Initially, I think, I'd been offended by Rublev's decision to stop talking. But now, though I've seen many good movies since then, it's still one of my favourites, and along with some of the other Tarkovsky films, I watch it every five or six years.

From Russia with impact

Katie Mitchell on the influences of two Russian virtuosos.

Come and See, the 1985 film by Elem Klimov, is the story of two children coping with life on the run from the Germans during the occupation of Russia in the Second World War. Early on in the film the little boy gets too close to a bomb exploding in the forest and his eardrums burst. For the next thirty minutes you hear everything through his ears, with all the normal sounds distorted or dulled. It's almost unbearable, and it was the first time I saw how sound could suck you into someone's head. As I watched more, I realised that sound was being used all the time to disturb and unsettle the viewer. There were abstract sounds, subliminal low hums or whirs, or noises like the buzz of flies over an overturned bowl of soup or the sound of a motorcycle in the fog. Then I saw how the director Elem Klimov made violence against animals and nature a part of his anti-war message. There were the rolling eyes of the dying cow behind which the little boy cowered as the laser-like shafts of gunfire passed overhead. There was the broken-winged heron shaking in the rain, wounded by the same shell that deafened the boy. There was the way in which the grass and fir tree were torn up by a shell, showering the forest with brown and green fallout. Sometimes these images were more disturbing than those of violence done to people.

But nothing could top the way Klimov filmed the soldiers burning the population of a village to death in a barn. Unlike many other films, *Come and See* gave the impression that it was happening in an agonisingly slow real time. And it was the tiny human details that struck you – the way in which one soldier vomited, another was drunk, a third stroked his petite lap dog, another lay dead in the bracken, with the brown liquid of a suicide draught dribbling out of the side of her mouth. Finally, in the aftermath, when flame-throwers were used to burn the rest of the village, there was the image of a young woman who had been gang-raped, struggling to walk down the mud road with only a top on, blood and shit caking her thighs, and a whistle rammed down her throat which sounded each time she took a breath.

It was almost impossible to watch this film without feeling violently sick. The thing that overwhelmed me most was the way in which everything I watched and heard was driven by one guiding idea – that war is wrong. It made me realise that many western war films get nowhere near articulating the reality of their subject because their motives are mixed or different – for many, war is portrayed as exciting and titillating rather than wrong. I've watched this film again and again, shown it in rehearsal rooms as a way of catapulting actors into the reality of war, and drawn repeatedly on its images in my theatre work. It is, above all, the film which provides the guiding principle for my use of sound, both abstract and literal.

Moving picture
Richard Linklater

Director, writer, *Slacker*, *Before Sunrise*, *School of Rock*, *Before Sunset*

I remember as a kid sitting through a triple-bill of *If...*, *Countdown* and *The Frozen Dead*, back to back. I was eight years old. I remember seeing *Taxi Driver* for the first time, and I kind of wandered out of the theatre in a daze, and didn't even remember they were showing *Mean Streets* next. This was in the early '80s, when *Mean Streets* wasn't on tape, so almost a year later I had to take a vacation from work when it showed up back on the schedule. But I was in such a daze after *Taxi Driver*, I just went 'Whooa', you know? And I remember sitting through Louis Malle's six-hour *Phantom India*, a wonderful documentary about India. It finished at something like five-to-one in the morning; it's meant to be watched one hour a week. I remember these endurance things. I saw Fassbinder's *Berlin Alexanderplatz* – not in one night, because it's 15 hours long, but in a weekend.

CONTEMPT

Tale of a monstrous national demagogue:
A Face in the Crowd

The other director to whom I owe an enormous debt of gratitude is Andrei Tarkovsky. Compared to the merciless and forensic takes of Klimov, Tarkovsky is more lyrical and poetic. His shots are notoriously slow and long, like when he shows a sick man try to walk across a drained pool with a lit candle that the wind keeps blowing out, for what feels like half an hour; or a woman, soaked by rain, pelt through the corridors of a printing house to check that she has not made an error in a Soviet book. He gives you the confidence to take your time in your work and follow your ideas through visually.

Then there's his idiosyncratic use of nature – the leitmotifs of wind through the trees and grass, or the mixture of fire and water, as when a wooden house burns down while rain drips from the eaves of a nearby dwelling. Weather is used repeatedly to communicate or support the psychological condition of the characters, like the endless rain in *Nostalgia* as a man, longing for home, travels through Italy; or the sunlight on the sand as a little boy remembers his dead mother.

And there's the bold use of dreams, like the slow motion of a mother washing her hair in a bowl while plaster from the ceiling falls all around her. These images haunt me and sometimes find their way into my work – literally, like the rain falling at the end of *The Three Sisters*, or the mother washing her hair in a bowl in *A Dream Play*. At other times his work provides a benchmark with which to measure my aesthetic choices. I don't think a single design process goes by without my referring to some image or frame from one of his films.

I also love the stories that are told about him and his perfectionism. For the opening take of *The Sacrifice*, Tarkovsky apparently spent hours picking all the tiny white flowers which littered the fields in the background of the shot, because he wanted a dense green texture.

Above all, Tarkovsky introduced me to the work of the actor Erland Josephson, who played the lead in *The Sacrifice*, and whom I finally tracked down at the Royal Dramatic Theatre in Stockholm, where I fulfilled my dream of working with him in productions of Strindberg's *Easter* and Beckett's *Krapp's Last Tape*.

Marty and me

Debbie Isitt wouldn't be where she is today without Scorsese.

I first saw Scorsese's *Raging Bull* when I was 15 years old and working in my Dad's video shop. My Dad had been a boxer in his youth, and I overheard him raving about it to customers as they came through the doors. One night I took the video home. Robert De Niro's performance as heavyweight champ Jake La Motta was awe-inspiring. As a child I had cried my way through *King Kong*, and La Motta got to me in a similar way. He was a man who was consumed with anger and jealousy, trained in violence and unable to escape his demons; he was exploited and yet he exploited others; there was no way out, it was downhill all the way. The film supplied a different vision of New York from the one in *King Kong* – still black and white, but glittering with glamorous, gangster-tinged society and shot through with intense emotional pain. I needed to know who the film-maker was. That's when I fell in love with Scorsese.

At 17 I wanted to be an actor. I had read up on Scorsese and De Niro, and knew all about the Lee Strasberg school of theatre in New York and the Method. I couldn't imagine leaving Birmingham and jetting off to New York, so I applied to a theatre school in Coventry. Not so glamorous, but only half an hour away on the train. I met a fellow student who was also a fan of Scorsese and De Niro, and we created our own 'film school', watching *Mean Streets*, *Raging Bull* and *Taxi Driver* over and over again. I was struck by the force of De Niro's acting, and wondered how Scorsese had created the conditions to elicit such brutally honest performances and create such believable yet hauntingly beautiful visual worlds. I was fascinated by his use of slow motion and sound effects; the music pulled me into another world and the unexpected violence shook my very being. I swung from laughter to fear to anger to tears. These were human stories about life and death, guilt and retribution, and, with a Catholic teenager, they struck a chord.

My fellow student and I made a deal. I would direct and he would be act, and together we would explore the Method, working on plays that I would write. Like Scorsese and De Niro we would have an intense working relationship, grappling with the issues that were important to us: domestic violence, relationships, gang culture and revenge. The Snarling Beasties theatre company was born. We were heavily inspired by Scorsese films, so it was no surprise when theatre critics described our work as 'cinematic'. We wanted the audience to

CONTEMPT

experience the same power that we encountered in Scorsese's films – but at a live event. The scenes were short and snappy – like a movie – driving the narrative through to its often shocking and violent conclusion.

In the 1980s, when I was on tour with Snarling Beasties, I saw that Scorsese's *GoodFellas* was out on general release. I went alone to an early showing in a desolate town called Crawley. There was no one else in the auditorium. It was the one of the most amazing cinema-going experiences of my life. My knuckles were white from the emotional rollercoaster ride of danger and violence, truth and glamour; it was the best ride I've ever had.

Better than sex. When I left the cinema to make my way to the theatre, I understood the powerful epiphany that had occurred. I wanted to make films. It wasn't enough to make theatre – however profound and exciting the live experience was, it always disappeared with the end of every show. I wanted something that would remain after all the sets had been burned.

It was a few years before I found the opportunity to make a film. My first short was for the BBC. I told them I knew everything I wanted to know about making films from watching Scorsese, and there was much raising of eyebrows; but I got the commission.

Strung up: **Team America: World Police**

CONTEMPT

Moving picture
Philip Seymour Hoffmann

Actor, *Happiness*, *Magnolia*, *Capote*

I was in college in the mid '80s and *GoodFellas* came out and I remember going to the theatre around the corner not knowing much about it – I was young then. I remember the movie started and then all of a sudden the movie was over and I realised that I had been sitting forward, on the lip of the seat, all the two hours 25 minutes without realising what was happening. It never even crossed my mind to make myself comfortable. Still, to this day, that was one of the most exciting cinema experiences of my life. I stood up – pretty stiffly – thinking, 'I have never seen anything like this.' It was the most thrilling movie I had ever seen; I couldn't believe it. And to this day I think it is one of the greats – I mean, come on, how many people have tried to make *GoodFellas* over the years?

I had always been a fan of *The Big Shave*. It was a bold and simple concept: a man stands at his sink and shaves. He doesn't stop shaving, he just lets the blood pour into the sink as he scrapes off more and more of his skin. I love this film, it's startling and funny and deeply disturbing. My first short, *Johnny Watkins Walks on Water*, was about a miracle birth. During one scene when a young girl gives birth to her miraculously conceived child, I drew on the imagery of the blood in Scorsese's sink.

My first feature, *Nasty Neighbours*, was my *Raging Bull*. I believed Ricky Tomlinson was an actor with all the emotional range of De Niro, and I invited him to take the central character of Harold Peach. A world away from New York boxing, *Nasty Neighbours* was set in a working-class suburb of Birmingham, but Peach had his own demons to deal with: a manic wife, aggressive neighbours and an ever-increasing cycle of debt. Ricky threw his heart and soul into the improvisational method we chose for the film and later won awards at international film festivals. I don't think anyone watching *Nasty Neighbours* would compare the film with *Raging Bull*, but if they were to look for Scorsese's influence they would see it in the tragicomic figure brilliantly portrayed by Ricky, and in the soundtrack and editing techniques. Moreover, they would find it in the tone: not blatantly comic, but funny and sad and disturbing all at once.

Prior to making *Nasty Neighbours*, I worked on a series of short films with film editor Nicky Ager. I understood the power of collaborating with a like-minded person in the edit. Like Scorsese and his editor Thelma Schoonmaker, Nicky and I have forged a long-term working partnership, and to my mind the power of these intense relationships, with actors or editors, are at the heart of making a personal vision.

My latest film, *Confetti,* is not inspired (in subject matter at least) by Scorsese's films – I don't think he'd be interested in making a film about weddings – but gathering an ensemble cast as 'family' was a big part of how this film was made. The actors involved worked with me over long stretches of time, developing characters and ideas and then throwing themselves into a shoot where there was no script and nothing to rely on except instinct and trust. *Confetti* is a comedy but it was still influenced by Scorsese: an emotional rollercoaster infused with humour, glamour and gritty reality.

Scorsese taught me about truth, energy, frenetic pace, danger, guts, instinct and the emotional journey. He has been inspirational even though I have never met him. He taught me never to shy away from what you believe to be true, even if the truth is ugly. He taught me to go on a quest of discovery when you work, to live your film-making, to love your film-making. He taught me about passion and risk.

Scorsese once said that directing a film is harder than coal-mining. I know what he means. Film-making is a dirty business: you have to roll up your sleeves and get on with it. It's gruelling. You dig, dig, dig until you discover the material. Scorsese has influenced and inspired a generation of film-makers and changed the lives of audiences around the world. He fed my imagination and spoke to me, and for that I will be eternally grateful.

CONTEMPT

Wonder

'I've seen things you
people wouldn't believe'
Blade Runner

Kid stuff
Wonder

Jonathan Rosenbaum looks at the ways a film can open our eyes – wide.

Wonder is closer to being a feeling than a thought, and one that we associate with children – or perhaps with grown-ups recapturing some of the innocent, open-mouthed awe they had as children. Many of us experienced such awe as kids watching the classic Disney cartoon features or certain live-action fantasy adventures like the 1933 *King Kong* or the 1940 *The Thief of Bagdad*.

Other generations, for that matter, might recall feeling a comparable emotion before the vast spaces of the 1916 *Intolerance* (whose gigantic Babylon set would eventually be redressed for Kong's Skull Island) or the 1924 *The Thief of Bagdad* or the 2005 *King Kong* – or even in that hokey opening line, 'A long time ago, in a galaxy far, far away…'. Or what about the hushed sense of reverence that we bring to the virgin wilderness of *The Big Sky*, whose very title expresses our feeling of astonishment? It's a primal emotion, particularly as it relates to cinema in the old-fashioned sense: 35-millimetre projection in palatial theaters, the screen invariably much larger than we are ('Bigger Than Life', as the title of a Nicholas Ray 'Scope melodrama has it). Of course, with the advent of digital video, smaller screens, home viewing and a more detailed interest on the part of the public in understanding how various visual effects are achieved, some of this innocence and involvement has been altered. But our primal sense of wonder in the cinematic experience remains, in spite of everything; and without it I'm not even sure if we'd still be watching nearly as much.

If we consider the role played by our imaginations in 'completing' a film's image and sound – filling in the dark spaces that appear between the film frames without ever consciously seeing them, and doing pretty much the same thing with offscreen spaces, such as responding creatively to suggestive soundtracks by filling in additional images

Magical, no other word for it:
Hayao Miyazaki's **My Neighbour Totoro**

WONDER

of our own – this shouldn't be at all surprising. 'I want to give the audience a hint of a scene,' Orson Welles said early in his career. 'No more than that. Give them too much and they won't contribute anything themselves. Give them just a suggestion and you get them working with you.' In fact, he was referring explicitly to theatre and implicitly to radio when he said this in 1938, not to cinema at all. But the sense of wonder he brought to movies soon afterwards in *Citizen Kane* and *The Magnificent Ambersons* had a lot to do with adapting some of the discoveries he'd already made about other dramatic forms to express a certain wonderment about America. One might even add to this that the medium for expressing

Ridley Scott saw the future, and it was raining: **Blade Runner**

cinematic wonder, sought after and applied with the aggressive assault of a blunt instrument, though I think it would be lamentable to associate this kind of coercion too closely with wonder. The best kinds of wonder in movies are the ones that invite and encourage idle speculation rather than those that are designed to settle disputes, stop conversations cold, or simply intimidate. Wonder is a kind of question mark from which fear is not so much abolished as held in an exquisitely sustained abeyance, allowing the mind in a relaxed state to fill in the gaps with all sorts of possibilities. Terrifying and brutalising the spectator, by contrast, has zip to do with soliciting the gentler responses of wonder.

Charles Laughton's sublime *The Night of the Hunter*, charting the nightmarish pursuit of two children by an insane and deadly preacher (Robert Mitchum) across an Expressionist version of rural Depression-era America, certainly has its chilling moments. Yet these are mainly secondary to the sense of poetic wonder felt by these children about the world they're inhabiting and sometimes rushing through. There's a sinister edge to the preacher's nocturnal silhouette on horseback as seen by the boy protagonist from a distant hayloft while he hears the villain faintly singing 'Leaning on the Everlasting Arms'. Yet it's the boy's relatively calm sense of wonder about this threat – 'Don't he never sleep?' – that leaves the most profound impression. If fear were all he was experiencing, we wouldn't wind up with any sense of wonder at all.

Another thing that needs to be sharply distinguished from wonder is curiosity – especially the kind that killed the cat and that leads us remorselessly through whodunits. Let's call curiosity a very limited kind of wonder, restricted mainly to details of plot and character that fill out an incomplete jigsaw puzzle. Wonder is more spiritual and all encompassing than that, and therefore less geared as a rule to straight-ahead storytelling. As gifted a storyteller as Steven Spielberg is, the moment in *Close Encounters of the Third Kind* when the massive alien spaceship makes its landing is basically a stretched-out moment when the story stops and the spectacle takes over.

this wonderment is secondary; it's the feeling itself that remains primary – the experience of remaining an infant, basking in the warmth and expanse of a maternal screen and wondering where all this bounty comes from.

Of course, there's always been a brutal side to movies as well; the military term 'shock and awe' could be viewed as a kind of perversion of

The wonders of the future, as imagined in 1936: **Things to Come**

I'm reminded of the term used by the American film theorist Tom Gunning, 'the cinema of attractions', that links early movies to carnival sideshows rather than serial cliffhangers. Both are of course essential aspects of our experiences of movies, but the elements that provoke our wonder are more apt to exist as spectacle than as plot or action: the landscapes in an Anthony Mann Western like *The Naked Spur* or *Man of the West* or the fairy-tale waterfall in Nicholas Ray's *Johnny Guitar*.

And when we turn to independent cinema and art cinema, a sense that people and life are ultimately unknowable – or at least unfathomable – lies behind the sense of wonder about the world and the human condition conveyed in very different ways by Michelangelo Antonioni, Robert Bresson, John Cassavetes, Carl Dreyer, and Atom Egoyan (to restrict my list to just the first five letters of the alphabet).

The late science fiction writer Damon Knight titled his excellent collection of science fiction criticism *In Search of Wonder*, and it's certainly true that it's a sense of quiet amazement and bemusement that draws us to both sci-fi and fantasy, either on the page or on the screen. It's the main thing we bring away from outer-space yarns as disparate as *Forbidden Planet* and *2001: A Space Odyssey*, and stories about androids and future cityscapes as different from one another as *Metropolis*, *Blade Runner*, and *A.I. Artificial Intelligence*. On the other hand, wonder isn't at all what we bring away from sci-fi satires like Stanley Kubrick's *Dr Strangelove: or, How I Learned to Stop Worrying and Love the Bomb* and *A Clockwork Orange*, or Paul Verhoeven's *RoboCop* and *Starship Troopers*, because sarcasm and wonder rarely make compatible bedfellows.

The sense of immensity and monumentality conveyed in sci-fi films such as *Things to Come* isn't necessarily just a function of the way we feel about the future. There's another string of films conveying a similar sense of bottomless mystery about the historical past, ranging from Howard Hawks's 1955 bombastic and campy but awestruck spectacular *Land of the Pharaohs* to Kubrick's more muted and melancholy *Barry Lyndon*

'It's the feeling itself – the experience of remaining an infant, basking in the warmth and expanse of a maternal screen.'

(a kind of variant of Welles's aforementioned *Ambersons*) – or from the exquisite Hong Kong biopic *Actress*, (with Maggie Cheung as Ruan Ling-yu, the Chinese Garbo, working in the Shanghai film industry of the 1930s), to Richard Linklater's underrated saga about a Texas family of 1920s bank robbers, *The Newton Boys*.

Some film-makers, such as Alain Resnais and Andrei Tarkovsky take us on guided tours of metaphysical worlds, mysterious and uncharted labyrinths of the mind. I'd call them quintessential directors of wonder, above all because their appeal remains sensual and emotional rather than intellectual while plumbing the depths of our inner lives, the kinds of secrets and hidden desires we sometimes keep even from ourselves. If you think Resnais and Alain Robbe-Grillet's *Last Year at Marienbad* or Resnais and David Mercer's *Providence* are intellectual or cerebral puzzles, you aren't likely to catch their poetic handling of nocturnal moods and the imaginative, dreamlike currents that flow through both of them like uncanny, subterranean wiring.

There's another sense of the uncanny found in Tarkovsky's *Solaris* and *Stalker*, both deceptively derived from SF novels of ideas. I think that both films have relatively little to do with these ideas, and quite a lot to do with the gut feelings and intuitions of someone experiencing spiritual desolation and a feeling of awe about the universe he inhabits.

WONDER

Apart from the church hymn sung by Mitchum, I haven't yet said anything about music. Yet this clearly plays a substantial role in establishing our gaping sense of wonder in many of the above examples – Strauss's 'Blue Danube Waltz' in *2001: A Space Odyssey* and the eerie organ music resembling a spooky silent film accompaniment in *Last Year at Marienbad*; the romantically lush, Hollywoodish Miklos Rosza score in *Providence* and the ecstatic burst of the choral climax of Beethoven's Ninth Symphony in the final sequence of *Stalker*.

Which makes it only logical that some of the ultimate expressions of amazement in movies come to us courtesy of actual musicals. Consider the awe-inspiring geometric shapes of chorus girls in Busby Berkeley production numbers, the astonishingly gaudy spectacle of Marilyn Monroe and Jane Russell in *Gentlemen Prefer Blondes*, or even something as relatively modest as Donald O'Connor dancing wildly around a park pavilion on roller skates in *I Love Melvin* from the same year. For the truth is we can only gape at such soulful visions of glitz, grace, and synchronicity, and become gullible kids all over again.

Wonder in 20 films

Tih Minh (1918)
My favourite of the wonderful Louis Feuillade serials of the teens – all of which feature masked criminals, intricate schemes and subterfuges, resourceful servants, dopey lounge lizards, lovely natural locations (such as the Paris settings for *Les Vampires* or the Côte d'Azur settings here), jaw-dropping stunts and a perpetual sense of fantasy rubbing shoulders with documentary actuality.

Foolish Wives (1922)
Erich von Stroheim had never even been to Monte Carlo when he decided to rebuild it on the Pacific Coast in all its glory and play a master Russian swindler and seducer inside the gargantuan set. He robs unsuspecting American tourists blind, especially the ladies of his title, and the so-called Man You Love to Hate can't help but command our guarded respect.

Blonde Crazy (1931)
Cut to some low-grade urban hijinks in the thick of the Depression, as James Cagney and Joan Blondell perform their own sassy scams with and against one

another and sometimes get burned by other people. We can only admire the energy of all the con-artistry.

Ivan (1932)
Meanwhile, over in Russia, they're idealistically building huge dams, like the one in Alexander Dovzhenko's first talkie. But the fact that we never even see this one completed is part of the goofy conceit of this poetic fable, which shows more affection for a crusty old peasant who refuses to move a muscle than for all the labourers breaking their backs.

Sylvia Scarlett (1935)
A highly subversive bending of both gender and genre that tanked at the box office because audiences didn't know what to make of it. Katharine Hepburn disguises herself as a boy, and when Cary Grant (in a rare part exposing his Cockney origins) gets the hots for him (or is it her?), we're not sure whether to laugh or cry. Director George Cukor keeps all concerned on their toes, including us.

Ivan the Terrible (1944–46)
Sergei Eisenstein's underrated masterwork is at once a period saga, the greatest Flash Gordon movie ever made, a devastating portrait of Josef Stalin's paranoia, a critical self-portrait with psychoanalytical overtones and a Gothic nightmare of angularity. And to make matters worse (or better), the whole thing seems to be experienced through the eyes of a ten-year-old.

The Three Caballeros (1945)
Disney at its most avant-garde, mixing South American live-action and giddy animation with such abandon, and in so many riotous colours that explode into so many alternate and abstract counter-realities, that Busby Berkeley must have been eating his heart out. Donald Duck ogles señoritas and the universe expands.

Park Row (1952)
The great Samuel Fuller couldn't convince Fox to bankroll his action-packed hymn to the birth of New York yellow journalism – Darryl F Zanuck suggested he do it as a musical – so he sank his own money into this pocket *Citizen Kane*, filmed on a cosy period set and lost every penny. It's hyperbolically sincere and reverent about the invention of linotype and a statue of Benjamin Franklin (against which Gene Evans's editor-hero bashes out a villain's brains).

The 5000 Fingers of Dr T (1953)
The weird imaginings of children's author Dr Seuss expanded into a Surrealist nightmare with musical numbers about a diabolical piano teacher (Hans Conried) who imports 500 hapless kids to his castle to play his favourite exercise on

WONDER

a continuous keyboard. Perhaps I found this tacky monstrosity unforgettable at the age of ten because I was the same age as the hero (Tommy Rettig).

Ordet (1955)
What better begetter of stupefied wonder than a genuine miracle? It's said Carl Dreyer wasn't even religious, yet he made this heavy, rural chamber piece about family discord and faith into a challenging confrontation for believers and non-believers alike.

The Tiger of Eschnapur/ The Indian Tomb (1958)
Fritz Lang's return to European film-making after a long sojourn in the US was a big-budget remake of a fantasy that he'd originally co-written with his wife, Thea von Harbou, in the early '20s. This opulent fairy tale in colour was popular with the public, at least in Europe, but its deliberate childlike innocence alienated most critics, who should have known better.

Shadows of Our Forgotten Ancestors (1964)
The first feature of the visionary Armenian-born Soviet film-maker Sergo Paradjanov to reach the west, adapted from a Ukrainian novel and set in the Carpathian Mountains. This delirious merging of myth, folklore, history, poetry, ethnography, dance and ritual begins with the cutting down of a majestic tree in a forest, which is partially seen from the viewpoint of the toppling tree.

Playtime (1967)
To make his greatest film, Jacques Tati built an entire city on the outskirts of Paris and turned his own most famous character, Monsieur Hulot, into one of many extras, insisting democratically that 'the comic effect belongs to everyone'. Perhaps the cinema's greatest illustration of community triumphing over architecture.

Aguirre, Wrath of God (1972)
An opening title of this pie-eyed epic about a mad conquistador (Klaus Kinski) in search of El Dorado through awesome natural landscapes claims that it has some historical basis, but film-maker Werner Herzog freely admitted that he made the whole thing up – and put together a mad expedition of his own in order to film it. One doubts that *Apocalypse Now* (1979) would ever have been conceived without its shining example.

Céline and Julie Go Boating (1974)
Jacques Rivette's delicious fusing of Lewis Carroll with Vincente Minnelli (as updated by Jean Rouch) into an uncanny horror comedy. It was co-written by

the four lead actress – Juliet Berto and Dominique Labourier as the goofy, titular heroines in Paris, Bulle Ogier and Marie-France Pisier as phantom ladies in the old, dark house in the suburbs that the other two periodically visit – in collaboration with the Argentinian magical realist Eduardo de Gregorio; and over its 193 minutes, wonders never cease.

Perceval le Gallois (1978)
Eric Rohmer's overlooked musical, based on Chrétien de Troyes's 12th-century epic poem, and filmed on a deliberately artificial-looking soundstage, with perspectives as flat as medieval tapestries, preserves all the sweet innocence of the original and adds bright colours.

Where Is My Friend's House? (1987)
The first masterpiece by Abbas Kiarostami to have a sizable commercial success in Iran, named after a locally famous poem by Sohrab Sepehry, is a miniature epic about a rural schoolboy trying to return a classmate's notebook in a neighbouring village and getting lost. Kiarostami makes it a philosophical parable about the adventures and ethical challenges of childhood itself.

Distant Voices, Still Lives (1988)
Terence Davies's impressionistic memories of his Liverpool childhood has been faulted for its emphasis on domestic brutality, family rituals such as funerals and weddings, and singing in pubs and at parties. But as a lapsed Catholic, Davies endows all these everyday activities with the passion and intensity of luminous dreams.

Dead Man (1995)
Jim Jarmusch reimagines the black and white Western the way a Native American during the 19th century might have viewed it – as a genocidal nightmare about the arrival of capitalism. He also creates a warm friendship between a dying accountant from Cleveland named William Blake (Johnny Depp) and a Native American outcast named Nobody (Gary Farmer) – as well as many visionary experiences in the American north-west.

Howl's Moving Castle (2005)
In Hayao Miyazaki's truly inspired animated adaptation of Diana Wynne Jones's novel, people and objects undergo constant transformations according to their emotional and existential states of being. Furthermore, wisdom doesn't so much succeed callowness as peacefully coexist with it. So the teenage heroine may get turned into a 90-year-old housekeeper for a youthful magician in a walking castle, but whenever she feels romantic stirrings for him, she becomes a teenager again – a wonderful conceit.

Seeing is believing

Nicholas Royle talks to Nicolas Roeg about a lifetime in the movies.

Many of the protagonists in Nicolas Roeg's films – Chas Devlin (James Fox) in *Performance*, John Baxter (Donald Sutherland) in *Don't Look Now*, Thomas Jerome Newton (David Bowie) in *The Man Who Fell to Earth* – share a vital quality: belief. Chas believes in himself, and, to begin with at least, studying his reflection only strengthens his self-belief. Newton is credulous, perhaps, taking people at face value, but being an alien recently arrived from another planet, he has a pretty good excuse. John Baxter believes the evidence of his eyes as he follows a phantom child in a red coat around a fatefully wintry Venice. 'Seeing is believing,' he says.

Born in 1928, Nicolas Roeg became a moviegoer in the 1930s, long before cinema was granted the status of an art form. There was no great emphasis on scholarly appreciation or critical analysis of the moving image. Film schools had yet to be invented. People went to the movies without knowing the business inside out, like today. The first film Roeg saw was *Laurel and Hardy in Toyland*.

'The thing that struck me most of all about cinema was that I believed it,' says Roeg. 'I didn't think of it as drama. It wasn't like pantomime or going to the theatre.'

A child visiting the local multiplex today to see the latest Harry Potter or Peter Jackson has seen the previous films in the series and the trailer for the new film. He or she has probably read the book and acquired a roomful of merchandising paraphernalia. The film could hardly be more familiar to them when they sit down in the dark to watch it for the first time.

The complete reverse was true for the young Roeg. When he went to see *The Lives of a Bengal Lancer*, C Aubrey Smith didn't play the Major, he was the Major. 'I couldn't understand that he was also a leading actor, because he was the Major. I accepted it as reality. And that stayed with me for a long, long time. Film criticism was not as popular as it is today, so what you saw on screen was always much more surprising. Now, before we go to the

cinema we pretty well know all about the film. There's very little left to discover, which is rather sad. For me it was a time of total discovery and amazement and wonder.'

Roeg regrets how staid and clichéd our thinking about cinema has become, especially with regard to the way film is constructed. 'Very few people have the sense of wonder that I had when I was first going to the cinema. I didn't know anything about it. Now everybody knows everything about it.' An unexpected, but nevertheless logical, corollary of this has been the growing interest in TV reality shows. 'The one thing people don't know everything about is the reality show.' In an area of film-making where anything could happen, it's still possible to be taken by surprise.

'With film now, you know what the drama's going to be. You just think, 'Oh, that was well acted,' or 'Didn't they do that well?' They have so many How to Do It books and they talk

Moving picture
Damien Odoul

Director, writer, *Le Souffle*, *Errance*

I was 20 years old when I went to see Carl Dreyer's *Ordet*. It troubled me so much, I couldn't leave the cinema. It was the last screening of the night, and people were asking me to go so they could lock up and get home, but I couldn't get out of my seat! I wondered if cinema was becoming a physical experience for me. And it was the same with Sokurov's *Mother and Son*, Tarkovsky's *Andrei Rublev*, and Pasolini's *The Gospel According to St Matthew*. I have the same reaction when I see certain paintings by Caravaggio – you feel you're not the same person after looking at it. Mizoguchi said, 'Each time you look at something, you have to refresh your eyes before looking.' That's great advice for a film-maker, but it works for a spectator, too.

Mary Elizabeth Mastrantonio, Ed Harris and some watery CGI wizardry: **The Abyss**

about the three-act structure. I can hardly bear to be in the room with people who know all about how to make a movie. Fucked if I know how to make a movie. They read a script and then they have those meetings in which they say, "It's two thirds there. I think there's a third missing." What, every third page, or the first thirty pages? It's meaningless. A script isn't a film. It's the first stage, just like getting the money is the second stage. As far as I'm concerned, the script is happening while the director is making the film. The final draft is happening while he's making the film, and the final release draft is when it's cut. If you could only budget and get a script of the film of how it's going to be when it's cut you could shoot everything in about two weeks.'

Warner Bros sat on *Performance*, which Roeg directed with Donald Cammell, for three years before letting it be released, and then it arrived with the tagline 'Ten years ahead of its time…' Ironic, because in the last 30-odd years a more conservative attitude has tended to prevail. It's hard to believe that any major studio would greenlight a film such as *Performance* today, but the film retains the same power to surprise audiences as it had in the 1970s.

Two decades later, Roeg was making a very different kind of film, *The Witches*, with Jim Henson, storyboards and everything, but surprise was still important elements for the director. 'Jim Henson was a very nice man but we couldn't have been further apart in terms of our thoughts about things,' says Roeg. Mice were an issue. Henson favoured scale models, while Roeg preferred the unpredictability, the random scattering, of real rodents. He wanted to follow their natural instincts, their tiny moments of decision, this way or that. In the end, they had both, real and artificial.

'We had a mouse trainer, a prop man: he was fantastic,' Roeg remembers, refusing to reveal exactly how the mice were put through their paces. 'I don't like to say how we did it. It was an extraordinary thing. Jim Henson couldn't believe it. He was amazed. Of course, we had an electric mouse – it ran across the

Wonderful girls! That's
Footlight Parade

set, whirrr – but cut together with the real mice.' The real mice gave it the strangeness Roeg wanted, they kept it surprising. 'We didn't have CGI or anything. I think that CGI is a wonderful instrument, but it can be overused. It takes away the surprise.'

Hand in hand with surprise goes innocence. 'There are no rules in life, are there?' says Roeg. 'And if there are, you should learn them, but not necessarily obey them all the time. You must make your choices. That's how you maintain your innocence. It's the only thing I'd be arrogant about. I'd like to retain my innocence in some way. When I first encountered cinema it was with a sense of wonder.'

Is that sense of wonder still intact?

'Yes, very much so. But in Britain right now we're not really experiencing much of a sense of wonder at cinemas at all. When you think that the most important people are the marketing people. I've actually had people say to me, "We don't know how to market this." Just about scripts. I say, "But marketing, that comes later." If they don't know how to market it, they shouldn't be in marketing. The fairground barker doesn't say, "Oooh, they don't like tattooed ladies." He says, "Roll up, roll up, come and see the most extraordinary tattooed lady you've ever seen." For a marketing person to say "We don't know how to market it" is the stupidest thing in the world. It's the death of the salesman. Arthur Miller would have a laugh at that.'

Good news for Roeg fans is that the director is developing two new projects, a return to the horror genre with *Adina*, and a thriller, *Puffball*. When is shooting expected to start?

'Oh, God knows. We'll have to see how the marketing goes.'

Critics' choice
Future visions

Alphaville
(1965, Fr/It) d Jean-Luc Godard. *cast* Eddie Constatine, Anna Karina, Howard Vernon. Godard's dazzling mix of *film noir* and sci-fi riffs on alienation in a technological society.

Blade Runner – The Director's Cut
(1982/1991, US) d Ridley Scott. *cast* Harrison Ford, Rutger Hauer, Sean Young. The restored and reconfigured version of Scott's classic film, set in 2019 Los Angeles.

Metropolis
(1926, Ger) d Fritz Lang. *cast* Alfred Abel, Gustav Fröhlich, Brigitte Helm, Rudolf Klein-Rogge. Gothic horror meets sci-fi in a future mechanised society founded on slavery.

Silent Running
(1971, US) d Douglas Trumbull. *cast* Bruce Dern, Cliff Potts, Ron Rifkin, Jesse Vint. Man and his machines must save the world – even at the risk of madness.

Solaris
(1972, USSR) d Andrei Tarkovsky. *cast* Donatas Banionis, Natalya Bondarchuk, Yuri Jarvet. The socialist response to *2001: A Space Odyssey* is a lesson in sentimental humanism.

The Terminator
(1984, US) d James Cameron. *cast* Arnold Schwarzenegger, Michael Biehn, Linda Hamilton. Arnie's back from a future where machines rule – though a freedom fighter may save us yet.

Things to Come
(1936, GB) d William Cameron Menzies. *cast* Raymond Massey, Ralph Richardson. Film version of HG Wells's tale of 100 years of global warfare, destruction and re-civilisation.

The Truman Show
(1998, US) d Peter Weir. *cast* Jim Carrey, Ed Harris, Laura Linney, Noah Emmerich. TV's most audacious experiment – a real-life soap following a man from cradle to grave.

2001: A Space Odyssey
(1968, GB) d Stanley Kubrick. *cast* Keir Dullea, Gary Lockwood, William Sylvester. Apes, astronauts, a homicidal computer, a monolith and a clutch of jaw-dropping sets.

2046
(2004, Fr/Ger/HK/China) d Wong Kar Wai. *cast* Tony Leung, Chiu Wai, Gong Li, Faye Wong. A writer's emotional odyssey is intercut with scenes from his own allegorical sci-fi novel.

The *bigger*
picture

Cannes
do

Kieron Corless enters the madhouse that is the world's largest film festival.

It's a dinosaur, a brothel, a decadent, PR-led spectacle; it's a cinematic cornucopia, a sensitive barometer, a vital commercial showcase. There are as many strongly held and polarised opinions about the Cannes film festival as there are *festivaliers*, and right now there are more of both than ever. The number of accreditations for the 2005 edition stood at 21,000 for the festival, 9,500 for the market. The number of films invited to compete in the Official Selection for the much-coveted Palme d'Or has barely altered in recent years (21 in 2005), but much else around that high-profile core entity has. Cannes just keeps on growing; including all the market screenings, there were more than 900 new feature films shown there in 2005. That makes it by some margin the biggest film festival, not to mention the biggest film market, in the world.

It's also the second biggest media event after the Olympics, which means producers will move heaven and earth to display their wares at

Cannes. Far more than its closest rivals Venice and Berlin, the publicity generated by a prize at Cannes will impact colossally on a film's commercial prospects and seal a director's international reputation. Achieving this level of worldwide recognition and preeminence has been, like all success stories, a combination of good fortune and canniness. Set up as a rival 'free festival' in 1939 to counter Venice's fascist leanings, and its location on the Côte d'Azur was a strategic choice which has reaped unforeseen dividends. The iconography of topless starlets cavorting on sun-kissed beaches and of carefree Mediterranean licence persists in the popular imagination (and, to an extent, in reality), to the festival's enduring advantage.

The gorgeous location and clement May weather have also been instrumental in tempting those all-important American stars across the Atlantic, inaugurating a complex, longstanding engagement between Cannes and America, between – at its simplest – the auteur

cinema with which France and Europe have long been associated, and another kind, driven by profit and entertainment. More than any other forum, Cannes has thrown the tensions provoked by those different versions of what constitutes cinema into sharp relief; at certain periods they've been mutually enriching, at other times deeply antagonistic.

Which begs the question – does Cannes need Hollywood more than Hollywood needs Cannes? The European market is hugely important for the big contemporary Hollywood releases. Sending your stars to parade at Cannes ensures massive press and TV coverage and removes the necessity for tiresome and expensive slogging round European capitals. For the festival, the big American stars supply the glamour and allure upon which its reputation has been founded, and so enable it to stay ahead of its rivals. There's a mutual dependence, but a mutual suspicion and wariness too.

A resonant anecdote related by Mike Leigh, a Palme d'Or winner with *Secrets & Lies* in 1997, shines a humorous spotlight on this occasionally uneasy relationship. Leigh was first invited into the Cannes competition in 1996 with *Naked*, a big coup for a small British arthouse film. Arriving by limo at his film's evening screening, Leigh and his entourage were politely asked by a festival official to stand aside to let no lesser eminence than Arnold Schwarzenegger precede them up the red carpet. Delighted to learn that Arnie was coming to see their film, the team gladly complied, enabling a beaming, waving Arnie to sweep past them and bask in the crowd's exultant cheers. Leigh and co trooped up the steps after him only to discover that Arnie, his photo-op done with, had made a swift exit through a side-door of the Grand Palais, and was off down the Croisette to grab an early dinner.

So Cannes, as many observers have noted, is curiously schizophrenic. In 2005 Paris Hilton and George Lucas brought the place to a standstill, while a low-budget art film by the Belgian Dardennes brothers carried off the main prize. Those kinds of seismic contrasts produce endless dramas, which of course constitute any film festival's lifeblood. In Cannes' case they've often been political, the most recent example being the award to Michael Moore's *Fahrenheit 9/11* in 2004 shortly before the US presidential election. Cannes attracts controversy, and accusations of corruption, like moths to a lamp. Jury presidents Françoise Sagan and Dirk Bogarde (in 1979 and 1984 respectively) both went on record to claim the festival tried to influence their jurys' deliberations for the main awards. In 2003 the trade magazine *Variety* offered compelling evidence that films with French financial input had a much higher chance of being accepted into the competition than those without.

The latter accusation is a useful reminder that the festival is a vast commercial enterprise – a 'state business' in the words of film historian and producer Colin MacCabe. The festival's budget currently stands at 20 million euros per annum, a mix of private and public money. Cannes' long-term investment in cinema as an art form, its championing of the auteur, does not preclude hard-headed business acumen. The vast amounts of sponsorship and TV money sloshing around Cannes nowadays, supplied principally by L'Oréal and Canal+, brings huge numbers of 'corporate' audiences in its train who, along with the hordes of star-gazers, contribute to the festival's gigantism. It doesn't make for a relaxed experience. Trying to walk past the Palais can be akin to shoving your way through a crowds of city-centre shoppers on a Saturday afternoon, especially when some superstar is fluttering up the red-carpet. Several days of this, let alone nearly two weeks, can rapidly erode your good humour.

According to Cannes lore, there was a time when a journo really could just sit down and have a coffee with Alfred Hitchcock or Cary Grant, without first begging 82 publicists for the privilege. The innocence and intimacy of those early days have long been obliterated, epitomised by the replacement of the old, small-scale Palais by the Orwellian Grand Palais in 1983, nicknamed Le Bunker, a monumental and monumentally hideous building. Security around it is tight, to put it mildly. 'I've been fucking manhandled by those guys!' recalled one well-known American producer recently, still smarting from the experience. Actress Rita Tushingham recalls pressing up her nose up to

the window of the *Taste of Honey* party in 1962 'like a Dickensian waif', shut out by a security goon who refused to believe she was the star of the film, despite the fact she'd just been awarded the Best Actress prize. With its ruthlessly imposed hierarchies, endless black limos and overbearing security, 'it feels very fascistic', director John Boorman has noted. You shouldn't go to Cannes if you're feeling delicate or insecure.

The resulting near-hysterical atmosphere produces a phenomenon known as 'festival fever'. It's apparent at other festivals too, but with nothing like the intensity of Cannes, where so much more is at stake. Festival fever can break out in all kinds of ways. If you're Spike Lee, you might hint at setting about the 1989 Jury President with a baseball bat ('I have a Louisville slugger with Wim Wenders's name on it') for not bestowing honours on *Do the Right Thing*. In the typical Cannes audience, you might find yourself stamping and cheering or baying and hissing like a feral dog when the lights go up, much as you would have done in a Roman amphitheatre circa 100 BC. Numerous directors have spoken of this sacrificial element to the Cannes experience, and while many careers have been made at Cannes (or 'anointed' as the French critics like to put it), plenty of others have been killed stone dead. If you're a journalist you might suspend your critical faculties to entertain the most outlandish rumours, which seem to flourish in these febrile conditions. You enter a bubble when you go to Cannes, removed from the rest of the world and operating by its own rules; the behaviour it induces can seem quite baffling when recollected in later tranquillity.

If you're up for the challenge, though, Cannes has something for just about everyone. Parallel strands such as the Director's Fortnight and Critics' Week, dedicated to unearthing new, more experimental cinematic talent, mean the festival covers an enormous amount of ground. They also reveal the Cannes capacity for reinvention, exemplified more recently by new initiatives such as 'Tous les Cinémas du Monde' and 'L'Atelier du Festival'. For all its black tie conservatism, Cannes has managed to adapt and thrive. With a relatively new artistic director, Thierry Frémaux, at the helm, the festival's identity will undoubtedly shift again in its seventh decade. It might be a dinosaur, but the beast is a long way from extinction.

On locations

Do the Right Thing and the brownstones of Brooklyn. *Once Upon a Time in the West* and the Almería desert, as well as the wide shots of Monument Valley. *Cyclo* and the hustle and bustle of Ho Chi Minh City. *Don't Look Now* and the dark, narrow streets of Venice. *The Story of Qiu Ju* and rural China. *Days of Heaven* and the Texas landscape. These are just a few of the movies that fuelled my love of cinema, and the locations that seemed to play such a huge part of the story.

For me, the vital part of making a movie is choosing the location. While the story is being written, I'm always thinking, 'where can I set this?' My first feature, *The Warrior*, was shot in India, in Rajasthan and in the Himalayas. The script was written as a samurai film set in Japan; it was only later that I shifted the location to make it more do-able. The new location gave me the rules of the story. I suddenly had the desert, the crumbling forts, the amazing light, the faces of the people in the villages, the language that made me realise I wouldn't be making the film in English.

My second film, *The Return*, takes place in the flat, barren greenery of Texas. Some of the

Moving picture
Ray Harryhausen

Special effects maestro, *Jason and the Argonauts*, *The Seventh Voyage of Sinbad*

My parents took me to the movies every Saturday, and the fantasy films always struck a chord with me. I saw *The Lost World* and *Metropolis* when I was four years old. But the film that changed everything for me was *King Kong* in 1933. My aunt worked for Sid Grauman's mother, and Sid gave her three tickets to this gorilla picture he was opening at Grauman's Chinese Theatre on Hollywood Boulevard. I went with my aunt and my mother. There was a giant ape and pink flamingos in the lobby, and there was a stage show before the movie that lasted about an hour: a jungle show with dancers and a trapeze, people in animal costumes. Sid Grauman was a great showman. Then there was the movie itself. I wasn't scared, I was awe-struck. I had never seen anything like it before. For me, it is *the* fantasy film.

WONDER

Nature's own pursuit drama: one of many marvels in **Deep Blue**

You know when you've been bugged: **Microcosmos**

movie was shot in West Texas in Big Bend, and I can't deny that a part of me wanted to go there, as I love mountains – and I was inspired by the opening of *Paris, Texas* being shot there.

True North, my next film (hopefully) is set in the high Arctic, the story takes place in snow and ice. I like tough locations, places that challenge me and the cast and crew; they give me a setting for the film, but they also give me barriers and restrictions. I don't really like shooting in studios, I come from low budget film-making, making films in places that I could use for free: the high street around the corner, my parents' house while they were away on holiday. I never had the chance to build sets. I now see how it works, but deep down I like the realism and the restrictions of real locations; I like the fact they force me to be creative.

I was heavily influenced by a short conversation I had with Ken Loach when I was a student. I intended to make my student film

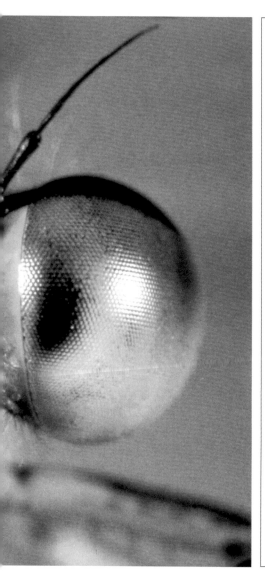

Moving picture
The Dardenne Brothers, Luc and Jean-Pierre

....

Directors, producers and writers,
La Promesse, Rosetta, The Son, The Child

Luc Dardenne: Our father wouldn't let us have a TV. But a neighbour's dad was an inventor and very keen on gadgetry, so they were the first family in the street to have a set. I'd go next door to watch without telling dad and be caught up in it while my friend's family usually sat there snoring. Well, they were the night I saw my first ever nude female, the teenage girl in Bresson's *Au Hasard, Balthazar*! I was transfixed; I couldn't believe I was the only one awake and watching. I went home flushed, and my dad asked, 'What have you been up to?' What could I say? 'Just playing.'

Jean-Pierre Dardenne: There were two cinemas in our village, but dad was very against us seeing movies. But when I was very small I used to visit our grandmother at the other end of the village. On one such visit I bumped into my school chums who lived in that part of the village and were going to see *The Adventures of Robin Hood* with Errol Flynn and Olivia de Havilland. They said I had to see it with them. I said I would, but my grandma said I had to ask dad. Because the film started quite soon, I had to run like mad across the village, and I turned up breathless: 'Can I see *Robin Hood*?'. Still he said no. So I had to run all the way back to my pals and tell them to go without me. So my most vivid memory is of a film I didn't see!

The Sheep Thief in India with non-professional actors, and I asked his advice on how to go about it. He told me to go there with my script, but rather than try to find exactly what I had written, to be open-minded to the place – to find somewhere that worked for the story and be free enough to change the script to fit the location, use the magic of the real places that I would find, use the local people and make them a part of the production; and, importantly, for the production and crew to become a part of the village or town we'd be living in for some time.

I was taught at the Royal College of Art film school by a brilliant production design tutor, Moira Tate, who taught me the importance of the production designer that a huge element of the movie hinges on a strong location, be it a set or a real place. I'm interested in making visually powerful films, so I love to work closely with a production designer and search for the best available location, if possible while writing the screenplay so I can actually put the unique places we find on to the page.

I'd go to the end of the world to find the place that is right for the film. As long as I am able to make films for the right price. Films are so expensive, that many get shot in places that offer the right tax deals, that offer cheap crew or that can easily cheat for a range of landscapes.

But for me, when I'm making my own more personal films, I would love to keep pushing to come up with stories that I can shoot in parts of the world I've never had a chance to experience. That's what excites me – the challenge of going to a new place, seeing it with an outsider's eyes. Taking in all the details that people who live in the place have maybe got so used to that they don't notice any more.

I remember in India while location hunting for *The Warrior* I made notes of all the insects and animals I would see every day. I put them in the script, those scorpions, wild dogs and dung beetles made it into the movie. They added texture. The close-ups sometimes give you a better idea of a place than a vast wide shot.

One day, if I can come up with the right script, I want to make a film in Hackney, or about London – but for now, as I sit at my desk and look out at the greyness of early January, I can't help but daydream about faraway places I want to shoot in: Latin America, for example. I recently drove from Texas to Monterrey in Mexico, and having had a tiny taste of the rich culture there I would love to make a movie there. If only I could find the right idea.

I also have the urge to return to India to shoot again in the desert. I look forward to being able to frame a character in close-up, standing in front of mud hut, with the vast, brooding, epic range of the Himalayas in the background...

Critics' choice
Animal magic

Babe
(1995, Aust) *d* Chris Noonan. *cast* James Cromwell, Magda Szubanski, Zoe Burton. This little piggy saves his bacon by learning the art of rounding up sheep.

The Best of Walt Disney's True Life Adventures
(1975, US) *d* James Algar. Polar bears rolling down ice caps by mistake, scorpions doing a barn dance, ducks slipping on a frozen pond. Cheesy fun.

Deep Blue
(2003, GB/Ger) *d* Peter Yates. *narrator* Michael Gambon. Exhilirating, comical and downright scary voyage to the bottom of the ocean.

Lassie Come Home
(1943, US) *d* Fred M Wilcox. *cast* Roddy McDowall, Donald Crisp, Dame May Whitty. The daddy of dog movies. Heart-warming fluff.

March of the Penguins
(2005, US) *d* Luc Jacquet. *narrator* Morgan Freeman. Love finds a way in this penguin chick-flick.

Microcosmos
(1996, Fr/Switz) *d* Claude Nuridsany. *narrator* Kristin Scott Thomas. Anthropomorphic doc on the lives of the insect inhabitants of a summer meadow.

One Hundred and One Dalmatians
(1960, US) *d* Wolfgang Reitherman, Hamilton Luske, Clyde Geronimi. *cast* voices: Rod Taylor, J Pat O'Malley, Betty Lou Gerson. Spot the finest version of Dodie Smith's dognapping classic.

Pom Poko
(1994, Japan) *d* Isao Takahata. A community of shape-shifting raccoons fights rampant urban growth in this one-of-a-kind 'toon.

Ring of Bright Water
(1969, GB) *d* Jack Couffer. *cast* Bill Travers, Virginia McKenna, Peter Jeffrey, Roddy McMillan. Substantial 'aahhh' factor when a civil servant takes his pet otter to the Scottish Highlands.

Winged Migration
(2001, Fr/Ger/Sp/It/Switz) *d/p* Jacques Perrin. Marvel at the incredible journeys that our feathered friends make each year.

Surreal to reel

A nightmare worthy of Dalí, and signed by Disney: **Fantasia**

Through overuse, 'surreal' is in danger of losing its meaning. Every week you read a review in which the incident or mood of a film is described as surreal, where perhaps 'unusual', 'strange' or 'odd' might have done the job better. I'm sorry, but *The Big Lebowski* isn't surreal. Neither is *The Hudsucker Proxy*, for that matter. And *Fargo*, for all its calculatedly offbeat atmosphere, bears no relation whatsoever to André Breton's *Manifeste du surréalisme*. It may seem harsh to pick on the Coen brothers, since it's hardly their fault that extended exposure to their work softens the brains of film-goers and critics. Although, if it's not their fault, whose fault is it?

It would be a great shame, anyway, if pedantry stood in the way of an appreciation of surreal cinema. For all the S-word's frequent appearance in reviews, blogs and fan sites, there have been very few films that can

WONDER

It's out of this world:
Close Encounters of the Third Kind

properly be described as surreal. Antwerper Harry Kümel's *Daughters of Darkness*, despite its emphasis on nudes and dunes on the Flemish coast (recalling the figures and landscapes of Belgian Surrealist Paul Delvaux), actually traces a more direct line back to the symbolist imagery of Leon Spilliaert. Kümel's slightly later *Malpertuis* owes more to the Surrealists, with imagery borrowed from De Chirico and, in particular, Magritte. The French language version uses Magritte's *La Mémoire* (which shows a bloodstained female bust, a grooved ball and a leaf) as a backdrop to its titles sequence, but Kümel's director's cut, recently released on DVD, prefers Sir John Tenniel's illustration of Lewis Carroll's Jabberwock.

Another Magritte painting is used in Alain Robbe-Grillet's 1982 film *La Belle Captive* in which a man, Walter (Daniel Mesguich), comes across an injured woman, Marie-Ange (Gabrielle Lazure), and takes her to a nearby villa; where another man, calling himself a doctor, locks them in a bedroom. They make love. Walter wakes up alone. A painting over the bed – Magritte's *La Belle Captive* – stirs echoes in his mind, recalling visions of a windswept beach framed by a theatre curtain. The narrative – a maze of false starts and dead ends – is typical Robbe-Grillet, and recalls his startling early novels. The novelist's films occupy a peculiar territory somewhere between genuine surrealist cinema and high-end porn. His fondness for mannequins, and actresses directed to resemble them, is reminiscent of the attention lavished on life-size dolls by the Surrealist Hans Bellmer.

Moving picture
Alexander Payne

Director, writer, *Election*, *About Schmidt*, *Sideways*

Every Tuesday afternoon at 2pm, the LA County Museum of Art shows a movie. A lot of old people go along, you know, deaf people, applauding names like Beulah Bondi in the opening credits. I go because I love old movies. About five years ago I went to see Robert Wise's *Somebody Up There Likes Me*, with Paul Newman and Piper Laurie. I'd seen it on TV as a kid and liked it fine, but when I saw it on the screen I realised it's an astonishing film, almost a perfect movie. At least that day it was. I had to rush home and write about it in my journal. The boxing in it is very gritty and realistic. Scorsese has to have seen this; well, we know he has, because he's seen everything. To show how successful Newman is, Wise has radio commentary of the fight playing over an empty city street: to show everyone, you show no one. Beautiful use of cinema.

There can be no denying the surrealist credentials of *Un Chien Andalou* and *L'Age d'Or*, directed by Luis Buñuel and written by him with Salvador Dalí. Narrative is rarely the strong suit of surrealism, and these films are little more than series of strikingly and authentically surreal images, deliberately shocking as well as funny, often with a satirical target (the Church, the Establishment). As pure cinematic surrealism they have probably never

WONDER

Moving picture
Tom McCarthy

Actor, *Meet the Parents*, *Syriana*; director, writer, *The Station Agent*

I've been trying to recall this London movie theatre I went to years ago, when I was living on Margaret Street just north of Oxford Street, I think it was somewhere around there... the Academy. You could sit, and behind every seat was like bench tables, you could drink and smoke. I remember a friend took me and we went and saw *Wings of Desire*, and I just loved

it. It felt right to me to be in that movie theatre and have a drink, there's that moment with Peter Falk and the cigarette, when everyone in the movie theatre lit up. The movie was so powerful for me, too, the quietness and the stillness, the images – it was one of those moments I'll always remember. It was a genius film, I thought, it really stuck with me, and at the same time there's something nice about being able to have a smoke and a beer and watch a great movie.

Moving picture
David Gordon Green

Director, writer, George Washington, All the Real Girls

The film that had the most impact on me was probably *2001: A Space Odyssey*. I saw it in Dallas, where I grew up. I was 14 or 15 at the time, and I saw it on my own. My parents had dropped me off, and my dad had told me it was a good science fiction movie. It was so crowded when I got there, the only place left was in the middle of the front row. Fifteen minutes into the movie, the reel broke. And it kept breaking and breaking and breaking every four minutes for about an hour and a half; the first reel just would not play. So after an hour and a half most of the audience had left. There were about six of us there, me still in the front row, when they brought in a new first reel of a 70mm print and started the film all over from the beginning. That was the first time I was totally beaten to death by a movie. It took my breath away and I realised the philosophical and religious power of an image and a sound: what movies were there for.

been surpassed. Buñuel's later work continued to display his affinity with the Surrealist movement, and Dalí went on to contribute effective sequences to Hitchcock's *Spellbound*.

With rebellion in the air, the 1960s was a good time for strange cinema. There was a pleasing sense of unreality about Lindsay Anderson's *The White Bus*, and *If....* certainly embodied the spirit of revolt that was central to Breton and co; but whether it was a surreal film or just a reversal of normality ('Run! Run in the corridor!') is open to debate.

You would have to be a jaded connoisseur of the surreal not to enjoy the exuberant weirdness of Alejandro Jodorowsky's *The Holy Mountain*, and arguably the images of small birds emerging from gunshot wounds are surreal, but it's difficult to know precisely what they reveal about the workings of the unconscious mind other than their being a visual reminder of the ants that swarmed out of Dalí's paintings into *Un Chien Andalou* through a black hole in the palm of a man's hand. The impossibly proliferating spiders in *Arachnophobia* remind us of this shot, too. Likewise the myriad shots of worms, spiders or cockroaches emerging from the mouths, noses and ears of corpses in a thousand horror films. Still, while these images may give us a welcome jolt, they're surely now too commonplace to be truly surreal.

A number of interesting directors have started out surreal and gone mainstream. The premise of Jerzy Skolimowski's wonderfully disturbing film *The Shout* – that a man can kill by raising his voice – is an idea the Surrealists would have loved, but his earlier *Barrier* was closer in tone and imagery to their vision. Fellow Pole Roman Polanski exhibited his own surrealist tendencies in *Cul-de-Sac*, but there has been little evidence of them since. David Lynch's short films were exercises in the absurd, and his *Eraserhead* perhaps represented the nearest thing to a successful marriage between narrative cinema and the ideals of the Surrealist movement, at least since 1930. The hamster-cheeked lady in the radiator ('In Heaven, everything is fine'), the grotesque appearance of the baby ('Oh, you are sick!'), the contorting midget chickens ('Just cut 'em up like regular chickens') – it's hard to think of a shot in the film that isn't surreal.

If Lynch's work became less overtly surreal as it moved into the mainstream, it has (with the regrettable exception of 1999's *The Straight Story*) at least remained Lynchian, an adjective that will always carry connotations of the surreal. It's an intriguing anomaly, and one that might have amused the Surrealists, that while artists have tended to outgrow their surrealist leanings in order to reach a wider audience, the visual iconography of the Surrealist movement has penetrated so far into our cultural consciousness in the forms of advertising and mass illustration that we almost no longer notice it. And yet, at the same time, every new Adam Sandler film will be hailed as a surreal comedy.

Still, having said that, *Punch-Drunk Love* had its moments.

WONDER

Contributors

Geoff Andrew was, until recently, senior film editor of *Time Out*. He is head of programming at London's National Film Theatre, and has written numerous books on the cinema, the most recent being a study of Abbas Kiarostami's *10* and *Film Directors A-Z*.

Emilie Bickerton holds a BA in anthropology and an MPhil in English literature, and writes on film, fiction and anthropology for publications in the US and UK. She also is on the Editorial Board of the *New Left Review*.

Don Boyd, since graduating from the London Film School in 1968, has directed or produced 30 feature films, some of them seminal works of British cinema (Alan Clarke's *Scum*, Derek Jarman's *The Tempest* and the multi-director film *Aria*). He also directs documentary films and is a professor of film at Exeter University.

Nick Bradshaw is currently a film and video postgraduate student at the California Institute of the Arts. Formerly deputy film editor of *Time Out*, he edits the film and DVD pages of *plan b*, an independent music and culture magazine, and has written for publications including the *Daily Telegraph*, the *Sunday Times*, the *Independent on Sunday*, *Sight & Sound*, *Cinema Scope* and Lovefilm.com.

Edward Buscombe's most recent book is *Cinema Today*, a survey of world cinema. His guide to 100 Westerns will be published in 2006.

Dave Calhoun is film editor of *Time Out*. Previously he was deputy editor of *Dazed & Confused* magazine. He has also written on cinema for the

Guardian, the *Independent on Sunday*, the *Observer*, *Sight & Sound*, the *Times* and *Uncut*.

Tom Charity is a freelance film critic and former film editor of *Time Out*. His books include *John Cassavetes: Lifeworks*, *The Right Stuff*, and *The Rough Guide to Film*. He is the chief film critic at Lovefilm.com and is a regular contributor to *Cinema Scope*, *Sight & Sound* and *Uncut*, among many other publications.

James Christopher is the chief film critic of *The Times*. He has written extensively about film and theatre for many publications including the *Evening Standard*, the *Sunday Express* and *Time Out*.

Kieron Corless writes for *Time Out*. He is co-author with Chris Darke of a forthcoming book about Cannes to be published in 2007.

Alex Cox is a film director, actor and screenwriter. Among his films are *Repo Man*, *Walker* and *Revengers Tragedy*.

Tod Davies is a writer. She also runs Exterminating Angel Productions – formerly a film and television production company, soon to go into online publishing.

Michael Eaton writes for film and radio, but mostly for television. His work includes *Fellow Traveller*, *Signs and Wonders* and the factual dramas *Shoot to Kill* and *Shipman*. He's also the author of a monograph on *Chinatown*.

Atom Egoyan has produced a body of work in film, television, and theatre. His installations have been exhibited at museums and galleries in Canada and abroad, including the Venice Biennale. production of Wagners *Die Walküre* was performed by the Canadian Opera Company in 2004 and will be reprised in 2006.

Gareth Evans is a writer, independent film programmer and the editor of moving image magazine *Vertigo*. Recent projects include the London International Gypsy Film Festival and Armenian Cinema since Independence.

Christopher Frayling is rector of London's Royal College of Art and its professor of cultural history. He is also Chairman of Arts Council England, a historian, critic and award-winning broadcaster. He has published many books on the arts, popular culture and film.

Wally Hammond is a former cinema manager and helicopter handler. He now works on the film desk at *Time Out*.

Debbie Isitt is a writer and director for both stage and screen. She won a BAFTA for her adaptation of Jacqueline Wilson's *The Illustrated Mum* in 2004; her latest feature film, *Confetti*, is released in 2006.

Malena Janson is a freelance film critic and journalist on the daily newspaper *Svenska Dagbladet*. She's also a lecturer and PhD student at the Department of Cinema Studies at Stockholm University.

Trevor Johnston writes on film for the Irish Film Institute and *Time Out*, for which he contributes a weekly survey of the films on television. He is also a regular contriutor to the *Time Out Film Guide*.

Terry Jones is a writer, actor and director. He was a member of Monty Python, and directed the films *Monty Python's Life of Brian* and *Monty Python's The Meaning of Life*; he is also co-author, with Alan Ereira, of a number of popular history books, including *Terry Jones' Barbarians* and *Terry Jones' Medieval Lives*.

Asif Kapadia is the director of the award-winning epic *The Warrior*. He is currently in post-production on his new film, *The Return*.

Guy Maddin is a film director. His five features and numerous shorts, including the award-winning *Heart of the World*, resurrect the images and codes of the silent era, early Russian cinema and Hollywood melodrama. His latest film, *The Saddest Music in the World*, stars Isabella Rossellini as the legless matriarch of a Depression-era Winnipeg brewery.

Conor McPherson is an actor, playwright, screenwriter and director of plays and films. His awards include the Evening Standard award for the screenplay for the film *I Went Down*. His most recent film as director was *The Actors*.

Katie Mitchell is a theatre director who has worked for the Royal Shakespeare Company, the Royal Court Theatre and the Royal National Theatre in London and the Abbey Theatre in Dublin. She has received two *Time Out* awards and one *Evening Standard* award for Best Director. She is currently an associate director at the Royal National Theatre.

Lisa Mullen was a staff writer for *Time Out* between 2000 and 2006. She is now a freelance writer on film, books, music and the arts.

Pete Paphides is chief rock critic at the *Times*, and he also writes for the *Observer Music Monthly*, *Mojo* and *Junior*.

Hannah Patterson is a film journalist, curator and documentary maker. Previous publications include *The Cinema of Terrence Malick* and *Critical Guides to Contemporary Film Directors*. She is currently commissioning editor of the forthcoming *Creative Essentials* series.

Christopher Peachment was film editor at *Time Out* in the 1980s. From there he went to the *Times*, where he was deputy literary editor and arts editor. He is the author of two novels, *Caravaggio* and *The Green and the Gold*. He is currently writing his third film script. His first, based on novel by James Ellroy, is due to start production later this year.

Chris Petit is a film-maker and writer. His feature films include

Radio On; his latest film is *Unrequited Love*. His novels include *Robinson*, *The Psalm Killer* and *The Passenger*. He is also known for his film collaborations with Iain Sinclair, among them *The Falconer* and *London Orbital*. He was editor of *Time Out*'s film section from 1973 to 1978.

John Pym worked for 13 years in the old Publications Department of the British Film Institute. For its past 12 editions he has been editor of the annual *Time Out Film Guide*. He has published a monograph on *The Palm Beach Story* and two books on the partnership of James Ivory and Ismail Merchant.

Tony Rayns is a London-based film-maker, critic and festival programmer with a special interest in East Asian film. He has been writing for *Time Out* since 1971, and is a contributing editor of *Sight & Sound*. His films include the documentary *The Jang Sun-Woo Variations*.

Jonathan Romney is film critic of the *Independent on Sunday*. He also writes regularly for *Sight & Sound*, *Modern Painters*, *Screen International* and *Film Comment*. His latest book is *Atom Egoyan*.

Jonathan Rosenbaum is film critic for the *Chicago Reader*. His books include *Discovering Orson Welles*, *Essential Cinema*, *Movie Wars*, *Dead Man*, *Movies as Politics*, *Greed*, *Moving Places*, *Placing Movies*, and, as editor or co-editor, *This Is Orson Welles* and *Movie Mutations*.

Nicholas Royle is the author of five novels, including *The Director's Cut*, which he is adapting for the cinema, and *Antwerp*, which has been optioned. He is a regular contributor to *Time Out* and the *Independent*. A short story collection, *Mortality*, is forthcoming.

David Rudkin is a dramatist and screenwriter, and one of British theatre and cinema's most distinctive talents. His acclaimed work for the screen includes *Testimony*, *December Bride*, *The Woodlanders* and *Penda's Fen*.

Sukhdev Sandhu is the author of *London Calling: How Black and Asian Writers Imagined A City* and *I'll Get My Coat*. He is the chief film critic of the *Daily Telegraph* and won the British Press Awards' Critic of the Year prize in 2005.

Iain Sinclair came to London in the early 1960s to attend a film school in Electric Avenue, Brixton. In 1967, with Robert Klinkert, he made a documentary about Allen Ginsberg. After 25 years of other activity – including gardening, book-dealing and a little writing – he made four essay-films with Chris Petit.

Ben Slater is a curator, writer and author of the book *Kinda' Hot: The Making of Saint Jack in Singapore*.

Ben Walters is *Time Out*'s deputy film editor. He is the author of a short biography of Orson Welles and a monograph on *The Office*, and has written on film and television for *Sight & Sound*.

Peter Watts is features writer for *Time Out* and also writes about cinema for *Uncut*. He believes that Steve Martin is the thinking man's Woody Allen.

Jessica Winter is a contributor to the *Village Voice* and *Time Out*, and also writes for *Minneapolis City Pages*, *Sight & Sound* and the *Guardian*. She is an associate editor at *Cinema Scope* and author of the *Rough Guide to American Independent Cinema*, to be published in 2006.

Peter Whitehead caught the pivotal moments of Swinging Sixties London in films: *Wholly Communion*, *Tonite Let's All Make Love in London* and others. He has also been a falconer and is now a prolific novelist.

Jason Wood is a film programmer and writer. Recent books include *100 American Independent Films*, *Nick Broomfield: Documenting Icons* and *Contemporary Mexican Cinema*. His writing has also appeared in *Sight & Sound*, *Vertigo* and *Time Out*.

Useful websites

Essential reference

Internet Movie Database (IMDb)
www.imdb.com
● The indispensable film-related internet site (based, believe it or not, in Bristol).

Ain't It Cool News
www.aintitcool.com
● Probably the most famous film site of all, this is still the first port of call for the skinny on upcoming blockbusters and DVD fare.

Alternative buzz

Images
www.imagesjournal.com
● A collection of smart, serious essays on classic cinema (The Western, Italian Gothic Horror, Cliffhangers).

Senses of Cinema
www.sensesofcinema.com
● This Australian-based (but thoroughly international) journal is probably the most impressive contribution to film scholarship on the web.

Bright Lights
www.brightlightsfilm.com
● Quarterly film commentary, this describes itself as 'a popular-academic hybrid', which seems to mean intelligent, witty criticism without jargon.

Cinema Scope
www.cinema-scope.com
● About 20 per cent of articles from this cutting edge international film journal find their way online.

Film Comment
www.filmlinc.com/fcm
● The online edition includes more reviews, fuller versions of interviews, a features archive and Amy Taubin's indie column.

The Film Journal
www.thefilmjournal.com
● Eclectic (and then some) essays and criticism out of Ohio, now aiming for an auteurist focus.

Film-Philosophy
www.film-philosophy.com
● Highbrow essays on Baudrillard, Deleuze, Zizek; Godard, Bresson, Kiarostami, and others.

indieWIRE
www.indiewire.com
● News, festival reports, reviews and interviews from around the world. The emphasis is on low budget and foreign-language movies.

Offscreen
www.offscreen.com
● Monthly journal with academic essays on anything from Gus Van Sant to Bresson.

Reverse Shot
www.reverseshot.com
● Lively online quarterly with contemporary reviews and themed issues.

Strictly Film School
www.filmref.com
● Auteurist reviews and essays mapping film classics linked by theme and style.

24 Lies a Second
www.24liesasecond.com
● This relatively new online journal grew out of a Brian De Palma forum. It offers meaty articles by academics, cinephiles and fans on popular film-making.

Criticism: newspapers

The Guardian
film.guardian.co.uk
● Superior site with extra online news, features, quizzes and archive of *Guardian* and *Observer* reviews.

Chicago Reader
www.chireader.com
● Leading critic Jonathan Rosenbaum writes here – but you have to pay to access the review archive.

LA Times
www.calendarlive.com
● The Calendar section includes Kenneth Turan's reviews and features.

The New York Times
www.nytimes.com
● In-depth reviews, features and more. Registration is required, but it costs nothing.

Criticism: magazines

Time Out
www.timeout.com/film
● Free reviews, news, interviews, trailers – and all of the *Time Out Film Guide*.

Village Voice
www.villagevoice.com
● Fully archived reviews and features by the estimable Jim Hoberman and the *Voice* team.

Box Office
www.boxoffice.com
● Worth a peak mostly for the collection of original industry reviews for classics from the 1930s on.

Filmmaker
www.filmmaker magazine.com
● Indie features and interviews.

MovieMaker
www.moviemaker.com
● Inside dope from film-makers in the online edition of the quarterly.

The New Yorker
www.newyorker.com
● Wit and wisdom from Anthony Lane and David Denby. Capsules are archived online as 'The Film File'.

Screen International
www.screendaily.com
● Online version of the European trade paper. Part subscription, but breaking reviews are free.

Vertigo
www.vertigomagazine.co.uk
● Online version of the quarterly British magazine. Passionate and offbeat pieces about all aspects of the moving image.

Online critics

CineScene
www.cinescene.com
● Longish reviews 'by and for movie lovers'.

Culture Vulture
www.culturevulture.net
● Online arts mag with a strong film books section.

The Man Who Viewed Too Much
www.panix.com/~dangelo
● Reviews by the reliably witty and insightful Mike D'Angelo, former critic for *Time Out New York*.

DVD

DVD Beaver
www.dvdbeaver.com
● Another superb resource for the dedicated collector, with in-depth comparisons across DVD regions.

Masters of Cinema
www.mastersof cinema.org
● Less technical than 'DVD Beaver' (above – there are frequent links between the two), this is a calendar of worldwide art house releases, supplemented with scholarly articles and the best links we found for director sites.

Criterion
www.criterionco.com
● Not only the catalogue to the world's best DVD company, it also has excellent critical notes and forums.

DVD Journal
www.dvdjournal.com
● There's a more critical tone to this US online mag, with a useful DVD lexicon, and myriad DVD links.

DVD Reviewer
www.dvdreviewer.co.uk
● Much the same as DVD Times. Both offer extensive coverage of other regional releases from the fan's perspective.

DVD Talk
www.dvdtalk.com
● Comprehensive coverage of Region 1 (US) releases, with price comparisons, extras, forum and reviews.

DVD Times
www.dvdtimes.co.uk
● And similar stuff for Region 2 (UK). Includes DVD, cinema and hardware reviews, forums, competitions and industry news. High quality, detailed reviews too.

Films on the Net

Animate!
www.animateonline.org
● All the dope on the films by the contributors to *pp100-102*, and more.

Atom Films
www.atomfilms.com
● Large selection of US and UK short films and animations, including *The Critic* and the Aardman collection.

Film Watcher
www.filmwatcher.com
● Free showcase for short films (you can review them, too).

Internet Archive
www.archive.org/movies
● Free public domain films to download, including *The Power of Nightmares* and out of copyright classics *His Girl Friday*, *Charade*, *Salt of the Earth*, *White Zombie*.

One Minute Movies
www.bbc.co.uk/films/oneminutemovies
● The BBC's superficial film pages are a blot on their otherwise essential site, but these 60-second miniatures are fun. Send in your own.

Trailers

Apple Trailers
www.apple.com/trailers/
● From the US majors, for Macs or PCs.

UbuWeb
www.ubu.com/film
● Download films by Kenneth Anger, Bruce Conner, Guy Debord, Man Ray, Harry Smith, Jack Smith and more, all for free.

100 to watch

The following 100 reviews of key titles mentioned in this book have all been taken from the annual *Time Out Film Guide*. They are supplied with fuller credit information than their entries in the **Index of titles** (*pp269-280*). The credits abbreviations are: *d* (director), *p* (producer), *sc* (screenwriter/s), *ph* (director/s of photography), *ed* (editor/s), *pd* (production designer), *ad* (art director, where no *pd* credited), and *m* (composer/s).

After Life

(1998, Japan, 118 min)
d Hirokazu Koreeda. *p* Shiho Sato, Masayuki Akieda. *sc* Hirokazu Koreeda. *ph* Yukuru Sato, Shigeki Nakamura, Yutaka Yamazaki. *ed* Hirokazu Koreeda. *ad* Toshihiro Isomi, Hideo Gunji. *cast* Arata, Erika Oda, Taketoshi Naito, Sadao Abe, Kotaro Shiga, Yusuke Iseya.
● The second feature from the maker of the exquisite *Maborosi* returns to the theme of the relationship between life and death, but reverses the perspective. It is set in a limbo that looks like a slightly shabby school, where counsellors help new arrivals choose their most precious memory which is then recreated on a film to accompany them to eternity. The movie is about how we look back and make sense of our lives. With a strong documentary feel (many of the cast are non-professionals evidently drawing on personal experience), the film succeeds partly as an amusing and richly affecting portrait of what constitutes happiness for a wide range of modern Japanese; it is also, in passing, a little tribute to the way cinema connects with our dreams. Most poignantly, however, as it charts a revelatory encounter between a counsellor and one of his charges, it offers a subtle tribute to the healing power of love.

Age d'Or, L'

(1930, Fr, 63 min, b/w)
d Luis Buñuel. *p* Vicomte de Noailles. *sc* Luis Buñuel, Salvador Dali. *ph* Albert Duverger. *ed* Luis Buñuel. *ad* Pierre Schildknecht. *cast* Gaston Modot, Lya Lys, Max Ernst, Pierre Prévert, Jacques Brunius, Luis Buñuel.
● 'Our sexual desire has to be seen as the product of centuries of repressive and emasculating Catholicism… it is always coloured by the sweet secret sense of sin,' mused Buñuel in his autobiography *My Last Breath*. One might describe *L'Age d'Or* as 63 minutes of *coitus interruptus*, a scabrous essay on Eros and civilisation, wherein a couple is constantly prised apart by furious love-making by the police, high society and, above all, the Church. Financed by the Vicomte de Noailles, a dream patron who loyally pronounced the film exquisite and delicious, even as right-wing extremists were pelting it with ink and stink bombs, this is a jagged memento of that Golden Age before directors forgot the art of filming erotica (the celebrated toe-sucking is sexier by far than almost anything since), the revolutionary avant-garde lost its sense of humour, and surrealism itself fell prey to advertising-agency chic.

Aguirre, Wrath of God

(1972, WGer, 95 min)
d/p/sc Werner Herzog. *ph* Thomas Mauch. *ed* Beate Mainka-Jellinghaus. *m* Popol Vuh. *cast* Klaus Kinski, Cecilia Rivera, Ruy Guerra, Helena Rojo, Del Negro, Peter Berling.
● As in *Even Dwarfs Started Small*, the exposition of Herzog's film about the crazy, megalomaniac dream of the Spanish Conquistadors is both functional and extremely concentrated: each scene and each detail is honed down to its salient features. On this level, the film effectively pre-empts analysis by analysing itself as it proceeds, admitting no ambiguity. Yet at the same time, Herzog's flair for charged explosive imagery has never had freer rein, and the film is rich in oneiric moments. The extraordinary, beautiful opening scene illustrates the ambivalence. In long shot, the image of the conquistadors descending the Andes pass brings with poetic resonances: the men are situated between the peaks and the valleys, between conquered land and unexplored forests, between 'heaven' and 'earth', shrouded in mists. In close-up, the procession picking its way down the narrow path is presented and defined with specific accuracy: all the leading characters are introduced, the social hierarchy is sketched (the slave porters in chains, the women carried in chairs), and the twin poles of the expedition's ideology are signified through the loads it carries (a large Madonna figure and an even larger cannon). Neither 'reading' of the action contradicts the other: they are, rather, mutually illuminating.

Alphaville

(1965, Fr/It, 98 min, b/w)
d Jean-Luc Godard. *p* André Michelin. *sc* Jean-Luc Godard. *ph* Raoul Coutard. *ed* Agnès Guillemot. *m* Paul Misraki. *cast* Eddie Constantine, Anna Karina, Howard Vernon, Akim Tamiroff, Laszlo Szabo, Michel Delahaye, Jean-Pierre Léaud.
● One of Godard's most sheerly enjoyable movies, a dazzling amalgam of *film noir* and science fiction in which tough gumshoe Lemmy Caution turns intergalactic agent to re-enact the legend of Orpheus and Eurydice by conquering Alpha 60, the strange automated city from which such concepts as love and tenderness have been banished. As in Antonioni's *The Red Desert* (made the previous year), Godard's theme is alienation in a technological society, but his shotgun marriage between the poetry of legend and the irreverence of strip cartoons takes the film into entirely idiosyncratic areas. Not the least astonishing thing is the way Raoul Coutard's camera turns contemporary Paris into an icily dehumanised city of the future.

Atalante, L'

(1934, Fr, 89 min, b/w)
d Jean Vigo. *p* JL Nounez. *sc* Jean Vigo, Albert Riera. *ph* Boris Kaufman. *ed* Louis Chavance. *ad* Francis Jourdain. *m* Maurice Jaubert. *cast* Michel Simon, Jean Dasté, Dita Parlo, Louis Lefebvre, Gilles Margaritis.
● Originally released in 1934 in a mutilated version now restored, Vigo's first and only full-length feature (he died tragically young) is one of cinema's greatest masterpieces. Its story is very simple: newlyweds Dasté and Parlo find that living on a cramped Seine barge brings tension to their relationship, and strive to continue through compromise – but Vigo creates a rich array of comic, suspenseful and heartrendingly romantic moods to explore the nuances of every single emotion. Produced on a minute budget, it exudes an invigorating rawness, but the lyricism of the camerawork, the childlike wonder of the performances and the moments of genuine surrealism situate the film, poetically, between objective realism and subjective fantasy. Simon's bestial Père Jules brings magic and bizarre comedy into the brew as he dithers between jealousy and a desire that his life on the boat should continue uninterrupted; Dasté and Parlo reveal a vulnerable intensity in their chastely erotic scenes together. Acting, setting, script, music and photography, which includes startlingly beautiful special effects, merge to create the loveliest, least maudlin study of human desire ever committed to film.

Autumn Afternoon, An

(1962, Japan, 112 min)
d Yasujiro Ozu. *p* Shizuo Yamanouchi. *sc* Kogo Noda, Yasujiro Ozu. *ph* Yuharu Atsuta. *ed* Yoshiyasu Hamamura. *pd* Tatsuo Hamada. *cast* Chishu Ryu, Shima Iwashita, Keiji Sada, Mariko Okada, Teruo Yoshida, Noriko Maki, Shinichiro Mikami, Nobuo Nakamura, Eijiro Tono, Ryuji Kita, Kyoko Kishida.

●Ozu's final film is a movingly valedictory work, its familiar story of Ryu's elderly widower marrying off daughter Iwashita carrying even more poignancy than usual as a poised and wise reminder of passing time and the inevitable approach of mortality. The gentle humour's there as ever, but in the subplot showing former teacher Tono's twilight years beset by drink-sodden regrets, the emotions are darker and tougher than previously. The central performance is, of course, a marvel of no nonsense, unspoken expressiveness, set against exquisitely arranged colour compositions and the director's loveable repertory company is in fine fettle. Whether the film's making was affected by the death of Ozu's mother and the onset of his own final illness is hard to quantify, but it does feel like a leave-taking. A year after its release, the director died on his sixtieth birthday.

Avventura, L'

(1960, It/Fr, 145 min, b/w)
d Michelangelo Antonioni. p Amato Pennasilico. sc Michelangelo Antonioni, Elio Bartolini, Tonino Guerra. ph Aldo Scavarda. ed Eraldo Da Roma. ad Piero Poletto. m Giovanni Fusco. cast Monica Vitti, Gabriele Ferzetti, Lea Massari, Dominique Blanchar, Renzo Ricci, James Addams.
●Though once compared to Psycho, made the same year and also about a couple searching for a woman who mysteriously disappears after featuring heavily in the opening reel, Antonioni's film could not be more dissimilar in tone and effect. Slow, taciturn and coldly elegant in its visual evocation of alienated, isolated figures in a barren Sicilian landscape, the film concerns itself less with how and why the girl vanished from a group of bored and wealthy socialites on holiday, than with the desultory nature of the romance embarked upon by her lover and her best friend while they half-heartedly look for her. If it once seemed the ultimate in arty, intellectually chic movie-making, the film now looks all too studied and remote a portrait of emotional sterility.

Beau Travail

(1998, Fr, 90 min)
d Claire Denis. p Jérôme Minet. sc Claire Denis, Jean-Pol Fargeau. ph Agnès Godard. ed Nelly Quettier. pd Arnaud de Moleron. m Eran Tzur. cast Denis Lavant, Michel Subor, Grégoire Colin, Marta Tafesse Kassa, Richard Courcet.
●Denis' extraordinary movie centres on Galoup (Lavant) who, while holed up in Marseille, recalls his time as a sergeant-major in the Foreign Legion. In the desert, he drilled raw recruits while quietly nurturing feelings of respect and love for his superior, Forestier (Subor). Then, with the arrival of Sentain (Colin), a soldier Forestier honoured for bravery, Galoup

caved in to resentment, envy and hate. Though little is spelt out explicitly in this elliptical tale of repressed emotion leading to murderous jealousy, the film is admirably accessible and clear throughout. The director shows scant interest in the new recruit as an angelic incarnation of goodness – her concerns are with how a wide open colonial outpost may become a prison; how men may cope with an all-male society; how the physical may mirror the metaphysical. Hence, she and her team create a fixed, timeless world of mysterious, balletic rites, rippled with simmering homoerotic tensions. The intensity of mood and thematic resonance both derive almost entirely from the poetic juxtaposition of music and the stunning images of beauty and sustained, even surreal strangeness. Prepare to be blown away.

Berlin Alexanderplatz

(1979/80, WGer, 15 hr. 30 min)
d Rainer Werner Fassbinder. p Peter Marthesheimer. sc Rainer Werner Fassbinder. ph Xavier Schwarzenberger. ed Jiliane Lorenz. ad Harry Baer. m Peer Raben. cast Günter Lamprecht, Hanna Schygulla, Barbara Sukowa, Karin Baal, Helmut Griem, Ivan Desny, Udo Kier.
●This shattering adaptation of Alfred Döblin's masterpiece – made for TV in 13 episodes with a two-hour epilogue – offers a level-headed account of protagonist Biberkopf's key weakness: his quasi-sexual infatuation with the psychotic pimp Reinhold. Aided by great design, cinematography, and, not least, performances, Fassbinder tells the story surprisingly naturalistically. Then in the epilogue, he offers a disturbing meditation on his own fantasies about Biberkopf. This phantasmagoria is Fassbinder's most daring act of self-exposure: a movie time-bomb that forces you to rethink the series as a whole. The work of a genuine master with nothing left to lose or hide.

Bête Humaine, La

(1938, Fr, 104 min, b/w)
d Jean Renoir. p Robert Hakim. sc Jean Renoir. ph Curt Courant. ed Marguerite Renoir. pd Eugène Lourié. m Joseph Kosma. cast Jean Gabin, Simone Simon, Fernand Ledoux, Julien Carette, Blanchette Brunoy, Jean Renoir.
●Stunning images of trains and railway lines as a metaphor for the blind, immutable forces that drive human passions to destruction. Superb performances from Gabin, Simon and Ledoux as the classic tragic love triangle. The deterministic principles of Zola's novel, replaced by destiny in Lang's remake Human Desire, are slightly muffled here. But given the overwhelming tenderness and brutality of Renoir's vision, it hardly matters that the hero's compulsion to kill, the result of hereditary alcoholism, is left half-explained.

Bicycle Thieves

(1948, It, 96 min, b/w)
d Vittorio De Sica. p Umberto Scarpelli. sc Vittorio De Sica, Cesare Zavattini, Suso Cecchi D'Amico, Oreste Biancoli, Adolfo Franci, Gherardo Gherardi, Gararado Guerrieri. ph Carlo Montuori. ed Eraldo Da Roma. ad Antonio Traverso. m Alessandro Cicognini. cast Lamberto Maggiorani, Enzo Staiola, Lianella Carell, Gino Saltamerenda, Vittorio Antonucci, Giulio Chiari.
●A working class Italian, out of work for some time, has the bicycle stolen which he needs for a new job; he and his son wander round Rome looking for it. Often hailed as an all-time classic, Bicycle Thieves tries to turn a simple story into a meditation on the human condition, but its greatest achievement is in bringing the lives of ordinary Italian people to the screen. However, like so many of the films grouped together under the heading of Italian neo-realism, its grainy monochrome images and simple storyline never delve beneath the surface of the characters' lives to reveal the social mechanisms at work there. It is as if, just by portraying the events unobtrusively, De Sica imagines that they will yield up their essential truth by a process of revelation – a very appropriate image for a strain of liberal humanism strongly influenced by Catholicism. Observant and sympathetic it is, politically perceptive it is not.

Branded to Kill

(1966, Jap, 91 min, b/w)
d Seijun Suzuki. p Kaneo Iwai. sc Hachiro Guryu. ph Kazue Nagatsuka. ed Mutsuo Tanji. ad Sukezo Kawahara. m Naozumi Yamamoto. cast Jo Shishido. Nanbara Koji, Ogawa Mariko, Annu Mari, Isao Tamagawa.
●The film that got Suzuki fired by Nikkatsu, and it's not hard to see why. It starts almost straightforwardly as a bluesy gangster thriller in pared-down Melville mould. But as 'number three killer' Shishido (a Suzuki regular) moves from some beautifully staged hits to perverse obsession with an ultra cool femme fatale and a set-to with 'number one killer', the weirder the film becomes. Just as Shishido cracks up and enters a surreal nightmare world, so Suzuki breaks the film down into a bizarre but beguiling chain of absurdist, OTT, barely related elements. It looks a little like golden-age Godard (but far more stylish). The climax, oddly reminiscent of Point Blank (made the same year), shows how much further Suzuki was prepared to push even than Boorman, let alone Hollywood. Occasionally mystifying, but always witty, inventive and dazzling to look at.

Cat People

(1942, US, 73 min, b/w)
d Jacques Tourneur. p Val Lewton.

sc DeWitt Bodeen. *ph* Nick Musuraca. *ed* Mark Robson. *ad* Albert S D'Agostino, Walter E Keller. *m* Roy Webb. *cast* Simone Simon, Kent Smith, Tom Conway, Jane Randolph, Elizabeth Russell, Jack Holt, Alan Napier.

● First in the wondrous series of B movies in which Val Lewton elaborated his principle of horrors imagined rather than seen, with a superbly judged performance from Simon as the young wife ambivalently haunted by sexual frigidity and by a fear that she is metamorphosing into a panther. With its chilling set pieces directed to perfection by Tourneur, it knocks Paul Schrader's remake for six, not least because of the care subtly taken to imbue its cat people (Simon, Russell) with feline mannerisms. Its sober psychological basis is barely shaken by the studio's insistence on introducing, as a stock horror movie ploy, a shot of a black panther during one crucial scene.

Cercle Rouge, Le

(1970, Fr/It, 150 min)
d Jean-Pierre Melville. *p* Robert Dorfmann. *sc* Jean-Pierre Melville. *ph* Henri Decaë. *ed* Jean-Pierre Melville. *ad* Théo Meurisse. *m* Eric de Marsan. *cast* Alain Delon, André Bourvil, Yves Montand, François Périer, Gian Maria Volonté, André Eykan, Pierre Collet, Paul Crauchet.

● Melville's special achievement was to relocate the American gangster film in France, and to incorporate his own steely poetic and philosophical obsessions. He described this, his penultimate film, as a digest of the nineteen definitive underworld set-ups that could be found in John Huston's picture of doomed gangsters, *The Asphalt Jungle*. Darker, more abstract and desolate than his earlier work, this shows, set piece by set piece, the breakdown of the criminal codes under which Melville's characters had previously operated. Even in the butchered version distributed in Britain (dubbed and cut to 102 minutes) it's worth seeing: the mood remains, as does the film's central sequence, a superbly executed silent jewel robbery in the Place Vendôme.

Chinatown

(1974, US, 131 min)
d Roman Polanski. *p* Robert Evans. *sc* Robert Towne. *ph* John A Alonzo. *ed* Sam O'Steen. *pd* Richard Sylbert. *m* Jerry Goldsmith. *cast* Jack Nicholson, Faye Dunaway, John Huston, Perry Lopez, John Hillerman, Darrell Zwerling, Diane Ladd. Roman Polanski.

● The hard-boiled private eye coolly strolls a few steps ahead of the audience. The slapstick detective gets everything wrong and then pratfalls first over the finish line anyway. Jake Gittes (Jack Nicholson) is neither – instead he's a hard-boiled private eye who gets everything wrong. Jake snaps tabloid-ready photos of an adulterous love nest that's no such thing. He spies a distressed young woman through a window and mistakes her for a hostage. He finds bifocals in a pond and calls them Exhibit A of marital murder, only the glasses don't belong to the victim and the wife hasn't killed anyone. Yet when he confronts ostensible black widow Evelyn Mulwray (Dunaway) with the spectacular evidence, the cigarette between his teeth lends his voice an authoritative Bogie hiss. Throughout, Gittes sexes up mediocre snooping with blithe arrogance and sarcastic machismo. It's the actor's default mode, sure, but in 1974 it hadn't yet calcified into Schtickolson, and in 1974 a director (Polanski), a screenwriter (Towne) and a producer (Evans) could decide to beat a genre senseless and dump it in the wilds of Greek tragedy. 'You see, Mr *Gits*,' depravity incarnate Noah Cross (Huston) famously explains, 'most people never have to face the fact that, at the right time and the right place, they're capable of anything.' As is *Chinatown*. The last gunshot here is the sound of the gate slamming on the Paramount lot of Evans' halcyon reign, and as the camera rears back to catch Jake's expression, the dolly lists and shivers – an almost imperceptible sob of grief and recognition, but not a tear is shed.

Citizen Kane

(1941, US, 119 min, b/w)
d/p Orson Welles. *sc* Herman J Mankiewicz, Orson Welles. *ph* Gregg Toland. *ed* Robert Wise. *ad* Van Nest Polglase. *m* Bernard Herrmann. *cast* Orson Welles, Joseph Cotten, Everett Sloane, Dorothy Comingore, Agnes Moorehead, Ray Collins, Paul Stewart, George Coulouris, Ruth Warrick, Alan Ladd.

● The source book of Orson Welles, and still a marvellous movie. Thematically less resonant than some of Welles' later meditations on the nature of power, perhaps, but still absolutely riveting as an investigation of a citizen – newspaper tycoon William Randolph Hearst by any other name – under suspicion of having soured the American Dream. Its imagery (not forgetting the oppressive ceilings) as Welles delightedly explores his mastery of a new vocabulary, still amazes and delights, from the opening shot of the forbidding gates of Xanadu to the last glimpse of the vanishing Rosebud (tarnished, maybe, but still a potent symbol). A film that gets better with each renewed acquaintance.

Come and See (Idi i Smotri)

(1985, USSR, 142 min, b/w & col)
d Elem Klimov. *sc* Ales Adamovich, Elem Klimov. *ph* Alexei Rodionov. *ed* V Belova. *pd* Viktor Petrov. *m* Oleg Yanchenko. *cast* Alexei Kravchenko, Olga Mironova, Liubomiras Laucevicius, Vladas Bagdonas, Victor Lorents, J Lumiste.

● Soviet Belorussia, near the Polish border, 1943. Florya, a young partisan, left behind as his unit moves to prepare for a renewed German advance, returns to his village to find only a mass of bodies, including those of his family, and later witnesses the entire population of a nearby town being machine-gunned and burnt to death. This epic, allegorical and traumatising enactment of the hellish experience of war (especially its effect upon a generation of the Soviet people) is rendered by Klimov – albeit unintentionally – as a disorienting and undifferentiated amalgam of almost lyrical poeticism and expressionist nightmare.

Conversation, The

(1974, US, 113 min)
d/p/sc Francis Coppola. *ph* Bill Butler. *ed* Walter Murch. *pd* Dean Tavoularis. *m* David Shire. *cast* Gene Hackman, John Cazale, Cindy Williams, Allen Garfield, Frederic Forrest, Teri Garr, Robert Duvall, Harrison Ford.

● An inner rather than outer-directed film about the threat of electronic surveillance, conceived well before the Watergate affair broke. Acknowledged as the king of the buggers, Hackman's surveillance expert is an intensely private man. Living alone in a scrupulously anonymous flat, paying functional visits to a mistress who plays no other part in his life, he is himself a machine; and the point Coppola makes is that this very private man only acquires something to be private about through the exercise of his skill as a voyeur. Projecting his own lonely isolation on to a conversation he painstakingly pieces together (mesmerising stuff as he obsessively plays the tapes over and over, adjusting sound levels until words begin to emerge from the crowd noises), he begins to imagine a story of terror and impending tragedy, and feels impelled to try to circumvent it. In a splendidly Hitchcockian denouement, a tragedy duly takes place, but not the one he foresaw; and he is left shattered not only by the realisation that his soul has been exposed, but by the conviction that someone must have planted a bug on him which he simply cannot find. A bleak and devastatingly brilliant film.

Crimes and Misdemeanors

(1989, US, 104 min)
d Woody Allen. *p* Robert Greenhut. *sc* Woody Allen. *ph* Sven Nykvist. *ed* Susan E Morse. *pd* Santo Loquasto. *cast* Caroline Aaron, Alan Alda, Woody Allen, Claire Bloom, Mia Farrow, Joanna Gleason, Anjelica Huston, Martin Landau, Jenny Nichols, Jerry Orbach, Stephanie Roth, Sam Waterston.

●In the first of two loosely interwoven stories, rich, philanthropic ophthalmologist Judah Rosenthal (Landau), afraid his lover (Huston) will reveal all to his wife (Bloom), decides to dispose of the former with the help of a hit-man friend of his brother. In the second, more comic story, earnest, impoverished documentarist Clifford Stern (Allen), falls for the producer (Farrow) of a TV tribute he has reluctantly agreed to make about the brother-in-law he hates (Alda), a conceited, successful maker of sitcoms. Judah and Clifford meet only in the final scene: what links them throughout is guilt, stemming from an obsessive interest in matters of faith and ethics. It's an extremely ambitious film, most akin perhaps to Hannah and her Sisters, the narrative and tonal coherence of which is sadly lacks, though the assured direction and typically fine ensemble acting manage partly to conceal the seams. Dramatically, the film seldom fulfils its promise, and its pessimistic 'moral' – that good and evil do not always meet with their just deserts – looks contrived and hollow. Intriguing and patchily effective, nevertheless.

Days of Being Wild

(1990, HK, 94 min)
d Wong Kar-Wai. p Rover Tang. sc Wong Kar-Wai. ph Christopher Doyle. ed Kai Kit Wai. pd William Chang. m Chan Do-ming. cast Leslie Cheung, Andy Lau, Maggie Cheung, Carina Lau, Tony Leung, Jacky Cheung.
●Wong Kar-Wai's second feature is a brilliant dream of Hong Kong life in 1960. A young man of Shanghainese descent drifts through a series of casual friendships and uncommitted affairs, unconsciously pining for a relationship with his mother, who has started a new life in Manila. He finally takes off for the Philippines, where he sets himself up for the ultimate fall... The terrific, all-star cast enacts this as a series of emotionally unresolved encounters; the swooningly beautiful camera and design work takes its hallucinatory tone from the protagonist's own uncertainties. The mysterious appearance of Tony Leung only in the closing scene heralds a sequel that will sadly never be made. But this is already some kind of masterpiece.

Deer Hunter, The

(1978, US, 182 min)
d Michael Cimino. p Barry Spikings, Michael Deeley, Michael Cimino, John Peverall. sc Deric Washburn. ph Vilmos Zsigmond. ed Peter Zinner. ad Ron Hobbs, Kim Swados. m Stanley Myers. cast Robert De Niro, John Cazale, John Savage, Christopher Walken, Meryl Streep, George Dzundza, Chuck Aspegren.
●This is probably one of the few great films of the 1970s. It's the tale of three Pennsylvanian steelworkers, their life at work, at play (deer-hunting), at war (as volunteers in Vietnam). Running against the grain of liberal guilt and substituting Fordian patriotism, it proposes De Niro as a Ulyssean hero tested to the limit by war. Moral imperatives replace historical analysis, social rituals become religious sacraments, and the sado-masochism of the central (male) love affair is icing on a Nietzschean cake. Ideally, though, it should prove as gruelling a test of its audience's moral and political conscience as it seems to have been for its makers.

Dr Strangelove: or, How I Learned to Stop Worrying and Love the Bomb

(1963, GB, 94 min, b/w)
d/p Stanley Kubrick. sc Stanley Kubrick, Terry Southern, Peter George. ph Gilbert Taylor. ed Anthony Harvey. pd Ken Adam. m Laurie Johnson. cast Peter Sellers, George C Scott, Sterling Hayden, Keenan Wynn, Slim Pickens, Peter Bull, Tracy Reed, James Earl Jones.
●Perhaps Kubrick's most perfectly realised film, simply because his cynical vision of the progress of technology and human stupidity is wedded with comedy, in this case Terry Southern's sparkling script in which the world comes to an end thanks to a mad US general's paranoia about women and commies. Sellers' three roles are something of an indulgent showcase, though as the tight-lipped RAF officer and the US president he gives excellent performances. Better, however, are Scott as the gung-ho military man frustrated by political soft-pedalling, and – especially – Hayden as the beleaguered lunatic who presses the button. Kubrick wanted to have the antics end up with a custard-pie finale, but thank heavens he didn't; the result is scary, hilarious, and nightmarishly beautiful, far more effective in its portrait of insanity and call for disarmament than any number of worthy anti-nuke documentaries.

Dog Day Afternoon

(1975, US, 130 min)
d Sidney Lumet. p Martin Bregman, Martin Elfand. sc Frank R Pierson. ph Victor J Kemper. ed Dede Allen. pd Charles Bailey. cast Al Pacino, John Cazale, Sully Boyar, Penelope Allen, Beulah Garrick, Carol Kane, Charles Durning, James Broderick, Chris Sarandon.
●At first sight, a film with large, self-conscious ambitions where a bank siege (the film is based on a real incident that occurred in the summer of '72) seems a metaphor for Attica and other scenes of American overkill and victimisation. But it turns into something smaller and less pretentious: a richly detailed, meandering portrait of an incompetent, anxiety-ridden, homosexual bank robber (played with ferocious and self-destructive energy by Pacino) who wants money to finance a sex-change operation for his lover. The film's strength lies in its depiction of surfaces, lacking the visual or intellectual imagination to go beyond its shrewd social and psychological observations and its moments of absurdist humour.

Double Indemnity

(1944, US, 106 min, b/w)
d Billy Wilder. p Joseph Sistrom. sc Billy Wilder, Raymond Chandler. ph John F Seitz. ed Doane Harrison. ad Hans Dreier, Hal Pereira. m Miklós Rozsa. cast Barbara Stanwyck, Fred MacMurray, Edward G Robinson, Porter Hall, Jean Heather, Tom Powers, Fortunio Bonanova.
●Before he settled down to being an ultra-cynical connoisseur of vulgarity, Wilder helped (as much as any of his fellow Austro-German émigrés in Hollywood) to define the mood of brooding pessimism that laced so many American movies in the '40s. Adapted from James M Cain's novel, Double Indemnity is certainly one of the darkest thrillers of its time: Wilder presents Stanwyck and MacMurray's attempt at an elaborate insurance fraud as a labyrinth of sexual dominance, guilt, suspicion and sweaty duplicity. Chandler gave the dialogue a sprinkling of characteristic wit, without mitigating any of the overall sense of oppression.

Dracula

(1931, US, 85 min, b/w)
d Tod Browning. p Carl Laemmle Jr. sc Garrett Fort, Dudley Murphy. ph Karl Freund. ed Milton Carruth, Maurice Pivar. ad Charles D Hall. m Peter Tchaikovsky, Richard Wagner. cast Bela Lugosi, Helen Chandler, David Manners, Dwight Frye, Edward Van Sloan, Herbert Bunston.
●Not by any means the masterpiece of fond memory or reputation, although the first twenty minutes are astonishingly fluid and brilliantly shot by Karl Freund, despite the intrusive painted backdrops. Innumerable imaginative touches here: the sinister emphasis of Lugosi's first words ('I...am...Dracula') and the sonorous poetry of his invocation to the children of the night; the moment when Dracula leads the way up his castle stairway behind a vast cobweb through which Renfield has to struggle as he follows; the vampire women, driven off by Dracula, reluctantly backing away from the camera while it continues hungrily tracking in to Renfield's fallen body. Thereafter the pace falters, and with the London scenes growing in verbosity and staginess, the hammy limitations of Lugosi's performance are cruelly exposed. But the brilliant moments continue (Renfield's frenzy in his cell, for instance), and Freund's camerawork rarely falters.

Elephant Man, The

(1980, US, 124 min, b/w)
d David Lynch. p Jonathan Sanger.
sc Christopher De Vore, Eric Bergren,
David Lynch. ph Freddie Francis.
ed Anne V Coates. pd Stuart Craig.
m John Morris. cast John Hurt, Anthony
Hopkins, Anne Bancroft, John Gielgud,
Wendy Hiller, Freddie Jones, Michael
Elphick, Hannah Gordon.

● More accessible than Lynch's enigmati-
cally disturbing Eraserhead, The Elephant
Man has much the same limpidly moving
humanism as Truffaut's L'Enfant Sauvage
in describing how the unfortunate John
Merrick, brutalised by a childhood in
which he was hideously abused as an
inhuman freak, was gradually coaxed into
revealing a soul of such delicacy and
refinement that he became a lion of
Victorian society. But that is only half the
story the film tells. The darker side, underpinned by an evocation of the steamy,
smoky hell that still underlies a London
facelifted by the Industrial Revolution, is
crystallised by the wonderful sequence in
which Merrick is persuaded by a celebrated actress to read Romeo to her Juliet.
A tender, touching scene ('Oh, Mr Merrick,
you're not an elephant man at all. No,
you're Romeo'), it nevertheless begs the
question of what passions, inevitably
doomed to frustration, have been roused
in this presumably normally-sexed
Elephant Man. Appearances are all, and
like the proverbial Victorian piano, he can
make the social grade only if his ruder
appendages are hidden from sensitive
eyes; hence what is effectively, at his time
of greatest happiness, his suicide. A marvellous movie, shot in stunning black-and-
white by Freddie Francis.

Eloge de l'amour

(2001, Fr, 97 min, b/w & col)
d Jean-Luc Godard. presented by Alain
Sarde, Ruth Waldburger. sc Jean-Luc
Godard. ph Christophe Pollock, Julien
Hirsch. ed Raphaële Urtin. m Ketil
Bjornstad, David Darling, Georges Van
Parys, Maurice Jaubert, Karl Amadeus
Hartmann, Arvo Pärt. cast Bruno
Putzulu, Cécile Camp, Claude
Baignères, Remo Forlani, Philippe
Loyrette, Audrey Klebaner, Mark
Hunter, Jérémy Lippmann, Jean Davy,
Françoise Verny.

● The wilful difficulty of Godard lost him
his English audience with 1987's King
Lear. Though hardly a conventional narrative – passages of sombre grandeur vie
with sequences of irritating obscurity –
this offers evidence of a desire to communicate, which may recommend it to a new
audience. Autobiography appears to play
a part. In Lear he cast a director (Carax) to
play Edgar – a name given to the director
(Putzulu) at the centre of Eloge. To sum-
marise: in the first half (shot memorably

in b/w), Edgar muses in voiceover about
a project he wishes to make (a play, a
movie or an opera); three couples are pro-
filed, as is the young actress he hopes to
cast. The second half, in colour-drenched
DV, flashes back two years to describe a
conflict between a Hollywood producer
and an elderly couple whose Resistance
story he wants to film; their granddaugh-
ter (Camp) is the young actress. How these
parts comment on each other is unclear.
What is clear is that Godard's obsessions
(anti globalisation, the role of art and cinema in life, etc) are as passionately held as
ever, though their precise meaning
remains elusive.

Eraserhead

(1976, US, 89 min, b/w)
d/p/sc David Lynch. ph Frederick
Elmes, Herbert Cardwell. ed/pd David
Lynch. m Fats Waller. cast Jack Nance,
Charlotte Stewart, Allen Joseph, Jeanne
Bates, Judith Anna Roberts, Laurel
Near.

● Lynch's remarkable first feature is a
true original. There's little in the way of a
coherent story: nervy Henry, living in a
sordid industrial city of smoke, steam and
shadows, is forced to marry his girlfriend
when she pronounces herself pregnant,
and finds himself the father of an all-
devouring, inhuman monster. But almost
like a surrealist movie, it has its own weird
logic, mixing black comedy (concerning
nuclear families and urban life), horror
and sci-conventions, and pure fantasy.
Best seen as a dark nightmare about sexuality, parenthood and commitment in
relationships, it astounds through its
expressionist sets and photography, the
startling, sinister soundtrack, and relent-
lessly imaginative fluency. Only the
sequence that gives the film its name – a
dream within the dream about Henry's
head being lopped off and turned into a
pencil-eraser – fails to work, and that's a
small reservation for a film with so many
cinematic coups.

Far from Heaven

(2002, US/Fr, 107 min)
d Todd Haynes. p Jody Patton, Christine
Vachon. sc Todd Haynes. ph Edward
Lachman. ed James Lyons. pd Mark
Friedberg. m Elmer Bernstein. cast
Julianne Moore, Dennis Quaid, Dennis
Haysbert, Patricia Clarkson, Viola Davis,
James Rebhorn, Celia Weston, Michael
Gaston, Ryan Ward, Lindsay Andretta,
Jordan Puryear, Bette Henritze.

● Like RW Fassbinder before him, Haynes
reworks Sirk's All That Heaven Allows to
masterly effect. Unlike Fear Eats the Soul,
however, Far from Heaven retains the post-
war suburban New England setting –
Hartford, Connecticut, 1957 – a time and
place of deceptively tranquil well being,
prior to the liberating turmoil of the '60s.
Cathy and Frank Whitaker (Moore and

Quaid) appear to have it all. He's a TV
sales exec, she's a happy wife and mother
with fine friends and a wonderful maid.
Then she finds Frank leads a double life.
And because their circle has no truck even
with guilt ridden homosexuals, she's so
isolated that her most comforting
moments are conversations with their gardener – trouble is, Raymond (Haysbert) is
black. While Haynes' script has its
moments of humour, it wisely steers clear
of condescension and camp while exploring a maze of taboos, confusions, prejudices and double standards. Elmer
Bernstein's music, Sandy Powell's costumes and Ed Lachman's camera hit all the
right notes, but Haynes' immaculate confection is finally best served by the extraordinary acting. Exultant in both its
artifice and its cruel honesty, it's a movie
Sirk would make today – and, as such, it's
quite brilliant.

Five Obstructions, The

(2003, Den/Bel/Switz /Fr/Swe/Fin/
GB/Nor, 90 min, col & b/w)
d Jørgen Leth, Lars von Trier.
p Carsten Holst. sc (idea) Lars von Trier.
ph Dan Holmberg. ed Camilla Skousen,
Morten Højberg. **The Conversations**
with Jørgen Leth, Lars von Trier,
Carsten Holst. **The Perfect Human,
1967** d Jørgen Leth. sc Ole John, Jørgen
Leth. ph Ole John, Henning Camre. ed
Knud Hauge. m Henning Christiansen.
cast Claus Nissen, Maiken Algren.
The Perfect Human Cuba d Jørgen
Leth. cast Daniel Hernández Rodríguez,
Jacqueline Arenal, Vivian Rosa. voice-
over Jørgen Leth. **The Perfect Human
Bombay** d/cast/voice-over Jørgen Leth.
The Perfect Human Brussels
d Jørgen Leth. p Marc-Henri Wajnberg.
sc Jørgen Leth, Asger Leth. ph Adam
Philp. cast Patrick Bauchau, Alexandra
Vandernoot, Marie Dejaer. voice-over
Patric Bauchau. **The Perfect Human
Cartoon** d Jørgen Leth, (animation)
Bob Sabiston. p Marc-Henri Wajnberg.
sc Jørgen Leth, Asger Leth. voice-over
Jørgen Leth, Patrick Bauchau.
**The Perfect Human, Avedore,
Denmark** d/sc Lars von Trier.
with/voice-over Jørgen Leth.

● In 1967, Jørgen Leth made The Perfect
Human, a short anthropological comedy
about a man in a room, which became a
favourite of the young Lars von Trier.
Years later, the latter came to Leth with an
offer he couldn't refuse: he would produce
five remakes of Perfect Human, each to be
directed by Leth according to von Trier's
diktat. In the first, Leth is sent to Cuba, and
instructed that no edit may last longer than
12 seconds. In the second, he is told to play
the lead himself and to shoot in the most
miserable place on earth – but to keep it off-
screen. A postmodern DVD of a movie – it

incorporates extracts from six versions of the same short film, each with its own 'making of' documentary – *The Five Obstacles* is a witty deconstruction process. The remakes appear to be of variable quality, but the heart and soul of the film comes in-between, as the two men meet, review the previous effort, and the producer lays down the rules for the next venture. Von Trier's ruthless instinct for his collaborator's soft spots may be sadistic, but it's vastly entertaining. When he really wants to punish Leth, he gives him complete freedom.

Frankenstein

(1931, US, 71 min, b/w)
d James Whale. *p* Carl Laemmle Jr. *sc* Garrett Fort, Francis Edwards Faragoh, John L Balderston. *ph* Arthur Edeson. *ed* Maurice Pivar, Clarence Kolster. *ad* Charles D Hall. *m* David Broekman. *cast* Boris Karloff, Colin Clive, Mae Clarke, John Boles, Edward Van Sloan, Dwight Frye, Frederick Kerr.
● A stark, solid, impressively stylish film, overshadowed (a little unfairly) by the later explosion of Whale's wit in the delirious *Bride of Frankenstein*. Karloff gives one of the great performances of all time as the monster whose mutation from candour to chill savagery is mirrored only through his limpid eyes. The film's great imaginative coup is to show the monster 'growing up' in all too human terms. First he is the innocent baby, reaching up to grasp the sunlight that filters through the skylight. Then the joyous child, playing at throwing flowers into the lake with a little girl whom he delightedly imagines to be another flower. And finally, as he finds himself progressively misjudged by the society that created him, the savage killer as whom he has been typecast. The film is unique in Whale's work in that the horror is played absolutely straight, and it has a weird fairytale beauty not matched until Cocteau made *La Belle et la Bête*.

General, The

(1926, US, 7,500 ft, b/w)
d Buster Keaton, Clyde Bruckman. *p* Joseph M Schenck. *sc* Buster Keaton, Clyde Bruckman, Al Boasberg, Charles Smith. *ph* Dev Jennings, Bert Haines. *ed* Sherman Kell. *ad* Fred Gabourie. *cast* Buster Keaton, Marian Mack, Glen Cavender, Jim Farley, Frederick Vroom, Joe Keaton.
● Keaton's best, and arguably the greatest screen comedy ever made. Against a meticulously evoked Civil War background, Buster risks life, limb and love as he pursues his beloved railway engine, hijacked by Northern spies up to no good for the Southern cause. The result is everything one could wish for: witty, dramatic, visually stunning, full of subtle, delightful human insights, and constantly hilarious.

Gloria

(1980, US, 121 min)
d John Cassavetes. *p* Sam Shaw. *sc* John Cassavetes. *ph* Fred Schuler. *ed* George C Villasenor. *ad* René D'Auriac. *m* Bill Conti. *cast* Gena Rowlands, John Adames, Buck Henry, Julie Carmen, Lupe Guarnica, Basilio Franchina.
● Notwithstanding Cassavetes' own dismissal of this crime thriller fantasy as a commercial chore he made for Disney so that his wife could act opposite a kid, it's clear from the opening montage that we're in the hands of a master. The film moves gracefully from painted credits through an exhilarating aerial survey of Manhattan by night to a vexed woman struggling to leave a crowded bus, all to the soulful strains of Bill Conti's lovely jazz/orchestral score. Rowlands is typically superb as the tough talking New York moll – half-whore, half-mother – reluctantly lumbered with a prematurely macho Latino boy (Adames) whose family have been killed by the Mob. As they go on the run, antagonism inevitably turns into affection, but Cassavetes and the two leads keep maudlin sentimentality at bay until the very bitter end, when the film basically 'fesses up that movie-style happy endings are the stuff of pipe dreams. Terrific.

Godfather, The

(1971, US, 175 min)
d Francis Ford Coppola. *p* Albert S Ruddy. *sc* Mario Puzo, Francis Ford Coppola. *ph* Gordon Willis. *ed* William H Reynolds, Peter Zinner. *pd* Dean Tavoularis. *m* Nino Rota. *cast* Marlon Brando, Al Pacino, James Caan, Richard Castellano, Robert Duvall, Sterling Hayden, John Marley, Richard Conte, Diane Keaton, John Cazale, Talia Shire.
● An everyday story of Mafia folk, incorporating a severed horse's head in the bed and a number of heartwarming family occasions, as well as pointers on how not to behave in your local trattoria (i.e. blasting the brains of your co-diners out all over their fettuccini). Mario Puzo's novel was brought to the screen in bravura style by Coppola, who was here trying out for the first time that piano/fortissimo style of crosscutting between religious ritual and bloody machine-gun massacre that was later to resurface in a watered-down version in *The Cotton Club*. See Brando with a mouthful of orange peel. Watch Pacino's cheek muscles twitch in incipiently psychotic fashion. Trace his rise from white sheep of the family to budding don and fully-fledged bad guy. Singalong to Nino Rota's irritatingly catchy theme tune. Its soap operatics should never have been presented separately from Part II.

Gojira (Godzilla)

(1954, Japan, 98 min, b/w)
d Ishiro Honda. *p* Tomoyuki Tanaka. *sc* Ishiro Honda, Takeo Murata. *ph* Masao Tamai. *ed* Yasunobu Taira. *pd* Satoshi Chuko, Takeo Kita. *m* Akira Ifukube. *cast* Akira Takarada, Momoko Kochi, Akihiro Harata, Takashi Shimura, Fuyuki Murakami, Sachio Sakai, Toranosuke Ogawa.
● Although its success ensured decades of sequels, this monster movie milestone is the product of an exact time and a place, 1950s Japan. Although the narrative template (nuclear testing, resurgent dinosaur, stomped-on city) was lifted from the previous year's Ray Harryhausen offering, *The Beast from 20,000 Fathoms*, the film is imbued with the traumatic atomic legacy of WWII. While US nuclear testing isn't mentioned by name, it's implicit that rampaging Gojira is its unwitting creation, inflicting massive civilian casualties and destroying the infrastructure built up by Japan's economic resurgence. And if the predominantly nocturnal mayhem suggest an effects team up against it, the spectacular destruction has a definite elegiac quality, while the final reel brings not Hollywood-style militaristic triumphalism, but heroic self-sacrifice from the professor who doesn't want his powerful nuclear gizmo falling into the 'wrong' hands. The dubbed 80-minute American version, with an inserted Raymond Burr, removes all reference to the war.

Grande Illusion, La

(1937, Fr, 117 min, b/w)
d Jean Renoir. *p* Frank Rollmer, Albert Pinkovitch. *sc* Jean Renoir, Charles Spaak. *ph* Christian Matras. *ed* Marguerite Renoir, Marthe Huguet. *ad* Eugène Lourié. *m* Joseph Kosma. *cast* Jean Gabin, Pierre Fresnay, Erich von Stroheim, Marcel Dalio, Julien Carette, Gaston Modot, Jean Dasté, Dita Parlo, Jacques Becker.
● Renoir films have a way of talking about one thing while being about another. *La Grande Illusion* was the only one of his '30s movies to be received with unqualified admiration at the time, lauded as a warmly humane indictment of war, a pacifist statement as nobly moving as *All Quiet on the Western Front*. Practically nobody noted the irony with which this archetypal prison camp escape story also outlined a barbed social analysis, demonstrating how shared aristocratic backgrounds (and military professionalism) forge a bond of sympathy between the German commandant (von Stroheim) and the senior French officer (Fresnay); how the exigencies of a wartime situation impel Fresnay to sacrifice himself (and Stroheim to shoot him) so that two of his men may make good their escape; and how those two escapees (Gabin and Dalio), once their roles as hero-warriors are over, will return home reduced being working class and dirty Jew once more. *The Grand*

Illusion, often cited as an enigmatic title, is surely not that peace can ever be permanent, but that liberty, equality and fraternity is ever likely to become a social reality rather than a token ideal.

Green Ray, The

(1986, Fr, 99 min)
d Eric Rohmer. *p* Margaret Ménégoz.
sc Eric Rohmer. *ph* Sophie Maintigneux.
ed Maria-Luisa Garcia. *m* Jean-Louis Valero. *cast* Marie Rivière, Vincent Gauthier, Carita, Basile Gervaise, Béatrice Romand, Lisa Hérédia.
●It's July, and Delphine (Rivière), a young Parisian secretary, is suddenly at a loss regarding her holiday; a friend has just backed out of a trip to Greece, her other companions have boyfriends, and Delphine can't bear spending August in Paris. She also hopes to find a dream lover, but receives only the unwelcome attentions of pushy predators, until… There's a whiff of fairytale to this particular slice of realism à la Rohmer, but what's perhaps most remarkable is that the film was almost completely improvised; though not so as you'd know it. It's as flawlessly constructed, shot and performed as ever, with France's greatest living director effortlessly evoking the morose moods of holidaying alone among crowds, and revelling in the particulars of place, weather and time of day. Deceptively simple, the film oozes honesty and spontaneity; the word, quite bluntly, is masterpiece.

Haine, La

(1995, Fr, 98 min, b/w)
d Mathieu Kassovitz. *p* Christophe Rossignon. *sc* Mathieu Kassovitz.
ph Pierre Aïm. *ed* Mathieu Kassovitz, Scott Stevenson. *ad* Giuseppe Ponturo. *cast* Vincent Cassel, Hubert Koundé, Saïd Taghmaoui, Karim Belkhadra, Edouard Montoute, François Levantal.
●Twenty-four hours in the Paris projects: an Arab boy is critically wounded in hospital, gut-shot, and a police revolver has found its way into the hands of a young Jewish skinhead, Vinz (Cassel), who vows to even the score if his pal dies. Vinz hangs out with Hubert (Koundé) and Saïd (Taghmaoui). They razz each other about films, cartoons, nothing in particular, but always the gun hovers over them like a death sentence, the black-and-white focal point for all the hatred they meet with, and all they can give back. Kassovitz has made only one film before (the droll race-comedy *Métisse*), but *La Haine* puts him right at the front of the field: this is virtuoso, on-the-edge stuff, as exciting as anything we've seen from the States in ages, and more thoroughly engaged with the reality it describes. He combats the inertia and boredom of his frustrated antagonists with a thrusting, jiving camera style which harries and punctuates their rambling, often very funny dialogue. The politics of

the piece are confrontational, to say the least, but there is a maturity and depth to the characterisation which goes beyond mere agitprop: society may be on the point of self-combustion, but this film betrays no appetite for the explosion. A vital, scalding piece of work.

Hana-Bi

(1997, Japan, 103 min)
d Takeshi Kitano. *p* Masayuki Mori, Yasushi Tsuge, Takio Yoshida.
sc Takeshi Kitano. *ph* Hideo Yamamoto. *ed* Takeshi Kitano. *ad* Norihiro Isoda.
m Joe Hisaishi. *cast* 'Beat' Takeshi, Kayoko Kishimoto, Ren Osugi, Susumu Terajima, Tetsu Watanabe, Taro Itsumi, Makoto Ashikawa, Yuko Daike.
●Kitano's Venice prize-winner mixes tenderness, violence and droll humour. A recently retired cop drifts towards a one-off crime, to help out a suicidal colleague crippled in a disastrous stake-out, and to take his terminally ill wife on one last trip around Japan. It's exceptionally assured, imaginative and idiosyncratic: the violence is sudden, brutal and almost all in the editing; the working of Kitano's own delightful paintings into the story is astonishingly resonant; the *mise-en-scène* as sharp and inventive as in *Sonatine*; and it's all held together by Beat Takeshi's unprecedentedly taciturn, impassive, but compassive performance, which is crucial to the film's emotional punch. Fans of Melville, Keaton, Hawks and Peckinpah should be especially impressed, but anyone with a modicum of patience, an open mind and a little love in their heart will probably recognise it as a masterpiece.

Heat

(1995, US, 171 min)
d Michael Mann. *p* Michael Mann, Art Linson. *sc* Michael Mann. *ph* Dante Spinotti. *ed* Dov Hoenig, Pasquale Buba, William Goldenberg, Tom Rolf. *pd* Neil Spisak. *m* Elliot Goldenthal. *cast* Robert De Niro, Al Pacino, Val Kilmer, Jon Voight, Amy Brenneman, Wes Studi, Dennis Haysbert, Tom Sizemore, Mykelti Wiliamson.
●Investigating a bold armed robbery which has left three security guards dead, LA cop Vincent Hanna (Pacino), whose devotion to work is threatening his third marriage, follows a trail that leads him to suspect a gang of thieves headed by Neil McCauley (De Niro). Trouble is, McCauley's cunning is at least equal to Hanna's, and that makes him a hard man to nail. Still, unknown to Hanna, McCauley's gang have their own troubles: one of their number is a volatile psychopath, while the businessman whose bonds they've stolen is not above some rough stuff himself. Such a synopsis barely scratches the surface of Mann's masterly crime epic. Painstakingly detailed, with enough characters, subplots and telling

nuances to fill out half a dozen conventional thrillers, this is simply the best American crime movie – and indeed, one of the finest movies, period – in over a decade. The action scenes are better than anything produced by John Woo or Quentin Tarantino; the characterisation has a depth most American film-makers only dream of; the use of location, decor and music is inspired; Dante Spinotti's camerawork is superb; and the large, imaginatively chosen cast gives terrific support to the two leads, both on glorious form.

Imitation of Life

(1958, US, 125 min)
d Douglas Sirk. *p* Ross Hunter.
sc Eleanore Griffin, Allan Scott.
ph Russell Metty. *ed* Milton Carruth.
ad Alexander Golitzen, Richard H Riedel. *m* Frank Skinner. *cast* Lana Turner, John Gavin, Sandra Dee, Juanita Moore, Susan Kohner, Daniel O'Herlihy, Troy Donahue, Robert Alda, Mahalia Jackson.
●There is a marvellous moment towards the end of Sirk's film which encapsulates the cruel cynicism that permeates his best work. As successful actress Turner, leaning over her dying black maid and long-term friend, lifts her head in tears, we see in the background a photograph of the dead woman's half-caste daughter, smiling. The romantic sentimentality of the moment is totally undercut by the knowledge that the girl, who has rejected her mother out of a desire to pass for white, has found a tragic release with her kindly parent's death. Sirk's last movie in Hollywood is a coldly brilliant weepie, a rags-to-riches tale of two intertwined families, in which the materialist optimism is continually counterpointed by an emphasis upon racist tension and the degeneration of family bonds. Despite the happy ending, what one remembers from the film is the steadily increasing hopelessness, given its most glorious visual expression in the scene of the maid's extravagant funeral, the only time in the film when her subordinate status and unhappy distance from her daughter are abolished. Forget those who decry the '50s Hollywood melodrama; it is through the conventions of that hyper-emotional genre that Sirk is able to make such a devastatingly embittered and pessimistic movie.

In a Lonely Place

(1950, US, 93 min, b/w)
d Nicholas Ray. *p* Robert Lord.
sc Andrew Solt. *ph* Burnett Guffey.
ed Viola Lawrence. *ad* Robert Peterson.
m George Antheil. *cast* Humphrey Bogart, Gloria Grahame, Frank Lovejoy, Robert Warwick, Jeff Donnell, Martha Stewart, Carl Benton Reid.
●The place is Hollywood, lonely for scriptwriter Dixon Steele (Bogart), who is suspected of murdering a young woman,

until girl-next-door Laurel Gray (Grahame) supplies him with a false alibi. But is he the killer? Under pressure of police interrogation, their tentative relationship threatens to crack – and Dix's sudden, violent temper becomes increasingly evident. Ray's classic thriller remains as fresh and resonant as the day it was released. Nothing is as it seems: the *noir* atmosphere of deathly paranoia frames one of the screen's most adult and touching love affairs, Bogart's tough-guy insolence is probed to expose a vulnerable, almost psychotic insecurity; while Grahame abandons femme fatale conventions to reveal a character of enormous, subtle complexity. As ever, Ray composes with symbolic precision, confounds audience expectations, and deploys the heightened lyricism of melodrama to produce an achingly poetic meditation on pain, distrust and loss of faith, not to mention an admirably unglamorous portrait of Tinseltown. Never were despair and solitude so romantically alluring.

Insignificance

(1985, GB, 109 min)
d Nicolas Roeg. *p* Jeremy Thomas. *sc* Terry Johnson. *ph* Peter Hannan. *ed* Tony Lawson. *pd* David Brockhurst. *m* Stanley Myers. *cast* Michael Emil, Theresa Russell, Tony Curtis, Gary Busey, Will Sampson.
● 1954. As Monroe, Einstein, DiMaggio and McCarthy, Roeg assembles an excellent cast of non-stars, confines them in anonymous hotel rooms, and lets them rip on all his favourite topics: life, love, fame, hate, jealousy, atomic firestorm and the whole damn thing. As usual with Roeg, the firmament is streaming with large ideas and awkward emotions, which grow larger and larger in significance, and most of which come together in a delightful scene when Marilyn (Russell) explains relativity to Einstein (Emil) with the aid of clockwork trains and balloons. Curtis is Senator McCarthy, still witch-hunting phantoms of his mind; Busey is the washed-up ballplayer, aching for Marilyn's return. It may be a chamber piece, but its circumference is vast.

In the Company of Men

(1997, US, 93 min)
d Neil LaBute. *p* Mark Archer, Stephen Pevner. *sc* Neil LaBute. *ph* Tom Hettinger. *ed* Joel Plotch. *pd* Julia Henkel. *m* Ken Williams, Karel Roessingn. *cast* Aaron Eckhart, Matt Malloy, Stacy Edwards, Emily Cline, Jason Dixie.
● Playwright Neil LaBute's film-directing debut is an impressively witty yet unsettling study of male insecurity, misogyny and rivalry. Away on a six-week business trip in a strange town, grouchy, resentful thirty-something execs Eckhart and Malloy decide to take revenge for their recently broken relationships by choosing a vulnerable, lonely woman for both of them (unbeknown to her) to date and dump. The scheme is put into action with deaf typist Edwards (a remarkable performance), but the best laid plans… Poised precariously but skilfully between realism and allegory, black comedy and straight drama, the movie makes the very most of its few locations by opting for a strangely timeless feel, and by focusing attention squarely on the three central performances and LaBute's clever, insightful script. Cruel, cool and pleasingly provocative.

In the Mood for Love

(2000, HK/Fr, 97 min)
d Wong Kar-Wai. *p* Wong Kar-Wai, Chan Ye-Cheng, Jackie Pang. *sc* Wong Kar-Wai. *ph* Tor Hor Feng, Lee Ping Bing. *ed/pd* Chan Suk-Ping. *m* Michael Galasso. *cast* Maggie Cheung, Tony Leung [Leung Chiu-Wai], Rebecca Pan, Lai Chin, Siu Ping-Lam, Chin Tsi-Ang.
● Wong's paean to the agony'n ecstasy of buttoned-up emotions is a kind-of sequel to *Days of Being Wild*, shaped and scored as a *valse triste*. In Hong Kong, 1962, Mr Chow (Leung) and Mrs Chan (Cheung) are neighbours who discover that their spouses are having an affair. He finds excuses to spend time with her, apparently intending to jilt her. Then they fall in love, but (aside from one reckless moment in a hotel) repress their feelings. He runs away to work as a journalist in Singapore; in 1966, covering De Gaulle's state visit to Cambodia, he's in Angkor Wat trying to unburden himself of the secret which overwhelms his life… Every charged frame of the film pulses with the central contradiction between repression and emotional abandon; the formalism and sensuality are inextricable. Career-best performances from both leads, Leung having a Cannes 'Best Actor' prize to show for his.

Irma Vep

(1996, Fr, 98 min)
d Olivier Assayas. *p* Georges Benayoun. *sc* Olivier Assayas. *ph* Eric Gautier. *ed* Luc Barnier, Tina Baz, Marie Lecoeur. *ad* François-Renaud Labarthe. *cast* Maggie Cheung, Jean-Pierre Léaud, Nathalie Richard, Alex Descas, Bulle Ogier, Lou Castel, Jacques Fieschi.
● Named after the slinky heroine of Feuillade's *Les Vampires* (which neurotic, idealistic director Léaud is here planning to remake), Assayas' partly improvised film charts the experiences of Hong Kong actress Cheung (playing herself) when she turns up in Paris to take the lead in Léaud's doomed movie. Crew members come on to her; journalists lecture her on the future of cinema, Léaud cracks up and is replaced by the gloriously seedy Castel, and Cheung starts having strange dreams. A delightfully nonchalant movie, complete with some nice satirical barbs aimed at contemporary French film culture, and fine performances throughout.

Jour se lève, Le

(1939, Fr, 87 min, b/w)
d Marcel Carné. *p* Brachet. *sc* Jacques Viot, Jacques Prévert. *ph* Curt Courant, Philippe Agostini, André Bac. *ed* René Le Hénaff. *pd* Alexandre Trauner. *m* Maurice Jaubert. *cast* Jean Gabin, Arletty, Jules Berry, Jacqueline Laurent, Bernard Blier, René Génin, Mady Berry.
● Possibly the best of the Carné-Prévert films, certainly their collaboration at its most classically pure, with Gabin a dead man from the outset as his honest foundry worker, hounded into jealousy and murder by a cynical seducer, holes up with a gun in an attic surrounded by police, remembering in flashback how it all started while he waits for the end. Fritz Lang might have given ineluctable fate a sharper edge (less poetry, more doom), but he couldn't have bettered the performances from Gabin, Berry, Arletty, and (as the subject of Gabin's romantic agony) Laurent. Remade in Hollywood as *The Long Night* in 1947.

Killers, The

(US, 1946, 105 min, b/w)
d Robert Siodmak. *p* Mark Hellinger. *sc* Anthony Veiller. *ph* Woody Bredell. *ed* Arthur Hilton. *ad* Jack Otterson, Martin Obzina. *m* Miklós Rózsa. *cast* Edmond O'Brien, Ava Gardner, Burt Lancaster, Albert Dekker, Sam Levene, Vince Barnett, Charles McGraw, William Conrad, Virginia Christine.
● If anyone still doesn't know what's signified by the critical term *film noir*, then *The Killers* provides an exhaustive definition. The quality isn't in the rather average script (elaborated from Hemingway's short story) but in the overall sensibility – the casting, the use of shadows, the compositions alternating between paranoid long shots and hysterical close-ups. After the brilliant opening murder scene, what follows is a series of flashbacks as Edmond O'Brien's insurance investigator looks into the circumstances of Lancaster's death. Ava Gardner is an admirably tacky femme fatale, and her fickleness/faithfulness provides the not very surprising denouement. Worth attention as a '40s thriller, but more than that as a prime example of post-war pessimism and fatalism.

Kind Hearts and Coronets

(1949, GB, 106 min, b/w)
d Robert Hamer. *p* Michael Balcon. *sc* Robert Hamer, John Dighton. *ph* Douglas Slocombe. *ed* Peter Tanner. *ad* William Kellner. *m* WA Mozart. *cast* Dennis Price, Alec Guinness, Joan Greenwood, Valerie Hobson, Audrey Fildes, Miles Malleson, Clive Morton, Hugh Griffith.

●The gentle English art of murder in Ealing's blackest comedy, with Price in perfect form as the ignoble Louis, killing off a complete family tree (played by Guinness throughout) in order to take the cherished d'Ascoyne family title. Disarmingly cool and callous in its literary sophistication, admirably low key in its discreet caricatures of the haute bourgeoisie, impeccable in its period detail (Edwardian), it's a brilliantly cynical film without a hint of middle-class guilt or bitterness.

King Kong

(1933, US, 100 min, b/w)
d Merian C Cooper, Ernest B Schoedsack. sc James Ashmore Creelman, Ruth Rose. ph Eddie Linden, Vernon L Walker, JO Taylor. ed Ted Cheesman. ad Carroll Clark, Al Herman. m Max Steiner. cast Fay Wray, Bruce Cabot, Robert Armstrong, Noble Johnson, Frank Reicher, Sam Hardy, James Flavin.
●If this glorious pile of horror-fantasy hokum has lost none of its power to move, excite and sadden, it is in no small measure due to the remarkable technical achievements of Willis O'Brien's animation work, and the superbly matched score of Max Steiner. The masterstroke was, of course, to delay the great ape's entrance by a thumbboard sequence of such humorous banality and risible dialogue that Kong can emerge unchallenged as the most fully realised character in the film. Thankfully Wray is not required to act, merely to scream; but what a perfect victim she makes. The throbbing heart of the film lies in the creation of the semi-human simian himself, an immortal tribute to the Hollywood dream factory's ability to fashion a symbol that can express all the contradictory erotic, ecstatic, destructive, pathetic and cathartic buried impulses of 'civilised' man.

Kiss Me Deadly

(1955, US, 105 min, b/w)
d/p Robert Aldrich. sc AI Bezzerides. ph Ernest Laszlo. ed Michael Luciano. ad William Glasgow. m Frank Devol. cast Ralph Meeker, Albert Dekker, Maxine Cooper, Paul Stewart, Gaby Rodgers, Cloris Leachman, Jack Lambert, Wesley Addy, Nick Dennis, Marian Carr, Jack Elam.
●A key film from the '50s, a savage critique of Cold War paranoia bounded by two haunting sound effects: at the beginning, the desperate, panting sobs of the girl hitching a lift from Mike Hammer on the dark highway, and her despairing plea to 'Remember me' as she disappears to her death; and at the end, the strange, groaning sigh that escapes as the Pandora's box containing the Great Whatsit is finally opened to unleash an incandescent nuclear blast. Aldrich's distaste for the unprincipled brutality of Mickey Spillane's hero is evident throughout the film; but nevertheless given a sort of dumb-ox honesty by Ralph Meeker, the character acquires new resonance as an example of mankind's mulish habit of meddling with the unknown regardless of consequences. Brilliantly characterised down to the smallest roles, directed with baroque ferocity, superbly shot by Ernest Laszlo in film noir terms, it's a masterpiece of sorts.

Knife in the Water

(1962, Pol, 94 min, b/w)
d Roman Polanski. p Stanislaw Zylewicz. sc Roman Polanski, Jerzy Skolimowski, Jakub Goldberg. ph Jerzy Lipman. ed Halina Prugar. m Krzysztof Komeda. cast Leon Niemczyk, Jolanta Umecka, Zygmunt Malanowicz.
●Polanski's first feature, a model of economic, imaginative film-making which, in many ways, he has hardly improved upon since. The story is simplicity itself: a couple destined for a yachting weekend pick up a hitch-hiker, and during the apparently relaxing period of sport and rest, allegiances shift, frustrations bubble up to the surface, and dangerous emotional games are played. Like much of Polanski's later work, it deals with humiliation, sexuality, aggression and absurdity; but what makes the film so satisfying is the tenderness and straightforward nature of his approach. With just three actors, a boat, and a huge expanse of water, he and script-writer Jerzy Skolimowski milk the situation for all it's worth, rarely descending into dramatic contrivance, but managing to heap up the tension and the ambiguities.

Land and Freedom

(1995, GB/Sp/Ger, 110 min)
d Ken Loach. p Rebecca O'Brien. sc Jim Allen. ph Barry Ackroyd. ed Jonathan Morris. pd Martin Johnson. m George Fenton. cast Ian Hart, Rosana Pastor, Iciar Bollain, Tom Gilroy, Eoin McCarthy, Frédéric Pierrot.
●Loach's film charts the experiences of an unemployed young Liverpudlian (Ian Hart) when he goes to join the Republicans in the Spanish Civil War, and for the first half-hour or so it seems that Jim Allen's script is going to be a sentimental celebration of fraternal unity among the good guys. Then, mercifully, things get more complex, as Hart's confusion and divided loyalties mirror the in-fighting that plagued the Left and led to Franco's victory. The film has its shortcomings – notably the didactic discussions on, for example, the ideology of collectivism – but Loach handles what is for him an unprecedentedly large canvas with aplomb. The action scenes in particular have a raw, plausible immediacy. Nor is this just a movie which simply fills us in on fascinating historical details; thanks to muscular performances (especially from Hart), it also packs an emotional punch.

Letter from an Unknown Woman

(1948, US, 90 min, b/w)
d Max Ophüls. p John Houseman. sc Howard Koch. ph Franz Planer. ed Ted J Kent. ad Alexander Golitzen. m Daniele Amfitheatrof. cast Joan Fontaine, Louis Jourdan, Mady Christians, Marcel Journet, Art Smith, Carol Yorke, John Good.
●Of all the cinema's fables of doomed love, none is more piercing than this. Fontaine nurses an undeclared childhood crush on her next-door neighbour, a concert pianist (Jourdan); much later, he adds her to his long list of conquests, makes her pregnant – and forgets all about her. Ophüls' endlessly elaborate camera movements, forever circling the characters or co-opting them into larger designs, expose the impasse with hallucinatory clarity: we see how these people see each other and why they are hopelessly, inextricably stuck.

Limey, The

(1999, US, 91 min)
d Steven Soderbergh. p John Hardy, Scott Kramer. sc Lem Dobbs. ph Ed Lachman. ed Sarah Flack. pd Gary Frutkoff. m Cliff Martinez. cast Terence Stamp, Peter Fonda, Luis Guzmán, Lesley Ann Warren, Barry Newman, Nicky Katt, Joe Dallesandro.
●Funny, touching, and as effortlessly assured, in its own relatively low budget way, as Out of Sight, this consistently imaginative, comic crime movie milks the fish-out-of-water theme for all it's worth, and then some. Stamp is superb as the ageing Cockney ex-con whose investigations into his daughter's death in LA lead him to surprise the locals not only with his (wonderfully OTT) rhyming slang, but with his hard-man resilience and ingenuity; moreover, he's given sterling support by Fonda (who as a rock impresario out of his depth in murky water inspires some lovely in-jokes about '60s counter-culture), Newman and Guzman (not, for once, typecast). Lem Dobbs' script is witty; Ed Lachman's images and Cliff Martinez' music are perfectly in keeping with the light, relaxed mood; and Soderbergh's customary playfulness with the narrative deftly underlines Stamp's obsession. A joy.

Magnificent Seven, The

(1960, US, 138 min)
d/p John Sturges. sc William S Roberts. ph Charles Lang Jr. ed Ferris Webster. ad Edward Fitzgerald. m Elmer Bernstein. cast Yul Brynner, Steve McQueen, Robert Vaughn, Charles Bronson, Horst Buchholz, James Coburn, Eli Wallach, Brad Dexter, Vladimir Sokoloff, Whit Bissell.

●Sturges' remake of Kurosawa's *Seven Samurai* is always worth a look, mainly for the performances of McQueen, Bronson, Coburn and Vaughn. The theme of the group of professionals coming together to defend a cause or undertake a useless task, mainly as an exercise for their narcissistic talents, was one that would be constantly reworked during the '60s. Numerous set pieces, like Coburn's knife fight, Vaughn's fly-catching and McQueen's jokes, stay lodged in the mind.

Man Who Shot Liberty Valance, The

(1962, US, 121 min, b/w)
d John Ford. *p* Willis Goldbeck. *sc* James Warner Bellah, Willis Goldbeck. *ph* William H Clothier. *ed* Otho Lovering. *ad* Hal Pereira, Eddie Imazu. *m* Cyril J Mockridge. *cast* John Wayne, James Stewart, Vera Miles, Lee Marvin, Edmond O'Brien, Andy Devine, John Carradine, Jeanette Nolan, Woody Strode, Denver Pyle, Strother Martin, Lee Van Cleef.

●Ford's purest and most sustained expression of the familiar themes of the passing of the Old West, the conflict between the untamed wilderness and the cultivated garden, and the power of myth. Stewart plays a respected senator who returns on a train (in an opening echoing that of *My Darling Clementine*) to attend the funeral of his old friend Wayne. In one scene, Stewart wipes the dust off a disused stagecoach, marking in a simple gesture the distance between the Old West inhabited by Wayne and the new West which he himself represents. In the central flashback sequence, it is revealed that it was not Stewart who shot the outlaw Liberty Valance (Marvin) but Wayne, the gun law of the Old West paving the way for the development of a new civilisation. For Ford, the passing of the Old West is also the passing of an age of romantic heroism. The only link between the two worlds is the desert rose, a flowering cactus hardy enough to survive the harshness of the desert and humanise the wilderness.

Man Without a Past, The

(2002, Fin, 97 min)
d/p/sc Aki Kaurismäki. *ph* Timo Salminen. *ed* Timo Linnasalo. *ad* Markku Pätilä, Jukka Salmi. *cast* Markku Peltola, Kati Outinen, Juhani Niemelä, Kaija Pakarinen, Sakari Kuosmanen, Annikki Tähti, Anneli Sauli.

●On arrival in Helsinki, a man (Peltola) is viciously mugged and given up for dead – but miraculously revives; without memory or any idea of who he is, the man wanders off into the city, moves in with the homeless living in freight containers around the harbour, and eventually begins to put his life (or someone else's?) back together after falling for a Salvation

Army woman (Outinen) at the soup canteen. A typically droll, deadpan comedy from Kaurismäki, complete with nods to '50s B-movies, rock'n'roll, and fairytale romance, but also, like its predecessor *Drifting Clouds*, addressing social and political issues (unemployment, homelessness, welfare, heartless capitalism) with the lightest of touches. Beautifully tender, funny and idiosyncratic, right down to some lovely stuff featuring a predictably melancholy dog.

Matter of Life and Death, A

(1946, GB, 104, b/w & col)
d/p/sc Michael Powell, Emeric Pressburger. *ph* Jack Cardiff. *ed* Reginald Mills. *pd* Alfred Junge. *m* Allan Gray. *cast* David Niven, Kim Hunter, Roger Livesey, Raymond Massey, Marius Goring, Robert Coote, Abraham Sofaer, Kathleen Byron, Richard Attenborough, Bonar Colleano.

●One of Powell and Pressburger's finest films. Made at the instigation of the Ministry of Information, who wanted propaganda stressing the need for goodwill between Britain and America, it emerges as an outrageous fantasy full of wit, beautiful sets and Technicolor, and perfectly judged performances. The story is just a little bizarre. RAF pilot Niven bales out of his blazing plane without a chute and survives; but – at least in his tormented mind – he was due to die, and a heavenly messenger comes down to earth to collect him. A celestial tribunal ensues to judge his case while, back on earth, doctors are fighting for his life. What makes the film so very remarkable is the assurance of Powell's direction, which manages to make heaven at least as convincing as earth. (The celestial scenes are in monochrome, the terrestial ones in colour: was Powell slyly asserting, in the faces of the British documentary boys, the greater realism of that which is imagined?). But the whole thing works like a dream, with many hilarious swipes at national stereotypes, and a love story that is as moving as it is absurd. Masterly.

Metropolis

(1926, Ger, 13,743 ft, b/w)
d Fritz Lang. *p* Erich Pommer. *sc* Fritz Lang, Thea von Harbou. *ph* Karl Freund, Günther Rittau. *ad* Otto Hunte, Erich Kettelhut, Karl Vollbrecht. *m* (original accompanying score) Gottfried Huppertz. *cast* Alfred Abel, Gustav Fröhlich, Brigitte Helm, Rudolf Klein-Rogge, Fritz Rasp, Heinrich George, Theodor Loos.

●UFA's most ambitious production, intended to rival Hollywood in its spectacular evocation of the 21st century city of Metropolis and its mechanised society founded on slavery. Thea von Harbou's script is a bizarre mixture of futuristic sci-fi and backward-looking Gothic horror;

it's at best garbled, and its resolution is, to say the least, politically dubious. Fritz Lang's direction, on the other hand, is tremendously inventive and exhilarating: no director before (and not that many since) had worked so closely with cameramen and designers to achieve such dynamic visual and spatial effects.

Mon Oncle d'Amérique

(1980, Fr, 126 min)
d Alain Resnais. *p* Philippe Dussart. *sc* Jean Gruault. *ph* Sacha Vierny. *ed* Albert Jurgenson. *ad* Jacques Saulnier. *m* Arié Dzierlatka. *cast* Gérard Depardieu, Nicole Garcia, Roger Pierre, Marie Dubois, Nelly Borgeaud, Pierre Arditi, Henri Laborit.

●After the disappointments of *Stavisky* and *Providence*, Resnais here retrieves his position as a great film innovator. *My American Uncle* takes three middle class characters (two of them from well-defined working class backgrounds) and leads them through a labyrinth of 'stress' situations. The tone hovers between soap opera and docudrama, consistently pleasurable if hardly gripping. Then it introduces its fourth major character, Henri Laborit, a bona fide behavioural scientist, who discusses his theories of biological and emotional triggers. Shortsighted critics seem to imagine that the fictional material merely illustrates what Laborit says, although Resnais inserts some jokey shots of 'human' mice to demolish any such notions. His triumph is to create a new kind of fiction: a drama that not only leaves room to think, but opens up fissures that thoughts flood into, some prompted by Laborit, others by personal reflections, yet others by dreams. Inevitably, it ends in a riddle, and one which proves that surrealism lives.

My Neighbour Totoro

(1988, Japan, 86 min)
d Hayao Miyazaki. *p* Yasuyoshi Tokuma. *sc* Hayao Miyazaki. *ph* Hisao Shirai. *ed* Takeshi Seyama. *pd* Kazuo Oga. *m* Joe Hisaishi. *cast* voices: Hitoshi Takagi, Noriko Hidaka, Chika Sakamoto, Shigesato Itoi, Sumi Shimamoto, Toshiyuki Amagasa, Tanie Kitabayashi, Yuko Maruyama, Masashi Hirose; (US version) Lisa Michaelson, Cheryl Chase, Greg Snegoff, Natalie Core, Kenneth Hartman, Alexandra Kenworthy.

●The film that first brought Miyazaki to international attention remains an animated achievement almost without parallel. The first half delicately captures both mystery and quietness as two little girls move with their father to a remote new home in the country while their mother recuperates from TB in hospital, and only gradually become aware that something's stirring in the trees outside. While younger viewers will adore the furry creatures, including the house-sized Totoro and the twelve-legged cat-bus, adults will perhaps best appreciate the film's delicate rendering of atmosphere (rainy afternoons in the country, as night falls), and its attuned understanding of the anxieties and wonders of childhood. And the lack of sentimentality will be utterly refreshing to those raised on a diet of Disney.

Night of the Hunter, The

(1955, US, 92 min, b/w)
d Charles Laughton. p Paul Gregory. sc James Agee. ph Stanley Cortez. ed Robert Golden. ad Hilyard Brown. m Walter Schumann. cast Robert Mitchum, Lillian Gish, Shelley Winters, Billy Chapin, James Gleason, Sally Ann Bruce, Peter Graves, Evelyn Varden.
● Laughton's only stab at directing, with Mitchum as the psychopathic preacher with 'love' and 'hate' tattooed on his knuckles, turned out to be a genuine weirdie. Set in '30s rural America, the film polarises into a struggle between good and evil for the souls of innocent children. Everyone's contribution is equally important. Laughton's deliberately old-fashioned direction throws up a startling array of images: an amalgam of Mark Twain-like exteriors (idyllic riverside life) and expressionist interiors, full of moody nighttime shadows. The style reaches its pitch in the extraordinary moonlight flight of the two children downriver, gliding silently in the distance, watched over by animals seen in huge close-up, filling up the foreground of the screen. James Agee's script (faithfully translating Davis Grubb's novel) treads a tight path between humour (it's a surprisingly light film in many ways) and straight suspense, a combination best realised when Gish sits the night out on the porch waiting for Mitchum to attack, and they both sing 'Leaning on the Everlasting Arms' to themselves. Finally, there's the absolute authority of Mitchum's performance – easy, charming, infinitely sinister.

Ninotchka

(1939, US, 110 min, b/w)
d/p Ernst Lubitsch. sc Charles Brackett, Billy Wilder, Walter Reisch. ph William H Daniels. ed Gene Ruggiero. ad Cedric Gibbons, Randall Duell. m Werner R Heymann. cast Greta Garbo, Melvyn Douglas, Ina Claire, Bela Lugosi, Sig Ruman, Felix Bressart, Alexander Granach, Gregory Gaye, Rolfe Sedan.
● This was the first time since 1934 that Garbo had been seen in the 20th century, and the first time ever that her material was predominantly comic (though it was hardly the first time she'd laughed, as the ads insisted). But her character still had an icy aura, at least at the outset – she plays a Russian comrade staying in Paris on government business, a situation providing writers Wilder, Brackett and Walter Reisch with rich material for imp-ish political jokes ('The last mass trials were a great success. There are going to be fewer but better Russians'). Then she meets the acceptable face of Capitalism in the form of Melvyn Douglas, and like many a lesser MGM star before her, succumbs completely to his suave looks and honeyed voice. The film's not quite the delight history says it is – by the late '30s, the famed Lubitsch touch was resembling a heavy blow, the elegant sophistication turning crude and cynical. Yet it's still consistently amusing, and Garbo throws herself into the fray with engaging vigour.

North by Northwest

(1959, US, 136 min)
d/p Alfred Hitchcock. sc Ernest Lehman. ph Robert Burks. ed George Tomasini. pd Robert Boyle. m Bernard Herrmann. cast Cary Grant, Eva Marie Saint, James Mason, Jessie Royce Landis, Leo G Carroll, Josephine Hutchinson, Philip Ober, Martin Landau, Adam Williams, Ed Platt.
● From the glossy '60s-style surface of Saul Bass' credit sequence to Hitchcock's almost audible chortle at his final phallic image, North by Northwest treads a bizarre tightrope between sex and repression, nightmarish thriller and urbane comedy. Cary Grant is truly superb as the light-hearted advertising executive who's abducted, escapes, and is then hounded across America trying to find out what's going on and slowly being forced to assume another man's identity. And it's one of those films from which you can take as many readings as you want: conspiracy paranoia, Freudian nightmare (in which mothers, lovers, gays and cops all conspire against a man), parable on modern America in which final escape must be made down the treacherous face of Mt Rushmore (the one carved with US Presidents' heads). All in all, an improbable classic.

Nuit et Brouillard

(1955, Fr, 32 min, b/w & col)
d Alain Resnais. p Anatole Dauman, Samy Halfon, Philippe Lifschitz. sc Jean Cayrol. ph Ghislain Cloquet, Sacha Vierny. ed Alain Resnais. m Hanns Eisler. narrator Michel Bouquet.
● Cloquet's camera tracks slowly through a deserted, autumnal Auschwitz, with its rusted wire, dilapidated huts and silent crematoria. This muted Technicolor 'now' is intercut with grainy monochrome records of 'then', as the commentary outlines the development and operation of the Nazi death camps. The achievement of Resnais' film is to find a tone appropriate to the desolating enormity of what took place. Cayrol's text presents the facts with a mixture of indignation, bewilderment and cool irony, complemented by Eisler's music, the austerity of which is cut with passages of great ten-derness. The subtext for film-makers is that unless you're certain you can match the emotional and intellectual range brought to bear here, far better to leave this particular subject well alone.

Once Upon a Time in America

(1983, US, 229 min)
d Sergio Leone. p Arnon Milchan. sc Leo Benvenuti, Piero De Bernardi, Enrico Medioli, Franco Arcalli, Franco Ferrini, Sergio Leone. ph Tonino Delli Colli. ed Nino Baragli. ad Carlo Simi, (NY) James Singelis. m Ennio Morricone. cast Robert De Niro, James Woods, Elizabeth McGovern, Treat Williams, Tuesday Weld, Burt Young, Joe Pesci, Danny Aiello.
● In 1968, Noodles (De Niro) returns to New York an old man after 35 years of exile, ridden by guilt. His cross-cut memories of the Jewish Mafia's coming of age on the Lower East Side in 1923, their rise to wealth during Prohibition, and their Götterdämmerung in 1933, provide the epic background to a story of friendship and betrayal, love and death. While Leone's vision still has a magnificent sweep, the film finally subsides to an emotional core that is sombre, even elegiac, and which centres on a man who is bent and broken by time, and finally left with nothing but an impotent sadness.

One and a Two..., A

(2000, Tai/Japan, 173 min)
d Edward Yang. p Shinya Kawai, Naoko Tsukeda. sc Edward Yang. ph Yang Wei-Han. pd Chen Bo-Wen. pd/m Peng Kai-Li. cast Wu Nianzhen, Elaine Jin, Issey Ogata, Kelly Lee, Jonathan Chang, Adrian Lin, Ko Su-Yun.
● Yang's most fully achieved film since A Brighter Summer Day offers a detailed and very moving account across three generations of a family of the ways people cope with crises and emotional setbacks. The problems, it humorously suggests, may change as one grows older, but the means of coping don't change much. The central focus is on family head NJ (Wu, a fine screenwriter and director in his own right), who bumps into his long-lost first love on the very day his mother-in-law goes into a coma, and finds himself wondering if he can erase the last 20 years and start over. This is one film which justifies a three-hour running time: each character is drawn with warmth and complexity, and each has to deal with issues which are all too recognisably real. The interweaving of story threads and the ability to keep larger perspectives in sight while not stinting on specifics both bespeak a true mastery.

Ordet

(1954, Den, 125 min, b/w)
d/sc Carl Dreyer. ph Henning Bendtsen.

ed Edith Schlüssel. *ad* Erik Aaes.
m Poul Schierbeck. *cast* Henrik
Malberg, Emil Hass Christensen,
Preben Lerdorff Rye, Cay Kristiansen,
Birgitte Federspiel, Ann Elizabeth.
● Dreyer's penultimate feature (*Gertrud*
followed a full decade later) is another of
his explorations of the clash between ortho-
dox religion and true faith. Based with great
fidelity on a play by Kaj Munk, it's formu-
lated as a kind of rural chamber drama, and
like most of Dreyer's films it centres on the
tensions within a family. Its method is to
establish a scrupulously realistic frame of
reference, then undercut it thematically with
elements of the fantastic and formally with
a film syntax that demands constant attention to the way meaning is being constructed. The intensity of the viewer's
relationship with the film makes the closing
scene (a miracle) one of the most extraordinary in all cinema.

Pickpocket

(1959, Fr, 75 min, b/w)
d Robert Bresson. *p* Agnès Delahaie.
sc Robert Bresson. *ph* Léonce-Henry
Burel. *ed* Raymond Lamy. *ad* Pierre
Charbonnier. *m* Jean-Baptiste Lully.
cast Martin Lassalle, Marika Green,
Pierre Leymarie, Jean Pelegri, Kassagi,
Pierre Etaix.
● Bresson is the dark Catholic of French
cinema. Here a young man, unwilling/
unable to find work, flirts with the idea of
pickpocketing: an initial, almost disastrous
attempt leads him on. Theft follows theft,
on the Paris Métro and in the streets, for
the activity occupies an obsessive, erotic
position in his daily life. Increasing skill
leads to increasing desire, and so to alienation from his only friend, and from the
moral counsel of the detective who watches over him with paternal concern. Black-
and-white images in the summer sun…of
hands flexing uncontrollably, of eyes
opaque to the camera's gaze…all part of a
diary/flashback that is in the process of
being 'written' by the thief himself in
prison. Read it as an allegory on the insuf-
ficiency of human reason; as a tone poem
on displaced desire; as Catholic first cousin
to Camus' *The Outsider*: one of the few
postwar European films that is both cerebral and resolutely sensual.

Private Life of Sherlock Holmes, The

(1970, GB, 125 min)
d/p Billy Wilder. *sc* Billy Wilder,
IAL Diamond. *ph* Christopher Challis.
ed Ernest Walter. *pd* Alexandre
Trauner. *m* Miklós Rozsa. *cast* Robert
Stephens, Colin Blakely, Irene Handl,
Christopher Lee, Tamara Toumanova,
Genevieve Page, Clive Revill, Catherine
Lacey, Stanley Holloway.
● A wonderful, cruelly underrated film.
Although there are some terrifically
funny moments, and on one level the

Wilder/Diamond conception of Conan
Doyle's hero does tend to debunk the
myth of the perfect sleuth (there are allu-
sions to his misogyny and cocaine addic-
tion), this alternative vision of Holmes
sets up a stylish and totally appropriate
story (concerning dwarfs, dead canaries,
and the Loch Ness monster) as a context
in which to explain the reason for
Holmes' forsaking of his emotional life to
become a thinking machine. Betrayal and
lost love are the elements that catalyse
this process, turning Holmes from a fallible romantic into a disillusioned cynic.
With a stunning score by Miklós Rozsa,
carefully modulated performances, lush
location photography, and perfect sets by
Trauner, it is Wilder's least embittered
film and by far his most moving.

Rashomon

(1951, Japan, 88 min, b/w)
d Akira Kurosawa. *p* Jingo Minoura.
sc Akira Kurosawa. *ph* Kazuo
Matsuyama. *ad* H Motsumoto.
m Takashi Matsuyama. *cast* Toshiro
Mifune, Machiko Kyo, Masayuki Mori,
Takashi Shimura, Minoru Chiaki,
Fumiko Homma.
● If it weren't for the occasional spasm of
gratuitous, humanist optimism,
Rashomon could be warmly recommended as one of Kurosawa's most inventive
and sustained achievements. The main
part of the film, set in 12th century Kyoto,
offers four mutually contradictory versions of an ambush, rape and murder,
each through the eyes of one of those
involved. The view of human weaknesses
and vices is notably astringent, although
the sheer animal vigour of Mifune's bandit is perhaps a celebration of a sort. The
film is much less formally daring than its
literary source, but its virtues are equally
plentiful: Kurosawa's visual style at its
most muscular, rhythmically nuanced
editing, and excellent performances.

Ratcatcher

(1999, GB, 94 min)
d Lynne Ramsay. *p* Gavin Emerson.
sc Lynne Ramsay. *ph* Alwin Kuchler.
ed Lucia Zucchetti. *pd* Jane Morton.
m Rachel Portman. *cast* William Eadie,
Tommy Flanagan, Mandy Matthews,
Leanne Mullen, John Miller.
● Set in and around a Glasgow tenement
block during a dustman's strike in the
mid-'70s, Ramsay's astonishingly assured
feature debut centres on a 12-year-old
(Eadie, excellent) who, haunted by the
(secret) role he played in a pal's accidental
death by drowning, gradually retreats into
a private world of solitude, strange friendships and consoling dreams of a new
home for his family. That's about it, story-
wise, but Ramsay's bold visual sense,
droll wit and tender but unsentimental
take on the various characters and their
relationships makes for a distinctly poet-

ic brand of gritty realism, and one of the
most impressive first features by a British
director in some years.

Sans Soleil

(1983, Fr, 100 min)
d Chris Marker. *p* Anatole Dauman.
sc Chris Marker. *ph* Sana Na N'Hada,
Danièle Tessier, Jean-Michel Humeau,
Mario Marret, Eugenio Bentivoglio,
Haroun Tazieff. *ed* Chris Marker.
m Michel Krasna, Mussorgsky,
Sibelius. *narrator* Alexandra Stewart.
● Imagine getting letters from a friend in
Japan, letters full of images, sounds and
ideas. Your friend is an inveterate globe-
trotter, and his letters are full of memories
of other trips. He has a wry and very
engaging sense of humour, he's a movie
fan, he used to be quite an activist (though
he was never much into 'ideology'), and
he's thoughtful and very well read. In his
letters, he wants to share with you the
faces that have caught his eye, the events
that made him smile or weep, the places
where he's felt at home. He wants to tell
you stories, but he can't find a story big
enough to deal with his sense of contrasts,
his wish to grasp fleeting moments, his
recurring memories. Above all he hopes to
excite you, to share his secrets with you,
to consolidate your friendship. Now stop
imagining things and go to see *Sans Soleil*,
in which Marker, the cinema's greatest
essayist, sums up a lifetime's travels, spec-
ulations and passions. Among very many
other things, his film is the most intimate
portrait of Tokyo yet made: from neighbourhood festivals to robots, under the
sign of the Owl and the Pussycat.

Scent of Green Papaya, The

(1993, Fr, 104 min)
d Tran Anh Hung. *p* Christophe
Rossignon. *sc* Tran Anh Hung.
ph Benoît Delhomme. *ed* Nicole Dedieu,
Jean-Pierre Roques. *ad* Alain Negre.
m Ton That Tiết. *cast* Yen-Khe Tran
Nu, Man San Lu, Thi Loc Truong,
Anh Hoa Nguyen, Hoa Hoi Vuong.
● The story of Mui, a peasant girl who
comes to Saigon to serve in the house of a
bourgeois family: grandmother, parents,
three sons and a maid. It's 1951, the influence of the West is beginning to make itself
felt, but already the old conventions are
beginning to crack. Tran's first feature –
shot, remarkably, in France – is sensuous,
evocative and politically ambivalent. It
focuses particularly on the servitude of
women. We watch in close-up as Mui
learns her duties: cleaning up after the
youngsters, running errands, cooking rice
and papaya for the family. At first these
are mere chores, but later, as she grows
into a woman, they take on a more fulfilling purpose. The movie's poetic-realist
design meshes detailed, patient observation and delectable, poignant travelling

shots; it grounds us in the quotidian duties of service and dissects contemporary Vietnamese social hierarchies, yet adds up to something much more subtle and enticing: a lyrical portrait of the human spirit in work and in love. Exquisitely controlled.

Searchers, The

(1956, US, 119 min)
d John Ford. *p* Merian C Cooper. *sc* Frank S Nugent. *ph* Winton C Hoch. *ed* Jack Murray. *ad* Frank Hotaling, James Basevi. *m* Max Steiner. *cast* John Wayne, Jeffrey Hunter, Vera Miles, Ward Bond, Natalie Wood, Hank Worden, Henry Brandon, Harry Carey Jr, Olive Carey, John Qualen, Antonio Moreno.
● A marvellous Western which turns Monument Valley into an interior landscape as Wayne pursues his five-year odyssey, a grim quest – to kill both the Indian who abducted his niece and the tainted girl herself – which is miraculously purified of its racist furies in a final moment of epiphany. There is perhaps some discrepancy in the play between Wayne's heroic image and the pathological outsider he plays here (forever excluded from home, as the doorway shots at beginning and end suggest), but it hardly matters, given the film's visual splendour and muscular poetry in its celebration of the spirit that vanished with the taming of the American wilderness.

Seven Samurai

(1954, Japan, 200 min, b/w)
d Akira Kurosawa. *p* Shojiro Motoki. *sc* Akira Kurosawa, Shinobu Hashimoto, Hideo Oguni. *ad* Asaichi Nakai. *cast* Takashi Shimura, Toshiro Mifune, Yoshio Inaba, Seiji Miyaguchi, Minoru Chiaki, Daisuke Kato, Ko Kimura.
● Kurosawa's masterpiece, testifying to his admiration for John Ford and translated effortlessly back into the form of a Western as *The Magnificent Seven*, has six masterless samurai – plus Mifune, the crazy farmer's boy not qualified to join the elect group, who nevertheless follows like a dog and fights like a lion – agreeing for no pay, just food and the joy of fulfilling their duty as fighters, to protect a helpless village against a ferocious gang of bandits. Despite the caricatured acting forms of Noh and Kabuki which Kurosawa adopted in his period films, the individual characterisations are precise and memorable, none more so than that by Takashi Shimura, one of the director's favourite actors, playing the sage, ageing, and oddly charismatic samurai leader. The epic action scenes involving cavalry and samurai are still without peer.

Sherlock Junior

(1924, US, 4,065 ft, b/w)
d Buster Keaton. *p* Joseph M Schenck.

sc Jean Havez, Joseph Mitchell, Clyde Bruckman. *ph* Elgin Lessley, Byron Houck. *ed* Buster Keaton. *ad* Fred Gabourie. *cast* Buster Keaton, Kathryn McGuire, Joe Keaton, Ward Crane, Jane Connelly.
● Keaton's third feature under his own steam is an incredible technical accomplishment, but also an almost Pirandellian exploration of the nature of cinematic reality. Buster plays a cinema projectionist, framed for theft by a jealous rival for his girl's hand, who daydreams himself into life as a daring detective. In an unforgettable sequence, Buster (actually fallen asleep beside the projector) forces his way onto the screen and into the movie he is projecting, only to find himself beset by perils and predicaments as the action around him changes in rapid montage. The sequence is not just a gag, but an astonishingly acute perception of the interaction between movie reality and audience fantasy, and the role of editing in juggling both. The timing here is incredible (a technical marvel, in fact); even more so in the great chase sequence, an veritable cascade of unbelievably complex gags (like the moment when Buster, on the handlebars of a riderless, runaway motor-bike passing some ditch-digging roadworks, received a spadeful of earth in the face from each oblivious navvy in turn). It leaves Chaplin standing.

Short Cuts

(1993, US, 188 min)
d Robert Altman. *p* Cary Brokaw. *sc* Robert Altman, Frank Barhydt. *ph* Walt Lloyd. *ed* Geraldine Peroni. *pd* Stephem Altman. *m* Mark Isham. *cast* Tim Robbins, Lily Tomlin, Tom Waits, Matthew Modine, Frances McDormand, Andie MacDowell, Annie Ross, Jack Lemmon.
● From the exhilarating opening, you know Altman's epic 'adaptation' of eight stories and a poem by Raymond Carver is going to be special. Like *Nashville*, it's a tragicomic kaleidoscope of numerous barely interlinked stories (plus a similarly portentous ending). Here, the focus is on couples whose relationships are, at one point or another, subjected to small, seismic shudders of doubt, disappointment or, in a few cases, disaster. A surgeon suspects his wife's fidelity; a pool-cleaner worries over his partner's phone-sex job; a waitress is racked by guilt after running down a child; a baker makes sinister phone calls to the injured boy's parents; the discovery of a corpse threatens a fishing-trip…and a marriage. The marvellous performances bear witness to Altman's iconoclastic good sense, with Tomlin, Waits, Modine, Robbins, MacDowell and the rest lending the film's mostly white, middle-class milieu an authenticity seldom found in American cinema. But the real

star is Altman, whose fluid, clean camera style, free-and-easy editing, and effortless organisation of a complex narrative are quite simply the mark of a master.

Singin' in the Rain

(1952, US, 102 min)
d Stanley Donen, Gene Kelly. *p* Arthur Freed. *sc* Adolph Green, Betty Comden. *ph* Harold Rosson. *ed* Adrienne Fazan. *ad* Cedric Gibbons, Randall Duell. *songs* Nacio Herb Brown, Arthur Freed. *cast* Gene Kelly, Donald O'Connor, Debbie Reynolds, Jean Hagen, Cyd Charisse, Millard Mitchell, Douglas Fowley.
● Is there a film clip more often shown than the title number of this most astoundingly popular musical? The rest of the movie is great too. It shouldn't be. There never was a masterpiece created from such a mishmash of elements: Arthur Freed's favourites among his own songs from back in the '20s and '30s, along with a new number, 'Make 'Em Laugh', which is a straight rip-off from Cole Porter's 'Be A Clown'; the barely blooded Debbie Reynolds pitched into the deep end with tyrannical perfectionist Kelly; choreography very nearly improvised because of pressures of time; and Kelly filming his greatest number with a heavy cold. Somehow it all comes together. The 'Broadway Melody' ballet is Kelly's least pretentious, Jean Hagen and Donald O'Connor are very funny, and the Comden/Green script is a loving-care job. If you've never seen it and don't, you're bonkers.

Some Like It Hot

(1959, US, b/w)
d/p Billy Wilder. *sc* Billy Wilder, IAL Diamond. *ph* Charles Lang Jr. *ed* Arthur P Schmidt. *ad* Ted Haworth. *m* Adolph Deutsch. *cast* Tony Curtis, Jack Lemmon, Marilyn Monroe, Joe E Brown, George Raft, Pat O'Brien, Nehemiah Persoff, Joan Shawlee.
● Still one of Wilder's funniest satires, its pace flagging only once for a short time. Curtis and Lemmon play jazz musicians on the run after witnessing the St Valentine's Day massacre, masquerading in drag as members of an all-girl band (with resulting gender confusions involving Marilyn) to escape the clutches of Chicago mobster George Raft (bespatted and dime-flipping, of course). Deliberately shot in black-and-white to avoid the pitfalls of camp or transvestism, though the best sequences are the gangland ones anyhow. Highlights include Curtis' playboy parody of Cary Grant, and what is surely one of the great curtain lines of all time: Joe E Brown's bland 'Nobody's perfect' when his fiancée (Lemmon) finally confesses that she's a he.

Son, The

(2002, Bel/Fr, 104 min)
d Jean-Pierre Dardenne, Luc Dardenne.

p Jean-Pierre Dardenne, Luc Dardenne, Denis Freyd. *sc* Jean-Pierre Dardenne, Luc Dardenne. *ph* Alain Marcoen. *ed* Marie-Hélène Dozo. *pd* Igor Gabriel. *cast* Olivier Gourmet, Morgan Marinne, Isabella Soupart, Rémy Renaud, Nassim Hassaïni, Kevin Leroy, Félicien Pitsaer.

● Olivier (Gourmet) is a good teacher of carpentry, but a touch gruff; even so, when he refuses to accept young Francis into his workshop, that doesn't explain why he takes to following the boy, as if he were spying on him. Might it have something to do with his own dead son, as his estranged wife insists? One strength of the Dardennes' follow-up to *Rosetta*, winner of the Cannes Palme d'Or, is that, once again, they ask us to discover certain crucial facts for ourselves: by the time we're faced with questions of ethical and spiritual import, we've done enough groundwork to assess the evidence properly. Wisely, the camera stays close to Gourmet, with the result that, notwithstanding his subtle understatement and a relatively taciturn script, we're privy to his every fleeting thought and nagging emotion. Never manipulative or sensationalist, the film is none the less deeply moving.

Sonatine

(1993, Japan, 94 min)
d Takeshi Kitano. *p* Masayuki Mori, Hisao Nabeshima, Takio Yoshida. *sc* Takeshi Kitano. *ph* Katsumi Yanagishima. *ed* Takeshi Kitano. *ad* Osamu Sasaki. *m* Joe Hisaishi. *cast* Takeshi Kitano, Aya Kokumai, Tetsu Watanabe, Masanobu Katsumura, Susumu Terashima.

● The terrific thing about *Sonatine* is its freshness, its ability to surprise. Basically, it's a slightly offbeat variation on the traditional yakuza thriller, with Kitano as Murakawa, the taciturn, influential hitman who, pushed by his boss to involve himself in an Okinawa gang war, comes to realise that he wants out. But what's truly arresting is the star/director's attitude towards the film's formal qualities. Structurally, the movie – like a sonata – is tripartite. It starts fortissimo with tempestuous scenes of gangland machinations and warfare. Then when Murakawa and his men take refuge in a coastal hideaway, their surreal, jokey seaside antics have all the light playfulness of a scherzo. While the final lyrical focus on death is virtually an adagio of moody introspection. Challenging, witty, adventurous and utterly singular.

Story of the Late Chrysanthemums, The

(1939, Japan, 143 min, b/w)
d Kenji Mizoguchi. *p* Nobutaro Shirai. *sc* Yoshikata Yoda. *ph* Minoru Miki, Yozo Fuji. *ed* Koshi Kawahigashi. *ad* Hiroshi Mizutani. *m* Senji Ito, Shiro Fukai. *cast* Shotaro Hanayagi, Kakuko Mori, Kokichi Takada, Gonjuro Kawarazaki, Yoko Umemura.

● Bristling with passion, Mizoguchi's film is a true find: a heartbreaker to end them all. Tokyo, 1885: a Kabuki actor of little self-awareness offends his famous father and transgresses tradition by insisting on his love for his brother's nurse. Trapped by the father's refusal to countenance their affair, dragged together into ignominy, she realises that only through her self-sacrifice can her love reclaim his familial glory. As the plot twists inexorably round their doomed affair, it says much more by showing less: an eloquently long tracking shot can follow remarkably understated scenes of intense emotion so that tears flow as if by magic. Unashamed sentimentality and anger controlled by extreme formal precision justify its reputation as the peak of Mizoguchi's film-making.

Sullivan's Travels

(1941, US, 91 min, b/w)
d Preston Sturges. *p* Paul Jones. *sc* Preston Sturges. *ph* John F Seitz. *ed* Stuart Gilmore. *ad* Hans Dreier, Earl Hedrick. *m* Leo Shuken, Charles Bradshaw. *cast* Joel McCrea, Veronica Lake, Robert Warwick, William Demarest, Franklin Pangborn, Porter Hall, Robert Greig, Eric Blore.

● Irresistible tale of a Hollywood director, tired of making comedies and bent on branching out with an arthouse epic called *Brother, Where Art Thou?*, who sets out to research the meaning of poverty. Suitably costumed as a hobo and starting down the road, discreetly dogged by a studio caravan ready to record the great man's thoughts and serve his needs, he angrily sends this absurd prop packing; only to realise much later, while sweating out a sentence on a chaingang, that severing the lifeline has left him to all intents and purposes a stateless person. He emerges a wiser and more sober man, having seen his fellow-convicts forget their misery in watching a Disney cartoon. The film has sometimes been read as a defence of Hollywood escapism, but what Sturges is really doing is putting down the awful liberal solemnities of problem pictures and movies with a message. Whatever, *Sullivan's Travels* is a gem, an almost serious comedy not taken entirely seriously, with wonderful dialogue, eccentric characterisations, and superlative performances throughout.

Sur mes lèvres

(2001, Fr, 119 min)
d Jacques Audiard. *p* Jean-Louis Livi, Philippe Carcassonne. *sc* Tonino Benacquista, Jacques Audiard. *ph* Matthieu Vadepied. *ed* Juliette Welfling. *ad* Michel Barthélémy. *m* Alexandre Desplat. *cast* Vincent Cassel, Emmanuelle Devos, Olivier Gourmet, Olivia Bonamy, Olivier Perrier, Bernard Alane, Céline Samie.

● Carla (Devos) does a bit of everything for a property development firm that takes her loyalty and talent for granted, and she does it well. But while the boss agrees to her hiring an assistant – she selects scuzzily good-looking but clueless ex-con Paul (Cassel) – her colleagues mostly treat her like dirt, ridiculing her frumpiness and taking credit for her work. It'd be worse still if they knew she's profoundly deaf, a disadvantage which she finds can be turned to her advantage. If only she and Paul, who has his own tormentors, could sort out their mutual wariness and their very different attitudes to life, they might savour some sweet revenge. Audiard's exquisitely elegant thriller is notable for its fresh, exploratory approach to genre. On one level, it's another bracing French film about the workplace, but filtered through Hitchcockian stylistic and thematic tropes. The plot has more than its share of wit and clever twists, there's insightful stuff involving voyeurism, shifts in power and point of view, and the sexual-romantic side is sensibly understated. And Devos and Cassel are both terrific.

Taboo

(1999, Japan, 101 min)
d Nagisa Oshima. *p* Eiko Oshima, Shigehiro Nakagawa, Kazuo Shimizu. *sc* Nagisa Oshima. *ph* Toyomichi Kurita. *ed* Tomoyo Oshima. *pd* Yoshinobu Nishioka. *m* Ryuichi Sakamoto. *cast* 'Beat' Takeshi Kitano, Ryuhei Matsuda, Shinji Takeda, Tadanobu Asano, Yoichi Sai, Tomoro Taguchi. *narrator* Kei Sato.

● Oshima's first feature in 14 years (and the first since the 1995 stroke which left him part-paralysed) adapts two short stories by Ryotaro Shiba about the Shinsengumi, a Shogunate militia of the 1860s notorious for both ruthless violence and homosexuality. Inducted into the force for his cool head and expert swordsmanship, the exquisite teenager Kano (Matsuda, son of the late Yusaku Matsuda) sets many hearts aflutter; the plot details the lust and sexual jealousies surrounding him in the barracks and the callous machinations of his superiors (directors Kitano and Sai) to put an end to the 'trouble'. Oshima conjures an odd mix of realistic elements (the settings, the kendo practice) and stylisation (Emi Wada's costumes, Sakamoto's excellent score) to produce one of his most bitter accounts of passion and individuality snuffed out.

Taxi Driver

(1976, US, 114 min)
d Martin Scorsese. *p* Michael Phillips, Julia Phillips. *sc* Paul Schrader. *ph* Michael Chapman. *ed* Marcia Lucas, Tom Rolf, Melvin Shapiro. *ad* Charles Rosen. *m* Bernard Herrmann. *cast*

Robert De Niro, Cybill Shepherd, Jodie Foster, Harvey Keitel, Peter Boyle, Leonard Harris, Martin Scorsese, Steven Prince, Diahnne Abbot, Albert Brooks.

● *Taxi Driver* makes you realise just how many directors, from Schlesinger to Friedkin and Winner, have piddled around on the surface of New York in their films. Utilising, especially, Bernard Herrmann's most menacing score since *Psycho*, Scorsese has set about recreating the landscape of the city in a way that constitutes a truly original and terrifying Gothic canvas. But, much more than that: *Taxi Driver* is also, thanks partly to De Niro's extreme implosive performance, the first film since *Alphaville* to set about a really intelligent appraisal of the fundamental ingredients of contemporary insanity. Its final upsurge of violence doesn't seem to be cathartic in the now predictable fashion of the 'new' American movie, but lavatorial; the nauseating effluence of the giant flesh emporium that the film has so single-mindedly depicted.

Things To Come

(1936, GB, 113 min, b/w)
d William Cameron Menzies.
p Alexander Korda. *sc* HG Wells.
ph Georges Périnal. *ed* Charles Crichton, Francis D Lyon. *ad* Vincent Korda. *m* Arthur Bliss. *cast* Raymond Massey, Ralph Richardson, Edward Chapman, Margaretta Scott, Cedric Hardwicke, Sophie Stewart, Ann Todd, Derrick de Marney.

● HG Wells thought *Metropolis* to be 'quite the silliest film', but a decade later Alexander Korda gave him enormous creative freedom to write a movie version of *The Shape of Things to Come*, which turned out to be just as silly. However, like *Metropolis*, it isn't just silly. It is a spectacular production wherein Wells takes his 'science versus art' preoccupations into the future (as seen from the '30s); and to make it work, only lacks the kind of pure cinematic form which a Powell/Pressburger would have given it, for its scale and love of 'ideas' pre-figure their films and make it just as unique in British cinema history. In the realm of 'prophetic science fiction', it is a genre landmark.

Time Out

(2001, Fr, 134 min)
d Laurent Cantet. *p* Caroline Benjo.
sc Robin Campillo, Laurent Cantet.
ph Pierre Milon. *ed* Robin Campillo, Stéphane Léger. *pd* Romain Denis.
m Jocelyn Pook. *cast* Aurélien Recoing, Karin Viard, Serge Livrozet, Jean-Pierre Mangeot, Monique Mangeot, Nicolas Kalsch, Marie Cantet, Félix Cantet, Olivier Le Joubioux.

● Like Cantet's first film, *Human Resources*, this sober, measured and terri-

bly sad movie explores that most subtle of distinctions: what it is that separates who we are from what we do. Middle-aged executive Vincent (Recoing) has been 'let go', although his redundancy seems self-inflicted, an existential torpor he does everything to conceal from his family. He's transferred his expertise to the UN, he claims, working as a business consultant and persuading old friends to invest in a hush-hush get rich quick scheme. It's insane, yet Vincent's pretence is virtually sufficient to his needs, his assumption of propriety and well-being as good as the real thing. Or put another way, a proper job is scarcely more meaningful than this hollow charade. In Cantet's own words, 'Vincent is the sincerest of liars, an actor of his own life.' It's a profound, measured portrait of a man driven – and driving – with no end in sight.

Touch of Evil

(1958, US, 108 min, b/w)
d Orson Welles. *p* Albert Zugsmith.
sc Orson Welles. *ph* Russell Metty.
ed Virgil W Vogel, Aaron Stell.
ad Alexander Golitzen, Robert Clatworthy. *m* Henry Mancini. *cast* Charlton Heston, Janet Leigh, Orson Welles, Joseph Calleia, Akim Tamiroff, Marlene Dietrich, Dennis Weaver, Ray Collins, Mercedes McCambridge, Lalo Rios, Zsa Zsa Gabor, Joseph Cotten.

● A wonderfully offhand genesis (Welles adopting and adapting a shelved Paul Monash script for B-king Albert Zugsmith without ever reading the novel by Whit Masterson it was based on) marked this brief and unexpected return to Hollywood film-making for Welles. And the result more than justified the arrogance of the gesture. A sweaty thriller conundrum on character and corruption, justice and the law, worship and betrayal, it plays havoc with moral ambiguities as self-righteous Mexican cop Heston goes up against Welles' monumental Hank Quinlan, the old-time detective of vast and wearied experience who goes by instinct, gets it right, but fabricates evidence to make his case. Set in the backwater border hell-hole of Los Robles, inhabited almost solely by patented Wellesian grotesques, it's shot to resemble a nightscape from Kafka.

2001: A Space Odyssey

(1968, GB, 141 min)
d/p Stanley Kubrick. *sc* Stanley Kubrick, Arthur C Clarke. *ph* Geoffrey Unsworth. *ed* Ray Lovejoy. *pd* Tony Masters, Harry Lange, Ernest Archer. *m* Richard Strauss, Johann Strauss Jr, Aram Khachaturian. *cast* Keir Dullea, Gary Lockwood, William Sylvester, Daniel Richter, Leonard Rossiter, Margaret Tyzack, Robert Beatty.

● A characteristically pessimistic account of human aspiration from Kubrick, this tripartite sci-fi look at civil-

isation's progress from prehistoric times (the apes learning to kill) to a visionary future (astronauts on a mission to Jupiter encountering superior life and rebirth in some sort of embryonic divine form) is beautiful, infuriatingly slow, and pretty half-baked. Quite how the general theme fits in with the central drama of the astronauts' battle with the arrogant computer HAL, who tries to take over their mission, is unclear, while the final farrago of light-show psychedelia is simply so much pap. Nevertheless, for all the essential coldness of Kubrick's vision, it demands attention as superior sci-fi, simply because it's more concerned with ideas than with Boy's Own-style pyrotechnics.

2046

(2004, Fr/Ger/HK/China, 129 min)
d Wong Kar Wai. *p* Wong Kar Wai, Eric Heumann, Ren Zhonglun, Zhu Yongde. *sc* Wong Kar Wai. *ed/pd* William Chang Suk-Ping. *ad* Alfred Yau Wai Ming. *m* Peer Raben, Shigeru Umebayashi. *cast* Tony Leung Chiu Wai, Gong Li, Takuya Kimura, Faye Wong, Zhang Ziyi, Carina Lau Ka Ling, Chang Chen, Wang Sum, Siu Ping Lam, Maggie Cheung Man Yuk, Thongchai McIntyre ('Bird'), Dong Jie.

● At least in the version premiered in Cannes 2004 (which one suspects may not have been the definitive final cut), this sumptuous follow-up to *In the Mood for Love* makes for a rapturous experience. It's not just the stunning sets, cinematography and music, which together give it the febrile intensity of a Puccini opera; it's also the subtlety, diversity and complexity that mark Wong's charting of the emotional odyssey undergone by writer Chow (Leung), as he passes through a series of relationships in the years immediately following a heartbreaking encounter (with Maggie Cheung in the previous film) that continues to shape his reactions to every woman he meets. Intercut with these new relationships are scenes from an allegorical sci-fi novel he's writing, set in the future but inspired by his own past. Over his protagonist's bitter-sweet infatuation, Wong builds layer upon layer of meaning, memory and desire, creating a work as cerebrally rewarding as it is sensually seductive.

Umbrellas of Cherbourg, The

(1964, Fr/WGer, 92 min)
d Jacques Demy. *p* Mag Bodard.
sc Jacques Demy. *ph* Jean Rabier.
ed Monique Teissure. *ad* Bernard Evein. *m* Michel Legrand. *cast* Catherine Deneuve, Nino Castelnuovo, Anne Vernon, Ellen Farner, Marc Michel, Mireille Perrey, Jean Champion.

● A novelettish story that in the hands of most directors would be no more than trivial is transformed by Demy into something rather wonderful: a full-scale all-singing musical whose inspiration is Hollywood but whose tone and setting are resolutely Gallic. Shopgirl Deneuve loves a poor mechanic who leaves her pregnant when he departs for military service. During his absence, she is courted by a diamond merchant and nudged into marriage by her ambitious mother... This bittersweet romance – whose underlying message would seem to be that people invariably marry the wrong person – is lavished with affection. Vivid colours and elegant camera choreography are bound together by Michel Legrand's sumptuous score. And never has an Esso station looked so romantic.

Vertigo

(1958, US, 128 min)
d/p Alfred Hitchcock. sc Alec Coppel, Samuel Taylor. ph Robert Burks. ed George Tomasini. ad Hal Pereira, Henry Bumstead. m Bernard Herrmann. cast James Stewart, Kim Novak, Barbara Bel Geddes, Tom Helmore, Henry Jones, Ellen Corby, Lee Patrick.
● Brilliant but despicably cynical view of human obsession and the tendency of those in love to try to manipulate each other. Stewart is excellent as the neurotic detective employed by an old pal to trail his wandering wife, only to fall for her himself and then crack up when she commits suicide. Then one day he sees a woman in the street who reminds him of the woman who haunts him... Hitchcock gives the game away about halfway through the movie, and focuses on Stewart's strained psychological stability; the result inevitably involves a lessening of suspense, but allows for an altogether deeper investigation of guilt, exploitation, and obsession. The bleakness is perhaps a little hard to swallow, but there's no denying that this is the director at the very peak of his powers, while Novak is a revelation. Slow but totally compelling.

Wild Bunch, The

(1969, US, 145 min)
d Sam Peckinpah. p Phil Feldman. sc Walon Green, Sam Peckinpah. ph Lucien Ballard. ed Lou Lombardo. ad Edward Carrere. m Jerry Fielding. cast William Holden, Ernest Borgnine, Robert Ryan, Edmond O'Brien, Warren Oates, Jaime Sanchez, Ben Johnson, Emilio Fernandez, Strother Martin, LQ Jones, Albert Dekker, Bo Hopkins.
● From the opening sequence, in which a circle of laughing children poke at a scorpion writhing in a sea of ants, to the infamous blood-spurting finale, Peckinpah completely rewrites John Ford's Western mythology – by looking at the passing of the Old West from the point of view of the marginalised outlaws rather than the law-abiding settlers. Though he spares us

none of the callousness and brutality of Holden and his gang, Peckinpah nevertheless presents their macho code of loyalty as a positive value in a world increasingly dominated by corrupt railroad magnates and their mercenary killers (Holden's old buddy Ryan). The flight into Mexico, where they virtually embrace their death at the hands of double-crossing general Fernandez and his rabble army, is a nihilistic acknowledgment of the men's anachronistic status. In purely cinematic terms, the film is a savagely beautiful spectacle, Lucien Ballard's superb cinematography complementing Peckinpah's darkly elegiac vision.

Wind Will Carry Us, The

(1999, Fr/Iran, 118 min)
d Abbas Kiarostami. p Marin Karmitz, Abbas Kiarostami. sc Abbas Kiarostami. ph Mahmoud Kalari. ed Abbas Kiarostami. m Peyman Yazdanian. cast Behzad Dourani, Farzad Sohrabi, Shahpour Ghobadi, Masood Mansouri, Masoameh Salimi.
● Another subtle, deceptively simple and richly rewarding work of genius from Kiarostami, this Venice prizewinner opens on a long shot of a car negotiating a dusty mountain road, with driver and passengers arguing about where they are. Those who have seen the Koker Trilogy, especially And Life Goes On..., may ask whether Kiarostami is simply repeating himself, but fans will know there's always more to his work than first meets the eye. Sure enough, once the car reaches the Kurdistan village of Siaf Dareh, the ambiguities and mysteries proliferate and interweave. Are the men in the village treasure-hunters, as they tell a boy, the telecom engineers as the villagers assume to be, or something more sinister? Why is their apparent leader curious about the boy's dying grandma? And why, when Tehran calls on his mobile and he needs to move to higher ground, does he always drive to the cemetery, where an invisible man sings through a hole in the ground? This engrossing and beautiful film succeeds on many levels. As witty, almost absurdist comedy, it offers lovely visual and verbal gags. And as an ethnographic/philosophical study of the relationships between ancient and modern, rural and urban, devotion and directionlessness, it's intriguing and illuminating.

Witchfinder General

(1968, GB, 87 min)
d Michael Reeves. p Arnold Louis Miller. sc Michael Reeves, Tom Baker. ph John Coquillon. ed Howard Lanning. ad Jim Morahan. m Paul Ferris. cast Vincent Price, Ian Ogilvy, Hilary Dwyer, Rupert Davies, Robert Russell, Patrick Wymark, Wilfrid Brambell.
● Filmed on location in the countryside of Norfolk and Suffolk on a modest budget, this portrait of backwoods violence

– set in 1645, it deals with the infamous witchhunter Matthew Hopkins, and the barbarities he practised during the turmoils of the Civil War – remains one of the most personal and mature statements in the history of British cinema. In the hands of the late Michael Reeves (this was his last film, made at the age of 23), a fairly ordinary but interestingly researched novel by Ronald Bassett, with a lot of phony Freudian motivation, is transformed into a highly ornate, evocative, and poetic study of violence, where the political disorganisation and confusion of the war is mirrored by the chaos and superstition in men's minds. The performances are generally excellent, and no film before or since has used the British countryside in quite the same way.

Woman of the Dunes

(1964, Japan, 127 min, b/w)
d Hiroshi Teshigahara. p Kiichi Ichikawa, Tadashi Ohono. sc Kobo Abé. ph Hiroshi Segawa. ed F Sushi. m Toru Takemitsu. cast Eiji Okada, Kyoko Kishida.
● An entomologist finds himself trapped by mysteriously tribal villagers, and forced to cohabit with a desirable but inarticulate woman in an escape-proof sandpit. Leaving aside all the teasing questions of allegorical meaning, Teshigahara's film is a tour de force of visual style, and a knockout as an unusually cruel thriller. It builds on its blatantly contrived premise (taken from Kobo Abé's novel) with absolute fidelity and conviction, which leaves the manifest pretensions looking both credible and interesting, and centres its effects on the erotic attraction between the man and woman, filmed with a palpable physicality that remains extraordinary.

Z

(1968, Fr/Alg, 125 min)
d Costa-Gavras. p Jacques Perrin. sc Costa-Gavras, Jorge Semprun. ph Raoul Coutard. ed Françoise Bonnot. ad Jacques d'Ovidio. m Mikis Theodorakis. cast Yves Montand, Jean-Louis Trintignant, Jacques Perrin, François Périer, Irene Papas, Georges Géret, Charles Denner.
● Costa-Gavras' crowd-pleasing left wing thriller was based on the 1965 Lambrakis affair, in which investigation of the accidental death of a medical professor uncovered a network of police and government corruption. As Greece was under the Colonels at the time, the film was shot in Algeria, with a script by Spaniard Jorge Semprun and music by Theodorakis. The recreation of the murder and the subsequent investigation uses the techniques of an American thriller to gripping effect, though conspiracies are so commonplace nowadays that it's hard to imagine the impact it made at the time.

Index of titles

The following is a list of all film titles mentioned in *1000 Films to change your life*, supplied with basic credits – name, country of origin, running time, director and key team members. All films are in colour unless indicated by 'b/w'. Page numbers given in italics indicate a still from the film. 100 selected titles have full reviews and more extensive credits information in the **100 to watch** section (*pp251-266*). The annual *Time Out Film Guide*, which lists over 16,500 films, includes the majority of titles mentioned below.

Critics' choice

Moving picture